A VERY PRIVILEGED LIFE

By Mary Louchheim Evangelista

8" x 10" (20.32 x 25.4 cm)

Black & White on White paper

Designed by Ye Q Zhu

ISBN: 9781792935947

CreateSpace Independent Publishing Platform, North Charleston, SC

BISAC: Biography & Autobiography / General

Special thanks to Beth Philips, Deborah Howard, and Judy Ross for help in editing.

TABLE OF CONTENTS

"Putting first things first: Thousands have lived without love, not one without water."

From *First Things First*

Wystan Auden

"So perhaps the great world was on three sides fashionable order, nullity and on the fourth side experience, power, art and magnificence."

From *The Last Puritan*

George Santayana

A ***Menschenkenner*** is an astute judge of character, a connoisseur of human nature, a person who evaluates people and can judge wisely. Learning to know others took me three-quarters of a lifetime. Have I finally become a *Menschenkenner*, an interpreter of calculations, disputations, fraud? My well-intentioned parents protected me—until I was let loose.

My Lauchheimer great-great-grandparents lived on the Judenstrasse (street for Jews) in the town of Lauchheim, Germany. They took our last name from the place where they lived. The Judenstrasse was the only place Jews could live, although it wasn't an actual ghetto surrounded by high walls. It was a designated area and our family house still stands—now owned by a clock maker who told me that he was given it by the German government.

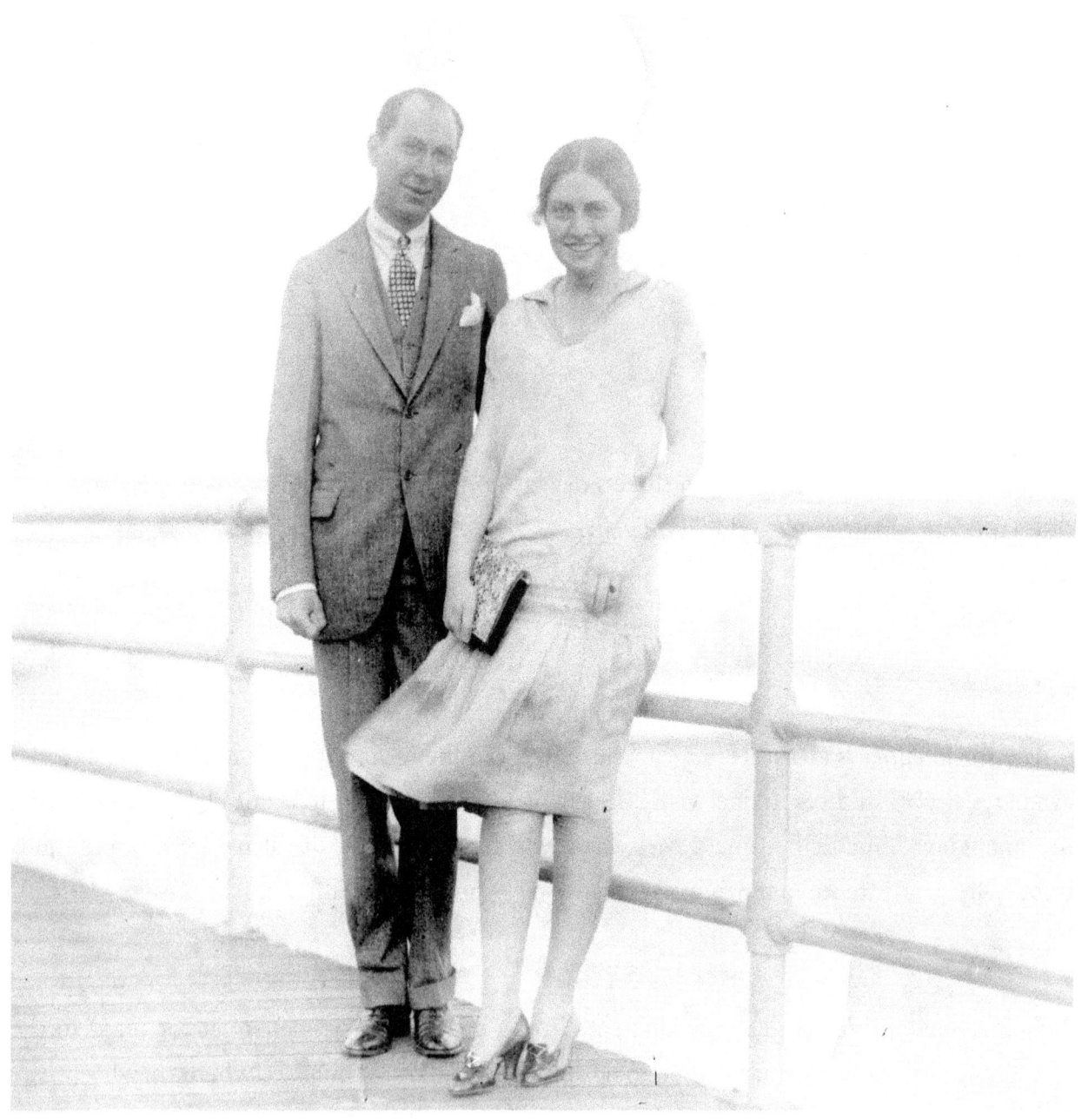

ABOVE:

My parents, Walter and Katie on their honeymoon, 1926.

FORWARD

My friend Mary is rather sophisticated. I know her from her summer habitat, an 1828 Cape Cod farmhouse. Her life as she tells it is a story which fascinates, from fortunate beginnings to adventures as a woman in the twentieth century. Mary is a person of vigor, wit, humor and strong mind. She keeps command, constantly communicating, reading, writing, and moving forward.

Sitting in one of her kitchen chairs, listening, I find focus in Mary's penetrating green-blue eyes, curious frowning tendency, and curliest of curly blonde hair. Kind-hearted and generous, neither effusive nor gushing in her provision of kindness and gifts, Mary is self-realized, a sociable woman in civilized circumstances, once a bit in the shadows imposed by dynamic parents and wealth. They collectively tried to shelter her from her Jewish roots, but now she stands strong.

Ellen Ross, June 2011

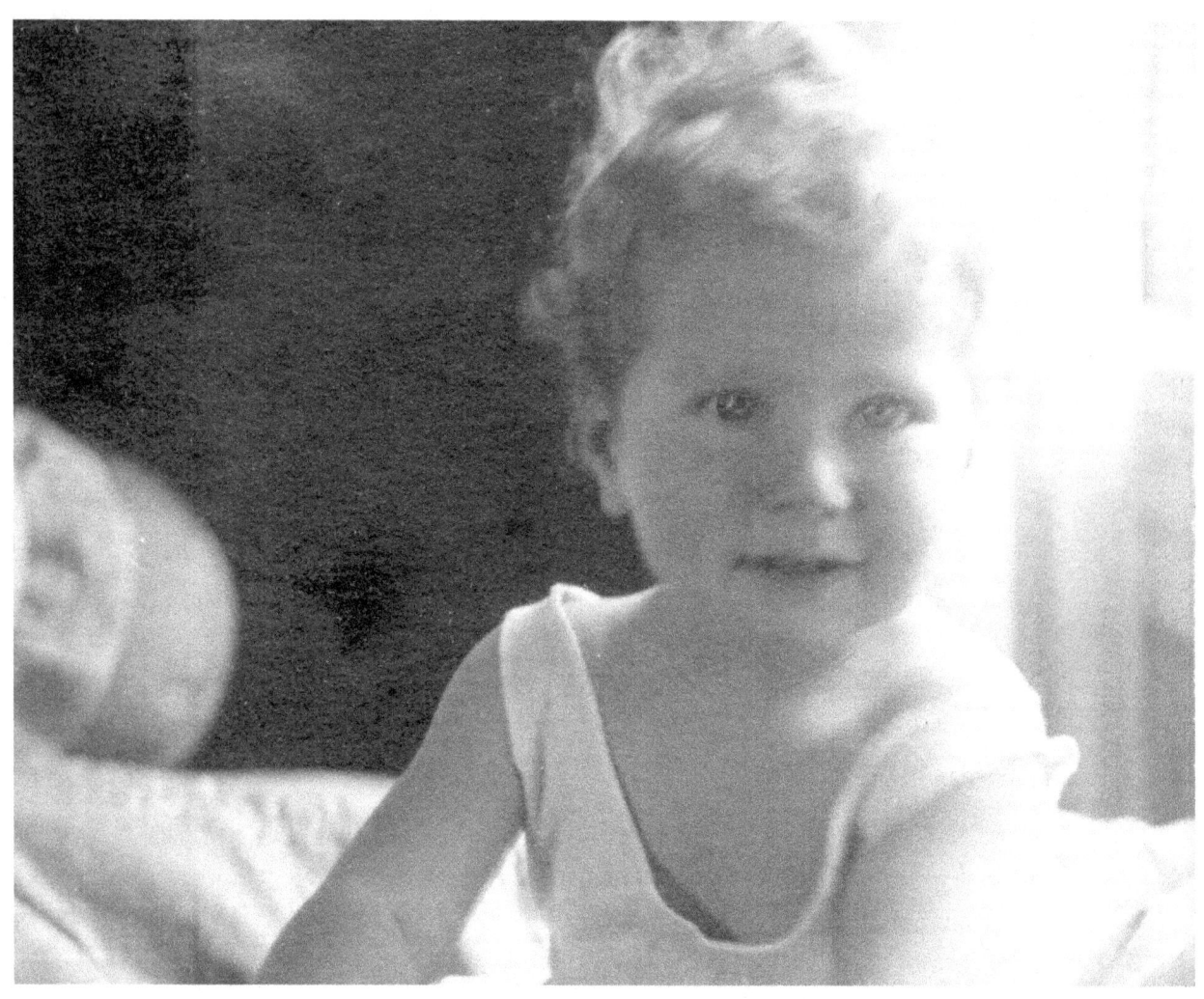

ABOVE:

Mary, one year old.

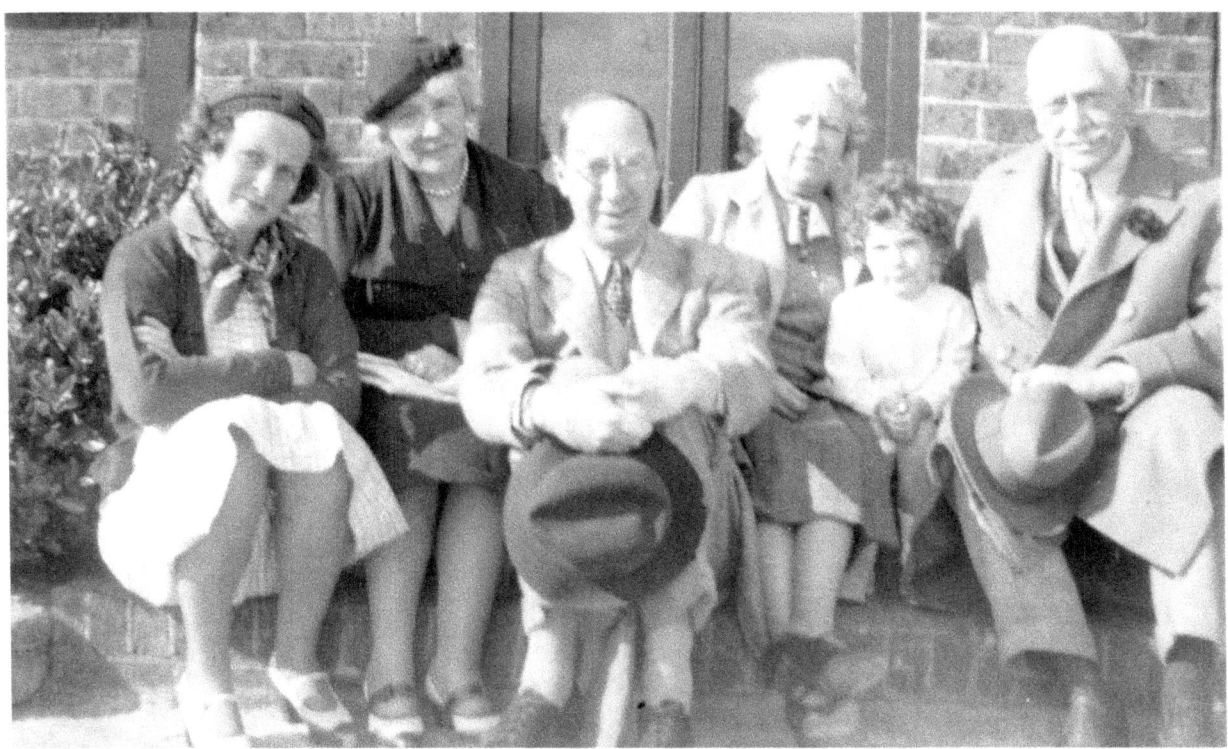

BEGINNINGS

I was born on Manhattan's Upper East Side, on May 18, 1930, three
blocks from where I live now and across Central Park from my mother's
birthplace, 47 West 86th Street, seven months after the Crash of
1929, and several years before the rise of Hitler in Germany. My
parents, Walter and Katie Louchheim, named me "Sandel" after my
great-grandfather, Schmuel Sandel Lauchheimer. My grandmother,
"Frankie" (Frances) Appel Louchheim, resentful of being given a
boy's name by her father, sent my parents a cable from Aix-les-Bains
instructing them to add "Mary." Because my Grandmother Frankie's
word was law in family matters, my name became Mary Sandel.

1

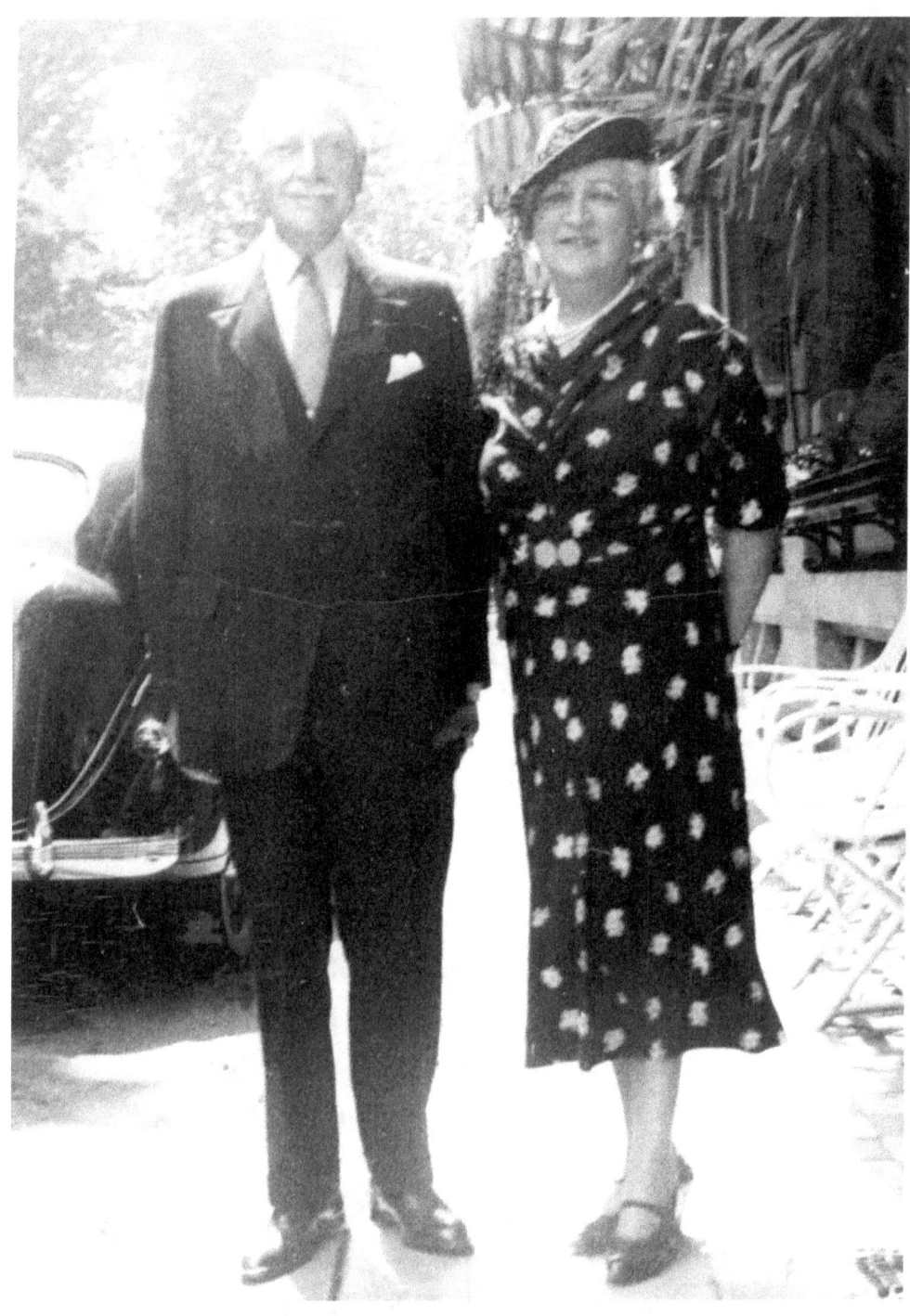

** Grandmother Frankie was raised by the ARAPAHO Indian tribe in Denver, Colorado, after her mother passed away. Frankie had many years' practice as head of the family.

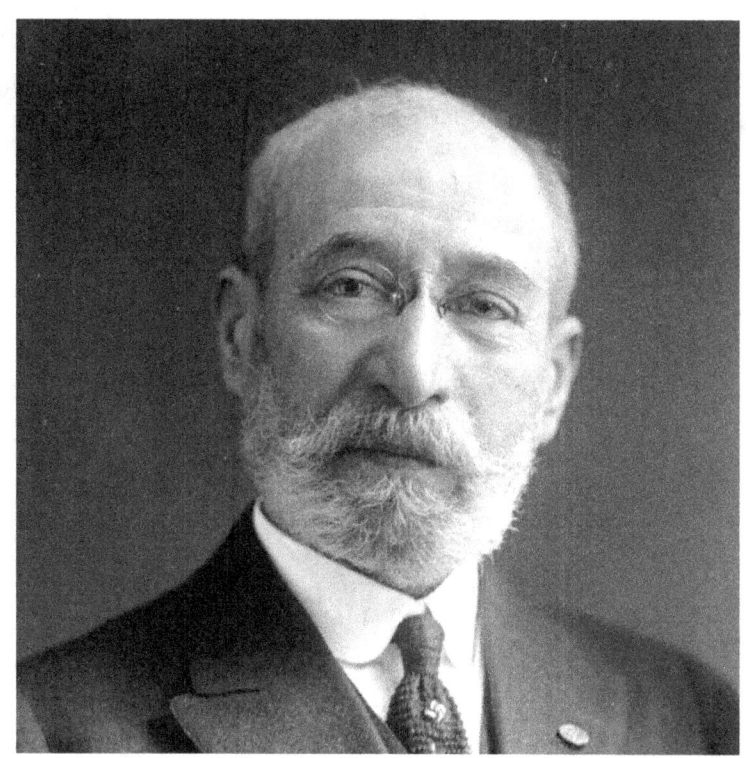

EXCERPTS FROM MARY'S BABY BOOK

Mary's outgoing, friendly nature is like great-grandfather, Fred Joseph's.

Her fair complexion and Roman face are traced to grandfather Leonard Scofield.

From grandmother Frankie, uncompromising vigor,

From Grandmother Adele Scofield, resourcefulness.
(That woman could make a quart of milk stretch forever.)

From father Walter a love of music and a touch of humor.

Aunt Florence, appreciation of art.

Mother Katie, natural charm and spirit of determination.

Great-grandmother Fannie Joseph, a love of sweets.

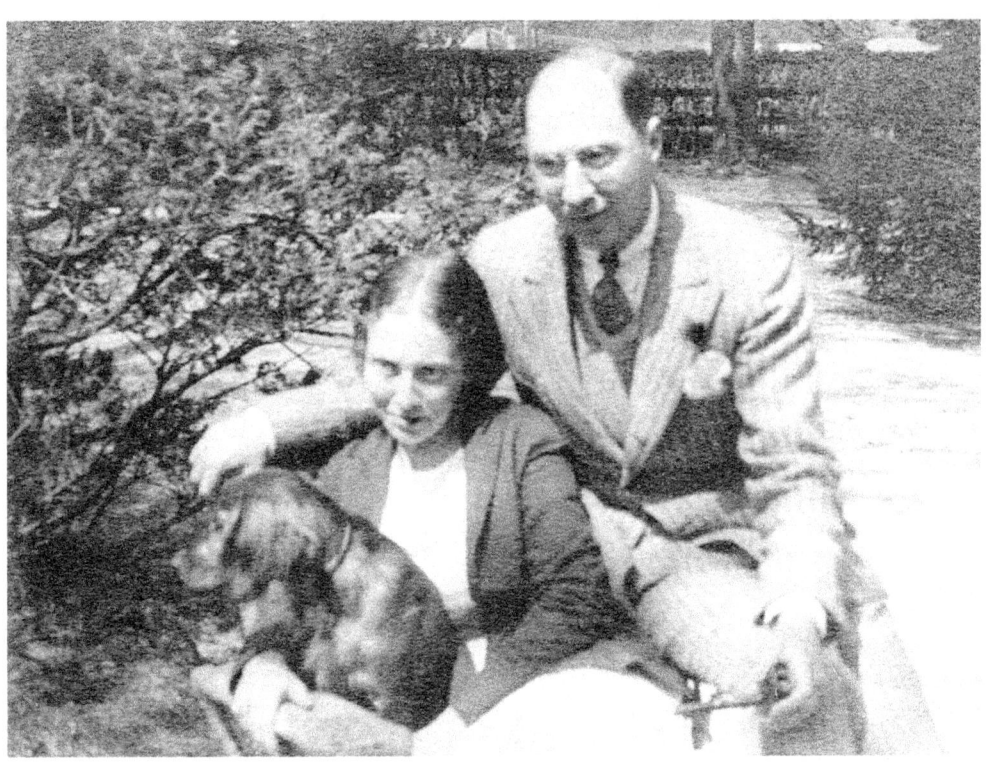

Neither of my parents wanted children, but Grandmother Adele insisted, "No happy family can exist without *kinder.*"

For three years, I was showered with attention as the "only kid on the block" until my sister, Judith Helen**, was born on August 24, 1933, in Red Bank, New Jersey. Grandfather Leonard Scofield objected to naming her Judith. "Judith is a Jewish name! Why do you handicap your child?" Once again, my parents were disappointed—another girl. We became dolls on the shelf, taken down and fluffed up in British outfits—dotted Swiss organdy with pink taffeta bows and "Mary Janes"—eliciting oohs and aahs from adults. I acquired a perennial frown, a pout grownups found beguiling. Surrounded by luxury, what did I have to sulk about?

** Helen was my father's youngest sister, fastidious, anorexic, and childless, a woman Judy grew to resemble.

I came to believe that boys were special, privileged, entitled—capable of handling money, strong, smart and achievers—more welcome than girls. Katie complained in her diary: "Motherhood is a dull and difficult job." Wanting a son, she was indifferent toward Judy and me, frequently referring to us collectively as "the young."

Her diaries reveal the anxiety she suffered as a young mother. Walter suggested nurses. It was the first of his noble and generous offers. When asked if she "raised" her children, my mother answered, "No, a series of incompetent, lonely, drill-sergeant governesses did. They were women who wanted obedience and perfection— clean hands and orderly rooms. I gained my little freedom to do nothing. I wanted neatness and order above all, a requirement my mother passed on to me."

My third birthday party took place in Elberon,** New Jersey. Many kids arrived, most of whom I'd never seen before. It was exciting to be the center of so much attention. My parents had hired a pony to give rides around our block. I waited eagerly for my turn but was told that, as hostess, I must allow my guests to go first. After everyone had ridden on the pony, it was my turn. That's when things began to fall apart: I was told that the pony was tired and had to go home.

**We left NYC at the start of the Depression—my mother didn't want to live amongst, as she put it "all the troubled folks looking for work"—and moved to Elberon, New Jersey where my mother and her family had summered. Walter commuted to his father's Wall Street brokerage firm, where he soon became known as the Stock Exchange cynic, spending his work hours reading poetry and observing insider trading.

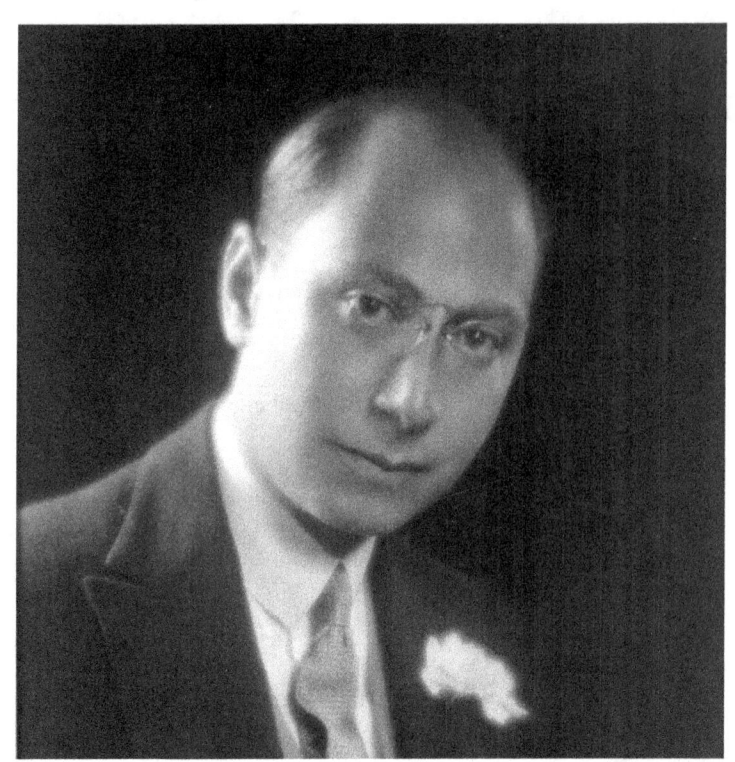

TOP RIGHT:
My father, Walter.

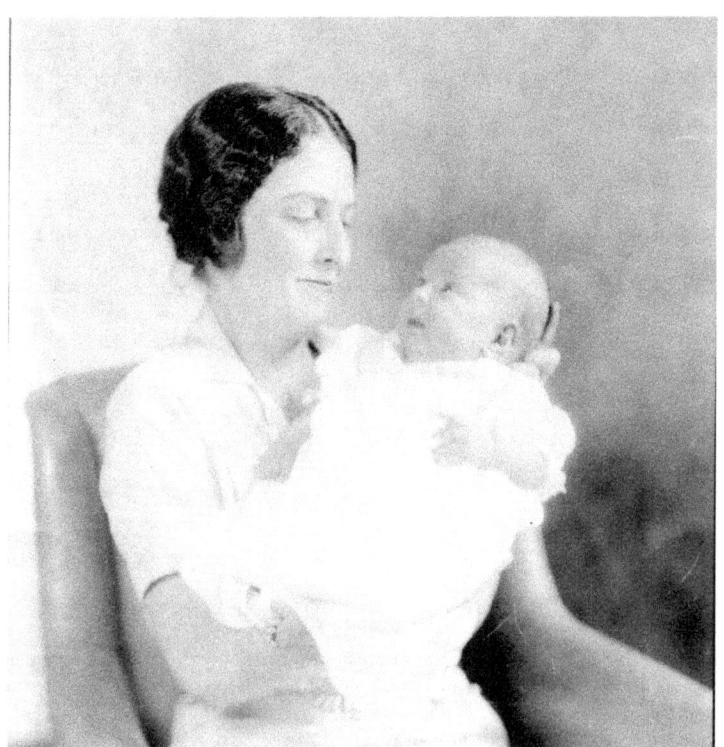

BOTTOM RIGHT:
My mother and me.

6

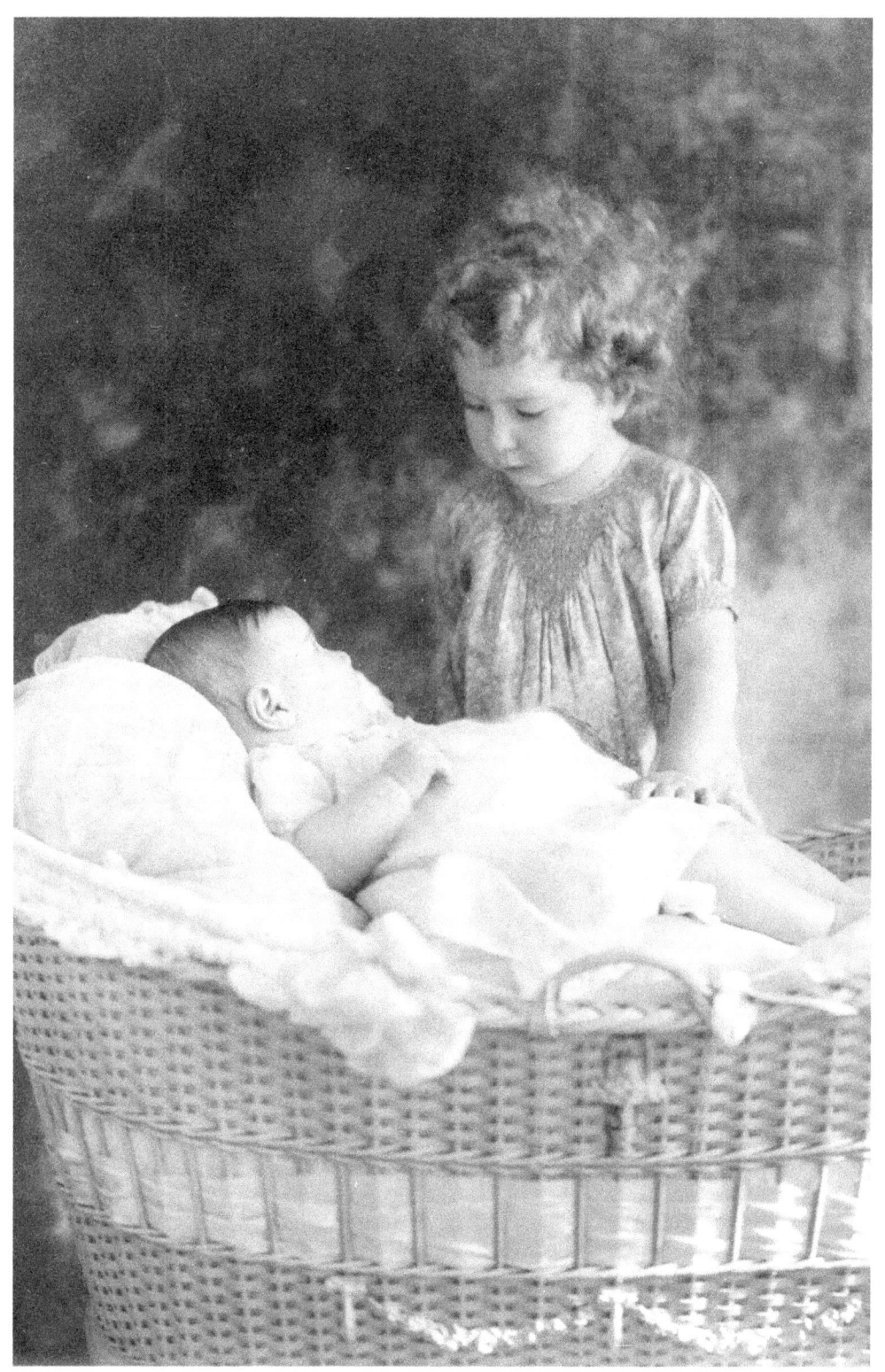

RIGHT:

Judy and me.

7

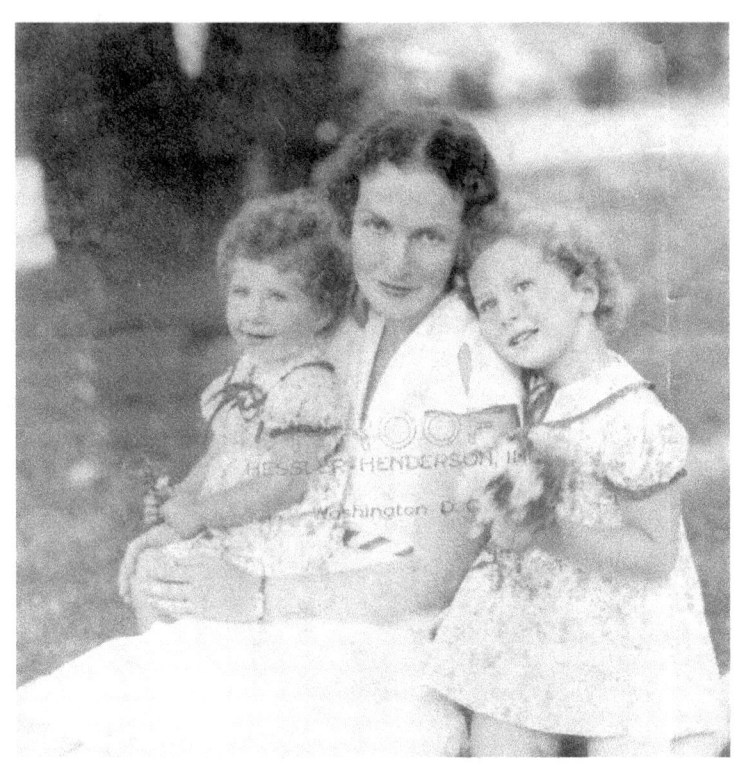

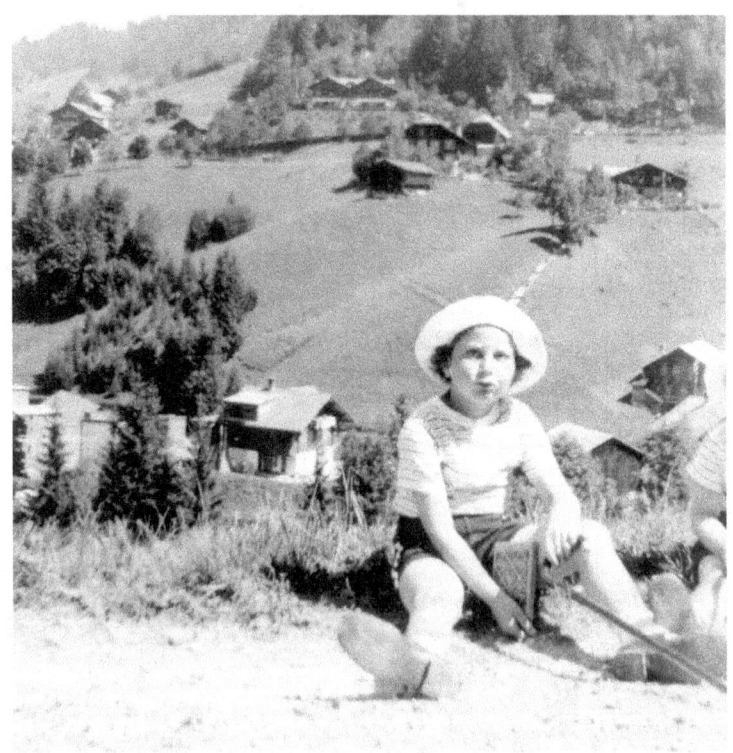

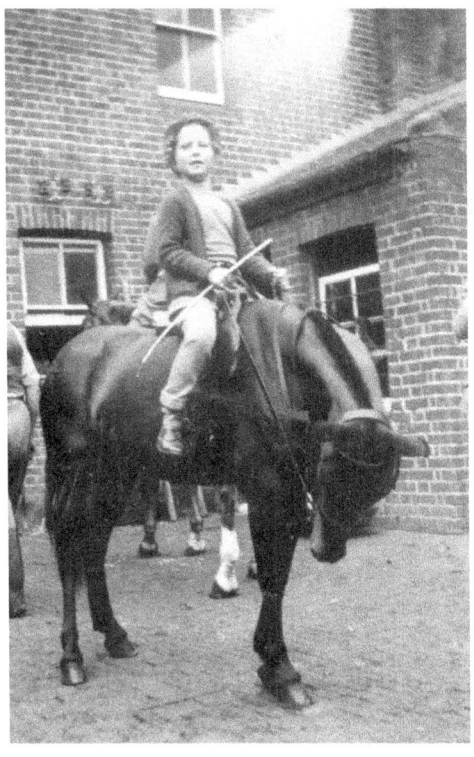

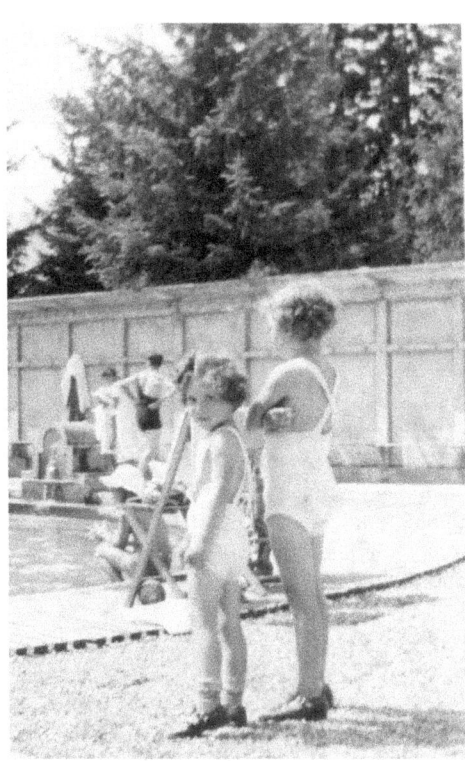

Compensation came in the form of summer travel abroad. Jews were not welcome at American summer resorts, and families like mine, who could afford to cross the Atlantic to escape the heat, jumped on the Cunard Line. Among the *petite histoires* that were entered in my Baby Book, my father wrote that I stood before a crowd in the First Class Lounge of the Queen Mary and sang "I Told Every Little Star." The story could well be apocryphal, but I like the idea of having had such *chutzpah* early on.

In Rottingdean, a coastal town near Brighton, England, we rode ponies and swam off rocky beaches, journeyed to Gstaad, high in the Swiss Alps, and sat around the Parkhotel Reuteler swimming pool , my father happily ordering special meals.

9

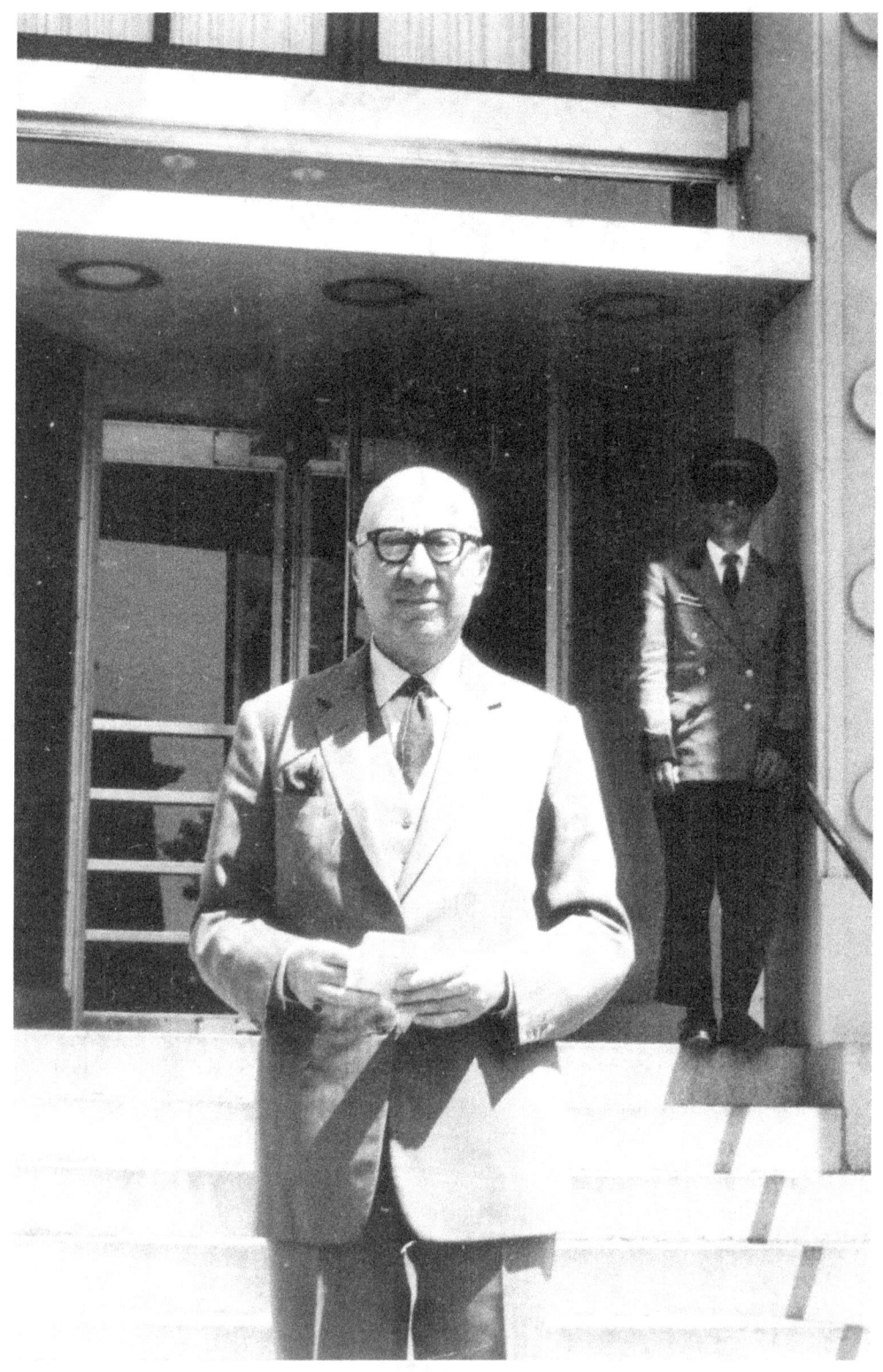

GEORGETOWN

FRANKLIN ROOSEVELT'S NEW DEAL

When Franklin Roosevelt was elected president in 1933 and the Democrats regained control of Congress, economic recovery was in the air. On June 6, 1934, Congress passed the Securities Exchange Act which provided for federal regulation of the stock market. Its goal was to prevent the fraudulent trading that led to the crash of 1929. My father was hired by Roosevelt to help create the Securities and Exchange Commission to oversee and monitor insider trading. His credentials were good. He had complained publicly about insider-trading and equally important, he and his clients had come out of the crash with fortunes intact. My mother urged him to accept the New Deal job offer – delighted at the prospect of escaping from the stodgy niche they occupied in anti-Semitic New York City. He became a committed New Dealer. He and Henry Morgenthau, Secretary of the Treasury, were among the many Jews to be included in Roosevelt's administration.

WASHINGTON D.C. offered an escape to a city where neither ethnic or religious background controlled what jobs you had or who your friends were. Roosevelt's personal magnetism inspired hope. My parents were comforted by his stentorian voice as he described newly created departments, reassuring Americans during his fireside chats, "The only thing we have to fear is fear itself." They sat, glued to our radio, their ears pressed against the box, confident that he would make it all happen. Norman Rockwell's illustrations on the covers of the Saturday Evening Post captured the faces of Americans who listened, and believed.

As Ben Cohen, a Roosevelt recruit famously remarked, "folks from everywhere in the U.S. came down to Washington to work for the Lord. There had never been a phenomenon in American life equal to the invasion of Washington by New Dealers—hundreds of men and women still in their twenties and thirties, brilliant and dedicated, trained in the law, economics, public administration, and technology, venturing into public life in order to restructure American society. They proposed new programs, drafted legislation, staffed the new agencies. They were active in the Administration, the Congress, the courts, and the news media. They fanned out all over America to discover the facts, planning ways of easing the pain of their foundering country. Many of them went on to be rich, famous, and powerful, but their early experiences in Washington were perhaps the most inspiring."

WE MOVED TO GEORGETOWN, WASHINGTON'S VENERABLE NEIGHBORHOOD

Paradoxically, the New Deal's goal of helping those out of work mingled with Georgetown elegance and a wish to impress. Washington, D.C. was a city of poor blacks, Southern rednecks, descendants of the Klu Klux Klan, ambassadors from countries around the world, and New Dealers—an eclectic mix, a city lacking in charm, beauty and warmth, the government buildings enlarged mausoleums.

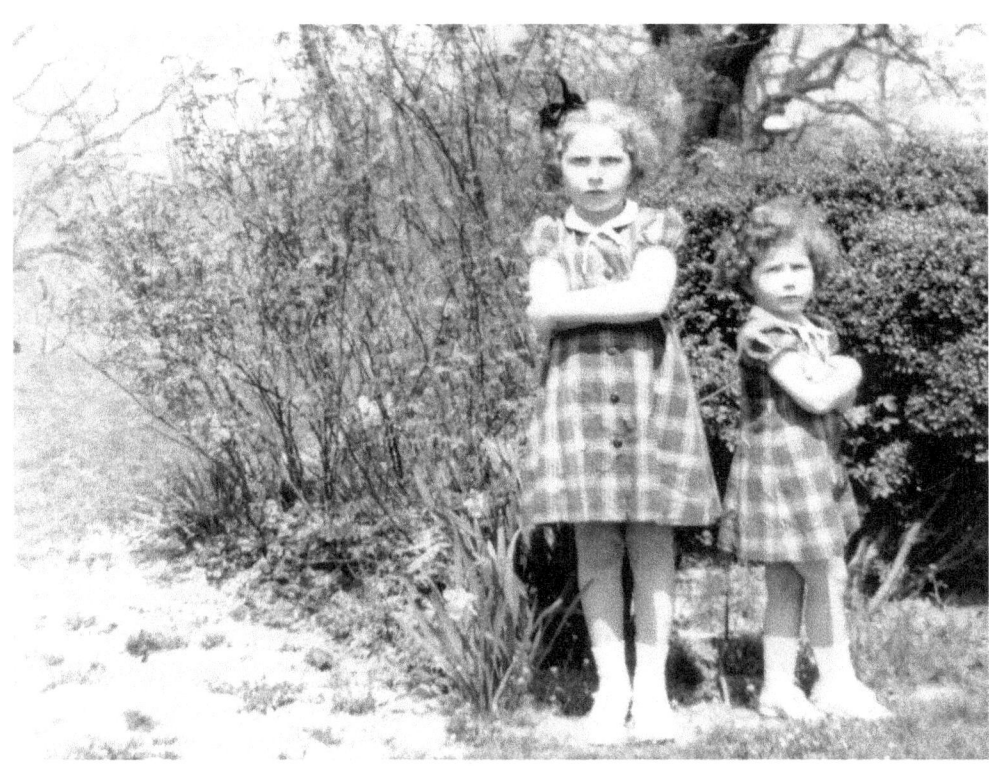

Built along the Potomac River during the Revolution, Georgetown's brick houses were home to black people who couldn't afford or weren't allowed to settle in the predominantly Republican white suburbs of Chevy Chase or Bethesda, where tall hedges surrounded columned, colonial-style residences. In 1934, most Georgetown homes in our immediate neighborhood were shanty-like, their front yards strewn with discarded stoves, sinks and toilet seats. My classmates lived too far away for play dates.

My parents, who considered themselves liberal, remained on unsure footing when it came to living with and addressing black people. **My mother called them "darkeys" or "the colored." A black chauffeur drove us the mile and a half to school.

** In 1970, attitudes changed and my parents became friends with Walter Washington, the first black mayor-commissioner of D.C. They also supported President Johnson during the passage of the Civil Rights and Voting Acts. When my mother rose to her aspired title −Assistant Secretary of State for Women's Affairs− in 1964, she chose Charlotte Hubbard, a black woman from Tuskegee, Alabama, to serve as Assistant Secretary of State for Public Affairs. Charlotte became the top black woman in Lyndon Johnson's administration and served in the State Department from 1964-1970. Pauline Gore, wife of senator Albert Gore and mother of Vice President Al Gore, chastised my mother for sending Charlotte to the University of Virginia to address a group of students. "Don't you know," said Pauline, "there are very few colored restrooms in the area?"

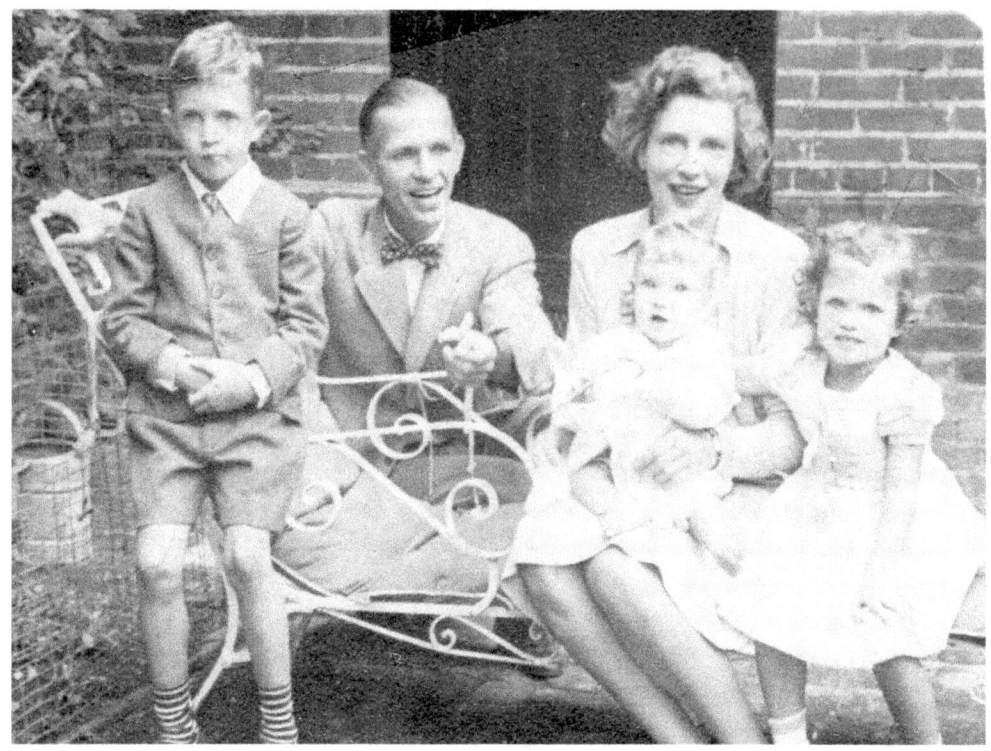

CHILDREN

Never Knew There Were Children.

I was a kid with low self-esteem—in awe of both my parents—my father, on Harvard's Board of Overseers, and my mother , a published poet.

Catherine Hiss, a Georgetown neighbor, confided: "I knew your mother for seven years before I discovered she had two children living in the house!" We were kept out of sight, hidden upstairs, secluded, smothered and shielded, like some embarrassment. In our house a hushed nothingness prevailed. The dominant mantra was "Do Not Disturb." Within our sterile nursery we lacked nothing. Few were permitted entry, as my father suspected all visitors of carrying dangerous microbes. Our time was spent crayoning—making stick figures of people, houses, clouds. Our conversations were empty of ideas. I welcomed almost anyone, entirely unaware of and unprepared for the world's manipulators.

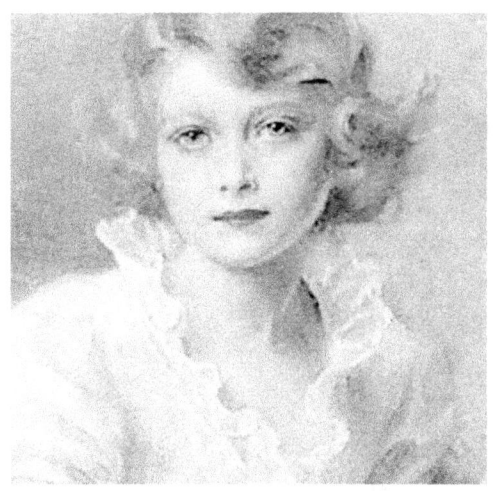

LEFT:

Portrait of Princess Elizabeth by Philip Alexius de Laszlo.

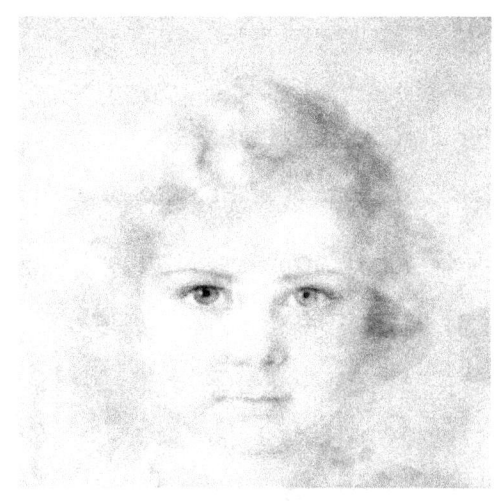

RIGHT:

Portrait of Mary.

There was a lot of friction between Judy and me. I resented having to bear the burden of her wellbeing and wanted to behave like a carefree child. Nothing we did could be spontaneous. We were expected to gush and smile and remain dignified and graceful, relating to the "help" who ran the household according to my father's orders. "Clean your room before the maid sees it." "Finish what's on your plate—the cook's feelings will be hurt if you reject her cooking."

FEAR was the prevailing emotion of my growing years: fear of black people, doctors, airplanes, boys—and kidnapping as a result of the famous Lindbergh kidnapping and murder of March 1932, after which small children became housebound. "Never leave the house alone," we were cautioned.

Our daily routines were fanatically observed. Every day we'd wake, dress, study, eat, sleep and then do it all over again. Our no-nonsense British governess, Rosina Darley, ruled our world. We went everywhere on "shank's mare" (on foot), dressed in identical outfits. Our clothes were made to order by Rowes of Bond Street, in London: a tailor came to measure us every year. We were the American counterparts of the British princesses, Elizabeth and Margaret Rose. For our daily trips to a playground a few blocks away, we were decked out in British tweeds, leggings and white gloves.

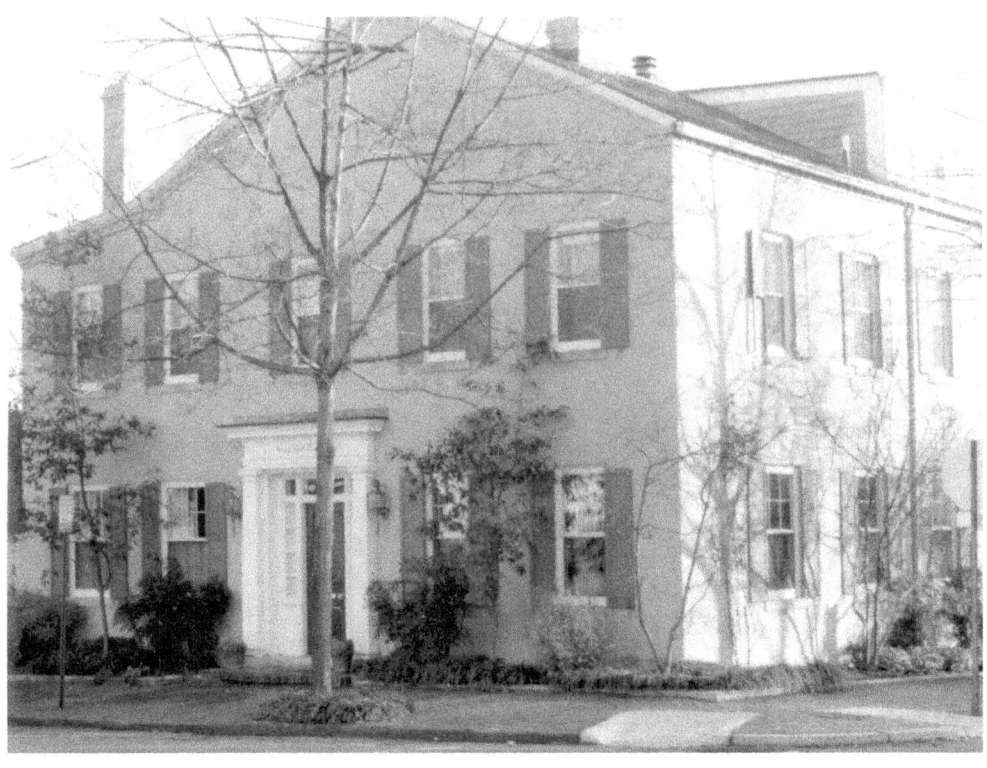

O STREET

Life In Our Big Empty House

2824 O Street became an entertainment center for New Dealers. Built in the Federal period and covering most of the block between 28th and 29th streets, it suited my parents' ambitions perfectly. Close to Rock Creek Park and Dumbarton Oaks, its well manicured garden was enclosed by brick walls. In its midst stood a Palonia tree so immense that its roots were perpetually pushing up the terrace flagstones. As a social attraction and a sign of wealth, it had one of the few heated swimming pools in all of Washington. The fact that they owned rather than rented their house gave them an aura of permanence that only "cave dwellers" possessed. Sophisticated and elegant New Yorkers, my parents soon became the de facto hosts of the nation's capitol. My father made a mean martini, played Bartok records and hung out

16

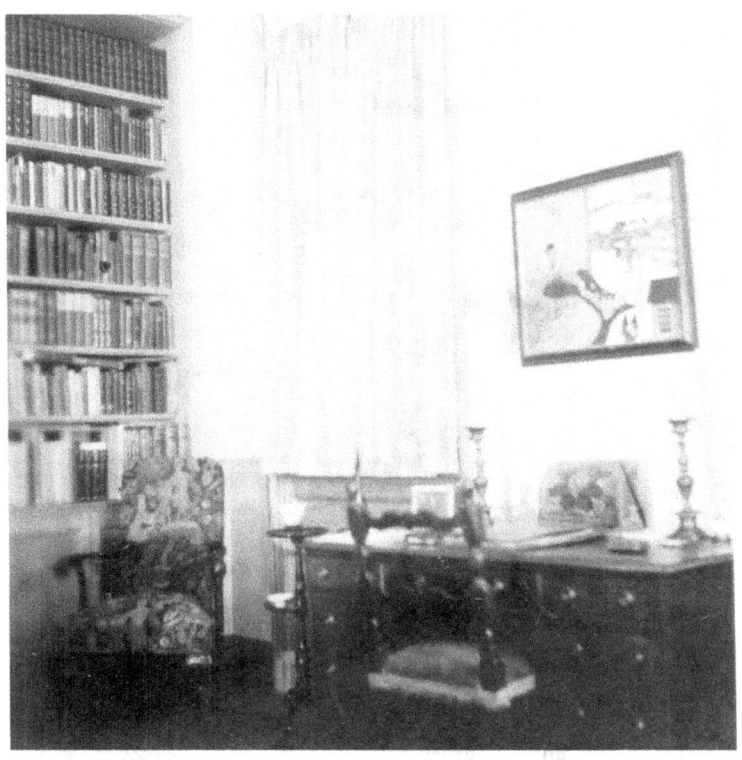

RIGHT:

Corner of living room at 2824 O Street with Peter Blume's "Pig's Feet" painting.

with the Juilliard String Quartet. Katie's clothes were made by an Italian dressmaker and a laundress came once a week to iron her linen/percale sheets. Our house was furnished with hand-stitched tapestries and velvet upholstery. Tea and coffee were served in Meissen china, on tablecloths embellished with our family crest (I'm not sure where we acquired a family crest). A succession of butlers and maids kept everything in order. I remember the living room and the dining room too as having the atmosphere of a public reception hall. Except when there were parties the house was depressingly silent. It was hard to believe a family actually lived there. On Sunday afternoons, my father hosted symposiums that introduced local Georgetown residents and New Dealers to Stringfellow Barr and Scott Buchanan, two gentlemen who established the Great Books curriculum at St. John's College in Annapolis, Maryland.

Paintings by Fernand Léger, Georges Braque, and Joan Miró—artist friends of Aunt Florence—hung on our living room walls. Bookcases contained first editions of poetry, philosophy, religion and art. The 1923 edition of the Encyclopedia Britannica, a twenty-eight-volume resource bound in dark red leather with deep gold lettering, contained everything there was to know. It was printed on thin tissue paper and marked EXTREMELY FRAGILE. We were allowed to use it for research but only when supervised.

If I needed help with homework, I was permitted to ask my father. His ability to conjugate Latin verbs was amazing as was his knowledge of American history. On evenings when he was home, he read Rudyard Kipling and Lewis Carroll aloud to us, clearly enjoying the cadence of the words. Friday nights, the designated children's radio hour, we listened to the "Lone Ranger" and "Henry Aldrich." Mostly, we read from the rich collection of books in our family library: Charles Dickens, Jane Austen, Honoré de Balzac, Aldous Huxley, Graham Greene, E.M. Forster, Evelyn Waugh, William Shakespeare, Rudyard Kipling, T.S. Elliot and W.H. Auden.

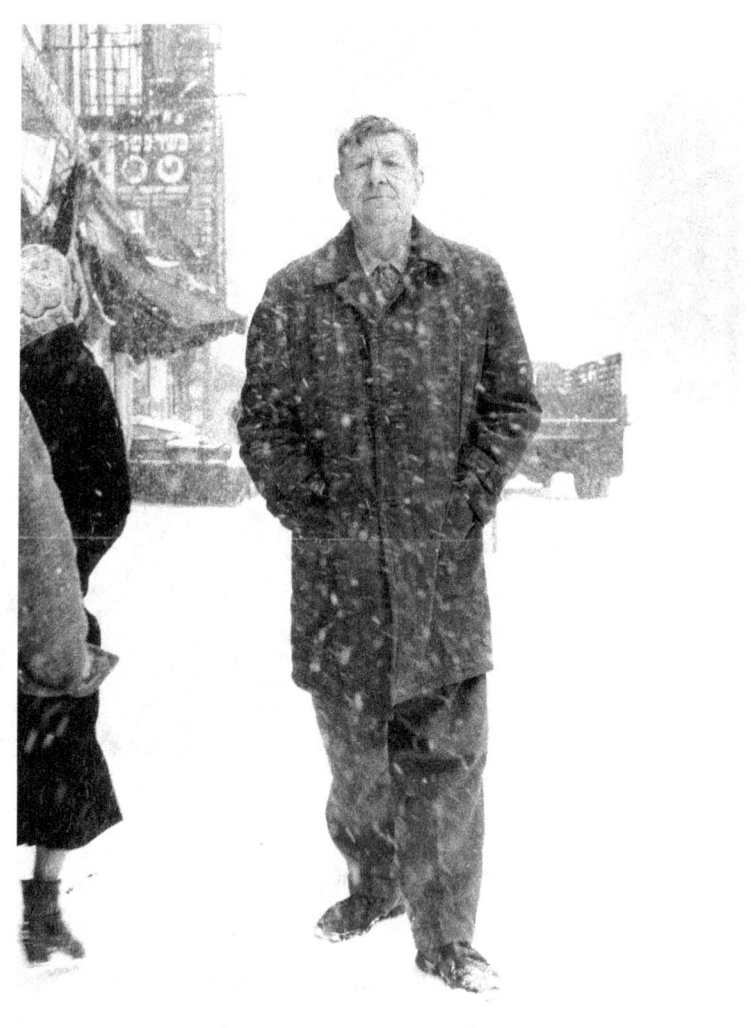

ABOVE:
W.H. Auden, photographed by Richard Avedon.

Auden lived with us for several months during the winter of 1940, hoping my father could help him get a visa. He was applying for a job in a boys' school. (The "truth" referred to in his poem below relates to the efforts my father made to obtain his visa). He wrote:

Suppose that I were Mary's father. . .Well,

These are the principles I would impress

Upon her growing mind. Thou shalt not spell

Deceiving or deception with an s:

Thou shalt not eat the slugs in watercress

Nor swallow ink or glue: Thou shalt not yell

At meals or spit upon thy governess;

And truth is not the proper thing to tell.

On rare occasions, Judy and I dined with the grownups, greeting them with a curtsy, perfected in our nursery, sitting silently on grandmother Frankie's needlepoint chairs, fearful that a guest would address us in a syrupy, pseudo-caring manner. I felt more like a stranger in my house than the visitors did.

CONSIDERATION FOR "THE HELP"

We never ate in restaurants—Katie remained fearful of tasting onions and garlic in prepared food. We were not allowed to enter our kitchen on O Street—disturbing the cook—"or being in the way." Katie lived in fear that she would be called on to cook if the cook quit. George and Lucille Banks lived with us for many years until one fateful day when George, the butler/chauffeur fell down the backstairs. "Drunk," my father muttered and fired them both.

Food was available only when served in our austere dining room. Meals followed a certain unspoken routine. If Judy and I were not seated at the dinner table by seven p.m., we had no dinner. No excuses were tolerated. The menus seldom varied. "Floating Island" dessert was the all-time favorite—a kind of yellow soupy liquid, on top of which puffs of whipped egg white stood stiffly.

Dinner table conversation was monitored and topics required approval. Comments about our school day, as long as they weren't derogatory, were acceptable; but silly remarks, jokes and uncontrolled laughter were strictly forbidden. I derived great pleasure in making Judy laugh and invariably was sent from the table and banished to my room. Ah, but the satisfaction of disrupting the dinner was far greater than that of the food I missed. Judy soon learned to be a perfect daughter, devoted, compliant and obedient, happy to stay at home and follow the rules.

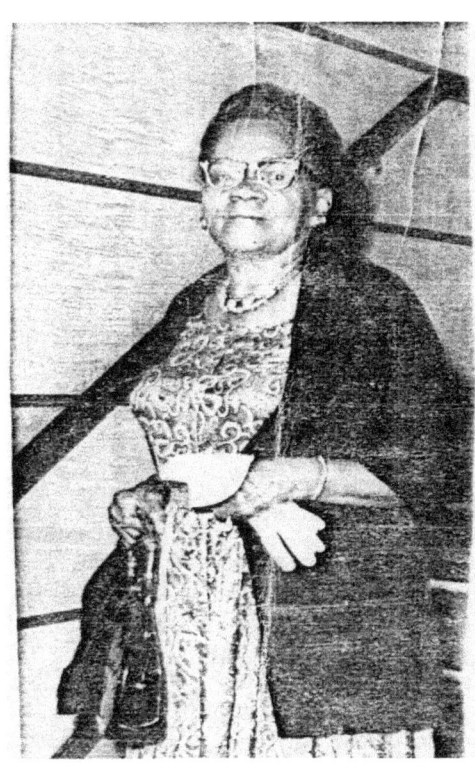

FRANCES PHIPPS

Frances Phipps, our black maid from Georgia, suffering badly from arthritis on both knees, waited on my parents with an unbelievable devotion for most of her life, trudging up and down flights of stairs, fussing over their fussiness**. She was rewarded with a modest salary along with one Sunday off every other week. On the morning of her "day off" she would cook a chicken, set the kitchen table and then go out on the street and try to hail a Washington, D.C. taxi to take her home. Taxis rarely stopped for black passengers.

Frances was very knowledgeable when it came to Washington society. Her opinions about who came to our house were always shared with Katie who listened to them carefully.

Practical and stubborn, she had special privileges. Even Katie was a little afraid of her. Devoted to my father, she had a temper equal to his. No one wanted to be on her wrong side.

** My father was a very fussy man. My daughter, Frances, was equally fussy. Frances Phipps called her, "Little Walter."

THE TELEPHONE ON O STREET

Our only telephone was lodged in my parents' bedroom. My father found the sound of its incessant bell irritating. I would shut myself in their room, lie lazily over the top of the bed and chat with a school friend. Invariably, a parent would enter and shuttle me off to my homework, declaring that whatever I had to say was not worth their monthly AT&T charges. Katie's fluency on the telephone however, her phone calls to Aunt Louise in far off New York City, lasted hours, and her dependence on it as an escape from home life made me aware of its tantalizing capabilities.

I remember my father's face when the phone rang during dinner. A cloud of annoyance passed over it. The phone calls were always for my mother and my father would say, "Katie, tell them to call back." Katie never did. I rather enjoyed the added tension these phone calls caused. They relieved the aura of stern obedience.

SEVENTEEN, a magazine for teenagers, was my connection to a less constricted world. The "page boy," a hair style for girls who didn't have frizzy hair like mine, was the rage, as was the "jitterbug," a dance that required a boy—I knew none.

Cigarettes and suntans and endless hamburgers from Hamburger Heaven—we spent our free time lying in the sun to achieve a bronzed look, chain-smoking.

SUMMER CAMP

1940

Gradually I became aware of the sizable gap between my parent's lives and mine. They went out to dinners, events, ceremonies, celebrations, and consequently had little time to deal with us. Judy compensated by living privately, with her stuffed animal family. They occupied her attention, distracted her from the pain of being a child in an all grown-up world. When she married, she took the animals with her.

I searched for escape routes, studying summer camp catalogs with their slick photos depicting halcyon days: sleeping in a tent, canoeing, swimming in sparkling lakes, riding horseback on sweetly shaded trails, singing around a campfire. Camp Aloha in Fairlee, Vermont seemed a dreamland.

Reality proved otherwise. The tents held too many bunks, a crowd scene with campers who mastered the art of complaining loudly and fighting over who goes first and who got more. Swimming was not in a lake but a mud hole, a pond filled with leeches. Canoeing facilities consisted of two canoes always occupied by older campers. Rain was frequent and tents leaked; counselors huddled and smoked, drinking warm beer.

I knew my parents would be angry if I asked to come home before the eight weeks were over. Somehow a *deus ex machina* saved me: I contracted whooping cough. Why was I the only camper to come down with it? For two weeks, I was isolated in the camp infirmary, a dark cabin, miles from everyone. My parents were traveling and couldn't come get me. My camp dream dissolved into a nightmare.

DOCTORS, HOSPITALS AND MEDICAL PROCEDURES

My mother took us to doctors, and I believed that they were infallible. Still, as a girl I developed a fear of them, fed by my father's fear that they would take control and perform strange, unnecessary procedures without consent.

My first medical experience in Norwalk, Connecticut, in 1940, confirmed these fears. On our trip to Vermont, I complained of stomach cramps. We pulled into the parking lot of Norwalk Hospital where the E.R. doctors announced that my ruptured appendix had to come out right then-and-there. I was rushed into the operating room and a black rubber mask slammed over my face. The intensity of the ether, coupled with the manner in which it was administered (the nurse said the mask would smell like orange juice and she lied), made me fearful of ALL medical procedures. However, I did not follow my father and sister into Christian Science.

I even developed the audacity to challenge doctors. On a routine visit to a gynecologist, I was advised to have a hysterectomy. Learning that I would lose my ovaries, I researched instead of simply following my gynecologist's advice and found Nora Coffey's HERS Foundation, in Bala Cynwyd, Pa., dedicated to helping women avoid unnecessary surgeries—exactly what I did.

MY PARENTS
WALTER AND KATIE

In their marriage, my parents complemented each other: Walter with his Harvard-honed intellect, Katie with her finishing-school charm. While Walter sought anonymity, Katie craved the spotlight. Every invitation that landed on Katie's desk elicited a positive response. She rarely missed an opportunity to show up, flash her winning smile and greet everyone with a warm political bear hug.

Walter idolized Katie—indulged her every whim and forgave all her indiscretions. He described her talents as "not strictly intellectual but unusual and creatively inspirational." I remember searching for lost diamond earrings (one of Walter's many extravagant gifts) among piles of autumn leaves on Georgetown sidewalks more than once. At that time, ear-piercing was strictly for the onion-and-garlic crowd.

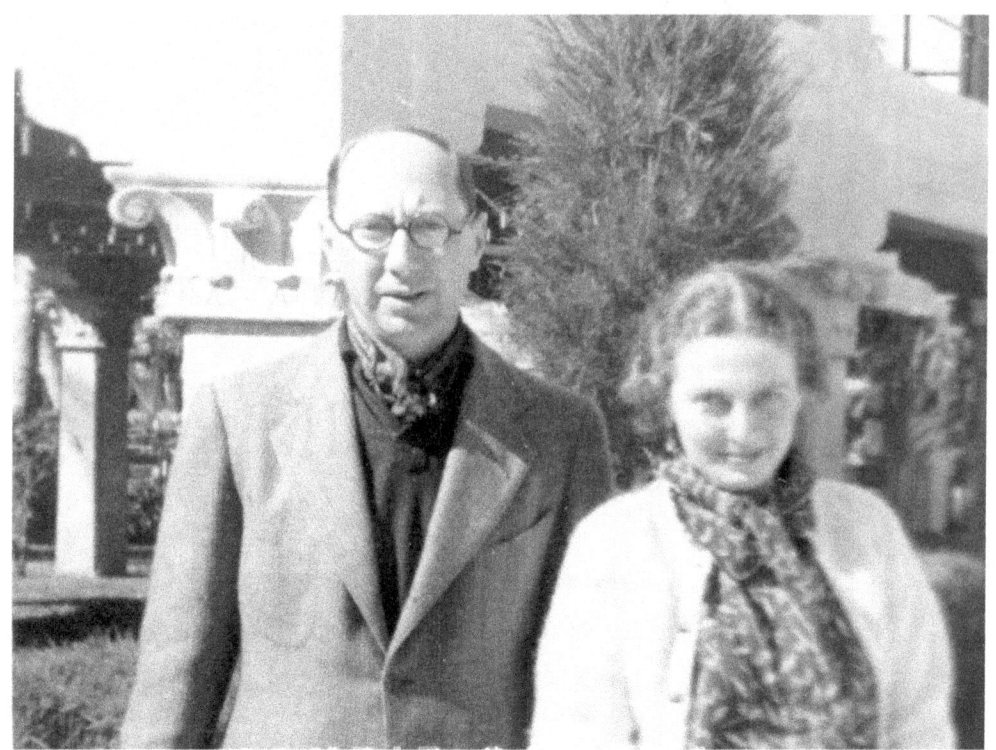

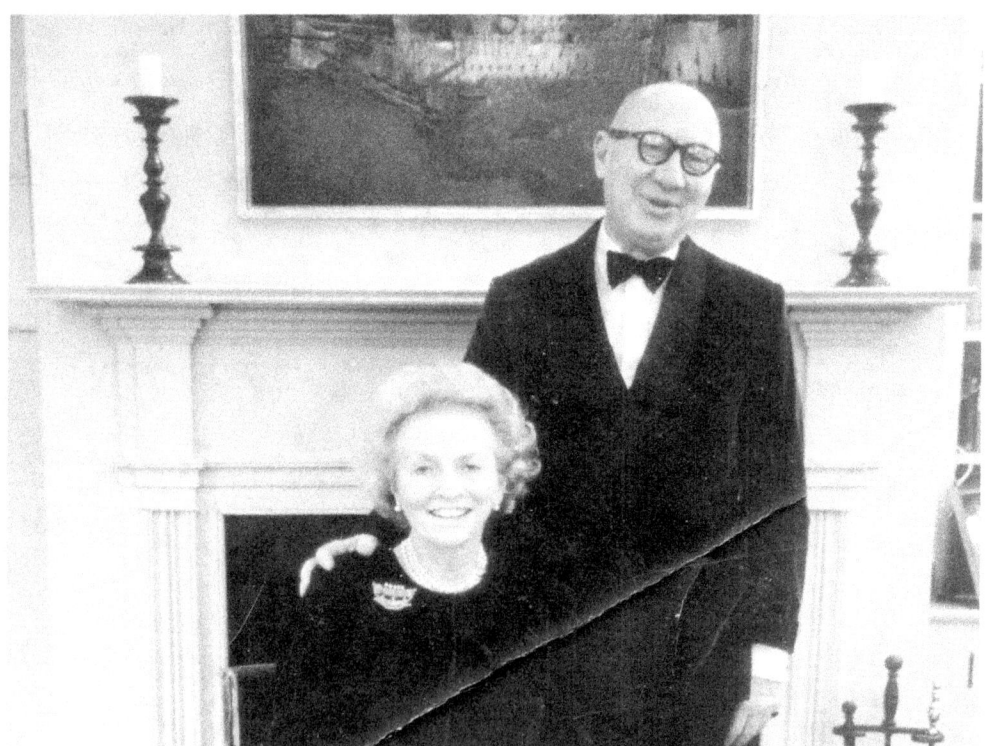

BOTTOM LEFT:

*Walter and Katie thirty
years later in front
of their Georgetown
fireplace.*

WALTER

As a young girl, I saw my father infrequently. Much of his life was spent behind closed doors. His need for privacy, listening to his fine collection of classical recordings, chamber works by Beethoven, Mozart and Brahms on 33 1/3 recordings in his room, or reading the Bible and correlative passages from Mary Baker Eddy's Christian Science textbook, or even writing and sending anonymous letters of advice regarding U.S financial policy to Presidents Truman, Kennedy and Johnson consumed his evening hours. My mother's social calendar—cocktails and formal dinners both at home and elsewhere—pleasures I'm not sure he shared in equal measure, tired and bored him but his devotion to her and her ability to attract and include interesting people in his life kept him endlessly occupied.

On rare evenings when he was just home, he chose musically inclined stories to read to Judy and me. The books he chose all possessed musical language. He was particularly fond of Rudyard Kipling's Jungle Books, full of such cadenced names as Mowgli and Baloo and such alliterative descriptions as "the great green greasy Limpopo River." When we were older, he liked to read Samuel Taylor Coleridge's visionary (opium induced) poem, *Kubla Khan*—"In Xanadu, did Khubla Khan a stately pleasure dome decree/ Where Alph the sacred river ran from caverns measureless to man down to the shining sea." Although music was his passion and he played his well-worn classical recordings for hours on end, I do not recall ever being invited to listen with him. It was his time alone.

It was often said that Walter lacked the gift of suffering fools gladly. However, at my birthday parties he would become the charming ringmaster, reciting his favorite "shaggy dog" stories and directing the Lemon Dance, operating the arm of our Victrola—lifting it to eliminate the dancing couple stuck holding the lemon.

Although my parents led separate lives, they complemented each other. They worked very well as a team. Deep down, my father enjoyed my mother's ability to attract the "right people." My father provided the props—the money, the gourmet food and imported wines necessary to produce the grand show.

Ours was not a cozy home, but a stage set for entertaining. My father performed to perfection, choosing elegant, sophisticated furnishings with an eye for impressing guests—Aubusson carpets, velvet upholstery, iridescent taffeta and tasseled drapes. Cutting-edge magazines—*The Nation, the Paris Review, The Economist, The New Yorker*—were scattered casually about for effect.

In this decorative effort, my father had the help of his sister, Florence. Her paintings by such currently acclaimed artists as Juan Miro, Fernand Leger and Pierre Matisse, were virtually unknown in the pseudo-colonial homes of Washington's wealthy Southern elite—the so-called "cave-dwellers."

Choosing the perfect outfit for each occasion consumed his attention and he derived great pleasure in arranging ties, shirts, handkerchiefs, and in winter, scarves and overcoats in colorful, blended harmonies. For each activity, he had suitable clothing. He became known as a perfectly outfitted gentleman. Our attic was filled with his clothing, each one carefully inscribed with its date, and the season when it would be appropriate to wear it, and the activity for which it would be suited.

28

Our cooks prepared five-course banquets, including mock-turtle soup and crab bisque, while Negro butlers serving with white gloves poured wines flown in from Provence cellars. These and other gourmet items graced the menus my father crafted for my mother's celebrity dinners.

My father spent his life surrounded by girls, and later, women. As a boy, his two sisters dominated family life and as a husband and father, his wife and two daughters, including his mother and mother-in-law Adele, made women once again the determinators. Adele, Katie's mother, was financially destitute and dependent on Walter for monthly support. His dollars never really covered her expenses and there was much handwringing and despair over her shortage.

Frankie, Walter's mother, was lonely. As a widow, living in her gracious Plaza Hotel apartment, she wanted Walter to visit frequently. And somehow, he found these visits to his mother intolerable. So much so, that he would select the longest route possible to arrive at the Plaza— leaving Washington on the B&O Railroad, which landed him in New Jersey and required a ferryboat ride across the Hudson to get to New York City, in preference to the Pennsylvania Railroad which had a direct route from Penn Station, on West 34th street. After a short visit with her in her apartment, my father would hasten downstairs to consume a sumptuous lunch at the Plaza's Persian Room, and jump on the B&O train back to Washington, getting home later that same evening in time to help Judy or me with homework.

During my father's long stretch of government service, Marie Cuthill remained his loyal and extremely devoted secretary. My mother resented her constant presence. in our house and never knew how to deal with her. She could not accept her as a friend. Marie was made from different cloth. Petite, dainty, well coiffed, her outfits emphasizing her eighteen-inch waist, the clicking sounds of her high-heeled shoes creating stress in my mother's face, she followed my father around with her shorthand pad at the ready, her equally subservient spaniel, Pukka, trailing the procession. Shortly after my father became a member of the Christian Science Church, Marie joined him every Sunday morning. It was rumored that Marie and my father were having an affair, although no proof was ever forthcoming.

Sometime during the late 1930's, my mother found a solution for Marie's evergreen presence. She rented a cottage in a dense forest in Blue Ridge Summit, Virginia, and invited Marie to serve as our surrogate mother. We left our forest glen to drive to Leesburg but only when Marie's cigarette supply ran out. Our days were spent learning to sew rickrack on the hems of skirts. It was the longest and dullest three months ever, but kept us out of Washington's serious summer heat wave and Marie from my father. As time passed, my mother lost interest in her whereabouts and I guess my father did, also.

Quite in contrast to Washington's political and social goings on, my mother chose Chatham, Massachusetts, on the elbow of Cape Cod, a small fishing village discovered by her liberal Democratic friends, as a summer respite from Washington's humidity and mosquitoes. Here, with Chatham's year-round stodgy Republican fishermen residents, she felt most at home and persuaded my father to buy an old farmhouse on a hill overlooking Stage Harbor. and a plot in the local Christian cemetery.

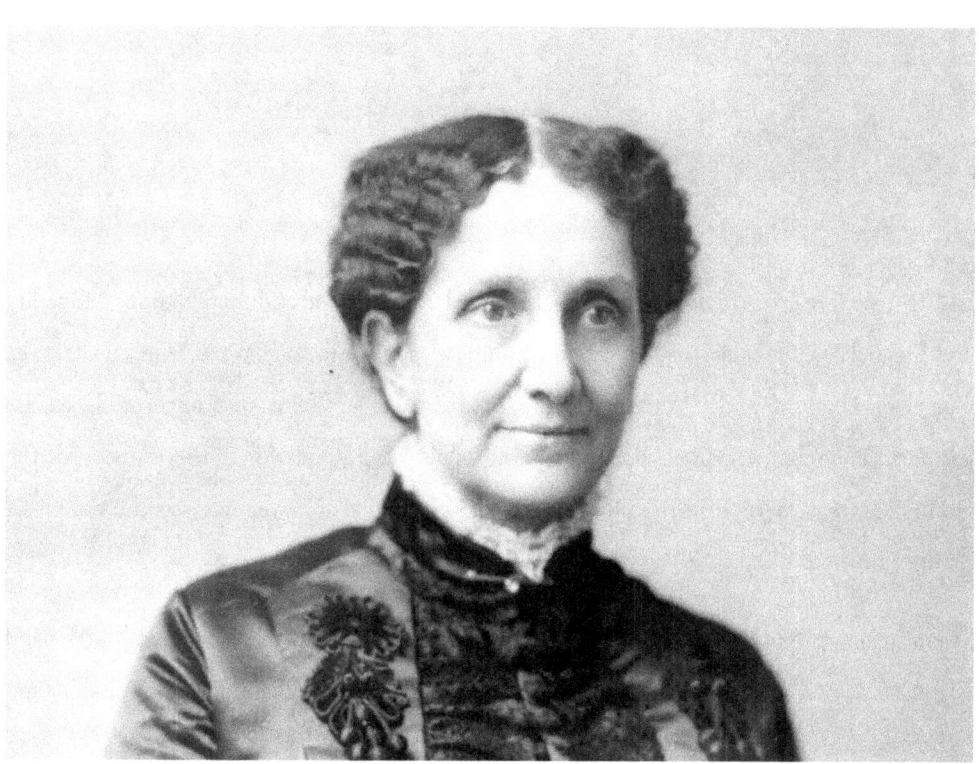

Hating the feeling of sand in his shoes, my father took to identifying and feeding local birds and encouraged my daughter, Didi, to assist him. And to be sure that he would be able to worship on summer Sundays, as he had recently converted to Christian Science, he organized and financed the building of a Christian Science church (now Unitarian) a mile from his house.

Christian Science had become a very important part of his life, a sort of protective insurance against doctors and medicine—a religion he had learned about from his mother-in-law, Adele—a religion which had ironically brought them closer together and would ultimately attract my sister and cause her premature death as well as his own.

In 1944, my father was invited to participate in the Bretton Woods (United Nations Monetary and Financial) Conference in New Hampshire, as an advisor to the United States delegation. Called by Lord Maynard Keynes, who believed that government spending could activate national economies, and that deficit spending could be a good thing. The purpose of the Conference was to stabilize the fluctuating dollar. Its signal achievement was the establishment of the World Bank.

When plans to build a national highway through the city were announced, my father and Elizabeth Rowe, a friend/neighbor, joined the National Capital Planning Commission, and organized protests. They warned against growing modernization and disruption of L'Enfant's original plans. L'Enfant had written: "Washington needs avenues providing reciprocity of sight, ensuring a rapid intercourse with all parts of the city."

Music was his passion, however, and when his friend, the renowned concert violinist, Yehudi Menuhin visited us in Georgetown, he persuaded my father to rent a chalet in Gstaad, Switzerland, in summer, where for many years, Yehudi organized chamber music festivals. Almost as dear to him as his faith in teachings of Mary Baker Eddy were the weekly chamber music concerts offered in the Coolidge Auditorium of the Library of Congress (a most incongruous confluence of controversy and composure.) My father never failed to attend these Friday night concerts and wanting to share his love of music with the great unwashed humanity beyond the Hudson, he underwrote live broadcasts of every program. I don't know whether he ever received responses of gratitude from listeners but Robert Mann, the first violinist of the Juilliard Quartet, wrote, "When I was a teenager in Portland Oregon, I dreamed of the ideal future as I listened to the radio broadcasts of the Budapest Quartet from the Library of Congress."

32

"A miracle came to pass and then I was playing on the Library's Stradivarius instruments in the Coolidge Auditorium and the music was indeed reaching out through our country in broadcasts just like the Budapest. These broadcasts were made possible by the generosity of Walter Louchheim. But even more wonderful was the friendship that grew between Walter and myself." Robert Mann and the Juilliard Quartet honored Walter by playing an all-Beethoven memorial concert in the Coolidge Auditorium, in March, 1973, shortly after he died.

Devoted throughout his life to study, my father became interested in the Great Books program developed by Stringfellow Barr and Scott Buchanan, Deans of St. John's College, in Annapolis, Maryland. The vision inspiring the program, according to Buchanan, was that the "great books of European thought are the classics and are the best instruments of education, to teach the real, traditional liberal arts. The Bible was selected as the best model, as it has become the scriptures of the whole race. This is the most read book on the list and its inspiration has spread backward and forward throughout all the classics." Its intention was to promote study beyond confines of the college. Its main audience was the already intellectually aware.

In 1943, my father persuaded Barr and Buchanan to lead seminars based on their program in his living room. Many of his friends and neighbors attended. It was a great source of pride to him that erudite discussions were being held in his home under his aegis. It nicely supplemented his reputation for having the most knowledgeable collection of classical records in Washington.

It was usually at more informal lunch parties, where the guests suspected he was teasing them, that my father brought out his "shaggy-dog" jokes. Only he could tell them. It's as if they grew out of his brain. One of my favorites was The Left-Handed Teacups (my father and I were both left-handed).

"A man went shopping for left-handed teacups. None of the shopkeepers could oblige. Flnally, a clever shop owner went to the rear of his store, and turned all the cup handles to the left. Triumphantly returning to his customer he said, "yes, of course. Here are some cups made especially for left handed people."

Georgetown was my father's preferred residence and driving his smartly polished black Jaguar over its old cobblestones gave him great satisfaction.

Tennis was my father's only sport. He had the ability to place the ball wherever he wanted it to land and seemed to enjoy teaching me. I was always amazed by his ability to stand in one place on the court, reaching effortlessly from one side to the other, returning the ball, never missing and never exerting himself. His tennis outfit never varied: white flannel slacks and a La Coste cashmere sweater. He never seemed to sweat or even get overly warm like the rest of us.

We were surprised when my father in his retirement years accepted an offer of membership in the remote and lofty Cosmos Club, an eating establishment for men of some local distinction. Not a club-joining sort of person, we were amused when we learned that it wasn't long before he became known there as its nattiest dresser. Perhaps advancing age brought many changes to my father—the most surprising his casting a vote for Richard Nixon for U.S. President. Having galloped into Washington as an ardent Democrat and New Dealer, he walked ever so slowly out of town as a Republican inheriting his father's ardent commitment to the Republican Party.

In 1968 Walter said, "Our army in Vietnam is like the Crusaders who went to rescue Christianity from the Muslims but it turned out to be an excuse to slaughter people." Regarding integrated education, Walter asked, "Why integration?" "Why not separate but equal schools?"

The night before he died, February 19, 1973, he phoned and asked me to come to say "goodbye." He spoke in an everyday—I'm going away and take care of this until I come back sort of—manner, saying, "Your mother needs a new stove. Please take care of getting one for her." Because he was always in denial about being sick, I knew nothing. And my mother rarely entered our kitchen, so this request for a new stove struck me then as it does now, symbolic of one of the great tragedies of their marriage. Katie had no interest in food preparation, while for my father, the pleasure of eating was what life—his life—was all about.

I wrote for his Memorial service—

"My father had a facility for simplifying and clarifying.

His wit was dry, like the Martinis he was famous for making. He maintained perfumed surroundings, elegant in all matters.

Suits, shirts, ties and even socks were carefully combined—the colors subtle, the textures various.

He preferred privacy, hated unexpected visitors (and unstimulating guests.)

Patience he had little of, punctuality a requirement.

He favored work as pleasure, rejected idleness as unprofitable.

His musical ear was that or a professional. He excelled at recognizing melodies, motifs and their composers.

Making final visits: Along with my mother, who cheered and encouraged him, came Judy who lavished him with trifles, Frances Phipps who pampered him knowingly, Charney, my daughter Didi's dog, who obeyed and appreciated him, and the rest of us whom he loved on short, not too routine—disturbing visits—and on Monday January 29, 1973, I made my last one."

Mayor Walter Washington came and personally installed a No Parking sign in front of our house. Katie purchased an oxygen mask at the corner drug store that didn't work. The RN nurse refused to work without written instructions. Katie heard a rattle in Walter's breathing. An insufficient dose of Demerol was administered. Judy read the Christian Science lesson. My father spoke these words with determination: "I want to die in peace, like Ivan Illich," "Tell your mother to let me die without all this fuss."

Several weeks after his death, February 23, 1973, my mother hosted a Memorial service at the Coolidge Auditorium of the Library of Congress. The Juilliard Quartet played his four favorite Beethoven quartets. The end of his life mirrored his dispassionate approach to himself—never blow your own horn. He was the most se!f-effacing person—willing to put Katie in center stage, he became the forgotten man.

Excerpts from condolence letters praising him:

a Renaissance man whose sensitivity made it possible for him to understand and appreciate all the major aspects of our cultural life to an extent and in such depth as is seldom given to one

— Donald Cook, Chairman of American Electric Power

an urbane, cultured English gentleman rarely seen without a furled umbrella

his warmth and humor combined with his rare wisdom and good judgment made him a friend whom I and many others valued

— Arthur Sulzberger, C.E.O., *New York Times*

the crackling conversations and controversies over issues that really count and that pervading sense of empathy even when we were at each others' throats on issues concerning gold, the dollar, or the domestic economy all evoked some of the fondest memories

—Walter Heller, Economist

he could have been one of the Medicis but with a heart. I always learned from chats with him, whether on· money or music, but more than that, came away bolstered by his warmth

—Frank Freidel, Harvard University Press

while we are much richer for having known him, we are much poorer for having lost him.

—Scott Reston, Columnist, Washington Post

KATIE, MY MOTHER, AKA KATHLEEN BARBARA (SCHOENFELD) — SCOFIELD

High School Graduate becomes Assistant Secretary of State

Katie, the only child in a house full of arguing grownups, grappled with her agressions and anger. She railed against her mother's stiff formal, Germanic conventions, best observed when in her diary she described the furniture in their house. The shades were always found drawn to protect the purple velvet chairs from becoming sunbleached, chairs–built to fit no human shape. And she missed having a father in residence. The Joseph's house 47 West 86th St, was dominated and ruled by women.

She developed social skills to override her contemporaries and in 1960, reached the top of the National Democratic Party as Chairman. When John Kennedy became President, she created a Department for herself as Assistant Secretary of State for Women's Affairs. With car and chauffeur, she rose above the "secretarial pool."

Well-bred women were scarce in political caucuses in 1938. My mother was a novelty—outspoken, observant and available—always willing to sacrifice a home chore for an exciting round of political talk. But more important, she had enough money and Walter's reluctant permission to travel. He knew that if he tried to force her into being a homebody, he would lose her. So he settled.

At home, in her smartly furnished Georgetown town house, she was simply "Mrs. Walter Louchheim," wife of an internationally respected economist, but out there, in the real world, she amazed and impressed newspaper columnists and television reporters with her smart-ass

38

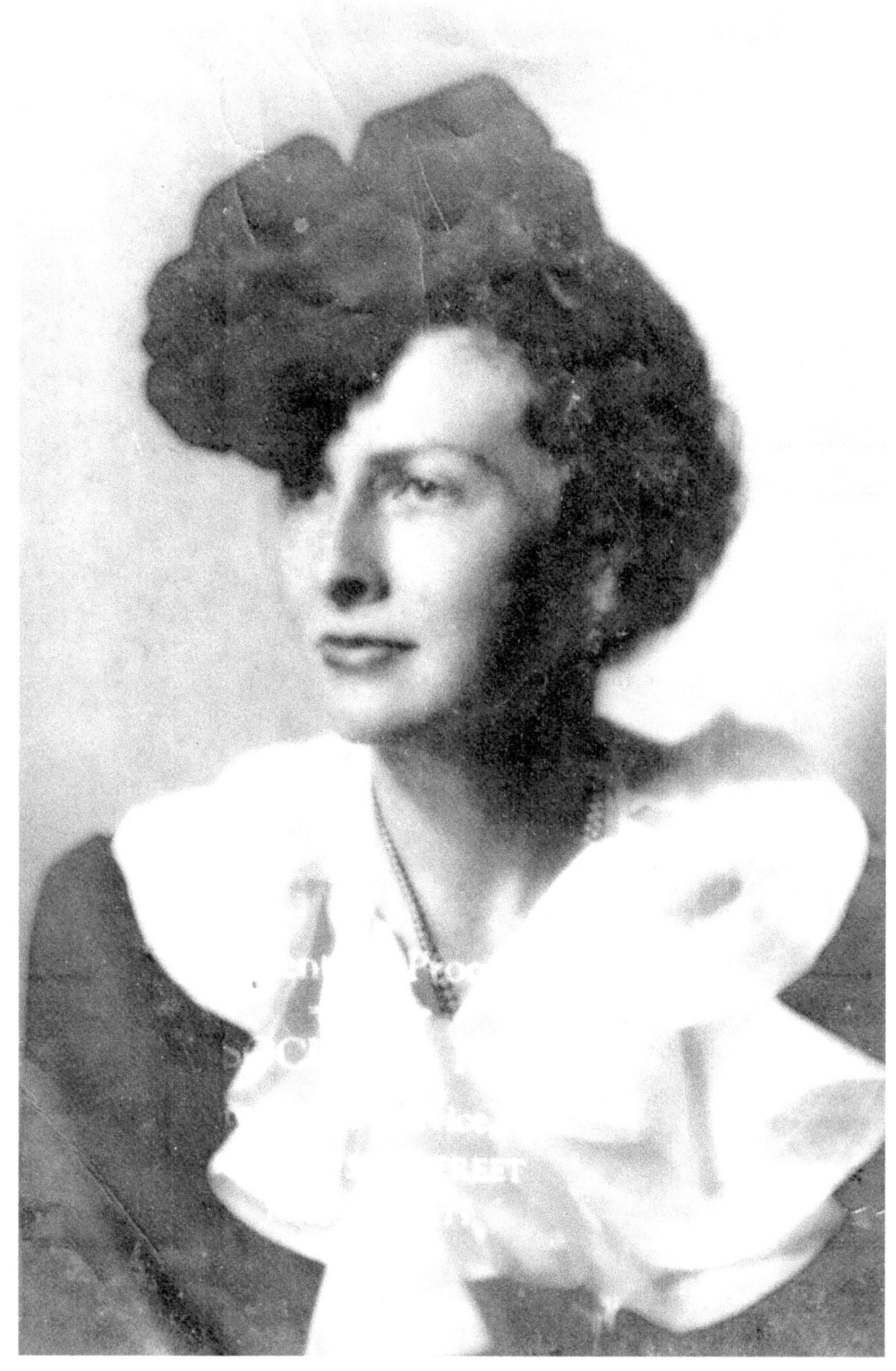

responses and savvy. Secretly insecure, lacking a college education, she overcame the loss, becoming a published poet.

Katie had verve, charm and a gift for oratory. She loved having people around her—people with important titles. A natural beauty, with a tongue like a dragon, she was capable of dazzling put-downs. I don't remember seeing much of her when I was growing up. At home, she was on the phone, composing poetry on her Royal typewriter, entertaining a group of Democratic women from Tennessee, napping with her door closed, or dressing in evening finery, wearing all her jewelry. Her beauty and people-maneuvering, her pert

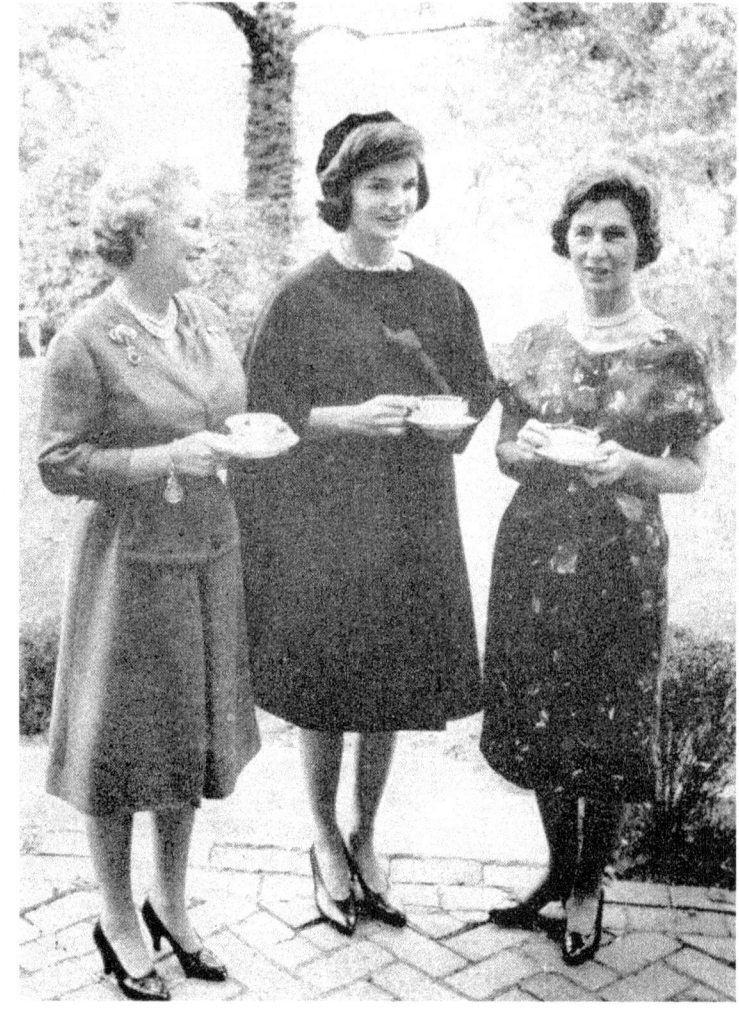

ABOVE:
Katie with Jackie Kennedy and her mother.

sarcasms and clever one-liners combined with her winning smile, frequently enlisted an entire room of folks—visiting ambassadors, political punsters, Supreme Court Justices, even Vice Presidents. I had no appreciation for the effort involved in her "friendships." I know that she nurtured them, hosted dinners in their honor, and was quick to help a cause or campaign. It

40

For My Daughter at Christmas

My dearest daughter, this year, Mary
let's vary
our traditional Christmas ritual,
skip our habitual
shopping and instead, let's try to find
a special kind
of gift; an imperishable shimmering thought,
all wrought
of spangled meaning, a permanent
ornament
to hang upon our tree of love.

Let's see what Merry Christmas really means!
Do our dreams
of brotherly love, good will and peace
suddenly cease
to seem improbable? Does our littleness
gladly confess
the inadequate, tawdry quality
of its reality,
and yearning for divinity, remember
each December
to hang its shiny hopes upon the tree?

What motivates this frantic giving?
Is just living
never enough, do the pretty parcels hide
good deeds denied?
To find what we want won't be simple,
the tinsel,

the bow, the mistletoe and holly berry
all have very
special magic meanings; but gifts are laid
away, greens fade
and then our tree will barren be.

I've found a gift, but what I got
I'm afraid is not
For keeps, it's a Christmas angel's gadget,
I suspect.
Come, look out the window, see how near
the cold clear
stars have come; I've borrowed one, the same
they claim
the weary kings pursued; take it, it can teach
us much, reach
for its spangled scriptures, hang them on our tree.

Dear Mary, bring the yule log, hang the wreath,
stand beneath
our shimmering tree, and when on distant days
our dreary ways
consume us, look up again and see
our star—be
guided by it, note how the wheel of night
her light
augments; the wisdom of the stars,
lies, like ours,
in membership, one of another.
                                    KATIE LOUCHHEIM.

was difficult to refuse her. She had a way of persisting and beguiling. She would have made a great politician. Eugene McCarthy, running for U.S. President, credited her with pulling together various factions of the Democratic party. People-hopping, people-dropping, moving ever upwards on the Washington political/social ladder became her *façon de vivre*—innocent enough as a social maneuver, more damaging when passed on and practiced by me and my sister in marriage and divorce.

41

Writing poems to commemorate special family occasions, Katie's first volume of poetry, "With or without Roses," was published by Doubleday, in 1960. Abigail McCarthy praised her poems: "You with your elegant photogeneity. Writing the lyric of wry spontaneity." When Louise Bogan came to Washington as Poet Laureate to the Library of Congress in 1945, she encouraged and advised her, "depend on the verb and forget all those unnecessary adjectives."

Daisy Harriman's (Mrs. J. Borden Harriman) influence on my mother was most apparent when my parents entertained in the grand manner. A tall, autocratic woman with Grecian features and white hair framing her to-the-manor-born-face, Daisy was known for her Sunday night supper-salons in Georgetown where Washington policymakers dined. Katie was often conscripted to help organize those Sunday evenings and she learned from Daisy.

Katie put forth just the right amounts of formality and informality, just the right selection of food and wine–created a sparkling new stage on which she reigned. A Supreme Court Justice, a prominent journalist, several Senators and a sprinkling of Ambassadors and their wives made up the guest lists.

When my parents married, my mother was my father's inferior. He was her mentor. But, as time passed, the roles reversed; he learned to take orders from her and often felt demeaned by her. At large formal dinners, my mother presided at the head of the table, her commanding presence, learned from Daisy, controlled the flow and direction of conversation.

SOME EARLY KATIE POEMS:

MARCH 1978

The snow unbidden

Laid a downy cap

On all that was

Last night

And stilled the limbs

Of green and brown

And even stilled the sound of wind chimes

Where they hung

It stilled the footfalls

Of all moving things

But not the voices of birds who found

Within the branches stilled

A haven from which to trill

It's come, It's come—

The spring!

DINNER AT EIGHT

*The New Frontier*** by candle light*

Dine with Madame X tonight.

Down the white cloth public faces

Take their place-card plotted places.

Heads of missions, heads of bureaus,

Pentagon and Senate heroes,

Pundits flattering their sources,

Seven lavish succulent courses.

Small talk lost in big talk boomers

Rises to a roar of rumors.

Dear Madame X. you're a success—

Each guest is drowning out each guest.

Stocks are up but Laos falters,

Discourse dipped in wine can't alter

What is lost is not a nation

But the art of conversation.

*** The New Frontier was a phrase coined by candidate John F. Kennedy when he was running for U.S. President.

The UNINSTRUCTED DELEGATE   May 11, 48.

I feel like an instructed delegate. All I need is a badge that says Mrs. K.
Louchheim, representing those who do not know where to go but want to attend.
Want to be there, where the event is unfolding, where the moment is slipping
into all the other moments, wanting to witness it, wanting to see it drop into
the street of life. You came without a purpose, Mrs. L? Yes, I came without
purpose. I have only my badge and my pencil. And my curious mind, that
sees and feels and touches it, the event, and then turns away. Where does it
turn to? To another event, to another place that may yield another drop of
happening, another pattern of things that move into another street of forgetting. Is it fear of forgetting that brings you, Mrs. L? Yes, I suppose so.
I am unable to answer truthfully, for it is a question I have answered in so
many different ways. It is certainly fear of something. There are only two
motives that might bring me again and again with my badge and my pencil, fear
is one and the other is what we call an economic necessity. Of the later, I
know nothing, so it must be fear. And the pleasantest and most presentable
kind of fear is that which we call wanting to remember, or fearing we might
forget. It's something of the childhood will, the I want to see, show it to
me, please, I want to see it, and something of the adult that wants to store
and preserve. Some save paper and string, I save memories. Drops of things
that fall and will not fall again. And since its easier to be there and
witness than be absent and regret, I attend. And that's another kind of fear,
the fear of never knowing just what it is you want to witness and the going
and going and going — the trying always to find out what it is that beckons.
You see, if I knew what it was I wanted to witness, I could perhaps stay
quietly here and not go anywhere at all. Just look out the window, note the
colors and seasons and weather and write down what goes on in my mind. Perhaps
its fearing that nothing might go on in my mind, perhaps that's the fear
that takes me everywhere. The fear of being alone with my mind.

But the unistructed delegate has compensations. There is no one this delegate
must report back to, please, placate. You can go at anytime, and if you do
not like what you see or hear, you need not write it down. There is no one
waiting for your report.
But that is just what troubles the uninstructed delegate. There must be
someone to approve, or criticize, or react with a nod. You cannot report
to yourself forever. Or even for a short time. Its very frustrating. And
you don't like it. Far better a small part, a small portion to cover and
observe, than this large unlimited area where you can wander so freely. Here
reporting to a loose leaf note book is very unsatisfactory. There are always
so many ways of not doing even that. No paper, no ink, no pencil, no desk,
no time. And the notebook says nothing at all about these excuses. When you
move it about and touch it only to put further out of reach, it accents this
denial very selfishly.
But if you want to report to someone, then you must chose. And this is difficult.
Choosing, again the child, is frightening. If its only one person you must
report to, what if you should fail them? Being instructed too, limits you. You
have a purpose, a very limited purpose. What, just go out at sun down and see
the street lights go on? What about the mornings, when the early sky unfolds
and the day begins, must I never see it?
Isn't the uninstructed delegate the child after all? Isn't that what we're
discovering? Wanting to be unlimited, free, wanting no authority, not master?
And wanting to see and touch everything? To be an eternal sipper, until the
cup is empty?
"God will not stand for any lukewarmness. He demands silence or boldness. All
I know that suit him are extremes, art and the orders. Levitation is not his
proof of love. He is not lavish with it. But occasionally he raises up a monk
or a poet." Cocteau to Maritain.
And Yeats: "the intellect of man is forced to choose— perfection of the life
or perfection of the work."
Oh to start again and choose— we would know now that it must be the work.
For the life is never perfect, even as an unistructed delegate.

44

I SUBSCRIBE TO ALL THE MAGAZINES!

(girl at table with pile of magazines)

I admit, I'm just a normal, average girl,
about five feet four tall,
with a college degree and a job, snappy clothes,
and a good many nice average beaux
with college degrees, jobs and varying dimensions
but none of them have matrimonial intentions.
Now what does one do, if one's in this fix,
call on Mary Hayworth or Dorothy Dix?
I have, I've written and they've replied,
their advice is excellent but they assume
that what I'm worrying about is a nervous groom.
Once you're committed, these columns are great,
But they're no help at all, when you're on the third date.
So what does a normal nice girl do - sit home and dream?
No indeed, she subscribes to all the "how to" magazines.
She puts all her spare cash on subscriptions,
locks the door and studies the "how to" perscriptions.
She learns how to cream-peach velvet her skin,
how to limber, limber, limber, ten times, her limbs,
how to eat everything and keep oh so thin,
how to find a house to keep a husband -
Never mind the house, how do you get the man?
Here is a complete all-inclusive plan,
129 ways to get a husband, I can't lose,
I'll try 'em all, I'll pick and choose

Get a dog and walk it. I tried that,
my dog got in a fight with a cat,
I met lots of other dogs, no males,
Most dog walkers wear polish on their nails.

Have your car break down in a strategic place.
I chose the Pentagon. Just in case
you try it be sure you have ten bucks,
and Call Carl - he's the one with the towing trucks.

Join a hiking club. I just love long walks,
so do all government girls. And do they like to talk!
They have a wealth of fascinating anecdotes
about the good advice they didn't take from their folks,
they wish they'd stayed in Pasco or Kalamazoo or Troy
where there were lots of nice, eager, marriageable boys.

Sit on a park bench and feed pigeons.
Try it if you like statues or bums.
Attend a night school, take courses men like,
If I knew the answer to that, I'd be somebody's wife.

ABOVE:

*Poem by Katie
Lauchheim.*

45

ALGER HISS

Among the Washington friends who enjoyed the plentiful bounty served by Walter and Katie, Alger Hiss and his brother Donnie with their wives were always welcome. I recall a picnic on a humid Sunday in Rock Creek Park. Alger and his wife, Priscilla, arrived with a bean salad, but because mint juleps were being consumed, little attention was paid to food. Alger walked over and spoke to me as an equal, seemingly to take an interest in what I, a four-year-old, had to say.

When his trial as a Communist spy began, my parents decided they would not testify, would not maintain his innocence. Their position came as a shock to me. I couldn't believe the accusations flung at Alger or imagine him a traitor.

Alger was accused by Whittaker Chambers of sharing State Department documents with Russia. Typewritten papers, allegedly written on his typewriter, were used as proof. The accusations were taken to court and Alger was sent to Lewisburg Prison for five years. I could never believe that he was guilty.

BOTTOM:
Alger Hiss.

In 1983, I found written instructions from my mother to Harvard University Press regarding the publication of her book, The Making of the New Deal. She asked them to remove Alger's photo from her book; she was still troubled by their friendship. Ironically, in a book review, the only image accompanying the review of her book was a photo of Alger Hiss.

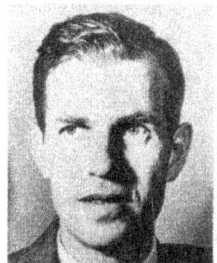

The Making of the New Deal: The Insiders Speak, edited by Katie Louchheim. Abe Fortas, David Riesman, Alger Hiss (shown here), and others recall historic moments, clashes of philosophy, and practical jokes from the time when they were restructuring American society. Harvard University Press; 378 pages; $20; October.

46

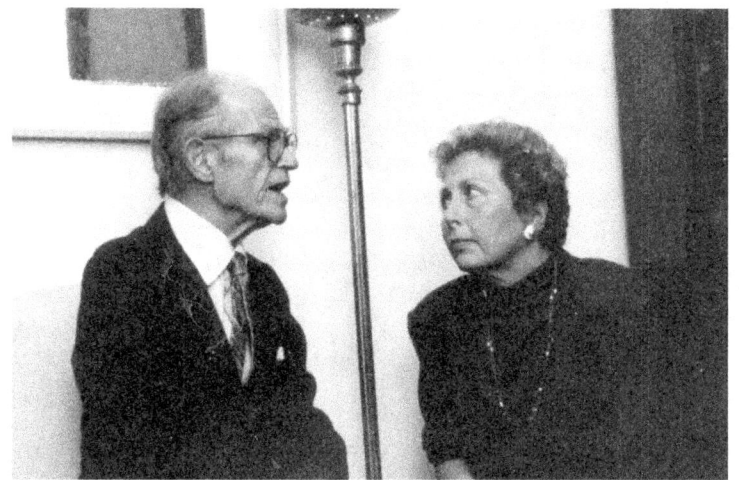

After serving nearly four years in prison on a perjury conviction, Alger moved to New York City, and in 1965 I spotted him ice skating at Wollman Rink in Central Park. His assurance on skates must have derived from years of skating on his pond in Vermont. I asked him to skate with my daughter, Didi, skating around the rink on her own. He was delighted to offer her his arm and off they went! We renewed our friendship and chatted about his "problems."

"I am unable to know when I am in danger or making trouble for myself. I have been told that I throw myself in front of a dragon."

Could this confusion have accounted for his undisclosed innocence?

When Alger lost his sight, I became one of his volunteer readers. His choice of books and newspapers kept me well informed.

My last meeting with him took place in 1992 in his apartment on East 18th Street. His memories were very clear, as if the events had taken place recently. He even remembered the picnic of very long ago—and the bean salad.

47

RELIGION, THE KILLER

Walter, Judy, and The Christian Scientists

Family diaries and treasured letters reveal the dominating role my grandmothers exercised. My grandmother Adele exerted a unique influence.

She either phoned or airmailed "loving" daily instructions and advice to Katie, reminding her of conjugal obligations and maternal duties. Katie was a most devoted daughter and probably suffocated from such intense affection. She wrote her mother daily and in one letter pleaded:"I cannot wait to see you again, Mummy dearest. I want you always by my side."

Adele's letters, stamped "Special Delivery," landed at our front door, a procedure that forced my father to sign for each letter. He never stopped resenting Adele's presence in his life. His verbal attacks on her were brutal. He developed a sneer when referring to her yet recognized Katie's dependence. Adele, in turn, became Walter's dependent, living in a studio apartment on East 72nd Street, waiting anxiously each month for his check.

In an effort to avoid the stigma of being Jewish, Adele subscribed to the preaching of Mary Baker Eddy, the Founder of Christian Science, and persuaded my father to join her. Almost immediately, their relationship became more cordial. Walter was terrified of doctors and rarely consulted them. Here was a religion that virtually did away with medicine, substituting reliance

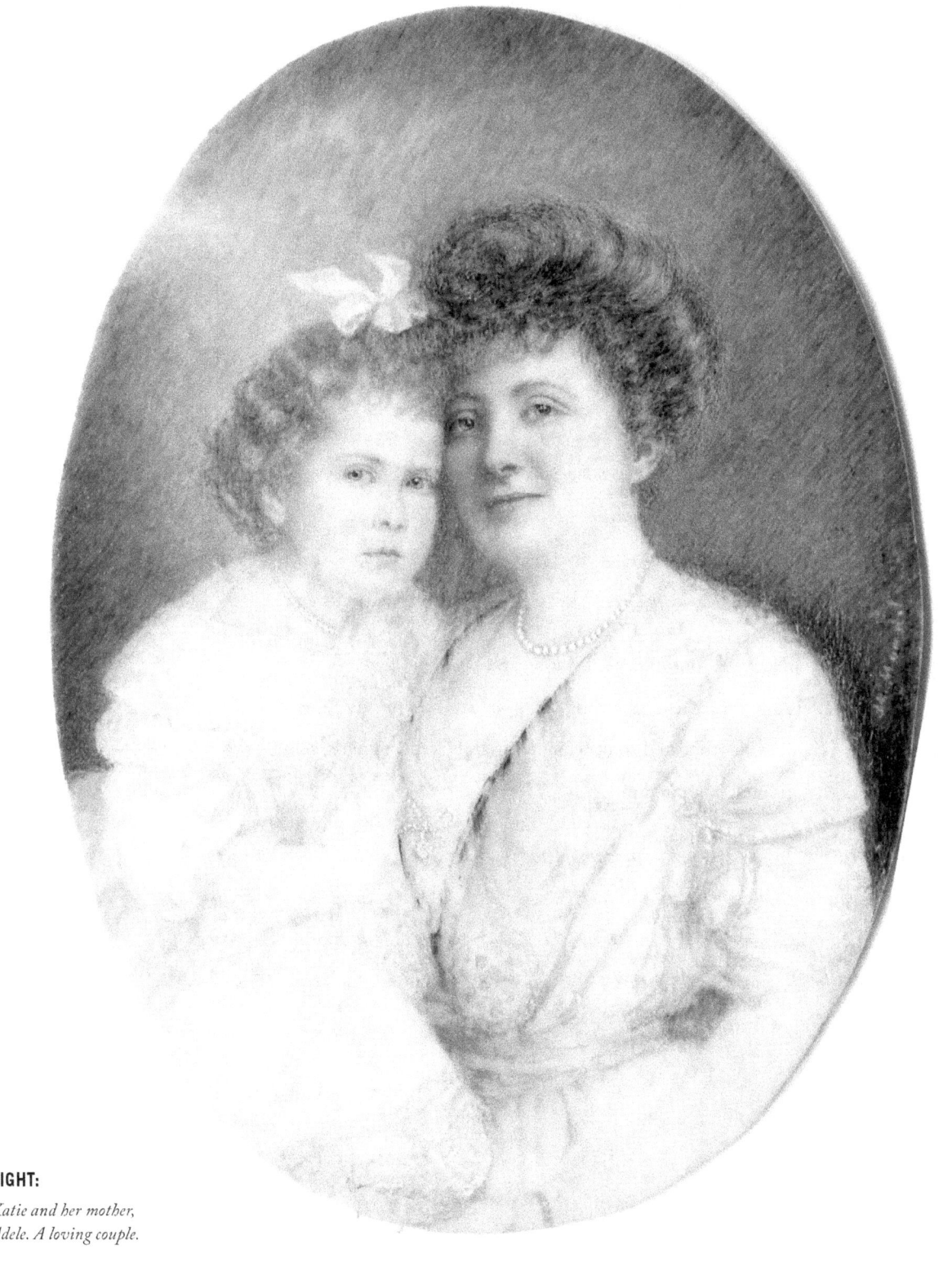

RIGHT:

Katie and her mother,
Adele. A loving couple.

49

on mind over matter. Mary Baker Eddy held that Christian Scientists could heal themselves through faith and should not seek the services of medical professionals when they become ill. Sickness was described as "being possessed of mortal error," curable by prayer and "right thinking."

Adele once wrote,

> I was surrounded by a great deal of 'error' materially called colds. Literally every one about me was suffering and when I was about to succumb, I repeated fervently to myself the credo: 'Become conscious for a single moment that life and intelligence are purely spiritual—neither in nor of matter—and the body will then utter no complaints'—and my error was conquered!

The belief that the mind could control the body was an appealing concept for an intellectual like my father. He became a regular Sunday churchgoer, forcing my sister and me to accompany him. At church, he stood and spoke eloquently and openly of dark feelings that he had kept suppressed and hidden in our family:

> People said I was moody and temperamental. I took advantage of the description, but this self-indulgence and self-righteousness brought no happiness. I never knew when a spell of despondency might descend or how long it would last. I only knew that it would come and spoil my good moods. I am happy to report that freedom from it is one of those things which has followed my study of Christian Science. I am indeed grateful.

The Church became both family and close friend to him, a man who, at home, saw most visitors as an intrusion.

My mother had no interest in Christian Science, which may well have saved our lives. Enjoying Sunday mornings in bed, her breakfast on a tray and the Sunday papers and telephone arranged around her, she declared her independence while Judy and I obediently shuffled off to Christian Science Sunday school.

My father's immersion in Christian Science coincided with my mother's emancipation. Traveling overseas for the United Nations Relief and Rehabilitation Administration (UNRRA**) in 1945, she cast off the heavy burdens of domestic life so repugnant to her. For the first time in forty-two years, my mother acted independently. She wrote my father asking his permission to stay in Europe longer. Crestfallen, he agreed. Leaving him to care for us girls, she declared her independence from home and marriage. In Madame Bovary fashion, she flew the coop. My father sensed that with Christian Science as his adopted religion, he would inevitably lose her. After UNRRA, she never really came back.

** UNRRA, United Nations Relief and Rehabilitation Administration, provided clothing and shelter for victims of World War II who had been displaced from their homes.

RELIGIOUS CONFUSION

On weekdays, Judy and I attended the National Cathedral School, in the shadow of the Washington National Cathedral. The school prided itself on turning out well-mannered, quasi-educated CHRISTIAN young ladies who could swing a field hockey stick, hold a china teacup properly, and recognize Latin origins in English words. The curriculum was aimed at preparing students for marriage to successful men and motherhood. The high point of the school year was the crowning of the most beautiful girl in the senior class as May Queen, followed by dances around a maypole—a defining image of the school's mission.

I had the misfortune to have been born Left Handed—a characteristic which both my grandfather and my father shared. School desks then and perhaps today were constructed to accommodate the right handed student. Two choices faced me and my teachers—swiveling in the chair in a sort of contortionist position or learning to write with my right hand. Miss Morse, my second grade teacher, bless her, held to the theory that I should choose which hand suited me best to go through life and after consultations with child psychologists and a variety of other pedagogists my left hand proclivity was confirmed.

I hated my last name: Louchheim. Teachers routinely, and with a seeming sense of satisfaction, stumbled over its pronunciation. Luchime? Lockhime? I squirmed. "How do you pronounce it? How do you spell it?" others queried, "and why are there two h's?" Underneath all the

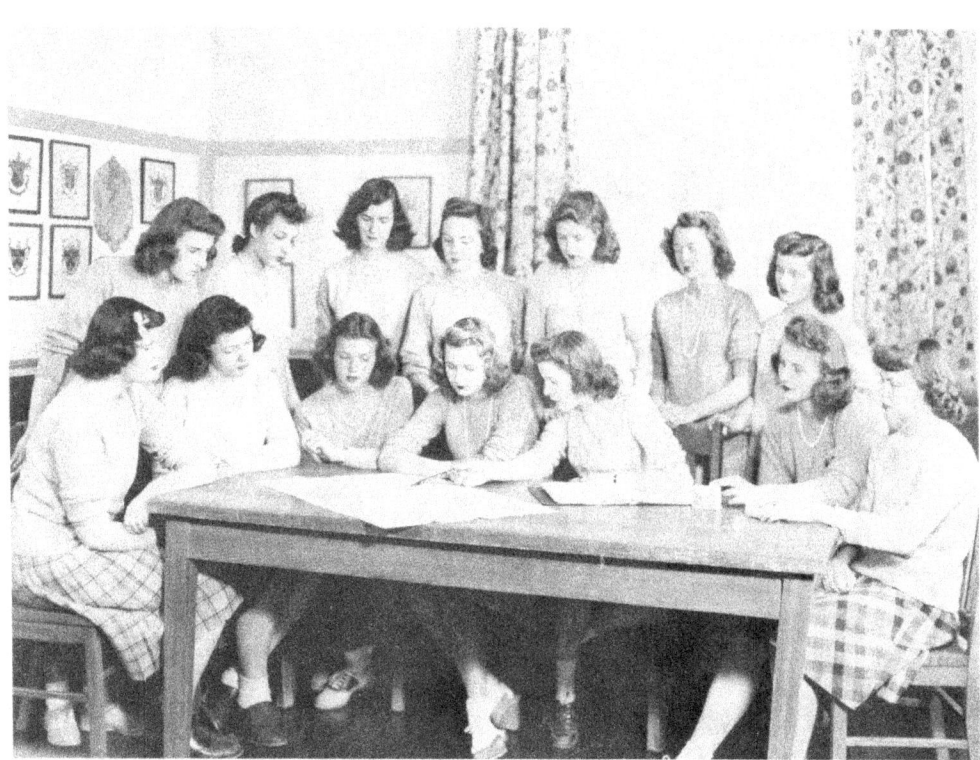

questions I felt the anti-Semitic sneers: " You Jew-girl, with the funny name and curved nose, you in the halls and classrooms of the Episcopal National Cathedral School for girls!" Grandpa Louchheim forbade us to change our name, although many did when Hitler's annihilation of Jews began.

My classmates spoke endlessly of boys—how to act coy, be a "dish," have big "boobs," a small ass—these were the qualities that could carry a girl through life, tethered to a boy soon to become a man.

I remained heavy, had no boy friends and wore frumpy clothes bedecked with bows and ribbons as if I were still a girl of six or eight.

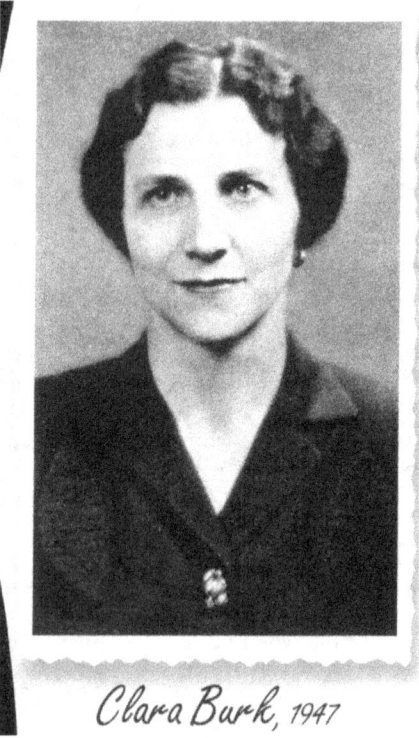

Clara Burk, 1947

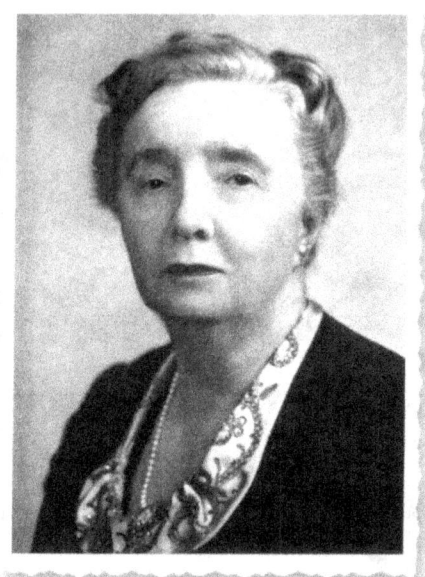

Elizabeth Johnson, 1951
History

At school, we recited the Apostle's Creed, while on Sundays, at a Christian Science Sunday School, we lowered our heads and repeated Mary Baker Eddy's prayers. No mention was made of our Jewish heritage. We had never set foot in a synagogue, tasted kosher food, or observed the Jewish Sabbath.

By the 1940's, I had learned to avoid the question, "are you Jewish?" I had no idea how Jewish girls behaved. I remember being the only girl in my class not admitted to ballroom dancing at "Miss Shippens Dancing School,"—a boy-girl thing. Being Jewish and overweight eliminated me, I'm sure.

54

It was a great surprise to me to be asked if I was Jewish, and to find myself at a loss. My parents had never taught me how to respond. Should I speak the truth? Or do as my mother often did—change the subject? I can't remember exactly, but I think I said something like "remotely Jewish." I was trying to be truthful without invoking the consequences of what I feared would be some kind of ostracism.

My mother insisted that we become fluent in French as a way to mask our Jewishness (as if Jews never spoke French). Mademoiselle Ayache arrived at 3 p.m. on school days. Although these lessons took up my only free hour before homework began, years later they enabled me to study at the Sorbonne and still later helped with Cotton's translations from Latin to French at the Lycée Francais. In 1982, command of the language also qualified me for piano study at Fontainebleau.

As the years passed, Judy became more and more deeply involved with Christian Science. After graduating Phi Beta Kappa from Radcliffe she became a Christian Science Practitioner, attempting to heal herself and her patient-friends with prayer. So much for a Radcliffe education. I believe that this strong commitment to Christian Science was instrumental in my father's death at 71, and Judy's at 62.

THE PIANO FRONT AND CENTER

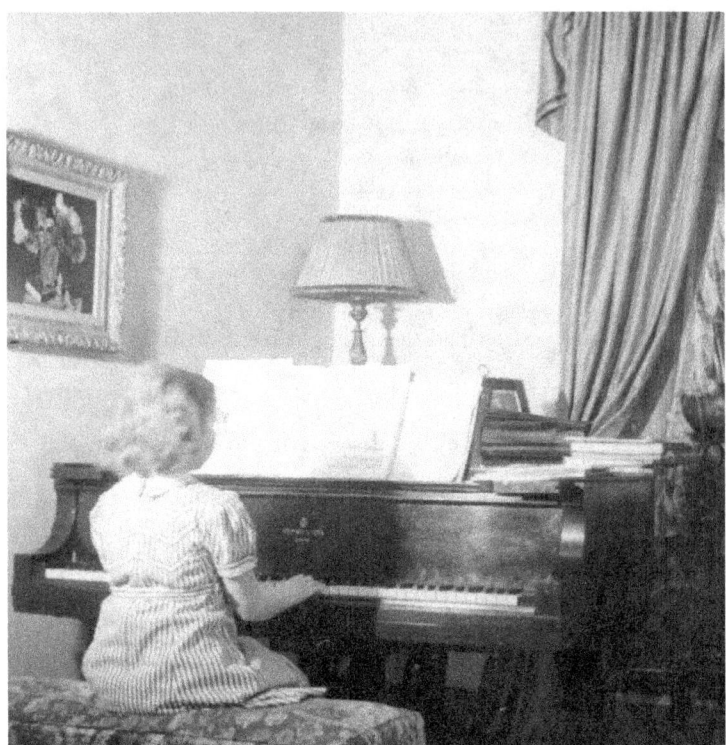

ABOVE:

*Playing grandmother
Frankie's Steinway.*

Singing brought my family together. Grandmother Frankie's grand piano, built for her by Steinway and Sons in 1911, was a revered piece of furniture in our living room. I was allowed to play it only for special occasions.

At Christmas we sang carols standing around the piano with Katie playing and Walter singing. We exchanged gifts under the tree—always practical items done up in fancy holiday paper, and overate festive foods. We assimilated! We were 100% Christians!

When guests assembled, I was propped up on the piano stool and told to play. My parents' friends politely endured my Haydn Sonatas, the ice in their glasses clinking restlessly. I found this quote from Johanna Klinkel, which seems a perfect description of the torture on both sides:

A cultural home without a piano is considered an impossibility—one can scarcely attend social gatherings without having to sit through some music by a family member—and what horrible music—forcing guests to listen without asking whether they enjoy it—how unfair to entice someone to a party and force him to listen to music.

GERTRUDE PRICE WOLLNER

Music Improvisation, 1944

I had a true friend and teacher in Gertrude Price Wollner. Gertrude didn't offer piano lessons in a conventional manner. She engaged in what she called "musical dialogues." Together, facing the piano, we would carry on a "conversation" by either rhythmically clapping hands or beating drums, the rhythms serving as dialogue. We exchanged phrases, which we then played on the piano. Gertrude called these sessions "improvisation—sharing the freedom and spontaneity of musical ideas." She believed that her teaching methods were "planting a seed." She must have planted one in me, as I grew to love our sessions and, in years to come, utilized her improv methods in many aspects of my life.

As a teenager, I felt that Gertrude's lessons were the closest experience to being set free. They opened my mind, which was otherwise crammed with *du must*, German rules passed down to me from my forebears who were known for elevating obedience and order to the very highest level of social behavior. Gertrude nurtured my love of making music, and she alone broke the pedagogical ice in which I was locked—encouraging me to explore rhythms and sounds on the piano.

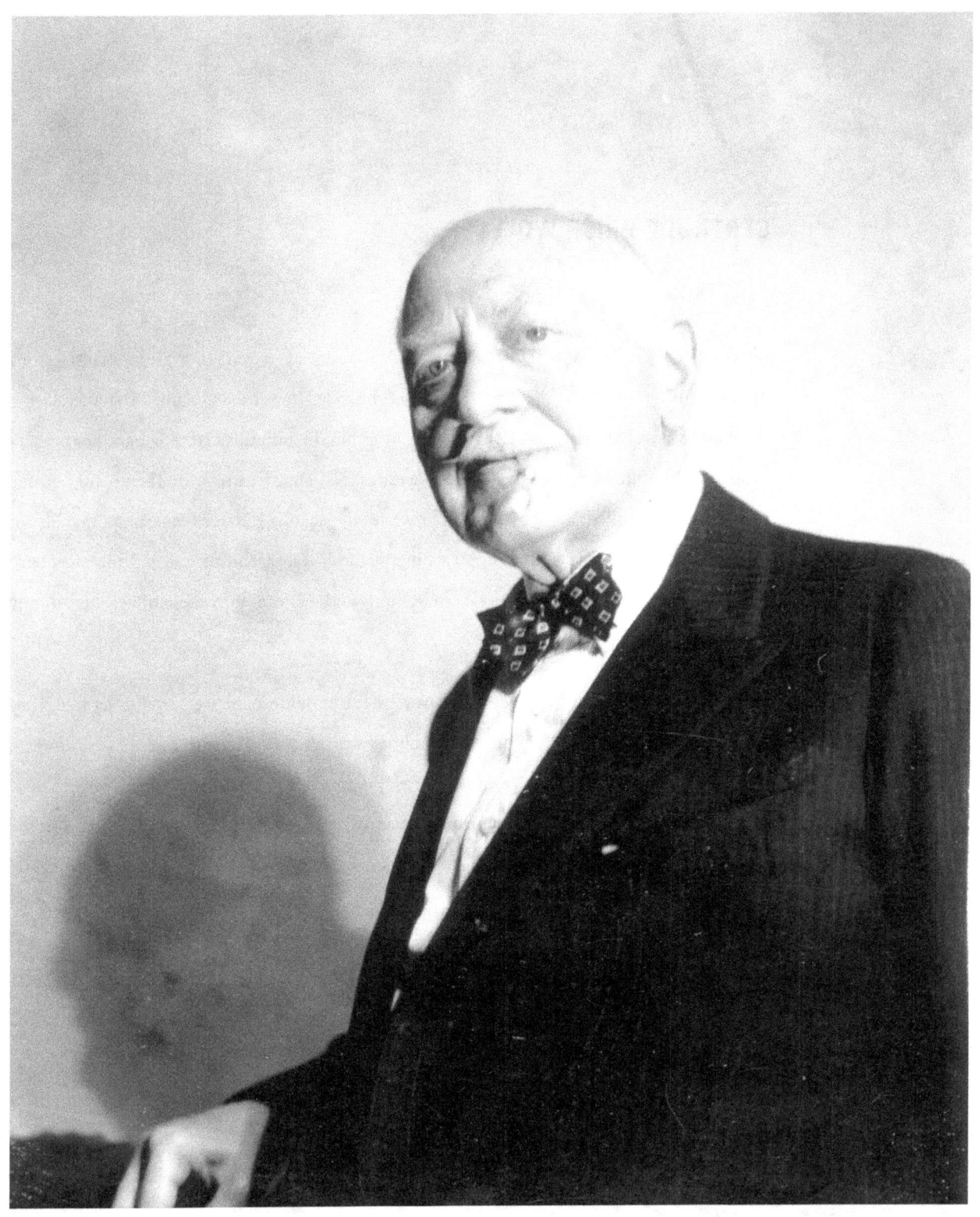

58

THE WAR YEARS

When World War II began, Judy and I were buffered from international news, and our lives continued unaffected. When the newspaper arrived at our door, we were given the comics. We could attach no reality to the reports of suffering we overheard. People went to war—some never returning—no explanation offered. I never dared ask, nor did I connect, the German spoken at home by my parents when they didn't want us to understand and the country of Germany where a terrible war was happening. I heard nothing about members of our family still in danger in Germany. We made blackouts for the windows so that no light could escape at night. My father donned a Civil Defense helmet and patrolled our neighborhood making sure no one violated the no-lights rule. He loved this role of policeman. Once in a while, an air raid siren would wail for a test drill. The government issued ration books limiting our consumption of gas, sugar, butter, meat and shoes. My mother decided that brown oxford lace-up shoes would serve all purposes and all seasons, and spent all my ration stamps on my totally ugly, brown oxford, lace-up shoes.

I visited my cousins Dody and Suzy Wilding in Scarsdale, New York. They were invited to a party and decided to drag me along. But catching sight of my shoes, they exclaimed, "You can't possibly go in those shoes!" I tried to explain that the shoes were purchased with my ration tickets (poor little rich girl!) but my cousins were too embarrassed to be seen with me. Their mother, Aunt Bede, called my mother the next morning and chastised her for not being more concerned about my appearance and social life.

59

My paternal grandfather, Walter Louchheim Sr., living in high style at the Plaza Hotel in New York, was a compassionate man. Recently, I came across letters he exchanged with his cousin, Salomon Ottenheimer, still living in Germany. Salomon claimed no harm would come to his family, as they were not a "political" threat to the Nazi party. "I have a good life here," Senna Ottenheimer declared. However, in 1938, the Nazis demanded that Salomon return the funds he'd invested in the U.S. and my Grandfather sent Salomon an affidavit that would allow his family to leave Germany. They were among the last Jews to leave. The Nazis soon took over their girdle factory in Göppingen to make ammunition.

Other family members rescued by Grandfather Louchheim included Ottie and Stephie Baer and Laura Kadden. Their correspondence indicated that they too felt no threat from the anti-Semitism everywhere. German Jews had assimilated into mainstream German life. They were not constricted by ghettos but lived where they chose.

My cousin, Inge Auerbacher was seven years old when Hitler came to power.

HOLOCAUST: *a time when Jews were singled out for total annihilation in all of Europe. Even though German Jews felt that they were part of German society, their assimilation into the culture meant nothing during the Nazi regime. Doors to the free world—the United States and South America—were closing rapidly, as each day new regulations were imposed on German Jews. In 1935, all Jews in Germany lost their citizenship.*

60

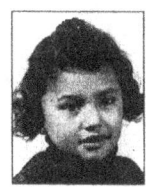

Name: Inge Auerbacher
Date of Birth: December 31, 1934
Place of Birth: Kippenheim, Germany

Inge was the only child of Berthold and Regina Auerbacher, religious Jews living in Kippenheim, a village in south-western Germany near the Black Forest. Her father was a textile merchant. The family lived in a large house with 17 rooms and had servants to help with the housework.

This card tells the story of a real person who lived during the Holocaust.

IDENTIFICATION CARD

For the dead and the living we must bear witness

United States
Holocaust Memorial Museum

ABOVE:

Cousin Inge Auerbacher, Holocaust survivor.

She wrote:

In 1942 my parents and I were loaded onto a transport with about 1,200 people and taken to Terezin, a concentration camp in Czechoslovakia. We lived there among rats, fleas, lice, and a total lack of hygiene. One third of the prison population died from malnutrition and disease. In 1945, the Soviet Army liberated our camp and I came to the United States with my parents. For four years afterwards, I suffered from tuberculosis and lost eight years of school. I was among the lucky ones.

Ships carrying Jewish refugees arriving in New York Harbor were turned back because of an antiquated U.S. immigration "quota" system. I wondered why my father hadn't made an effort to become involved in attempts to rescue the Jews being gassed in Nazi ovens. I never had this conversation with him, so I can only assume that he didn't want his Jewish background to become known.

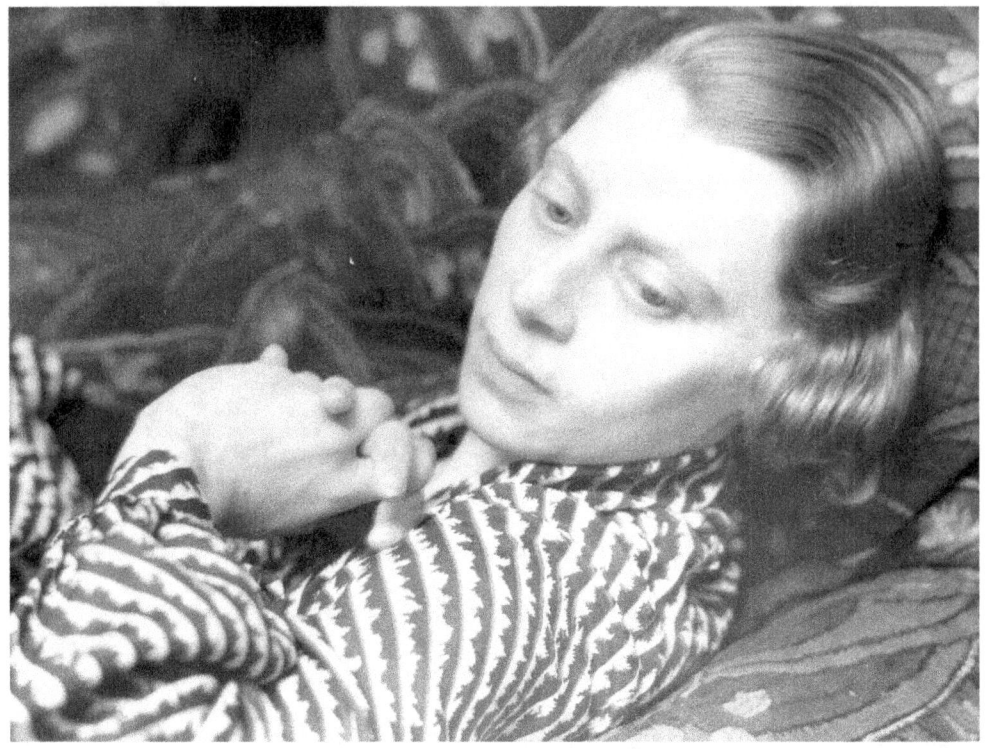

LEFT:
Photo of Florence by Francis Bruguière.

AUNT FLORENCE, MY FATHER'S YOUNGER SISTER

A maverick

Aunt Florence regarded me as the child she wished she had and took over my education as soon as I was ready to be shipped off.

During World War II, she sent me news clippings of men in trenches, bombs falling on civilians in Europe, entire cities in ruin, believing that I should be informed. By the 1940's, when I was just entering my teens, Florence was an established practitioner of "radical chic," a swinger, a freethinker, a chain smoker—some even thought, a Communist. She rarely associated with other Louchheim family members, whom she dismissed as bourgeois.

I was lucky. Visits with her during this period opened up my world to include artists arriving from Europe seeking asylum, meals at Horn & Hardart, the automat, and—most memorably— people who spoke to children in a natural way.

62

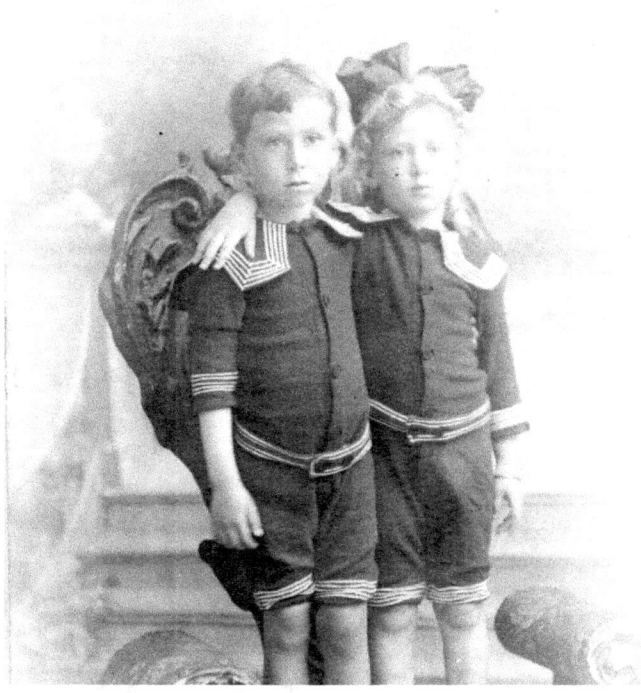

In 1941, my mother took more kindly to Florence when she offered to take Judy and me to visit poet Robert Frost's farm in South Shaftsbury, Vermont. We were the same age as his two granddaughters.

Frost insisted that we make daily treks to the surrounding hills to pick blueberries. We had to fill an entire bucket before he would allow us to go play. We were given eight cents for each bucket; it seemed like a fortune! Florence was permissive and encouraged us to do things we never dared—sleeping in a cow pasture, and waking to see big heads of curious cattle leaning over us, sitting on three legged stools, right under the udders, watching the milk come streaming out.

We were saddened at summer's end when reality returned and we weren't allowed to bring home a Beagle puppy that Florence had given us.

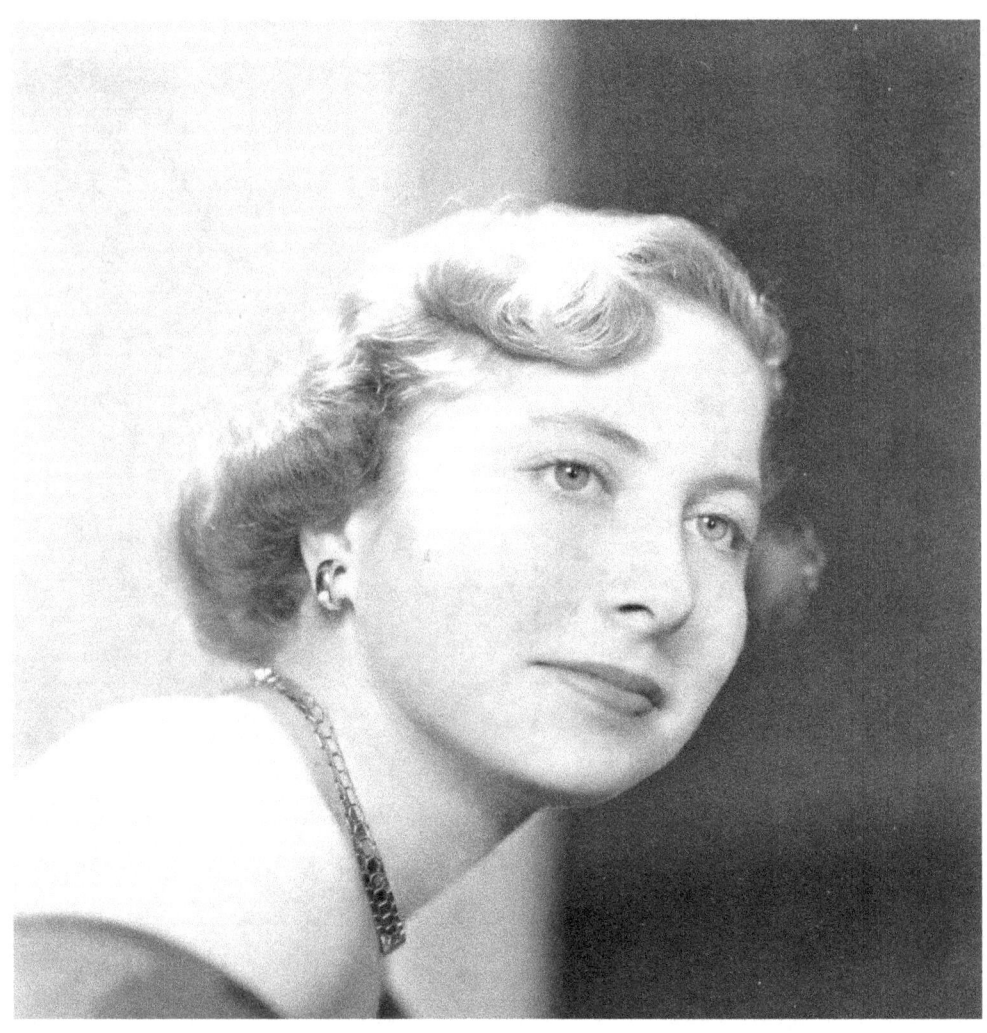

MARY THE DEBUTANTE

1948

My status in my family rose significantly when my parents decided to introduce me to Washington society. In Washington, D.C., as in many U.S. cities, 18-year-old girls are "presented" to society with a "coming-out" party and a debutante ball, a veritable must if funds were available. My parents saw the occasion as an opportunity to offer up their first born and join hands with the predominantly Christian community. The real society folks, Washington's Mayflower descendants, put on elaborate coming out parties in ballrooms and

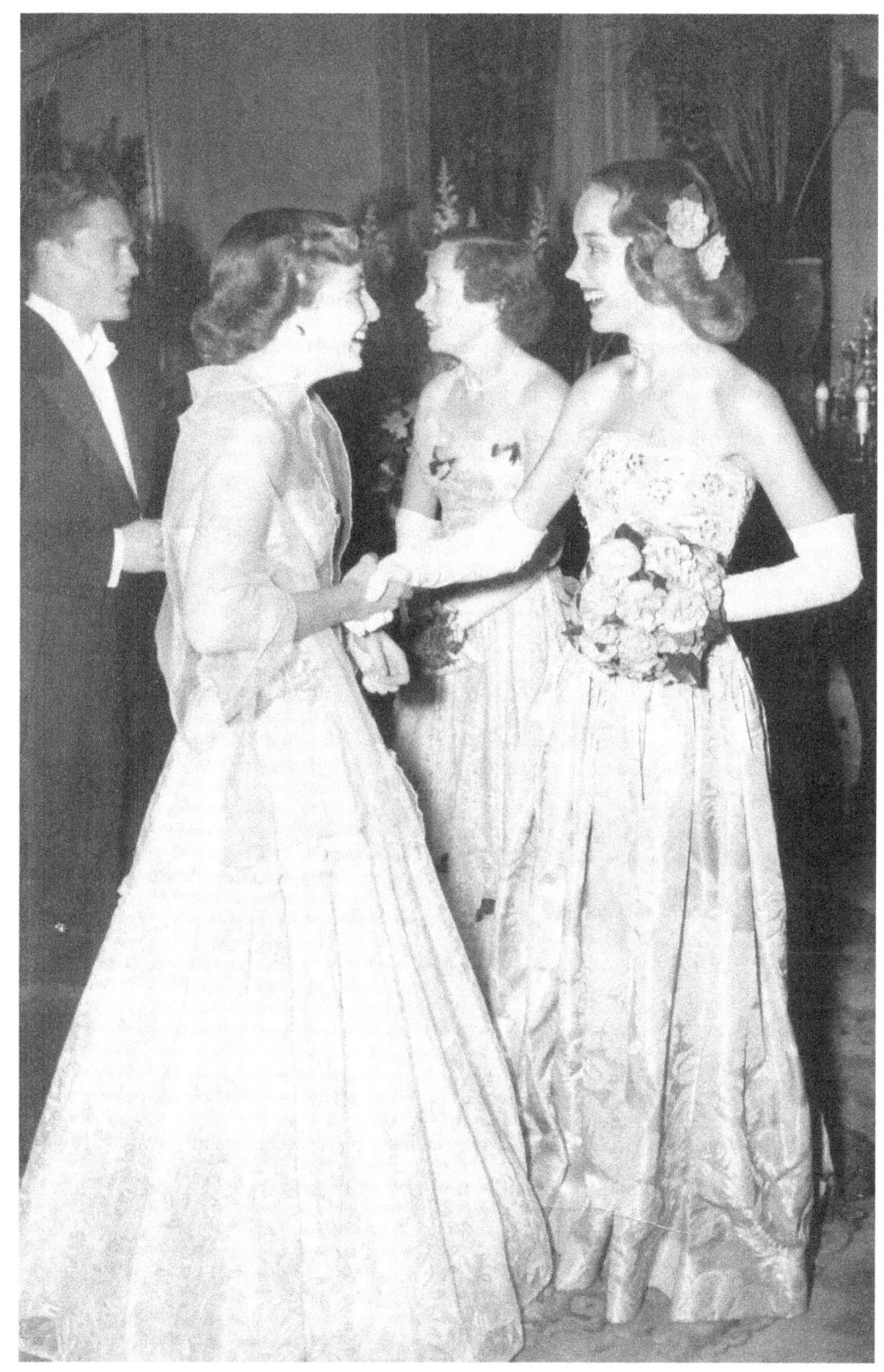

65

private clubs with entertainment provided by Meyer Davis & his Orchestra. However, because we were Jewish and not members of a social club. it would have been unseemly for Jews to spend excessive amounts of money to promote the family's available daughter, my party took place as a "tea" in our living room. I was planted in a receiving line between my mother and grandmother, dolled up in a dark green velvet "afternoon" gown. The guest list included old family friends, other debutantes and 'eligible" young men. My wardrobe expanded, from practical skirts with hems wide enough to let down and sweaters durable enough to pass on to Judy, to include frothy ball gowns and sequined headbands.

Reporters from The Washington Post took my picture and wrote about me, although there was not much to report. I had never done anything significant nor been anywhere of interest. Nevertheless, I became a PERSON with a social schedule, a wardrobe and male attendants.

HIGHER LEARNING

Freshman at Brown University

When it became time to think about college in my senior year, I was fortunate to have a caring and helpful advisor, Elizabeth Fry, who suggested that I apply to Brown University and guided me through the application. I got in with little sense of what I would do there. I remember loving European history, sneaking out of Biology Lab where we examined the inside of a sheep's head and the bowels of a pig, and studying with boys. Otherwise I was an ordinary student with an ordinary dating life.

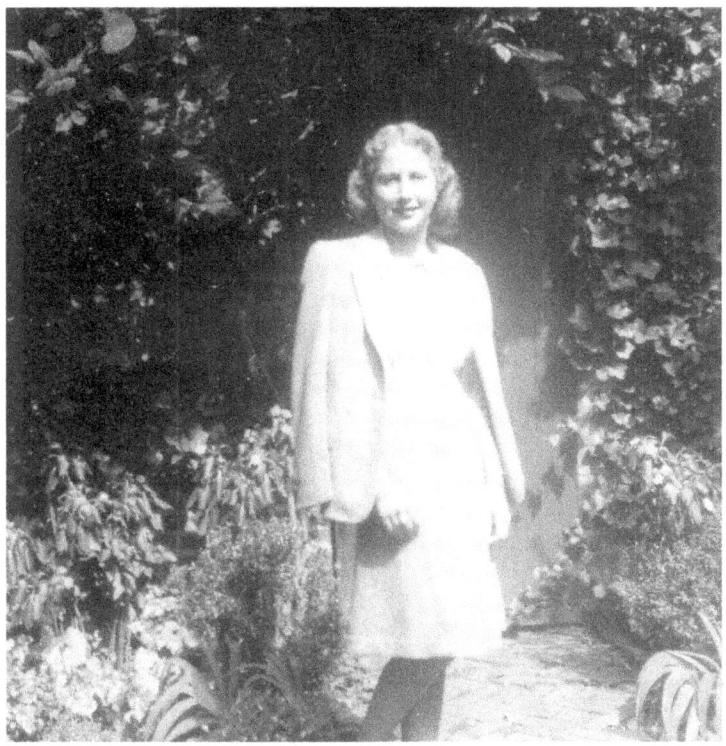

The distance between Washington, D.C., and Providence, Rhode Island, offered freedom from the endless lectures and strict rules of home. But my parents weren't happy with the way I was conducting my life at Brown. They complained that I was too far away with access to too many extracurricular, unchaperoned experiences. Katie contacted the Infirmary and asked them to keep tabs on my weight loss. I had put myself on a starvation diet. Having been noticeably overweight most of my teenage years, I was determined to fit into those styles designed for the far-too-thin. I hated being so closely supervised and jumped at the chance to spend my Junior year at the Sorbonne in Paris.

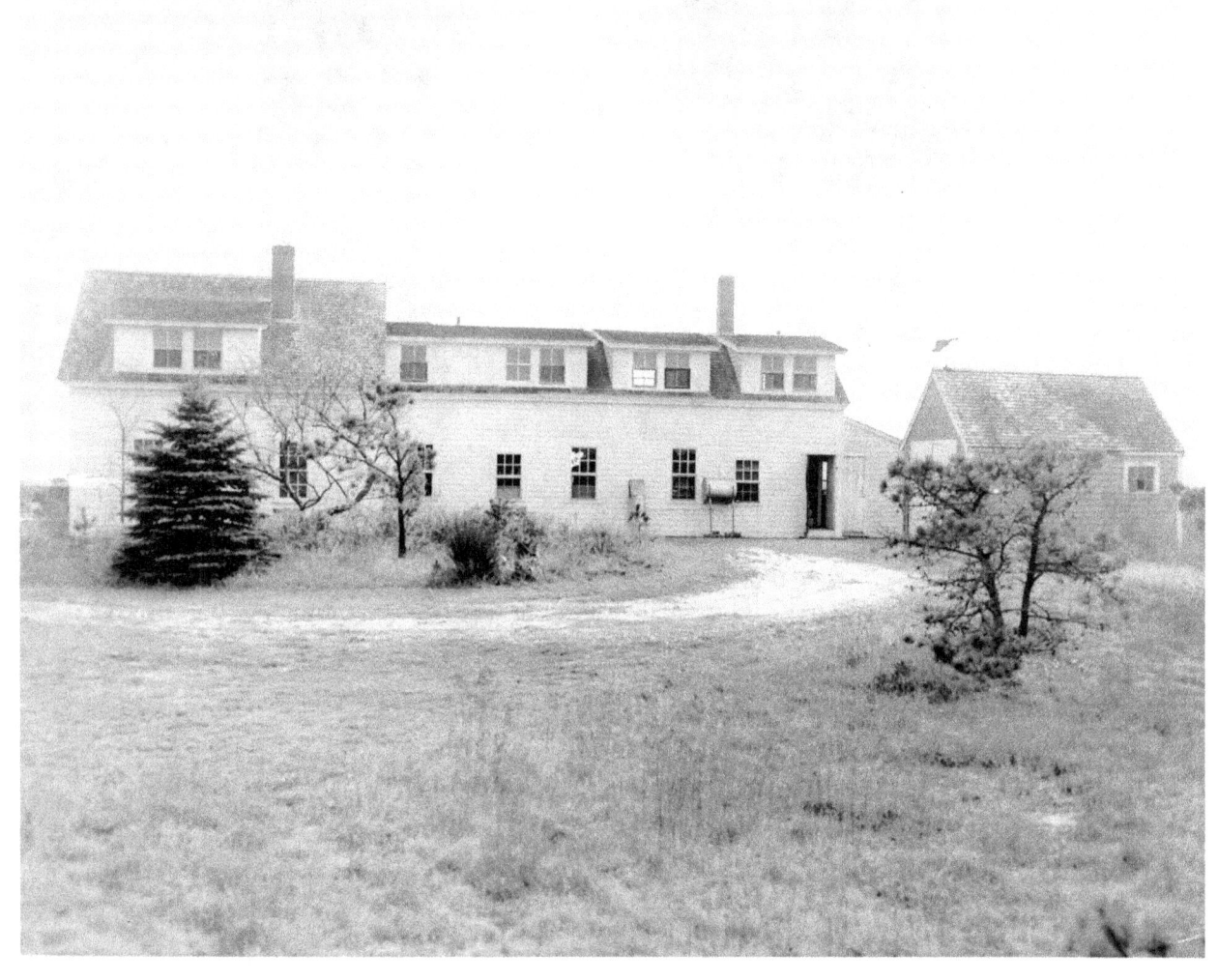

ABOVE:

*The house on Stage
Harbor Road before my
parents bought it.*

CHATHAM, CAPE COD

On fine evenings, in Chatham, one can see the surf, the rosy afterglow of the sunset behind the dunes and the homeward bound flight of the herons and egrets while gulls congregate on the sands. Chatham is the only town in Cape Cod surrounded on three sides by water—Pleasant Bay, Nantucket Sound, and the Atlantic Ocean. It's sixteen square miles of land are bounded by sixty-six miles of constantly changing waterfront. In its waters cod, haddock, scallops and clams are plentiful. Historically it has been the home of sea captains. In the late nineteenth century it also became a summer haven for Boston.

New England summer communities were gradually accepting Jews after World War II. Katie and Walter's Protestant New Deal friends urged them to try Chatham, a fishing village on Cape Cod, a twenty-three hour drive from Washington, D.C., a village where, twenty years earlier, on a visit, they had been turned away from The Chatham Bars Inn by a sign on the front desk warning, "NO Dogs, NO Jews."

How I hated that long twenty-three hour drive—no highways, only two-lane roads and no air-conditioning in cars. Conversation was impossible over the strong winds blowing in from open windows. And my father was such a courteous driver, never wanting to aggressively pass another car.

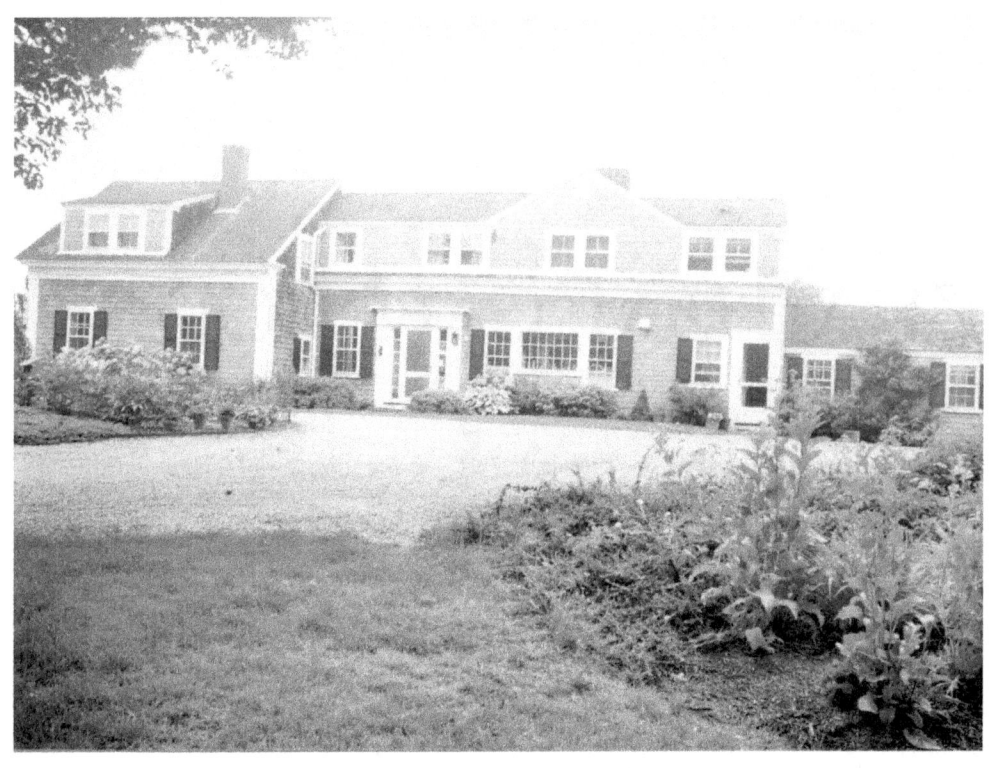

In 1948, after several summers renting cottages, my parents bought the perfect old farmhouse, beautifully situated on a small hill overlooking Stage Harbor, surrounded by pine trees—quiet, and peaceful. In her 1948 diary, my mother wrote about buying the house: *going back again and again and always liking it better, seeing the quail on the lawn, finding the little spruces buried in the overgrown wildness, watching the goldenrod and the wild asters grow thicker, the trumpet vine bloom heavily and climbing the roof and looking way out—out to the bar, past the cut through and down past the old mill to the Mill pond again Stage Harbor with its boats—that it should always be there, to look upon seemed miraculous.*

Perhaps it was the informality of our lifestyle there that made us a "family." We were even allowed to enter our kitchen! We grew closer. It was tough to impose family routines when Judy and I were able to break away on our bikes. Meals might be slightly off-schedule. Chatham provided an interfamily intimacy that our more austere winter schedules prohibited. Picnics to the "outerbeach" ferried by solemn-faced Captain Art Gould—linked us. Diving in the waves and rescuing sandwiches from the sand, even making communal small talk (my father hated that) made a family of us.

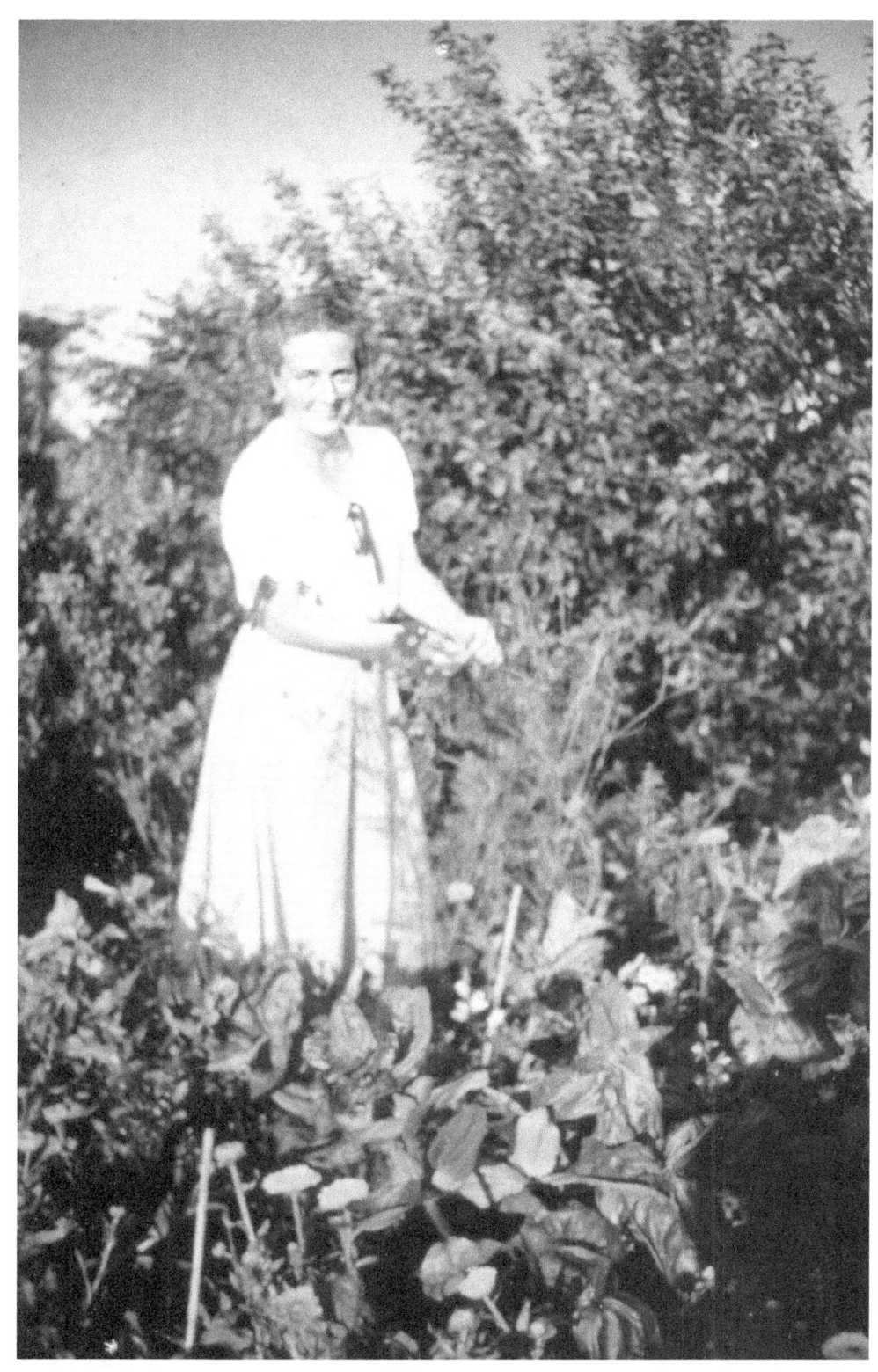

Chatham was a Katie-place and Walter was bored. Katie prided herself on being liked by Chatham's year-round residents. Walter remained aloof, looking down on the "boat-trailer" people and the summer tourists. Equipping himself with a strong pair of binoculars, he became an expert at identifying birds and bird calls, setting up feeding stations, and, in later years, paying my daughter Didi to spot them.

Being Jewish in Chatham brought its own set of irregularities. Owning a well-heeled summer house did not convey acceptance into the Yacht and Beach Club world of Chatham society. We were not invited to join. However, we were permitted to go to the Club twice a month, and only on days when it wasn't too crowded. It didn't surprise me that the whole town knew we were Jewish. Recently, I was able to bring up the subject with a neighbor, Mel Webster, a realtor. "There is no anti-Semitism in Chatham, not as far as I know." "We're not happy about having blacks, but I don't recall anything about Jews. After all, we've always had the Brandeis and Fleishmann families and they've never been a problem." "Jews with prestige and money are always welcome, as long as they don't flaunt their Jewishness or act like Jews."

Furthering her efforts to avoid being labeled Jewish, Katie bought a cemetery plot in Chatham's Seaside Cemetery. Although our families owned plots in Philadelphia (Louchheim) and Long Island (Joseph), Katie wanted to distance us as much as possible from the Semitic world she had left behind.

To insure his proximity to Christian Science services in Chatham, Walter helped facilitate the building of a Christian Science Church (now Unitarian) along with a Christian Science Reading Room—a revelation for Chatham residents, who were a mix of Catholic, Episcopal and Methodist.

TOP RIGHT:

Katie and me, Chatham, 1949.

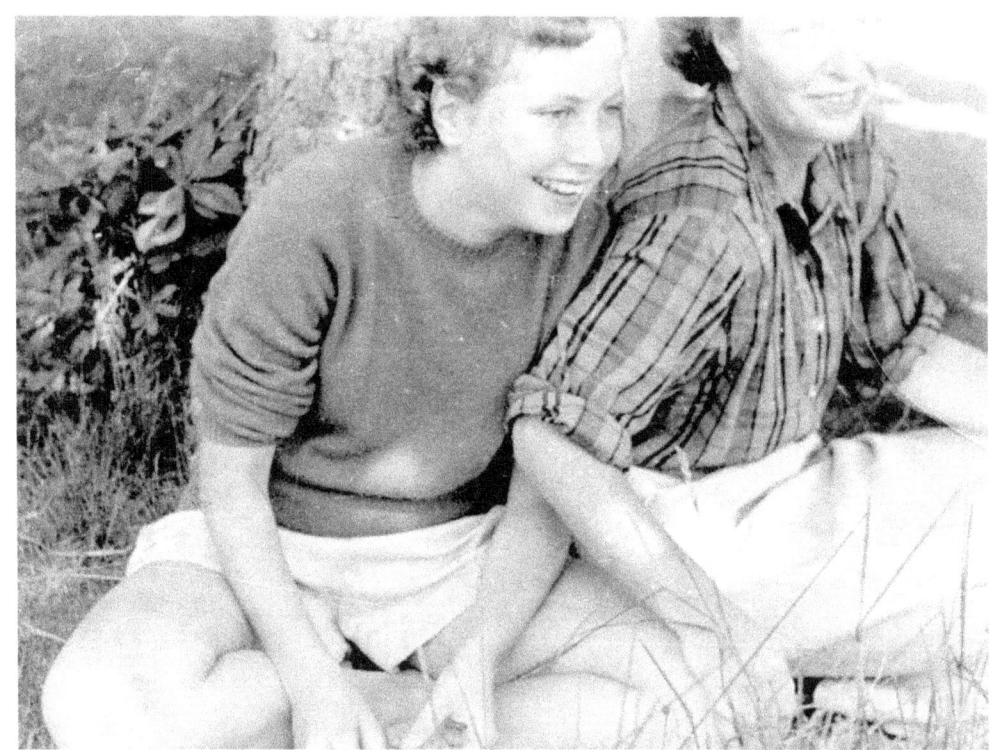

BOTTOM RIGHT:

Originally built as my father's Christian Science Church in Chatham, now the Unitarian Universalists Meeting House—photo by Cotton Coulson.

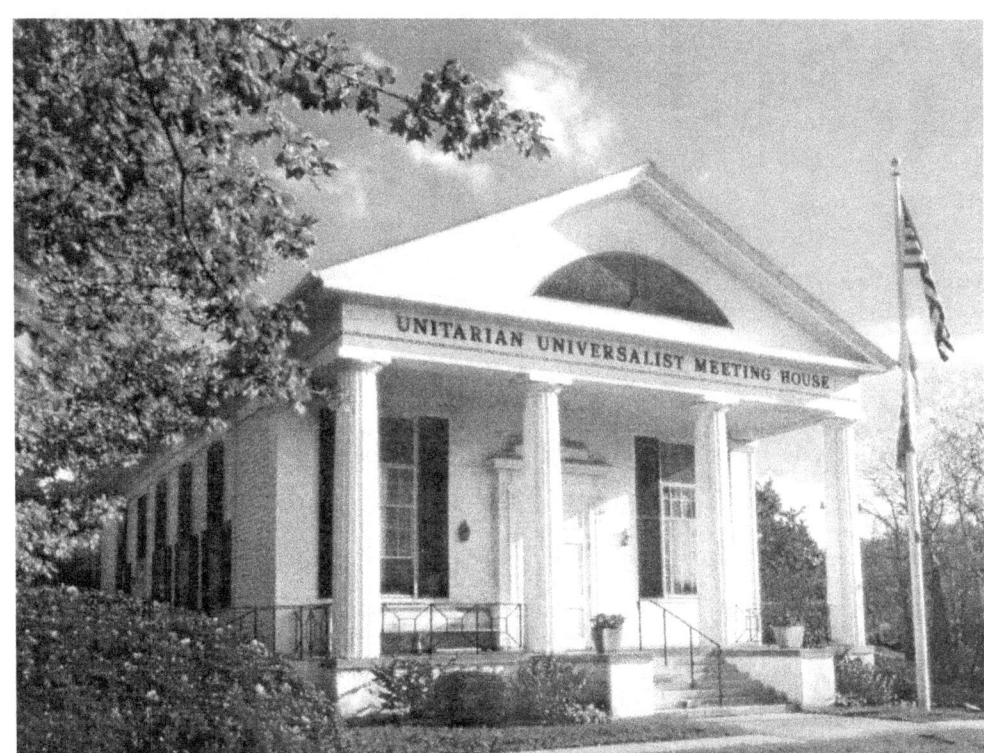

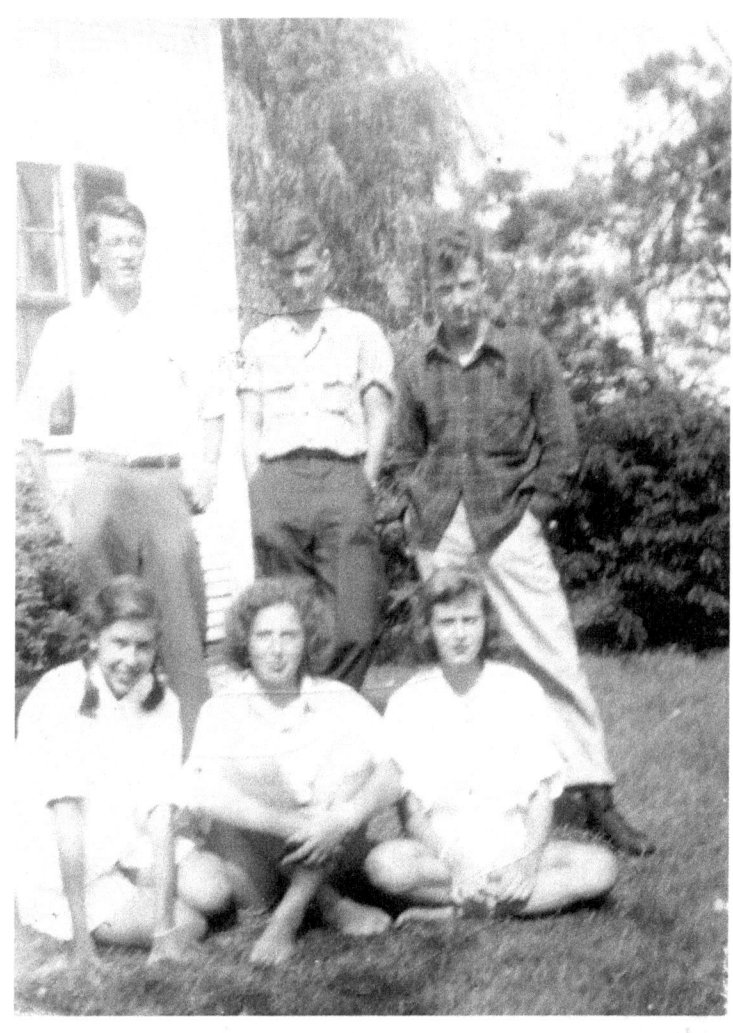

THE BUTTON

Katie's fascination with Spaulding Dunbar, a "hunk" who built boats in Chatham and talked New England patois, led to her buying one of his Catabouts, small sailboats he designed for beginners racing in Chatham's Stage Harbor. She carried on her romance *en plein air*. Rising at five a.m. on a summer morning, she would bicycle to his boatyard where they would zoom out of Stage Harbor for a day's fishing. Flushed, sunburned and radiant, she would return in

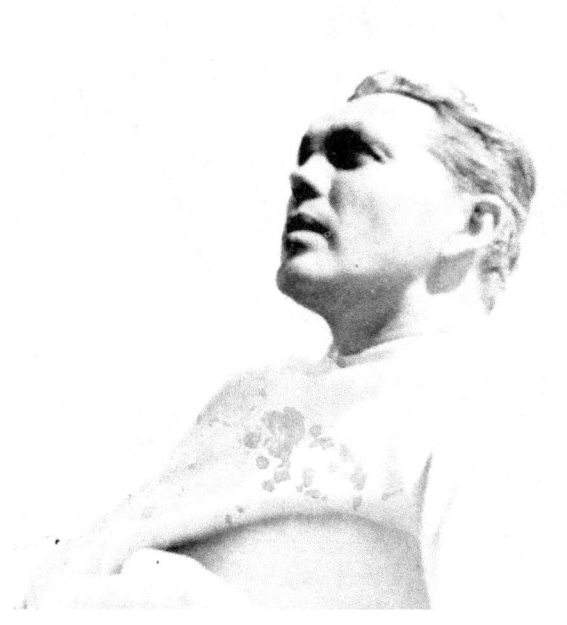

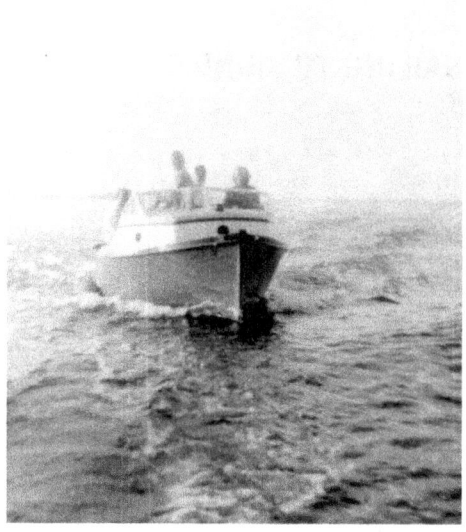

time to hand our maid a fish to prepare for dinner. Spaulding's tolerant, alcoholic wife, Doris, had grown accustomed to her husband's summer dalliances—Katie was not the first. She took pride in knowing that such an important woman cared about her husband.

Walter did not know how to "handle" the situation, so he did the only thing he could think of doing, he commissioned Spaulding to build Katie a fishing boat—one that she could operate by simply pushing a single button. "The Button" as it was christened, boasted a handsome, bright blue exterior and shiny white trim. Looking at it riding smartly on its mooring in Stage Harbor, one would believe it belonged to an "old salt." Katie felt very proud and insisted on being photographed on board by the renowned Chatham photographer, Richard Kelsey. It reminds me a bit today of the British comedienne, Mrs. Bucket posing on board her yacht at dockside in *Keeping Up Appearances*.

SAILING TO MONOMOY

Catabouts and Tig

Boys who sailed were the best. Sure of themselves. I watched them from the shore, envious, admiring their skill at maneuvering the tiller, always in complete control against Chatham's prevailing Southwest wind. Tig Woodland was capable of handling a boat in all weather, and I was one of those silly girls standing on the shore—admiring.

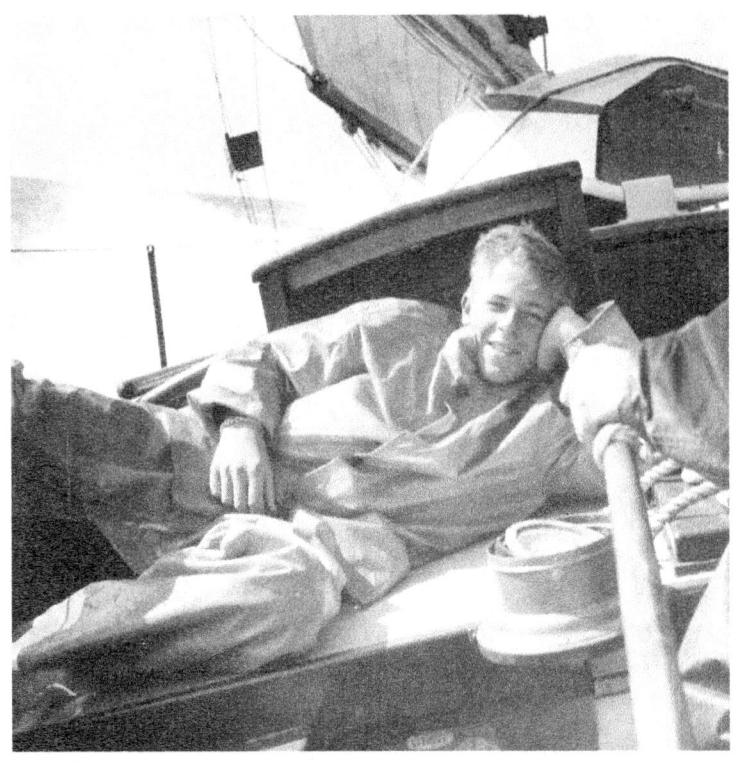

Judy and I had little confidence sailing our Catabout in Stage Harbor—gauging the wind velocity and tide direction. Gradually, our sailing proficiency increased, and with it, our social life. Tig (a.k.a. Henry Thompson Woodland, Jr.), a very secure member of the Chatham in-crowd, reached out and made efforts to include us.

He seemed willing to overlook our status as *Ausländers* and brought us into Chatham's exclusive social network. As one of Chatham's champion sailors, Tig loved the sea as much as he disdained the polished-brass-and-blazer look. He frequently referred to sailboat masts as "sticks" and large groups on a boat as "drowning parties." His dismissive backwoodsman spirit didn't jibe with his parents' friends. His stepfather, Elmer Jared Bliss, Commodore of the Edgartown Yacht Club, seemed to relish the formality his Yacht Club exuded.

Tig was related to just about everyone in Chatham and welcomed everywhere. His grandfather, Willard T. Sears, was architect for the Isabella Stewart Gardner Museum in Boston, and was

76

proud owner of a peninsular jetty in Chatham's Stage Harbor, which became known as "Sears Point." Tig's great grandfather was Francis Scott Key.

Tig flirted with all the girls except me, an overweight teenager. However, I was an acceptable companion on explorations outside Stage Harbor. I remember one sunny day in late August, Tig and I sailed to Monomoy Island, a thin strip of land lying just beyond Chatham, disobeying the rule about staying inside Stage Harbor. We secured the Catabout on the beach and began the mile walk to the far side of the island where seagulls laid their nests and osprey dove into the foamy waters.

Midway across the island, a heavy fog suddenly enveloped us. I grew fearful, but Tig stayed calm and determined, focused on our destination, an old Monomoyick Indian camping ground. We continued walking east without benefit of a compass, believing we would soon reach it. As time passed, the fog grew increasingly dense and darkness made walking treacherous. We stumbled over prickly clumps of dune grass and sharp clamshells. I was more than ready to turn back, but Tig convinced me that the fog would soon blow out to sea and we would come upon that campsite, a relatively unexplored treasure. The image of my father's stern face brought shivers and I decided to retrace my steps without Tig, so strong was my conviction that my punishment for breaking the boundary rules would be severe.

As soon as I was out of range of Tig's voice, I became really frightened. Now, not only would I suffer shame from my parents, I would be separated from Tig as well. Just then, I heard the sound of helicopter blades whirring overhead. Within a few feet of where I was standing, a Coast Guard helicopter appeared like a ship in a ghostly setting. Both doors sprung open, and Judy and a Coast Guard officer emerged. Yes, my parents had sent her to find us, and Judy, having overheard our plans the day before, knew just where we were headed. Thank God for eavesdropping siblings!

77

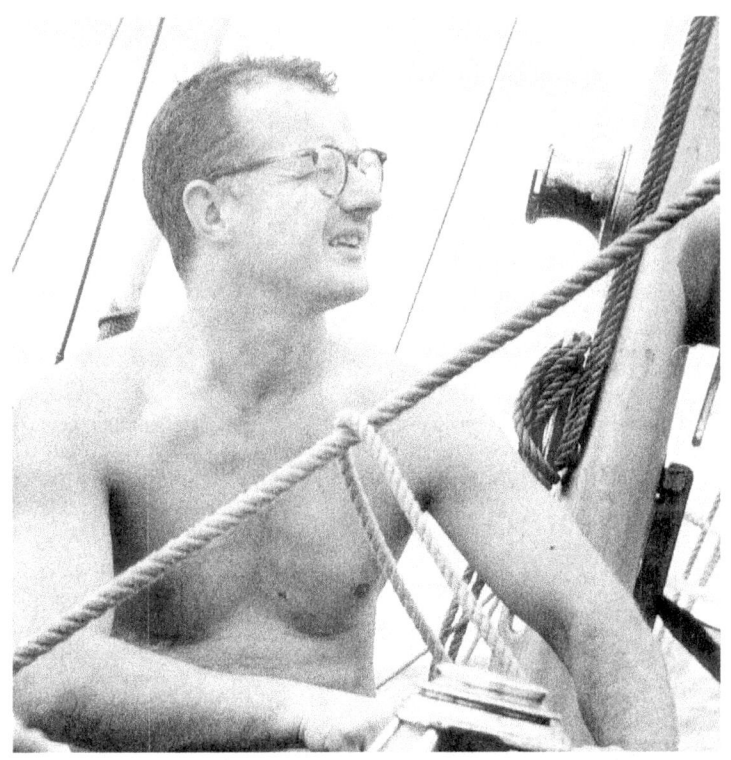

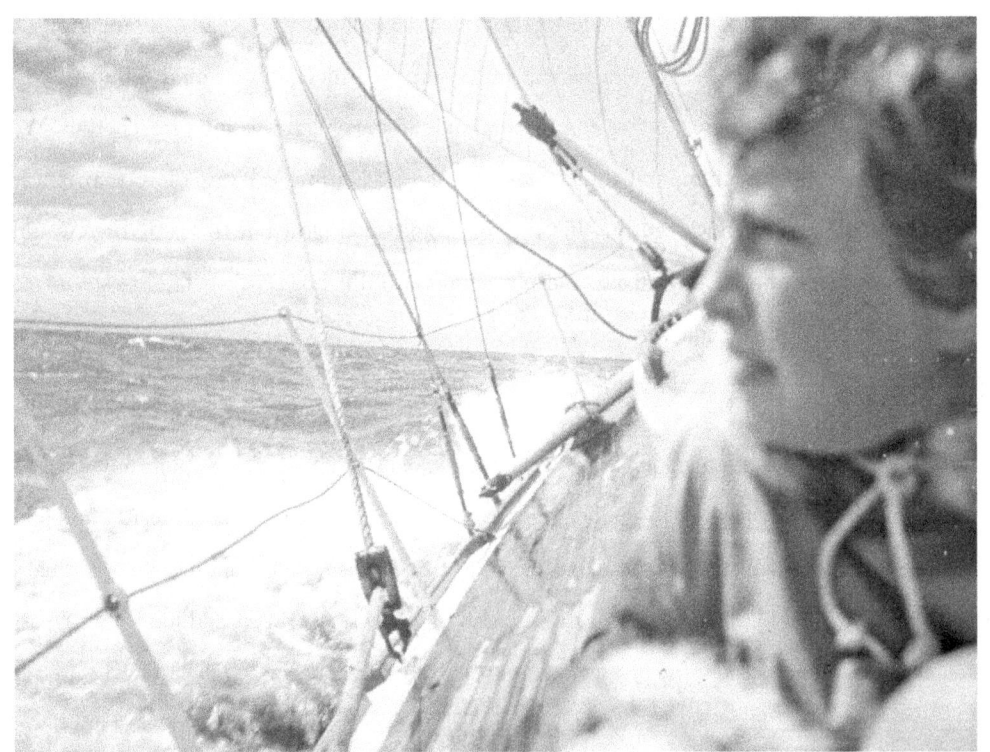

BOB COULSON

A Summer Romance

Tig ferried us to the Edgartown Regatta in his outboard. We "oohed" and "aahed" over Bob Coulson, who was collecting all the prizes. Bob and Tig often raced together. I was impressed by Bob's sailing ability. He was usually first to cross the starting line and always first to finish. We stood around him in admiration. He invited me to race with him and "work" the spinnaker. "Make sure it isn't luffing." I felt I had risen in the sailing world.

Suddenly, without warning, as we jockeyed about waiting for the starting gun, Bob picked me up and threw me overboard into Edgartown harbor! I panicked. Was this a kind of initiation, an honor? The new grey flannel shorts my mother had presented to me as, "regatta wear," along with a wrist watch from my grandmother and cash to rent a room for the night, would surely be ruined.

My admiration for Bob's skipper skills quickly dissolved in the cold water. I wished I could laugh like everyone else—just a collegiate prank, ha! ha! But my eyes desperately followed the fast disappearing stern of Bob's boat, as it moved away from where I was treading water in the midst of fifty boats jockeying to hit the starting line first.

My parents seemed glad to see me and welcomed me back, despite my damaged wardrobe and deflated ego. I was still their connection to the coveted gentile world.

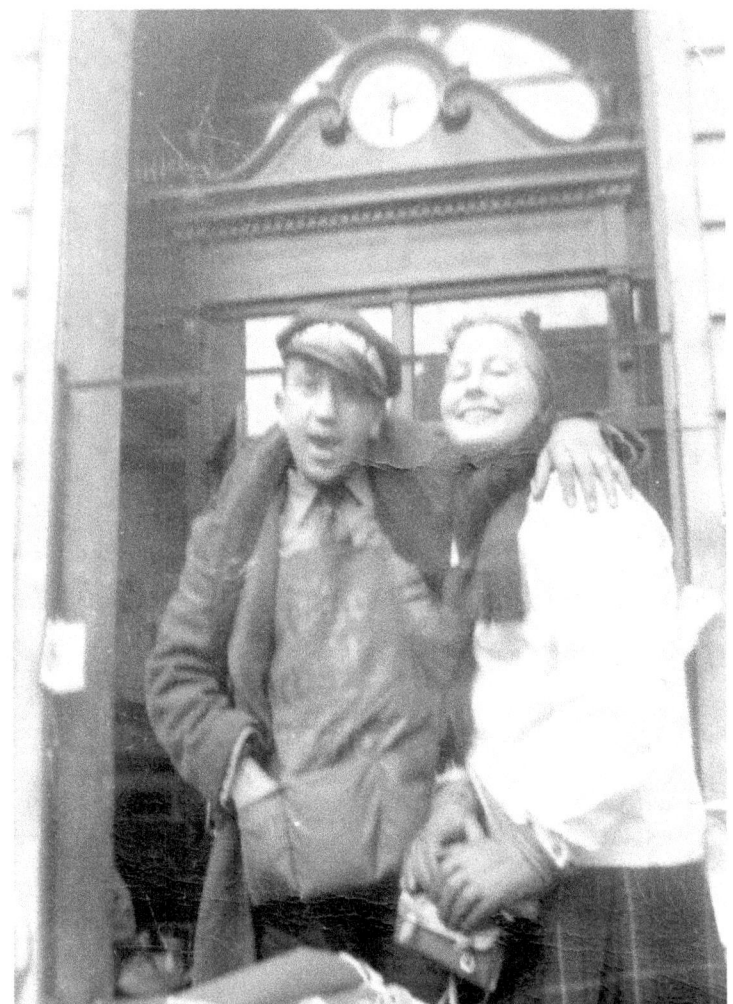

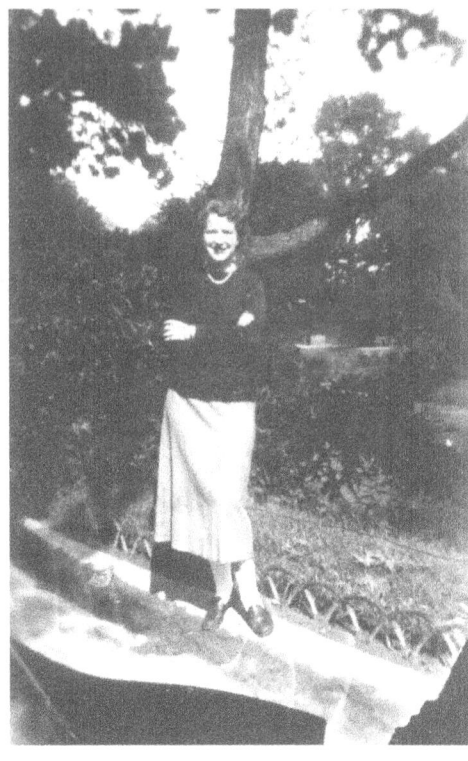

LEFT:
In Paris with Joe, the Newspaper Salesman.

ABOVE:
My Roommate Muriel Carl.

NO 2, RUE DE DOUANIER

Paris, 14th Arrondissment

Would the Parisians, who had lived through a terrible war and occupation, welcome a naïve American girl? Post World War II, Paris was still a beautiful but suffering city. It bore the restrictive effects of Nazi occupation. A depressing chill hung in the damp stone buildings. Bombs had not destroyed buildings, but neglect was evident in their crumbling façades and potholed streets where German tanks had driven recklessly over ancient cobblestones. Once in a while I felt the sharp edge of resentment from Parisians directed toward me— an American girl who had suffered so little.

Sitting in a café on Boulevard Raspail, I admired the poise of women trailing shopping carts, smoking Gauloises, reading *Le Monde*, bicycling home with freshly baked baguettes securely tied to the backs of their bikes. Could I fit in?

Muriel Carl and I settled on the fifth floor of Madame Eve's brownstone, numero Deux, Rue de Douanier, facing Parc Montsouri. Heat and hot water were severely rationed. Parisians were still experiencing many deprivations, and we were limited to one bath a week, with exactly six inches of water measured out by Madame Eve. (To avoid declaring income from our rent, she squirreled us away in her basement when the tax collector rang her bell.)

Super-practical Muriel was the daughter of a Fuller Brush salesman from Hartford, Conn. Her steamer trunk was filled with brushes for an amazing number of situations. Hating the morning odor of Gauloises mixed with brandy on our Metro commute to the Sorbonne, and eager to test our new independence, we spotted a MOTORCYCLE FOR SALE sign, pooled our emergency funds, threw in some Fuller brushes, and bought it. Neither of us had ever ridden one before. Living in Paris gave us courage to try.

To finance the bike, needing many costly repairs, we took a job in a *boite de nuit* (night club). I played piano and sang American show tunes, wearing saddle shoes and a plaid skirt. Although

French audiences preferred entertainers in more glamorous garb, we collected 12 to15 francs in the tip cup each night. When Madame Eve learned of our evening employment, she wrote our parents and I was soundly reprimanded: cut it out or come home!

My parents continued to send me letters, on a daily basis, expressing their concern about the war in Korea (1950-1953), in which the U.S. had become involved.

In one of her letters my mother cautioned:

there is always the possibility that something might happen OVER NIGHT! You must keep your valuables—passport, letter of credit etc. right beside you or sew it firmly into a small hankie and then pin the hankie to the middle of your bra—this way you can change it at night when you change to your evening bra. In case of need, hop the first plane, boat is fine, come any way you can—

Even worse, I started dating a young American writer, David Flavin, who asked me to marry him. When I called home in a state of flattered confusion, my parents invited him back to Washington so we could marry there. I sensed great concern in their voices. One hour after we arrived, Katie thanked him for escorting me back to America and told him (I'm not sure how politely) that I was far too young to marry. The fact that he was Catholic played a not insignificant part in the drama. My father frequently quoted Paul Blanshard to us on the dangers of Catholicism.

Bob Coulson wrote to me in Paris, letters with cartoons of his Harvard Law School professors wagging crooked fingers and students sleeping at their desks. His Harvard address and

Protestant name caught my parents' attention and they invited him to Washington. After a day sightseeing, Bob suggested that we get married and wanted to "clear" it with my father. Was he proposing? Confronted with another marriage proposal from a boy I scarcely knew, I nevertheless accepted without a moment's pause—like being asked to dance after being a wallflower for so many years.

Frumpish, overweight and unattractive, as I saw myself, the prospect of a future life glowed as an escape from parental control. To become the wife of a winning skipper of ocean races with impressive credentials and a piquant sense of humor! Did I know the significance of a marriage vow? My parents' marriage didn't offer much of an example. They slept in separate rooms, came and went at different hours and shared very few pleasures outside of the strict routine of eating.

Had I ever been "in love?" Naïve and overly supervised, I was hungry for age-appropriate privileges, like decision-making—or even risk. Neither of us knew what marriage meant, neither of us knew how to live together and have children together. It was thrilling and romantic, and a recipe for disaster.

A PROPOSAL APPROVED

When Bob made a formal request for "my hand," my father invited me into the library and described the Grandpa Louchheim Trust fund created for me, with an annual income of $3,000. Three thousand dollars sounded like a lot of money. Was it my dowry? Would it have been made available to me had I not been about to marry? My father was sweetening the deal, letting Bob know he was getting a rich girl, one who could pay her own bills. After our marriage, I paid all our monthly bills, while Bob used his inheritance to cover the substantial expenses incurred by his boat.

In the 1940's and 50's, girls were expected to go from college to marriage to motherhood within a half dozen years. A Liberal Arts degree unless followed by graduate school counted for little.

Managing a home, creating meals, bearing children—I hadn't been schooled in any of that, although our wedding gifts seemed to point in that direction. A dozen salad bowls, silver salt and pepper shakers, casserole cookers and countless kitchen utensils seemed to suggest that I had some familiarity with the kitchen.

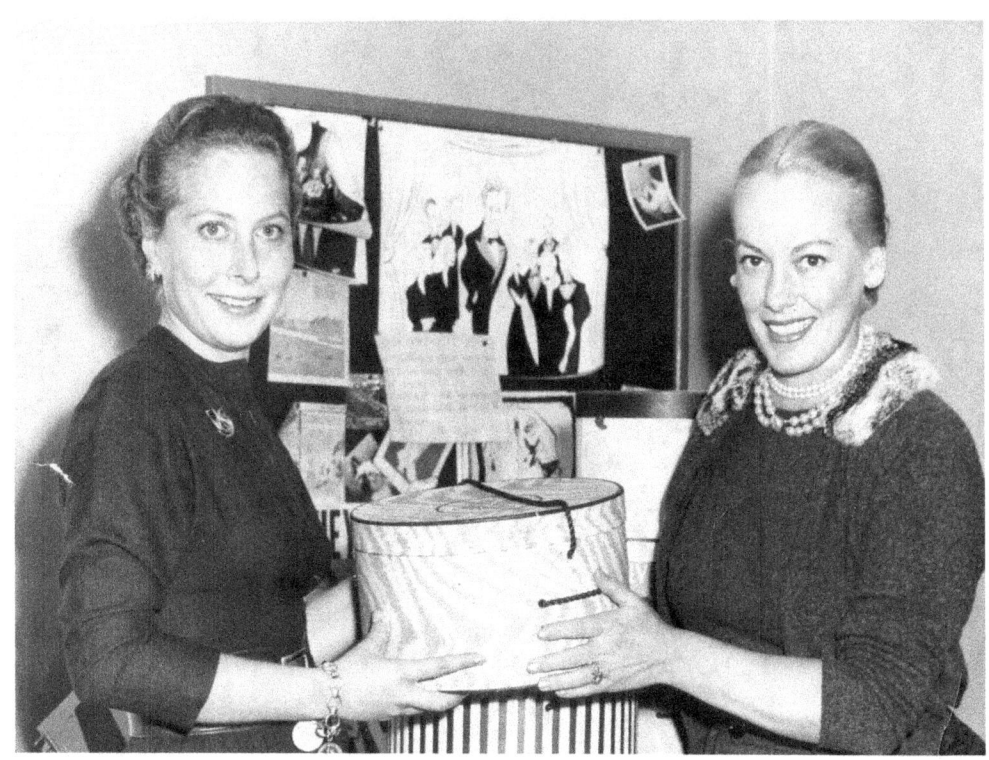

WEDDING PLANS: I ENTER THE CHRISTIAN WORLD

My parents were delighted that I was about to become a Christian. For years, they had wanted to join the Chatham Tennis club, to become a member of the Chatham Protestant community.

Katie threw herself into arranging our wedding with the same imagination and single-mindedness with which she had broached Washington society. Who should be maid-of-honor? Where was Grandma Frankie's wedding veil stored? I had existed as an annoying teenager, yet overnight I took center stage as an about-to-be blushing bride.

The minister at the Church of the Holy Spirit in Orleans, Massachusetts, announced in a pontifical manner that I needed to, be " baptized a Christian," before even approaching his altar. I found this to be a rather strange requirement but hadn't developed enough muscle

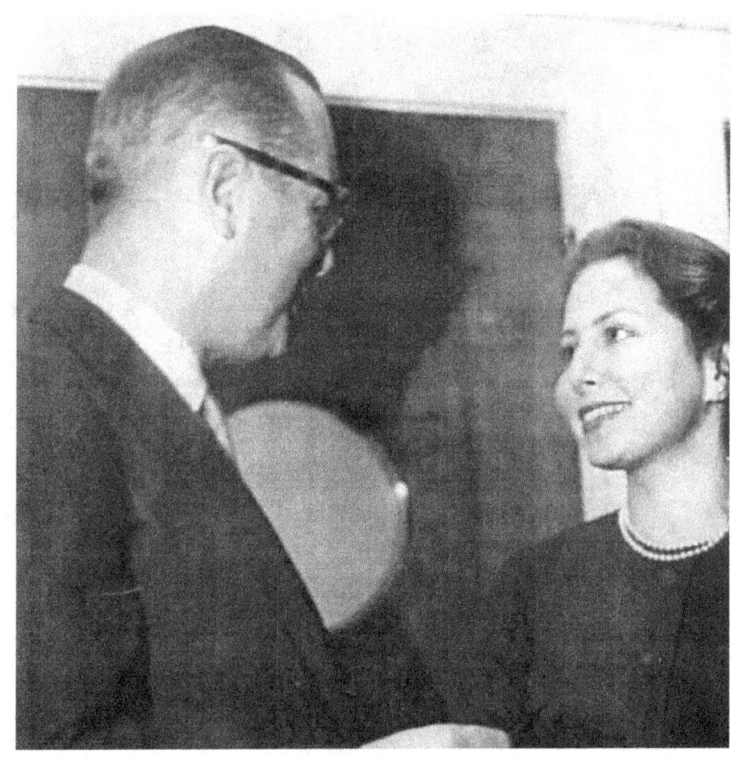

LEFT:

Mary and Robert Montgomery—a Hollywood movie star, offering me a small part in one of his films.

to question or challenge a member of the Christian clergy. Was this yet another poke at my Jewish background?

Our marriage ceremony was picture-book perfect. Standing with me at the rear of the church, my father delivered a few last minute aphorisms before walking me down the aisle: "compromise" on all issues, he advised. It didn't strike me as the *modus vivendi* in his marriage to my mother.

Bob's brother, Dick, was the jovial best man, and Judy, maid of honor. A retinue of friends outfitted in wedding froth surrounded us at the altar. I shook continuously—who knows why?—and had to be prompted by the minister several times before finding a speaking voice. Grandpa Louchheim cried and had to leave the church.

Guests at the Eastward Ho Golf Club reception milled about, waiting for us to go on our honeymoon, and roared with laughter when they learned that, instead of a romantic getaway, Bob and his racing crew were headed for Marblehead Harbor, and the start of a race from there to Nova Scotia. I was to follow four days later in a jeep, bringing an "ample supply" of canned food to Halifax to meet the racing crew. My parents seemed charmed by the idea of fitting our wedding date into Bob's ocean-racing schedule.

Bringing the "Finn MacCumhaill" back to Chatham harbor, we were becalmed in the Bay of Fundy for several days—no wind and an empty gas tank—a memorable experience.

MOTHERHOOD

Becoming a mother seemingly happened overnight. First, I was marching down the aisle in a white dress, surrounded by friends and relatives offering flowers and hugs. Then in an *Augenblick* I appeared with a protruding front, responsible for a new life—but still an emotional teenager having problems managing my own. Overwhelmed, inadequate, unprepared, I entered the world of motherhood with innocence and misgivings.

When I learned I was pregnant, in my senior year at college in Boston, having transferred there to accommodate Bob Coulson's Harvard Law school location, I wept in my clothes closet. Where else to hide? I knew no one in Cambridge. The ob-gyn I consulted was an uptight waspish, unsympathetic man, Dr. Judson-Smith.

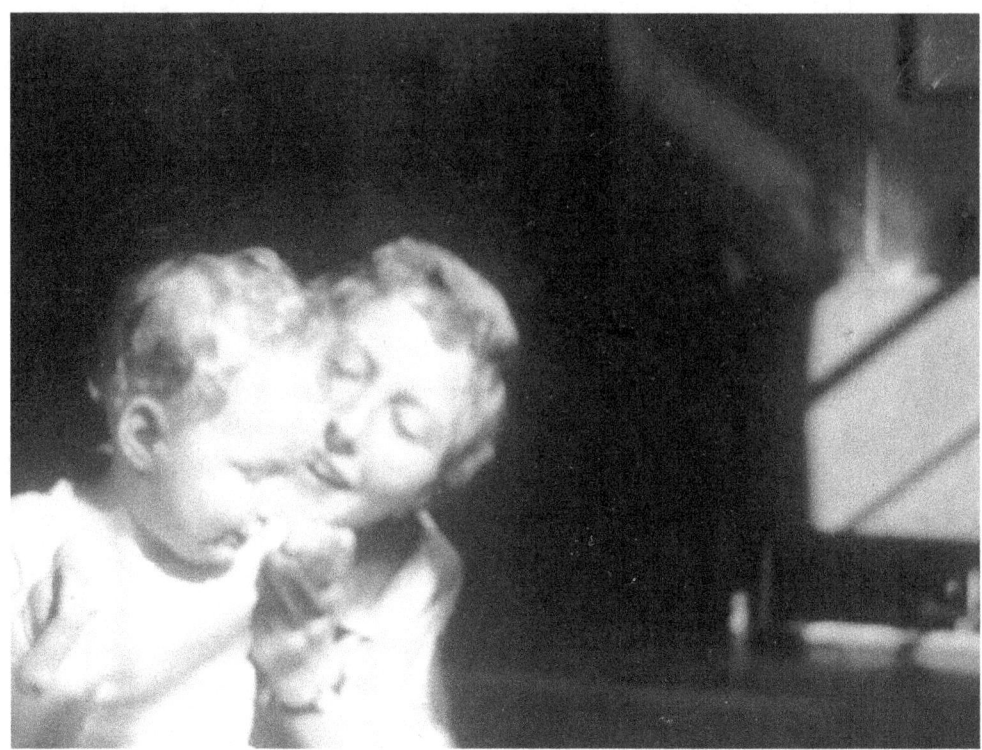

COTTON

May 16, 1952

I hid my pregnancy under a massive raincoat at Boston University. Mothers-to-be weren't college students in those days. "Cotton"—Bob announced that the baby's name had to begin with the letter "C"—weighing just 3 pounds, 14 ounces—they said it was because I had had the measles—arrived two weeks early just as I was taking final exams. I greeted him through the glassed-in walls of the "preemie" nursery, trying desperately to introduce myself as his mother. I knew nothing about babies, mothering, or home life. I had been attended by maids, governesses, controlled and directed by my all-knowing, elsewhere parents. Here was a live baby—underweight, needy. I had trouble mastering my fear of this new person entirely dependent on me. I begged the starchy nurses at Richardson House in Boston to let me hold Cotton, but hospital rules were rigid: a mother giving birth to a baby under five pounds had to keep her distance so as not to infect her child—reminiscent of my father's rules regarding

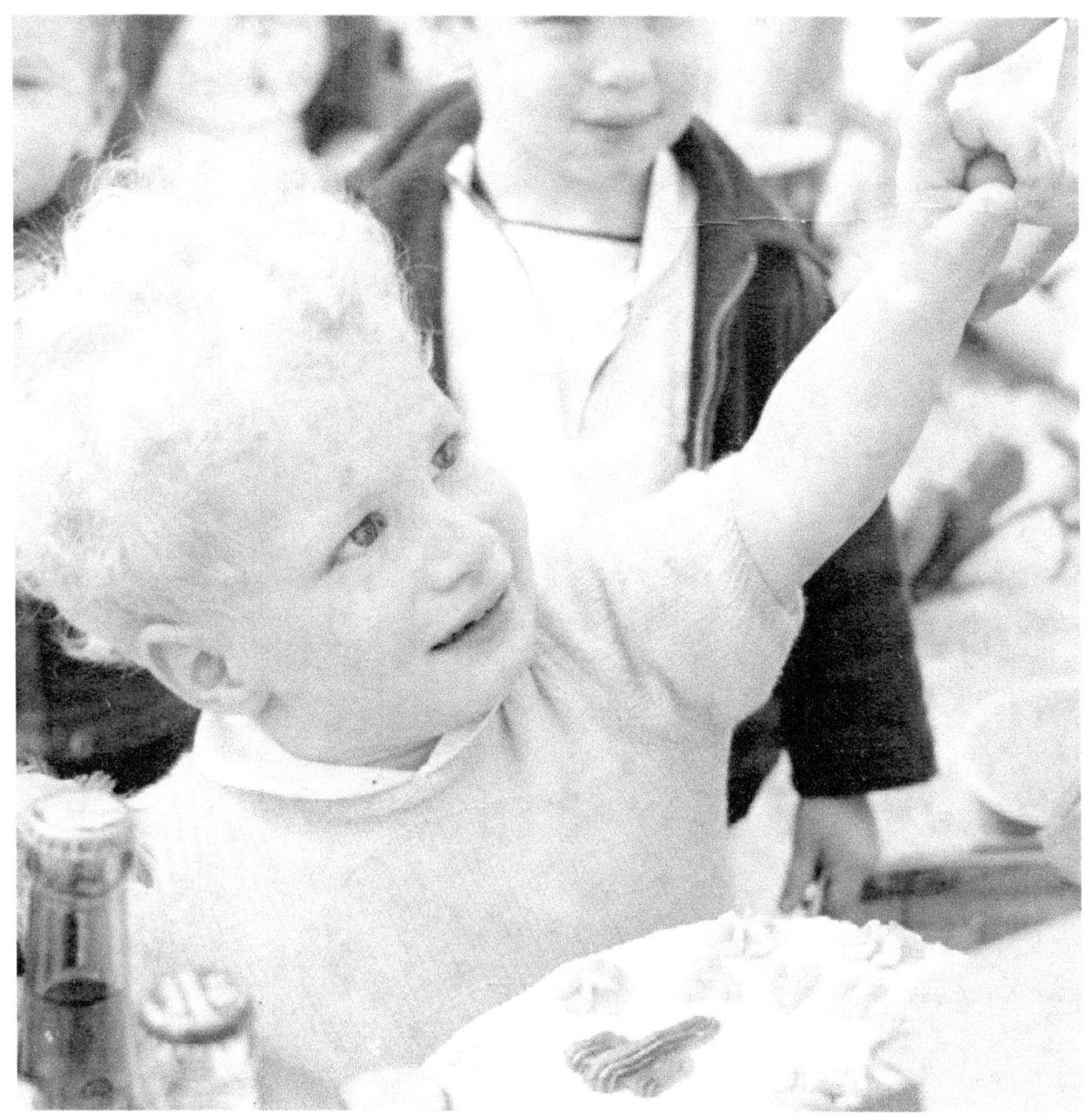

ABOVE:

*Cotton's birthday,
age 2. Singing
Beach, Manchester,
Massachusetts.*

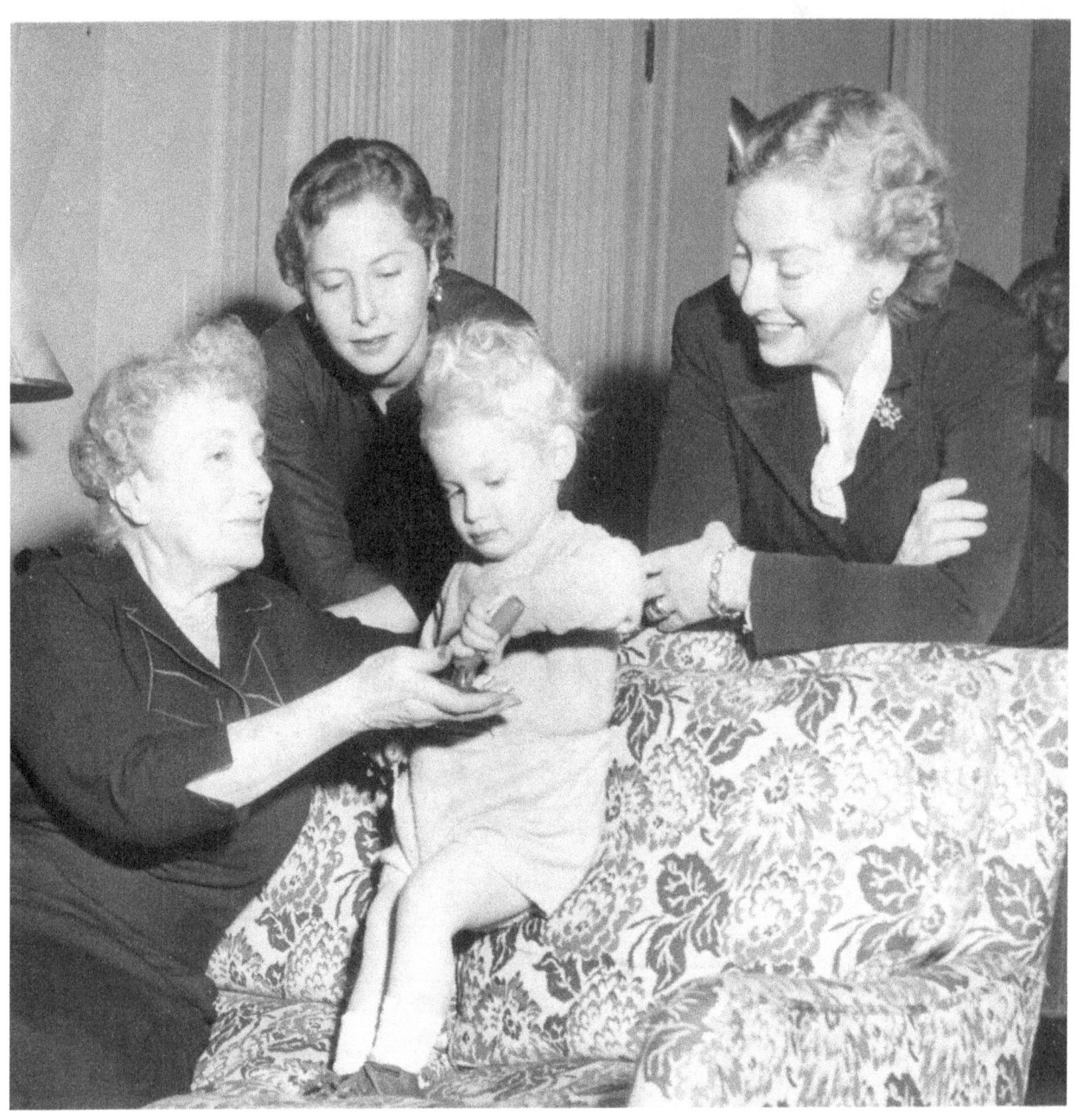

ABOVE:

Cotton and doting
Grandparents Adele and
Katie in New York City.

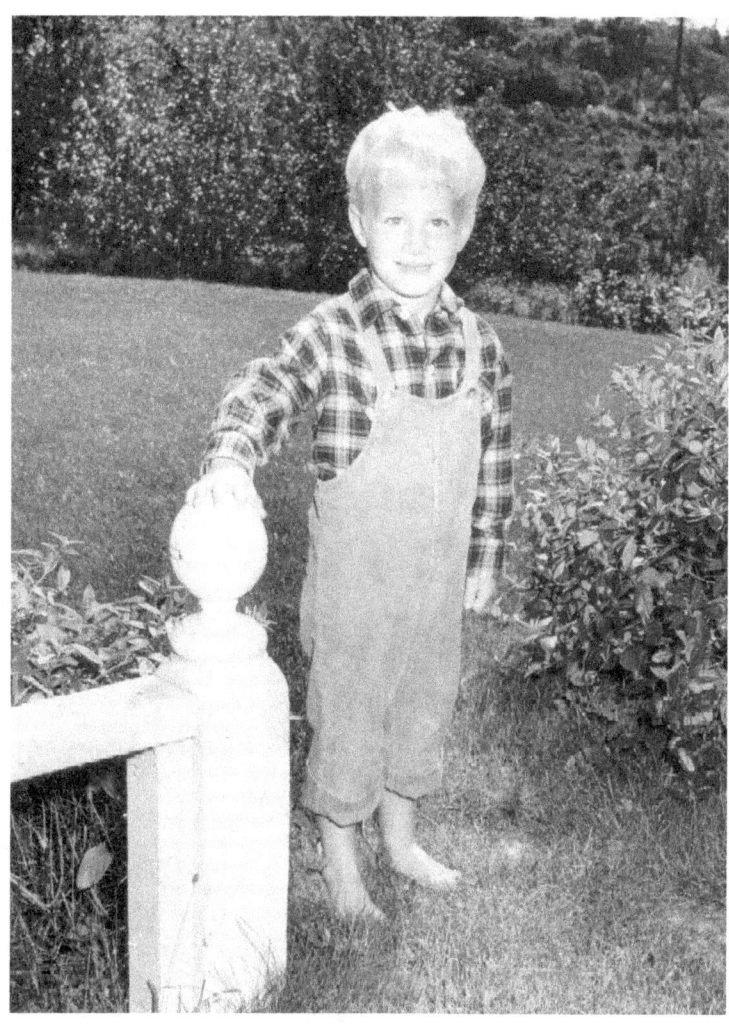

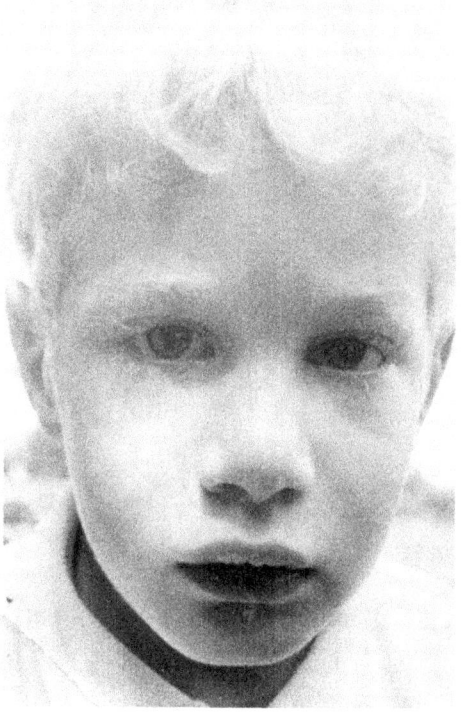

LEFT:

Cotton in Chatham.

ABOVE:

Photo of Cotton by Paul Mattisse.

our nursery. I was given a heavy metal breast pump to use at home and told to return to the hospital with breast milk every day. When Cotton reached the required 5 pound weight, they would release him. My mother visited, knitting a blanket for the crib, proudly announcing her new state of grandmotherhood. Bob's ribald humor kept her entertained. Bob's mother invited us to spend the summer at her palatial house in Marblehead. She insisted on hiring a baby nurse. "You'll need someone with practice," she explained. "I'll pay."

As it turned out, Nurse Van Tassell had practice—at keeping the baby to herself. Every time I tried to feed Cotton I was shooed away on some pretense. "The baby is sleeping—The baby is digesting—It's not good to pick up the baby too often—."

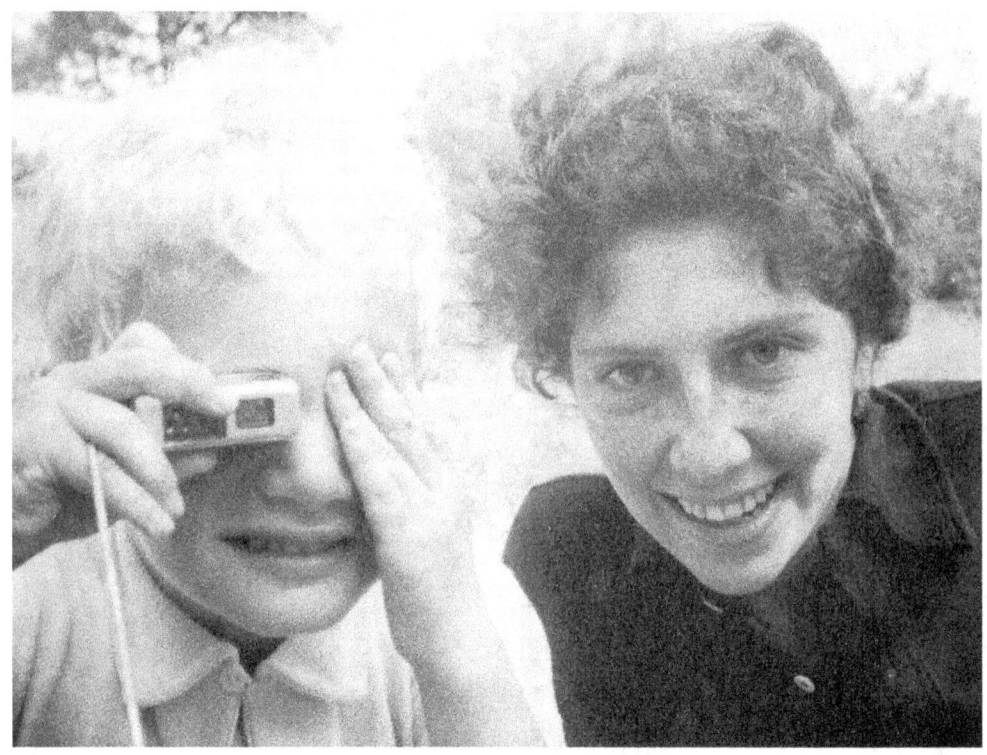

Discouraged, I reverted to the zombie I'd been in my parents' home—standing by while others more efficient took over. I was limited to pushing Cotton in his carriage once a day, terrified that he might wake up and cry—grateful for Dr. Spock's manual on baby care.

Since cooking had never been part of my life, frustration overtook me when I had to prepare meals in our two by four foot kitchen on Concord Avenue in Cambridge. Poor Bob Coulson ate hamburgers, frozen French fries and Bird's Eye beans for dinner almost every night. Years later, my children accused me of feeding them TV dinners. On some evenings, I resorted to that quick fix. They probably tasted better.

Judy, in her freshman year at Radcliffe, became our babysitter. She had been so closely coddled and cared for that when she finally left home, she felt frightened: many decisions to make and no one to tuck her in. I was able to help a little.

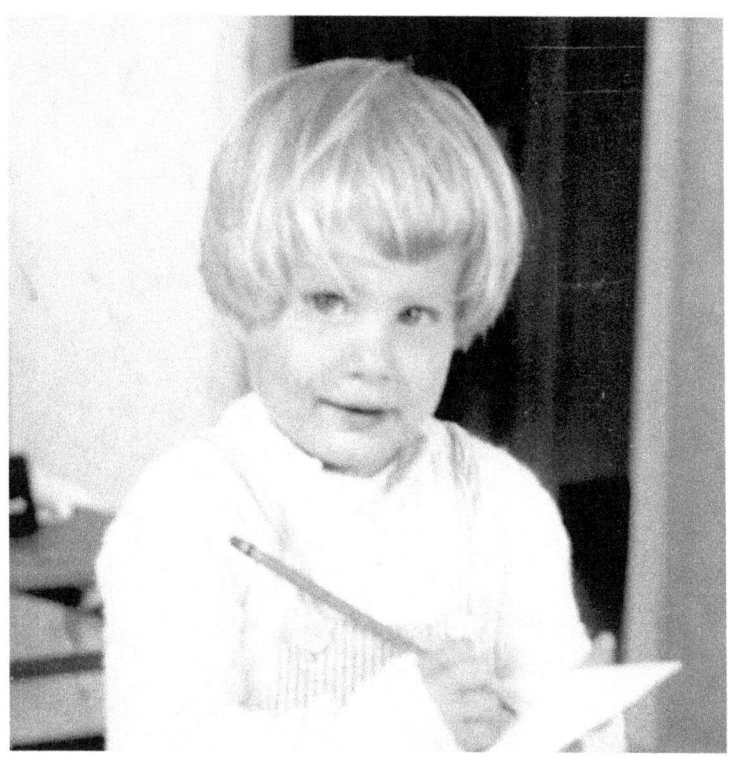

DEIRDRE (DIDI)

December 14, 1955

I greeted Deirdre's beautiful, trouble-free face with confidence. Cotton had given me a crash course in mothering. What a delightful baby Didi was! Deirdre (somehow "Didi" always replaced her lovely Gaelic name) managed, at a very early age, to take charge of her own life. Cotton's response to her arrival was mixed. He threw his tricycle into her crib and often barred her from his room. However, early in her infancy, she developed immunity to his assaults and grew stronger as a result.

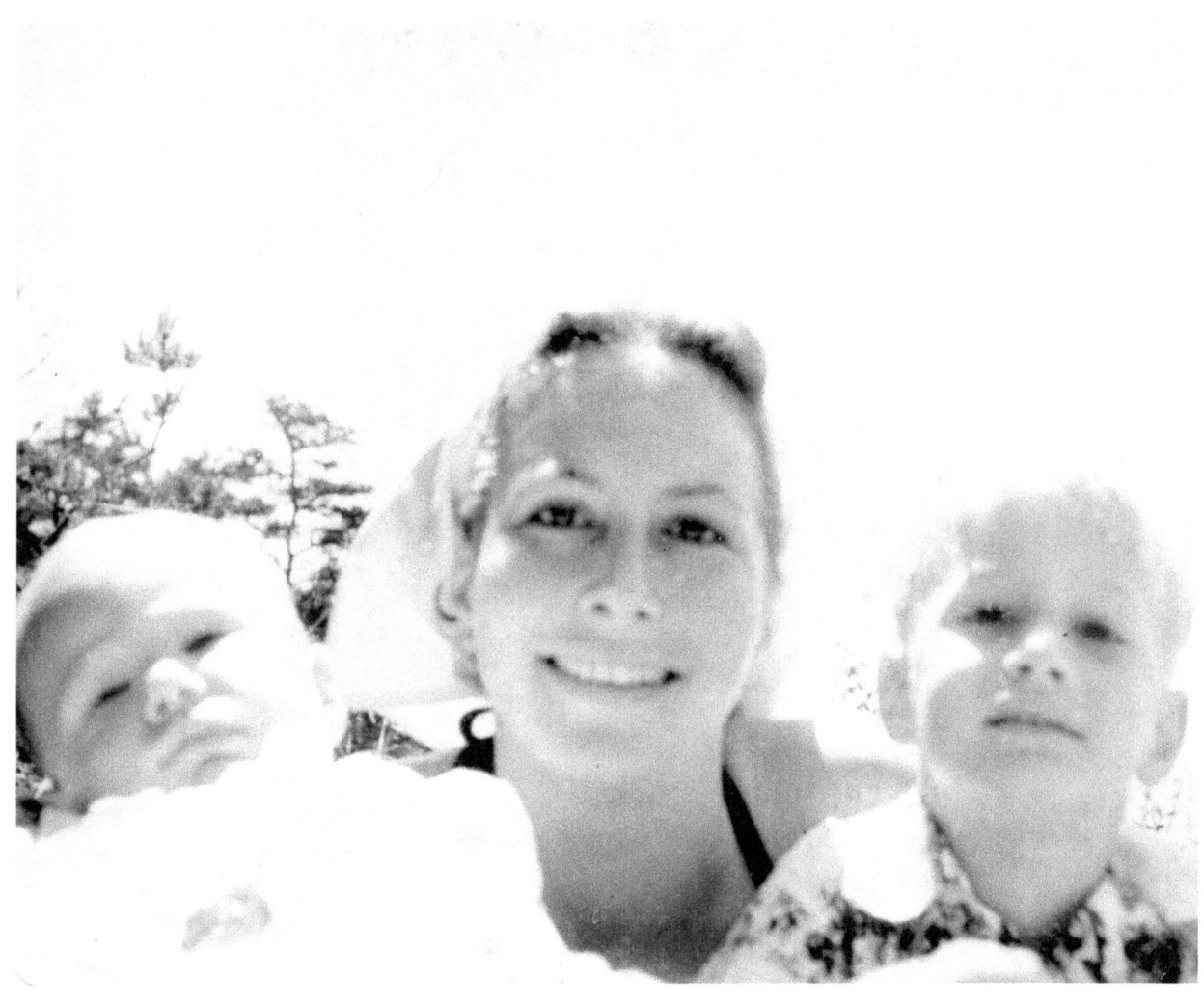

MOTHER MARY

I was determined to mother my children without helpers—probably a reaction to being overlooked by my parents when I was growing up. Much of my time was spent in a state of anxiety over where they were, what they were doing, and how to care for them when they got sick.

I remember the night Cotton and Didi created a new sport–hurling bits of banana against walls and furniture. They insisted on showing me how the game was played—breaking off bits

94

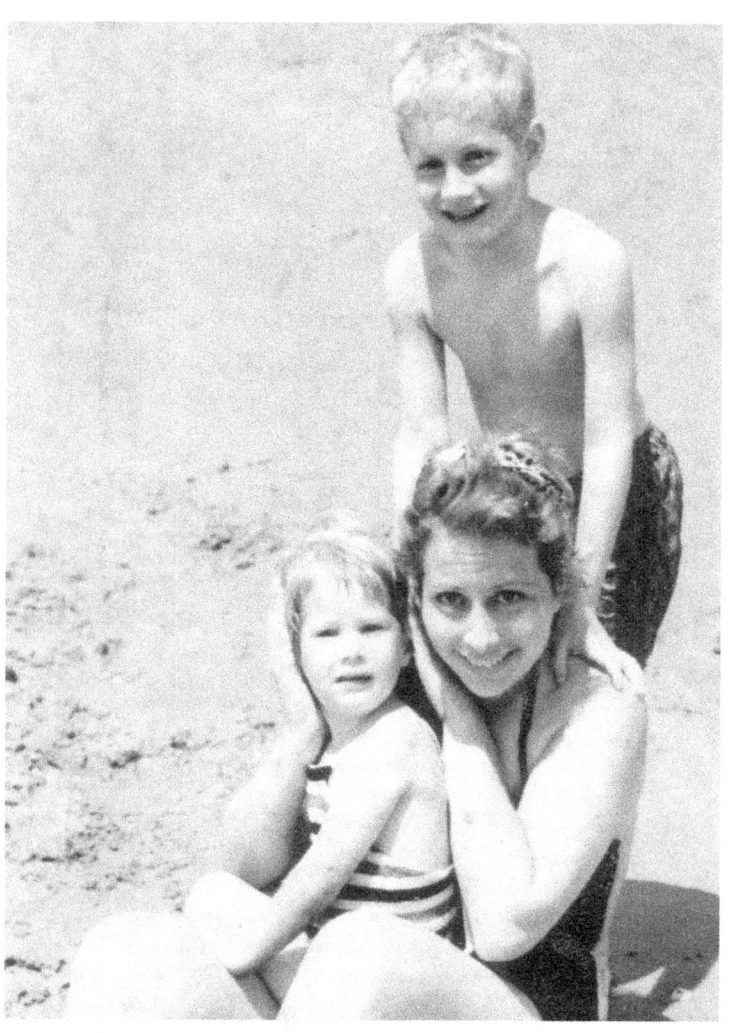

of banana and aiming it at a designated target. The entire six room apartment was covered with bananas—walls, couches, chairs and rugs.

Peeling dried banana from walls and rugs, I tried really hard to contain my anger.

Gradually, as my children matured, I came to lean less heavily on Dr. Benjamin Spock's parental advice and developed my own routines. Cotton and Didi were so very different in their sensitivities to food, sleep and play. Didi gobbled up everything while Cotton picked at his plate. Didi's daredevil spirit found an outlet riding horses. She chose Charney, a Hungarian Viszla, as her special canine pal.

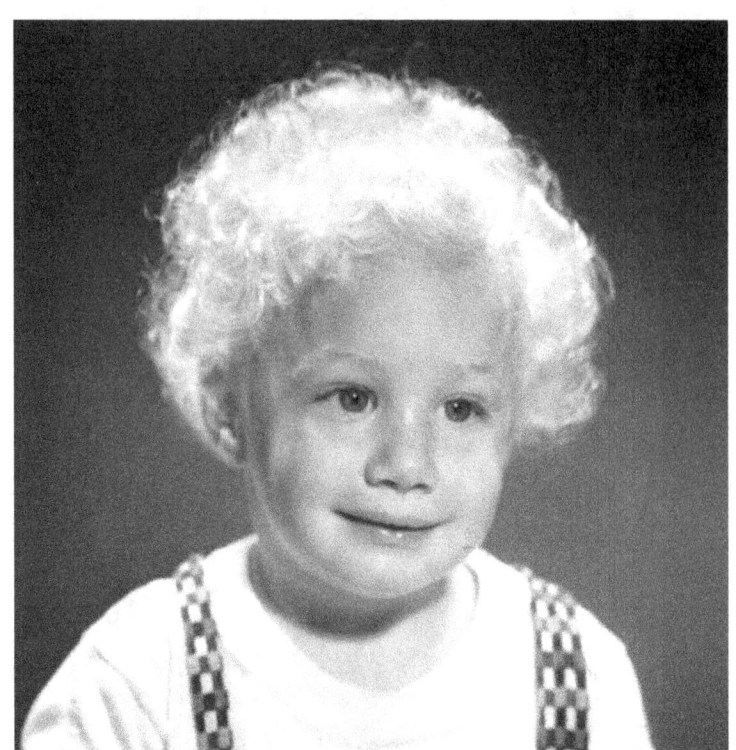

TOP LEFT:

Cotton.

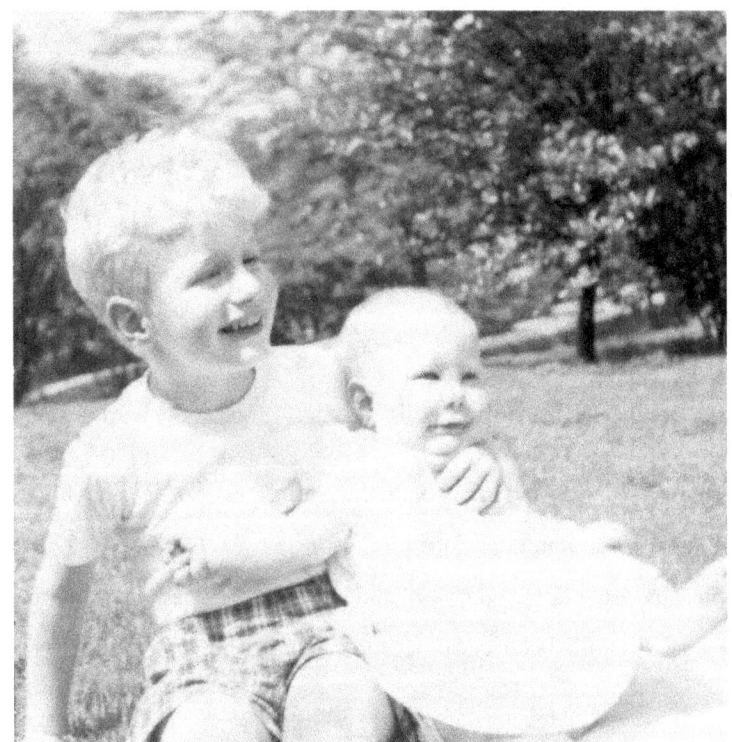

BOTTOM LEFT::

Didi and Cotton, 1956.

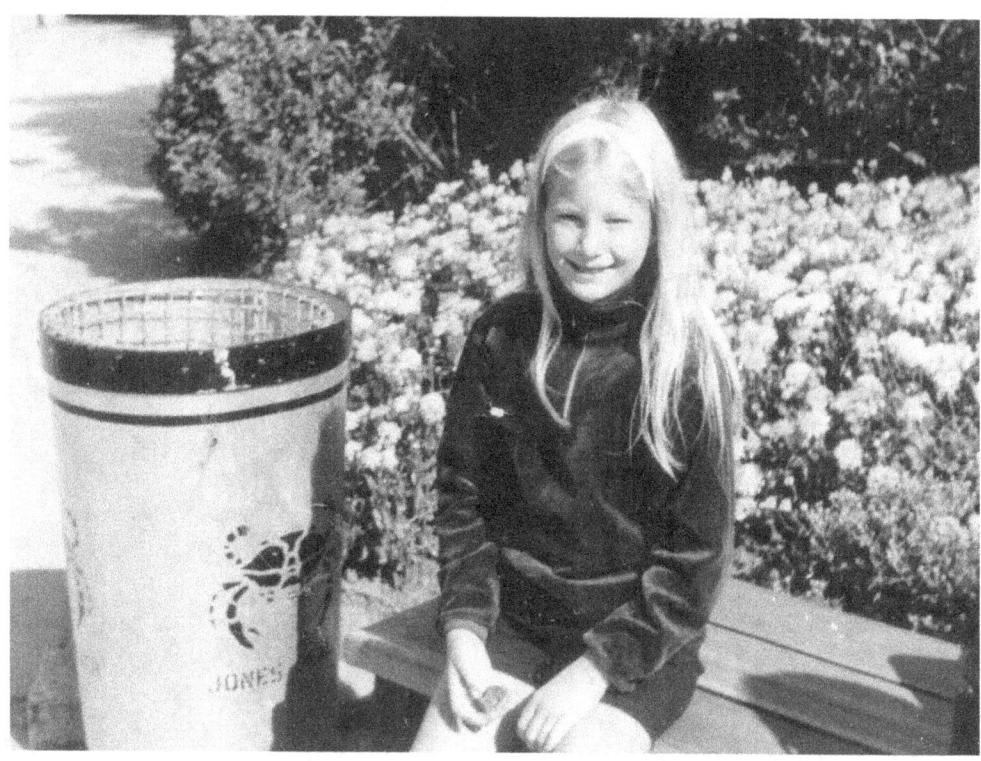

BOB AND ABBY COULSON, BOB'S PARENTS

The Protestant Coulson world was very different from my German/Jewish cocoon. In different ways, they were both terrible. Drinks were served every evening by Pearl, a black woman from the Bahamas. During the cocktail hour, Abby sat at a card table in her Marblehead living room playing Solitaire, her long nails clicking loudly against the plastic cards, while Bob Senior remained in an upstairs bedroom, fondled by one of his Wall Street secretaries.

Abby's aesthetic tastes and mine differed substantially, although I'm not sure mine were even developed. But there was this huge, I mean huge aquamarine ring—part of Abby's inventory in her Bahamas gift shop—which she offered to Bob for our engagement. It sat on my stubby unmanicured fingers in a wobbly manner and because I am left-handed, greatly curtailed my freedom of movement. As my courage in speaking up developed, I asked Bob if we could

97

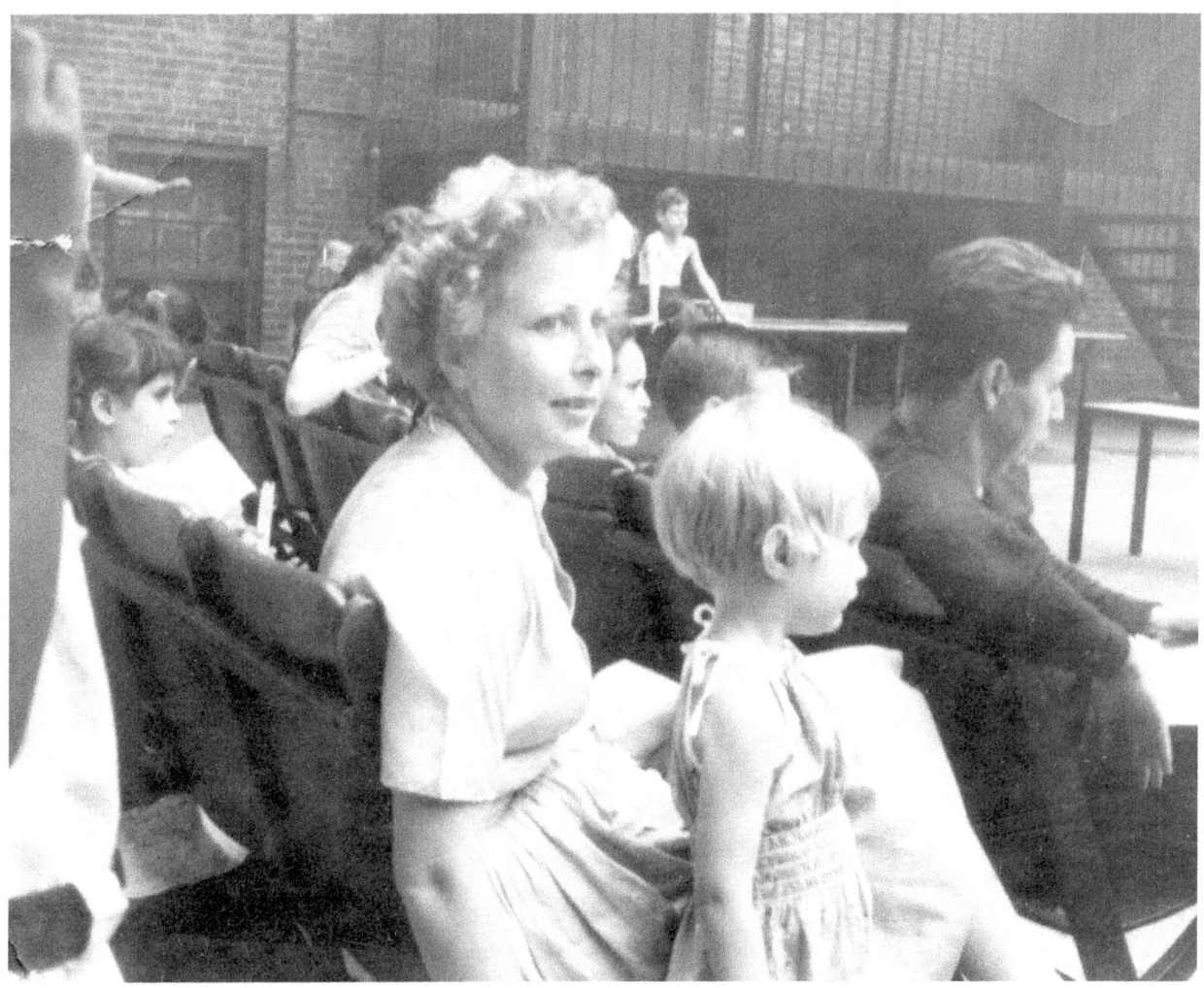

ABOVE:

Didi and me listening to Cotton sing at Union Settlement on 108th Street, N.Y.C.

symbolize our marriage with a smaller ring. More awkward exchanges followed, and in place of an engagement ring, I was given a half dozen British demitasse cups.

I learned that young Bob had never lived at home. At the age of four, he'd been sent off to a boarding school and continued growing up in a world of kindly academics who served as parent replacements. He had never experienced the day-to-day life of a child developing within a nurturing family. He and I had that sad reality in common.

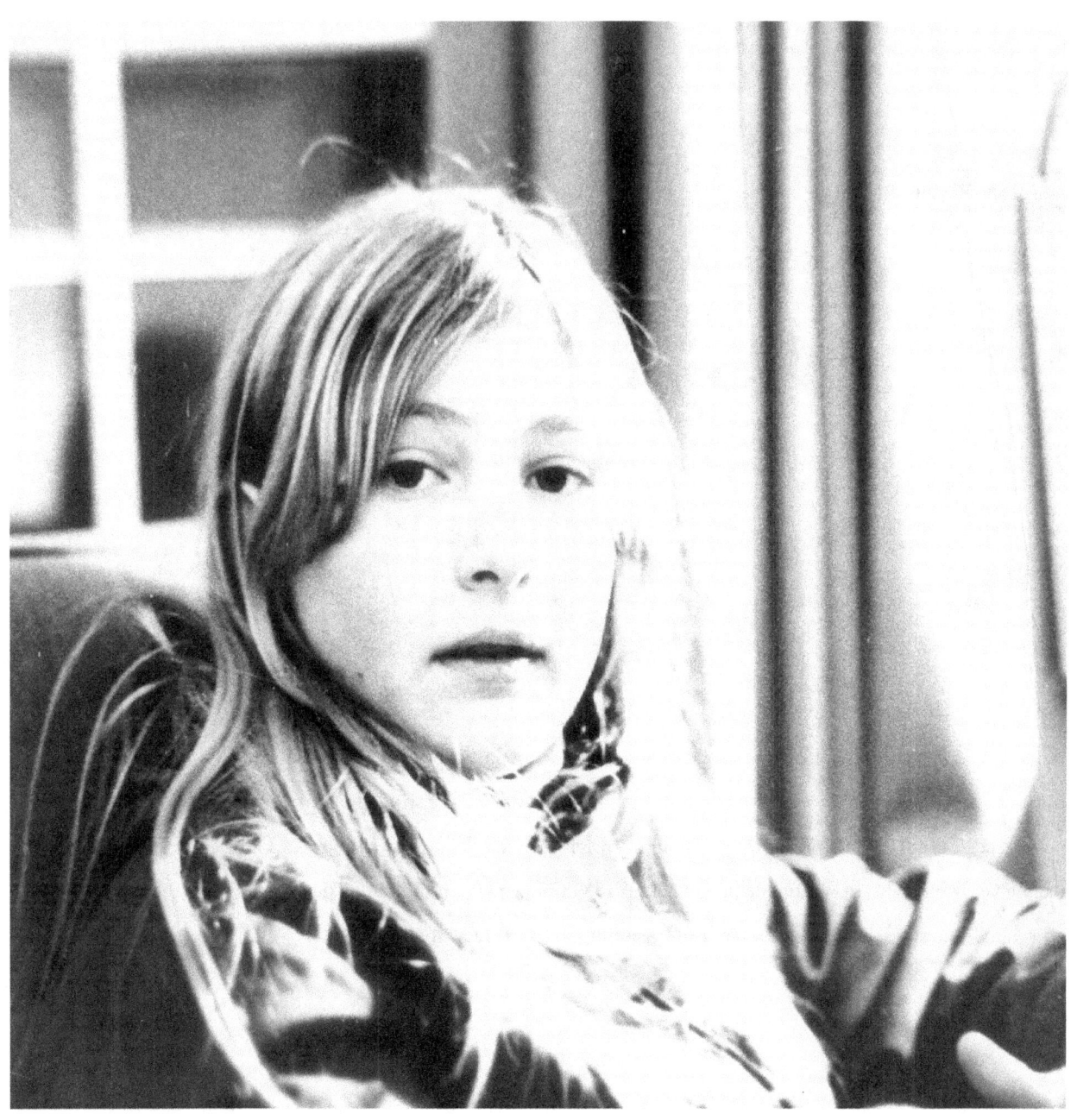

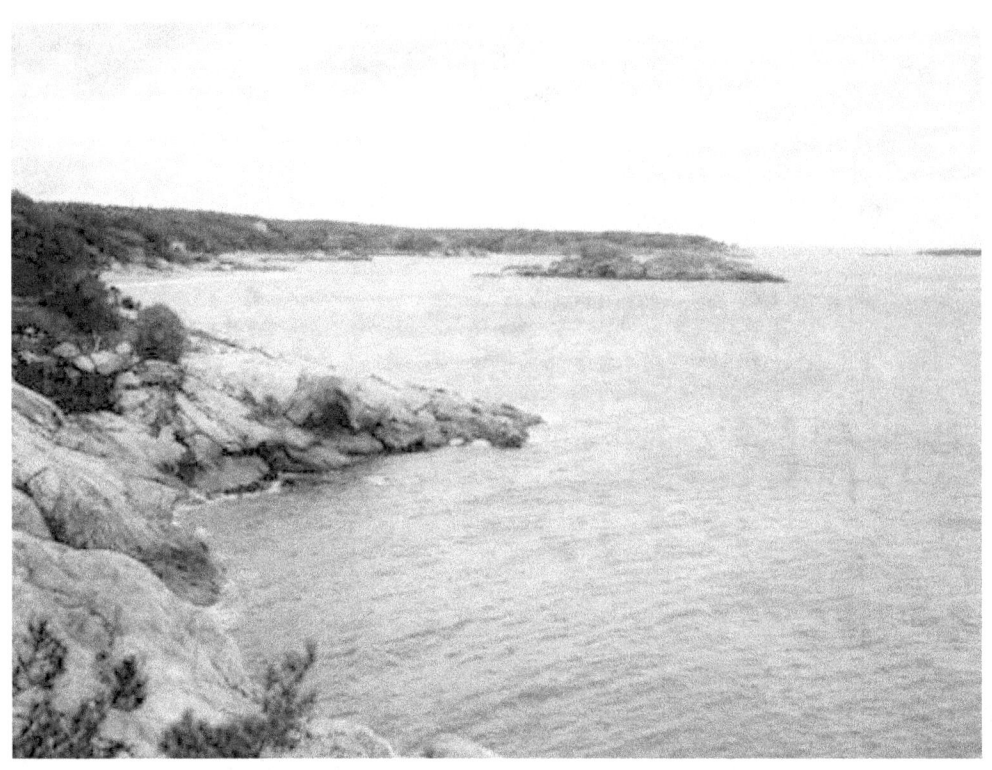

It took me a while to realize that Bob's focus on his sailboat would determine where we lived. After three years at Harvard Law School, he found a mooring for his boat in Manchester-by-the-Sea, Massachusetts, and we moved there. In frequent heavy snow and wind, the Manchester power station shut down, and snowplows couldn't reach us. Stranded, with Cotton and Didi, feeling very vulnerable in our fragile prefab**. I read Winnie-the-Pooh to them, *Tosca*, playing on the radio, and resolved that I was indeed beginning to function as their mother.

**Eaglehead was the Singing Beach Bob chose to build a house. Our "prefab" house was constructed of plywood – arrived on a truck and like a Lego, was put together in a half a day. Perched high on a rocky cliff overlooking the sea, there was a real possibility of someone falling overboard–down the cliff side.

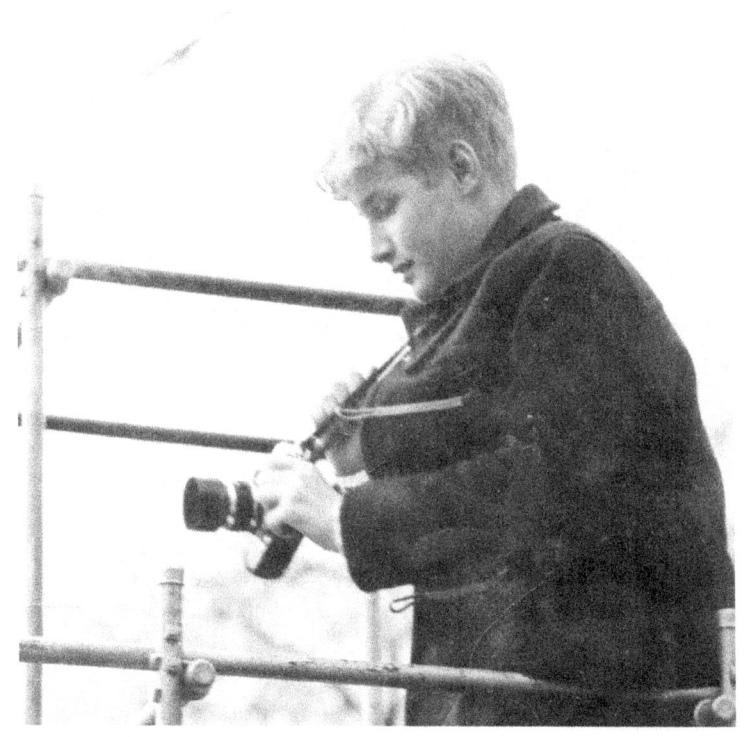

TOP RIGHT:

Cotton, young photographer, Central Park.

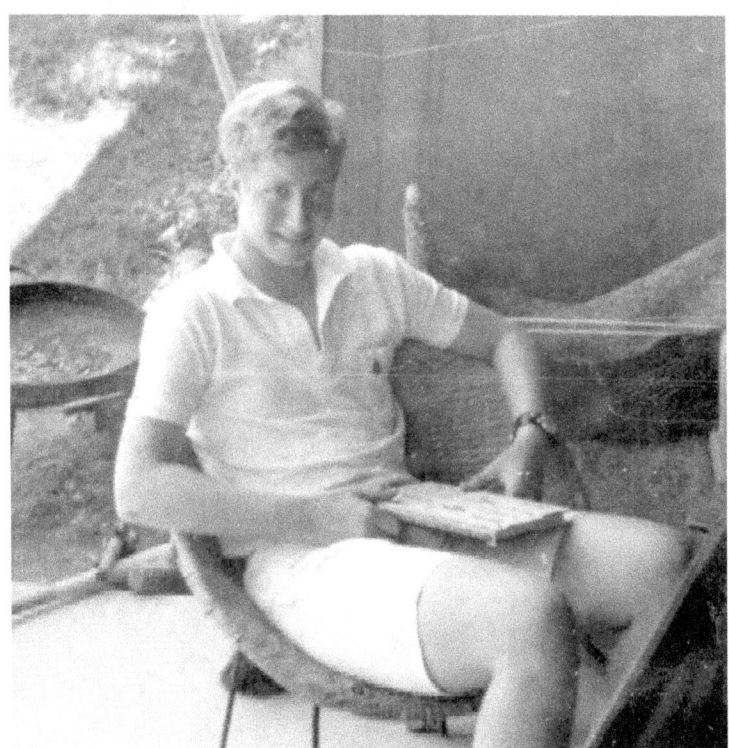

BOTTOM RIGHT:

Cotton.

101

DIVORCE

1957

One Sunday in Manchester I felt the need for organ music and a somber hour in church. The local Episcopal church service provided a nostalgic reminder of my National Cathedral School days, dozing during prayers in the Bethlehem Chapel.

A brown haired minister greeted us all as we left and grasped my hand rather firmly, saying, "You are new to the church. Stay a moment and let me know you." After the congregants left, he asked in a most sincere and caring way whether I would come again and what my religious background was. I described my lonely life with a boat-obsessed husband. Young married friends were content with tuna casseroles and tennis dates. He surprised me saying, "Why don't you divorce and find yourself a husband-companion who can share?" I was shocked to hear the word "divorce" from a prelate. I assumed divorce meant failure, abandonment and disruption. I was unable to imagine living on my own. Somehow, this churchman gave me the courage to move on and not settle.

Aunt Florence gave me another push. She took me to a psychiatrist when I despaired over Bob's boat obsession. Increasingly, Bob preferred sailing—"frostbite racing" in winters, long distance ocean racing in summers—to family life. I felt left out at home. She urged me to disregard my parents and break away from their rules and concern with appearances.

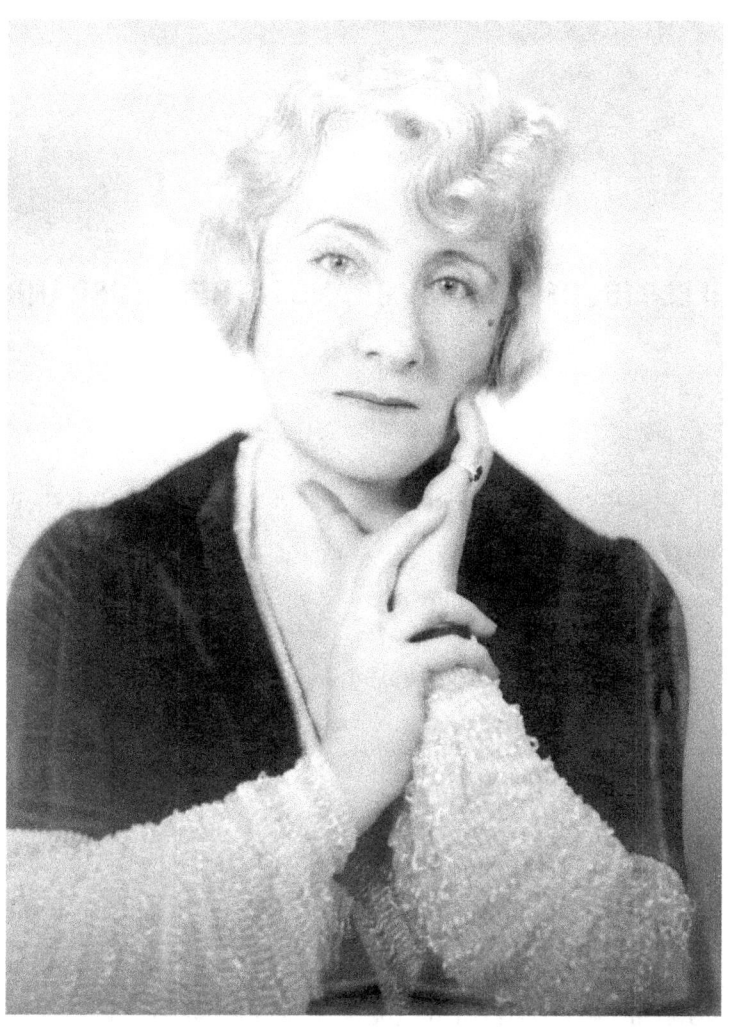

When my parents learned of my intention to divorce, they turned their backs on me, declaring that I was ruining my childrens' lives and bringing embarrassment to our family. Enter Adele, with some homilies.

Adele shook her finger at me–"You are disgracing your family", she maintained. "No one in our family has ever gone through a divorce!" Some years later, I discovered that my sanctimonious grandmother, Adele, and Leonard Scofield had separated and divorced after one year.

LEONARD SCHOENFELD (SCOFIELD), MY GRAND FATHER, HUSBAND OF ADELE JOSEPH

I never met my grandfather, Leonard Schoenfeld. I only saw photos and he looks particularly handsome and fit in his tracksuit, as the Captain of Harvard's Broad Jump team, handsome, even arrogant. I think my mother had a crush on him.

After his brief marriage to Adele Joseph, he was banished from her family when he failed to provide. He was included, however, at her dinner parties when an "extra" man was needed at the table.

Not interested in business, Leonard worked only occasionally in his family's Textile By-Products Company, in the Flat Iron Building in New York City, and preferred to "hang out" at the Manhattan Chess Club where he was always a winner. I found a letter he wrote to my mother explaining that he didn't have sufficient funds to cross the Atlantic to attend her wedding in Hamburg, Germany. Having money defined who you were in Leonard's German/Jewish circle.

Leonard suffered, ending his life in The Home for Incurables in the Bronx where Adele placed him, hiring a "reader" to come once a week to visit him. His hands shook too much from Parkinson disease to hold a book. He was moved to the Men's Ward where after a year, the reader stopped coming, and on June 18, 1937, he jumped from the Fifth floor bathroom window to his death.

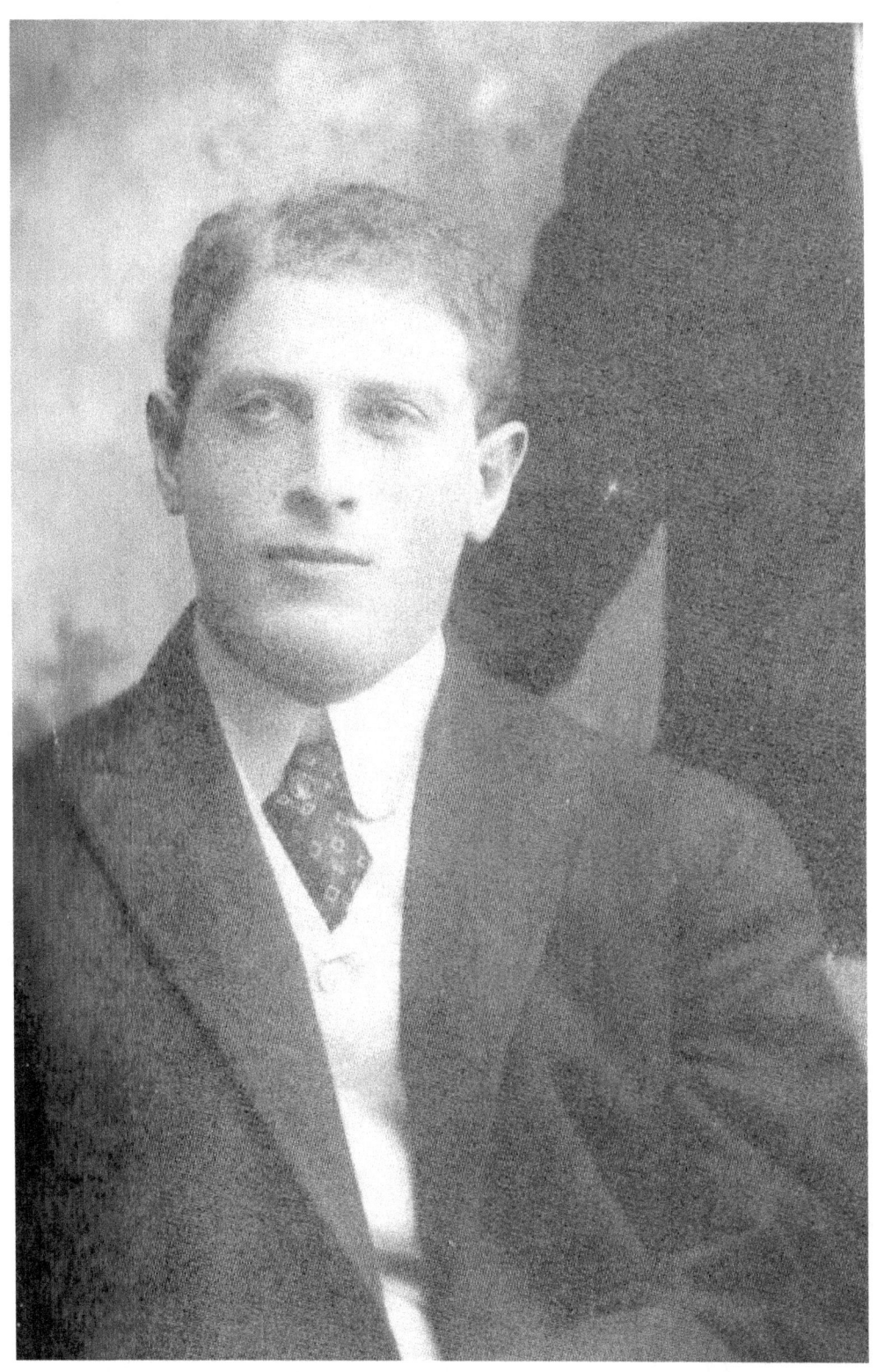

My mother never talked about her father with me but I imagine there must have been much pain connected to his death. In 1965, she wrote:

ABOUT MY FATHER

by Katie Louchheim

Now that you are long since safely dead
I remember what you never said
A fabulist, you shook the humbug tree
Of make believe, wound up life's toy for me.
You were vain, caught in the mirror bowing approval
Of that high Roman nose, those well set eyes
Women adored you flim flam and all
Even little girls worshipped your charms,
Swallowed your harmless lies.
You broke all hearts, your own beneath the
Well pressed suits
Must have known the lightening bolt of failure
How could you weather all their scorn? Did you
Commute daily from despair to dreams
Were you sure you could outwalk, outdance
Out please their taunts
Make for me a world where I would always be
Safe, fair, gay, loved in nice rooms by nice names
Protected by the luck you won me?

THE MARRIAGE MANTRA

'Every girl should marry before she's thirty,' was the message broadcast in women's magazines, girly novels and afternoon soaps during the fifties. How should one feel before marrying? Why did Katie put such stock in the institution? And why did that legal tie always open up such a can of worms for me? My mother preached Marriage-as-Security. "A woman on her own is looked down upon." And yet her marriages did little to improve her sense of self. She believed that Walter's money and Donald's publishing firm would take care of everything, but, apart from enjoying the physical comforts, she was very lonely. Marrying was the easy part. Breaking up—divorcing—took determination and money. Wanting out of a relationship cost me dollars and stress.

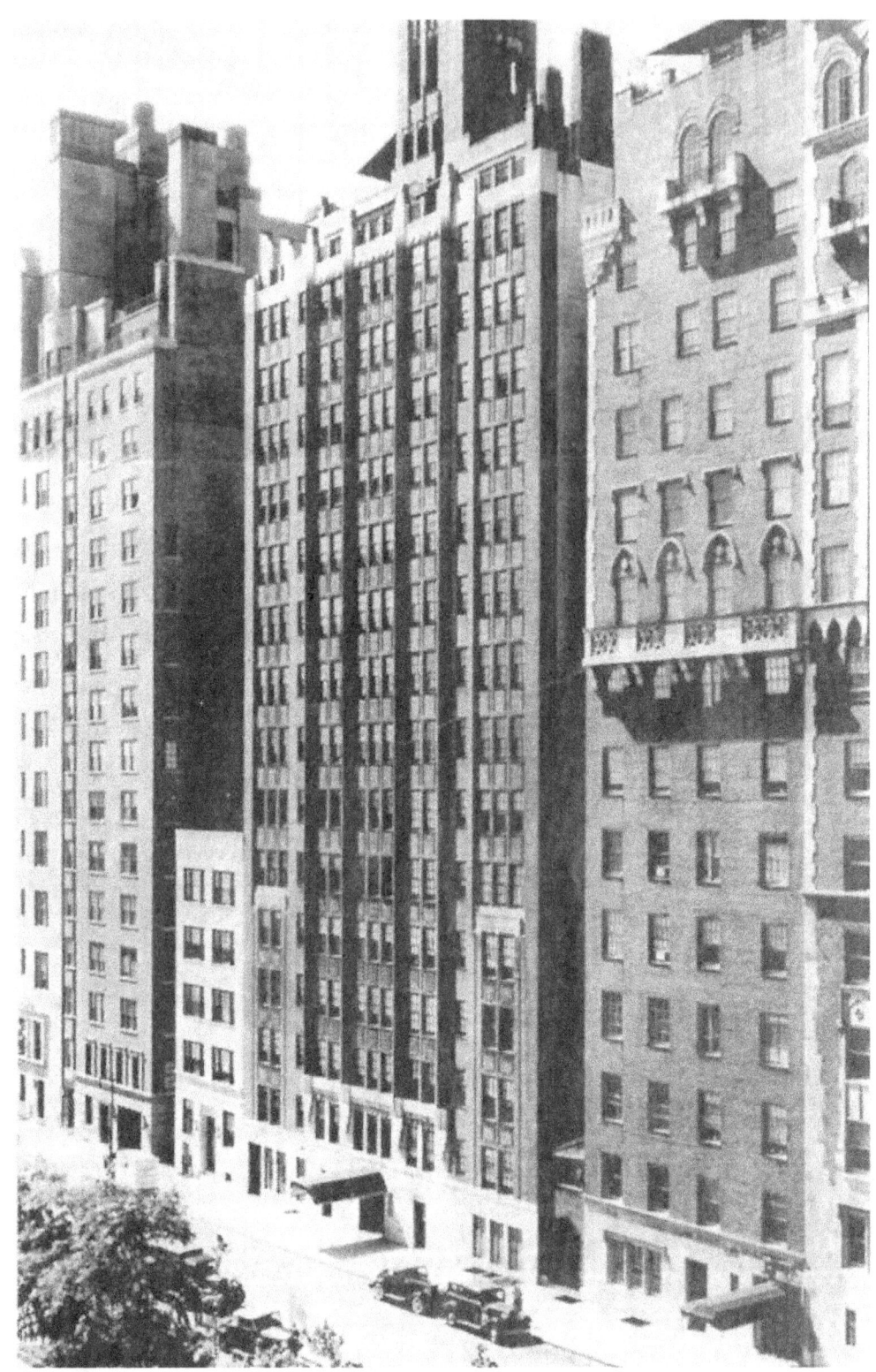

LEFT:

*7 Gracie Square
mentioned in The New
York Times.*

SEVEN GRACIE SQUARE

YORKVILLE

1955

When Bob was offered a position in his father's law firm, Whitman, Ransom and Coulson, we moved to New York City, to 7 Gracie Square on the East River, a neighborhood full of nabobs, wealthy, fancy folk. Gloria Vanderbilt lived in the building next door. Because our apartment was in the rear of the building surrounded by other high-rises, daylight was elusive and we were seemingly enclosed in a brick prison, an eternal night. I missed seeing people and sunshine.

I'm sure the previous owners were delighted to dump it for $7,000. They probably would have given it away just to leave. Our neighbors hated children and dogs. Whenever they had a chance they would open and close their front door with a loud slam—a statement intended to manifest their rage at finding us in residence next door. One day, my mother's photograph appeared on the front page of The New York Times, showing her standing alongside President Kennedy, proud of her new assignment as Assistant Secretary of State. Not long afterwards, the neighbors began smiling and inviting me in for drinks, even leaving small gifts on the doorstep for my children. Amazing what weight a news photo can carry.

Still very much a German neighborhood, Yorkville boasted storefront displays of tantalizing wursts and rich German chocolate cakes—fanciful pastries with miniature marzipan figures. Food shopping was always an adventure. I learned to make *choucroute*, an Alsatian favorite, with bratwurst and sauerkraut from Schaller & Weber on Second Avenue, the German meat vender where my grandmother Frankie shopped.

Cotton enrolled in the Collegiate School and joined the Knickerbocker Greys—a young man's military group drilling in the Seventh Regiment Armory, sporting handsome military outfits and carrying rifles. Cotton loved costumes and the military outfit was one of his favorites.

Didi longed for a dog of her own. Herb Ernest found a wonderful Hungarian Viscla named Chick Charney needing a home and arranged to have him flown to New York from the Bahamas. The poor dog arrived in Manhattan during one of our wintry blizzards. However, he survived and thrived under Didi's loving care and lived with our family seventeen years, the last four with my sister Judy in Darien, Conn., where he was forbidden to have contact with us. My father doted on Charney and allowed him to sit on his favorite chair and chew the leather insides of his Jaguar.

THE 1960'S

Rhythm and Band Instruments

At home, I held improvisation classes, making music with cymbals, drums and triangles, twirling and marching around our living room. Later, we heard different sounds when Cotton began strumming a guitar in Woody Guthrie-style, singing *This Land Is Your Land*. Didi's tootling on the clarinet added to the music making in our small apartment.

Olga Quelia, Andres Segovia's mistress, a classic guitarist, gave Cotton lessons in the back seat of her car, which was parked on 92nd street, in front of their brownstone. She claimed that she could not teach him inside their house as it might disturb Andres during his afternoon nap.

BRINGING ART HOME

The Museum of Modern Art (MOMA) encouraged members to borrow from its film library on weekends. We invited the neighborhood kids and, thanks to my father's old 16mm projector, watched outstanding feature films that I would fetch on Friday and return Monday morning. *Nanook of the North* was a favorite.

The Whitney Museum loaned members artwork from its permanent collection stored in the basement. I felt like a seasoned art collector, with a Joseph Stella abstraction, an Edward Hopper cityscape and three of Georgia O'Keefe's watercolors on our walls.

THE FORTY-DAY TEACHER'S STRIKE

In May, 1968, teachers at all New York City public schools went on strike. Community School Boards battled the United Federation of Teachers, headed by Albert Shanker. The strike lasted nearly two months. Cotton and Didi stayed glued to our living room television set watching soaps and sales pitches, but my "gotta-learn" gene took over and I searched for teachers willing to cross the picket line. The first ten I contacted refused to break the strike. I bought used textbooks and set up a temporary schoolroom in our apartment; found four teachers willing to help. Word spread fast in our Yorkville neighborhood—and children were eager to participate. A school was born.

AUNT FLORENCE AGAIN

Living in New York, as a young mother, I met Aunt Florence frequently. Her renegade spirit brought color to my otherwise routine life. She usually arrived with a carton of Pall Mall cigarettes, which she chain smoked while offering me a welcome shoulder. One night, on our way to a movie, we heard a harpsichord played across the hall from her apartment. Boldly, she knocked at the door and asked if we might come and listen. Anya and Aldo Bruzichelli, from Florence, Italy, welcomed us, explaining that Anya

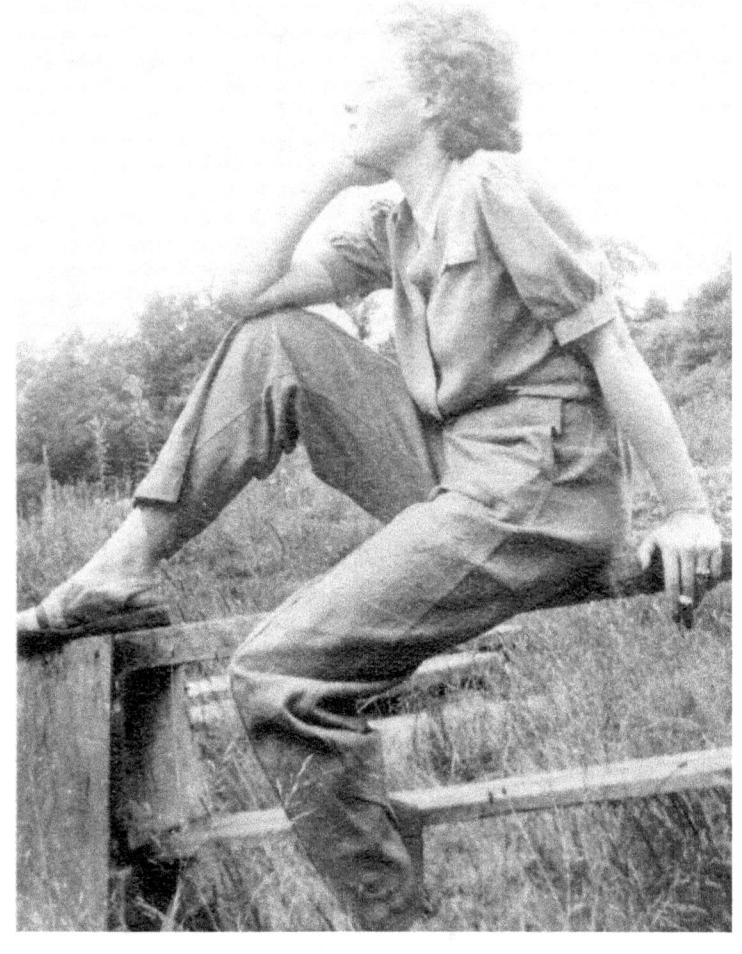

ABOVE:
Aunt Florence.

was studying harpsichord with the great Wanda Landowska. We met other guests—Vincent Bruno, a portrait painter and his wife, Ann, Xanti Schawinsky**, Anya's brother, philosophy professor Morris Grossman (a friendship lasting fifty years), and Leo Smit, a composer, who after meeting my mother months later, wrote music to accompany her poems. In one evening's chance visit, I acquired so many new and good friends.

**XANTI SCHAWINSKY: a Bauhaus graduate and obsessive chess player invited me to parties in his loft, and borrowed my Peugeot one weekend, making tire marks on large pieces of paper he placed on the streets surrounding Washington Square. Today, these "track paintings" are hanging in the Kunsthalle in Cologne, Germany.

MORRIS GROSSMAN

My first tete a tete conversation with Morris G., a shy, heavy bearded man in his late twenties, took place at 7 Gracie Square, and dealt with his interpretations of Descartes oft-repeated statement, "Cogito ergo sum." "I think therefore I am." Morris was surprised that I had not heard this proclamation—the daughter of a philosopher. We met at a harpsichord recital taking place in an apartment across the hall from my Aunt Florence's apartment, on 57th street, in New York City. That was 1957, when people weren't afraid to make contact with their across-the-hall neighbors.

And I guess my ignorance relating to Descartes' proclamation showed how infrequently my philosopher/father and I connected over conversations and ideas.

As things turned out, Morris was very good at explaining it and over the years (fifty years) he became the person I would turn to when I drew a blank over a word, a topic or a concept. Late nights on the phone we would chat, often about nothing. Once in a while, I found myself sound asleep the phone still in my hand and a dial tone ringing in my ear. Morris had hung up and gone to sleep, too.

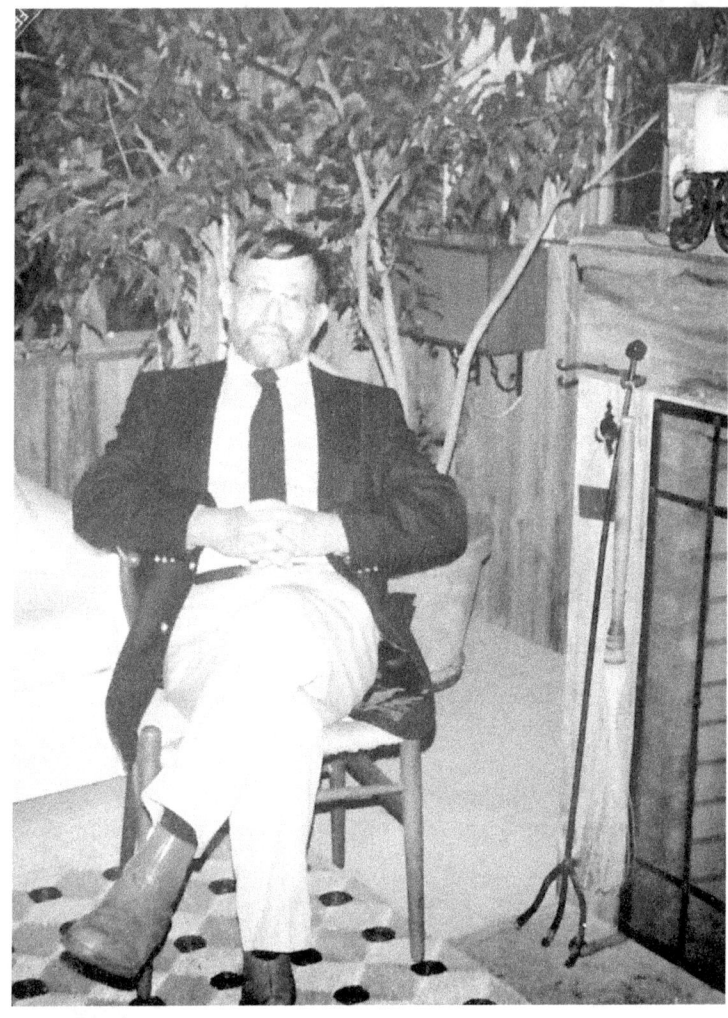

Occasionally, Morris and I met in Fairfield, Conn. an hour's train ride for me, and rallied on Fairfield University's tennis courts. As a professor, Morris taught philosophy at Fairfield University and was allowed to use their courts. We broke the monotony of our tennis with walks on Fairfield beach and deli sandwiches from Gold's delicatessen.

Many of our conversations ended in humorous arguments. I would often criticize Morris' voice when he answered the telephone. Here below I've copied his amused response to efforts he made to change the way his voice sounded when he answered the phone:

114

Aug 17, 1983

Dear Mary,

I'm practicing my "Hellos." Here's how I began, and what I worked up to.

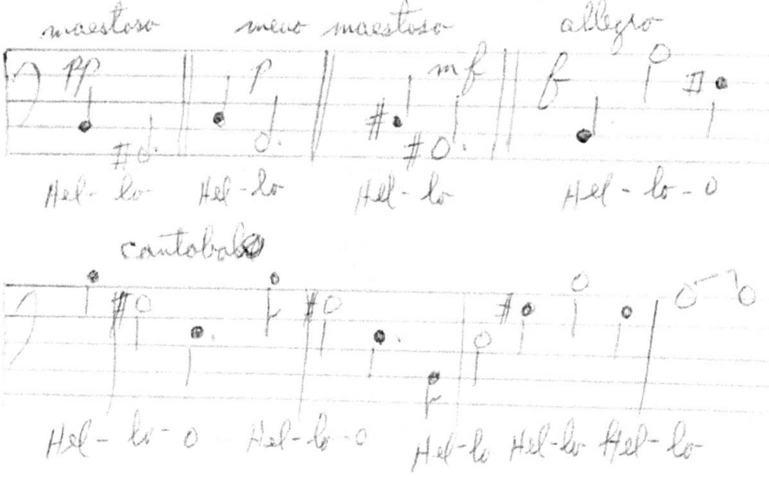

Practice my hellos on both your pianos. Then put them in your computer. Puis, ·modem à la monde!

I enclose the Woody Allen review I told you about.

I'm going to Montreal. See you on Sept. 1, or

before.

Love, Mom

F.P.A. Be good. But don't, like me, keep telling other people to be good, or how to do it. And don't let them tell you! Do it in your own inimitable Mary way. So good enough!

To Mary, Cotton, and Deedie, too,

The best to you, and you, and you;

Let old acquaintance be renewed,

Let feuding friends get nicely stewed,

Let glog be sipped while it's still hot

Lest old acquaintance be forgot,

Let sleigh bells ring, and doorbells too,

Let guests be many, Scrooges few,

Let Lido's sunny summer air

Suffuse warm thoughts through Gracie Square.

Just as a fire has lasting embers

The mind is warmed as it remembers

Times when it knew a brighter glow,

Places to which it now can't go,

Except as it ranges by a leap of will

Like a blue bird fluttering from sill to sill,

Perching where it may not stay

And staying only to fly away

To another window, and a different view,—

Why,—of Cotton, Deedie, and Mary, too!

Love,

Morris

116

CLARA MEYER

Living in New York City opened many new doors for me. One day, a petite, elderly woman pedaling toward me on a bicycle suddenly lost her balance and fell, trapped by the bicycle's weight. As I rushed toward her, she waved me away. "Please don't help," she said. "I need to be able to get up on my own,"explaining that she rode her bike every morning from her home on East 72nd Street to the New School for Social Research on West 12th Street. She added modestly, "I am a Dean at the New School."

Without question or explanation, Clara instantly adopted me into her busy life, even appointing me to the New School's Academic Selection Committee. I served as one of eight board members charged with hiring European scholars displaced by WWII, in need of jobs. For reasons I never understood, since I felt so lost in my own life, Clara grew to depend on my views, on my opinions, and on me.

I learned that she and her brother Albert belonged to the wealthy German Jewish world my grandmother Adele dreamed about. As Dean of the New School, Clara was unassuming, unconventional, and radical, reflecting the New School's function as a harbor for iconoclastic, independent-minded professors. She was often described as the "spirit" of the school. I was a frequent guest at her Victorian mansion on East 72nd Street, dining with composers John

Cage; Igor Stravinsky and his wife, Vera; Leonard Bernstein; conductor Arturo Toscanini; and Lincoln Kirstein, co-founder of the New York City Ballet. They all loved Clara and she fed them well. I was gradually able to overcome my fear of talking to "important" people. I wish I could remember some of their discourse, which probably included versions of inventing the wheel. I followed Clara around New York, bicycling everywhere. Clara didn't believe in "motor transport" and travelled exclusively by pedal.

I was summoned to escort Clara to a number of social events. One of my favorites was an annual dinner which took place at home of Joe and Ann Blumenthal on West 11th street. Joe was the publisher of the Metropolitan Museum's brochures and catalogs. Ann was his diligent wife. Clara was their very best friend. The regulars included Alger and Isabel Hiss, Alger's second wife, and a woman whose last name was Lehman. As soon as we arrived at their front door they issued directions: "coats on the bed and please wash your hands before you come to the table." The guest list and menu never varied. Ann prepared a round of beef saturated with legumes and well-flavored port. Joe carved. The desert of berries and cream was followed by Ann's special cake, sliced paper-thin.

Years later, as age overtook Joe and Ann, they moved to Washington, Connecticut. We stayed in touch. One wintry day, Ann called to say that she hoped Alger and I would drive up to say goodbye, as she and Joe had decided to die together, three days hence. Their suicide pact came as a shock. I'd become attached to them and it hurt to think of them disappearing forever.

Alger refused to make the trip, so I went alone.

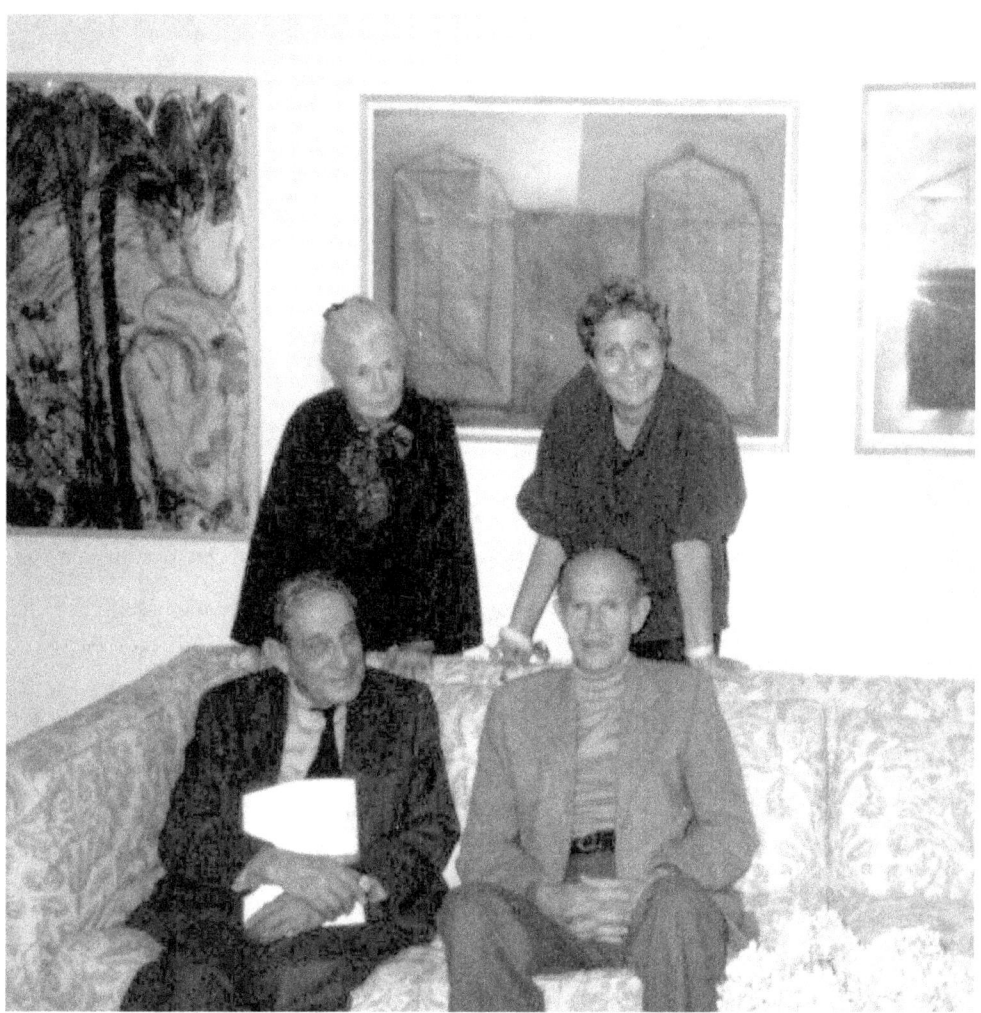

Joe and Ann and I had lunch together if as nothing out of the ordinary was about to happen. Not until I was behind the wheel of my car on the return trip did I feel seized by despair over two such wonderful people ending their lives in a cold, no-nonsense manner. They had no children, no relatives that I knew of and very few remaining friends.

And so off they went quietly into the Connecticut night.

JEROME LIEBERTHAL

I met Jerome "Bud" Lieberthal at a dinner party arranged by Clara Meyer's niece, Stella, and her husband, Milton Albert. Bud was a hugely attractive, gentle, caring person, with kindly green eyes and a warm smile. He spoke lengthily about the challenges of constructing a mega-shopping-center just outside Plattsburgh, a town which had served as home base to the U.S. Army's B-52 bombers, an overnight boom town that emptied when World War II ended. Financing the remainder of his shopping center was challenging as he had already maxed out his borrowing limits with banks and family. A bowling alley had negotiated a lease which may have given him the confidence to go ahead. Bud was motherly, compassionate and sympathetic. What a change from my standoffish father and Bob Coulson. Was this really what friends defined as Jewish warmth?

Bud drove us to Valcour, his family camp on Lake Champlain, twenty miles west of Plattsburgh, and invited us to join his sister, Horty, and her husband, Max Zera, with their two daughters, Helene and Barbara, at their Passover celebrations—our introduction to Jewish culture—which had not been part of my childhood. Max read the Hagadah during Passover, his strong voice declaring the story of the Jewish departure from Egypt—the hardships, and plagues followed by the songs of relief as they crossed the Red Sea—accompanied by the many homemade dishes prepared by Horty and Aunt Hansa, wonderful cooks, warm motherly women. Aunts and uncles, cousins, friends of cousins—old and young—read the Haggadah, sang songs of Jewish freedom, and overate. I learned to make pot roast and matzoball soup watching Aunt Hansa and Horty.

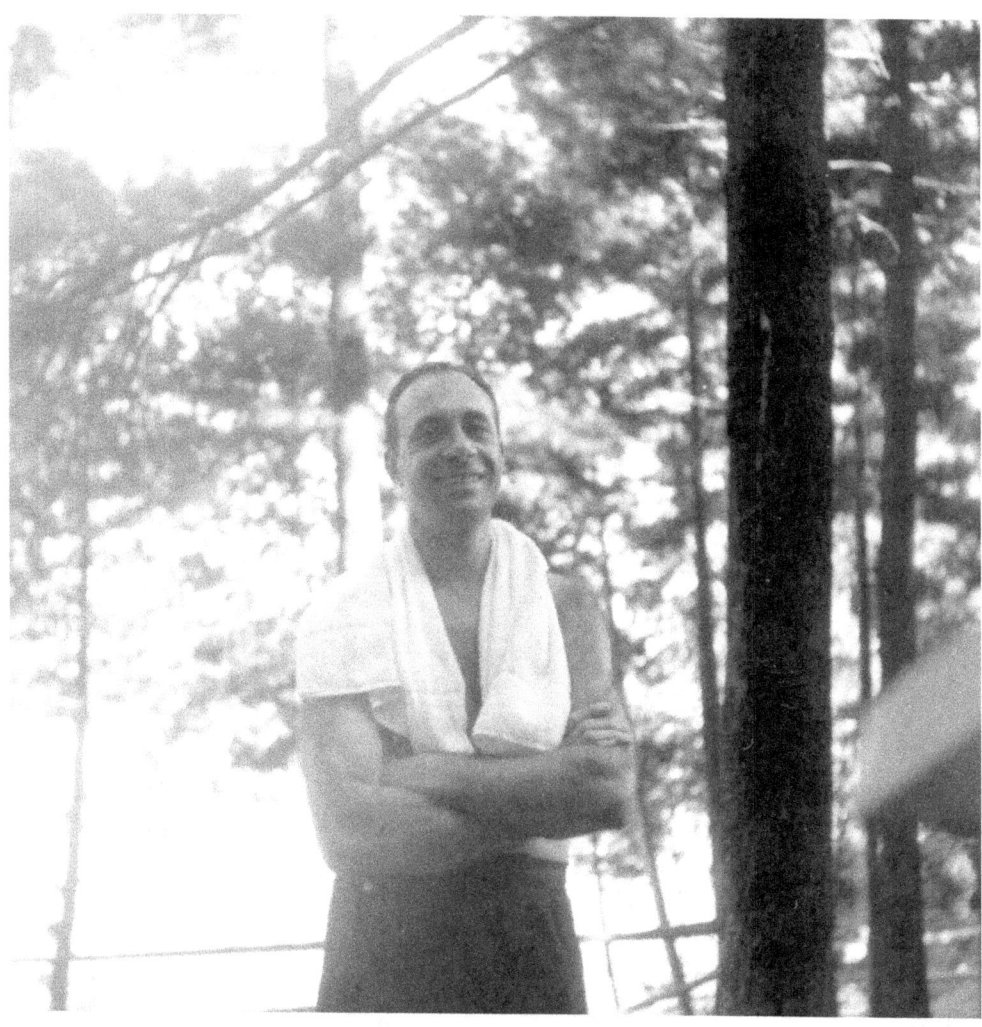

After we married, Bud asked if I would be willing to invest in his Plattsburgh Shopping Center, and we began what would prove to be a disastrous check-exchanging routine. I would write a check to his contractor and Bud would give me one of his own checks in return. Sadly, Bud had no prior experience in developing a business of such magnitude and I had no background in earning or lending money. His checks were undated and without funds to support them. Mine were cashed instantly. Soon, I was really out of money. Cotton took a job delivering flowers and Didi walked dogs to boost our income.

121

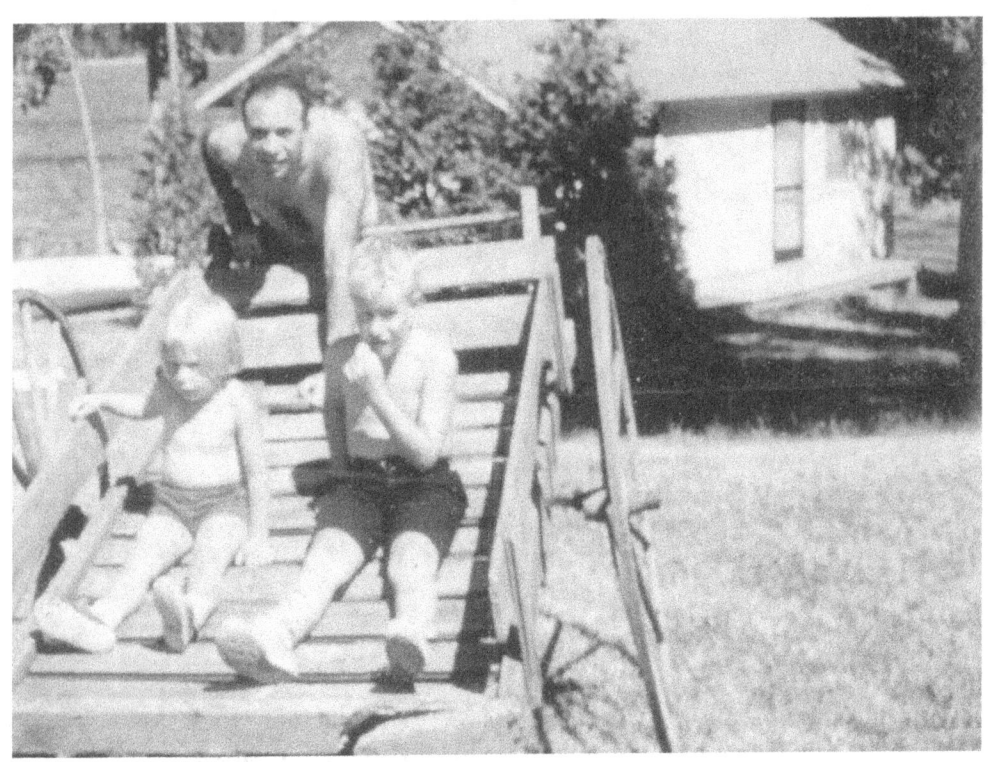

TOP LEFT:

Bud with Didi and Cotton at Valcour, Plattsbugh, New York.

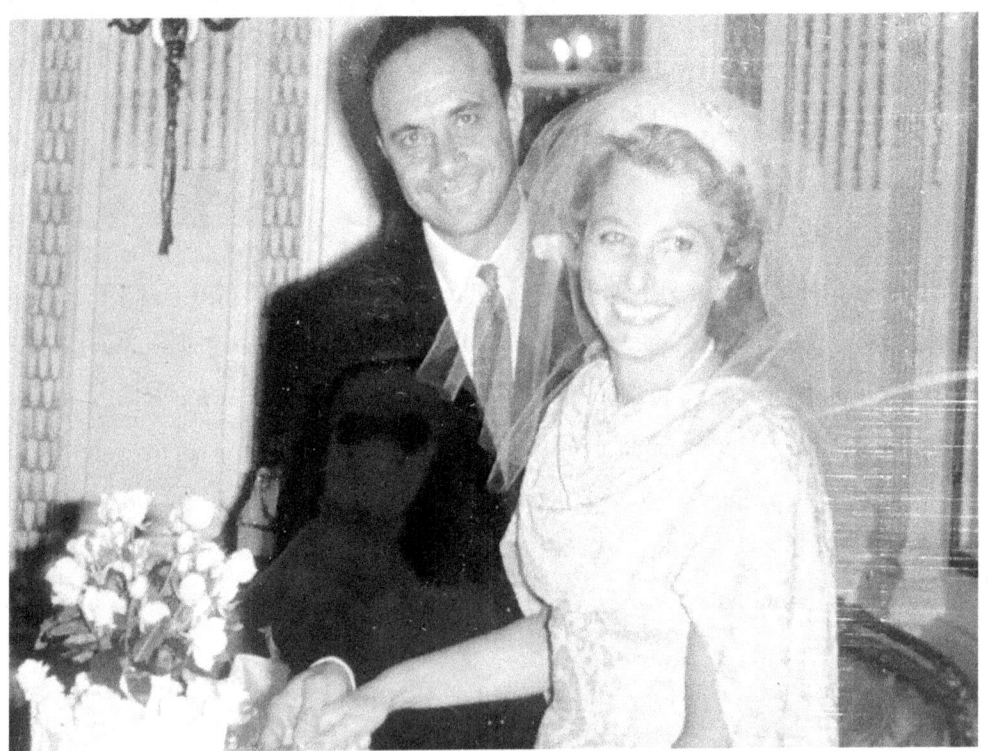

BOTTOM LEFT:

Marriage to Bud Lieberthal, 1961.

122

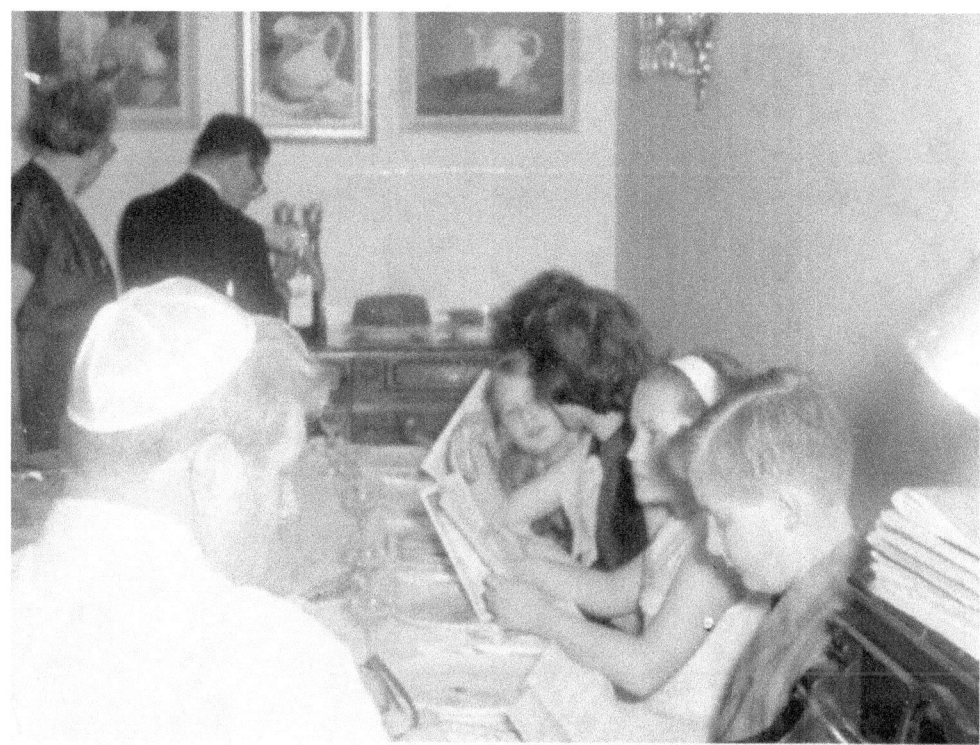

FRANCES ANNE LIEBERTHAL

1965

Bud's concerns and attentions toward Cotton and Didi were so special that I felt he would delight in having a child of his own. On October 28, 1965, our beautiful daughter Frances Anne** Lieberthal, a.k.a. "Kaffa," a most cherished and adored baby, was born at Doctor's Hospital. Lamaze classes in natural childbirth had helped me avoid anesthesia, and I was wide awake and joyful as Fran grabbed my thumb with her tiny fist. My obgyn, Dr. Millard Stone, had hired an anesthesiologist to assist in the birth and my greatest struggle was fighting off his all-too-eager services. I had been advised by my aunt Florence to involve my two older children in the new baby's arrival and I bought outfits—a doctor uniform for Cotton, a nurse uniform for Deirdre. Warnings of possible jealousy over the new baby seemed quite unnecessary..

**We chose the name Frances Anne to please my grandmother, Frankie Appel (Louchheim), who changed her name from Frankie to Frances when she married Walter Louchheim. Her father, Alexander Appel, never forgave her for making the change.

123

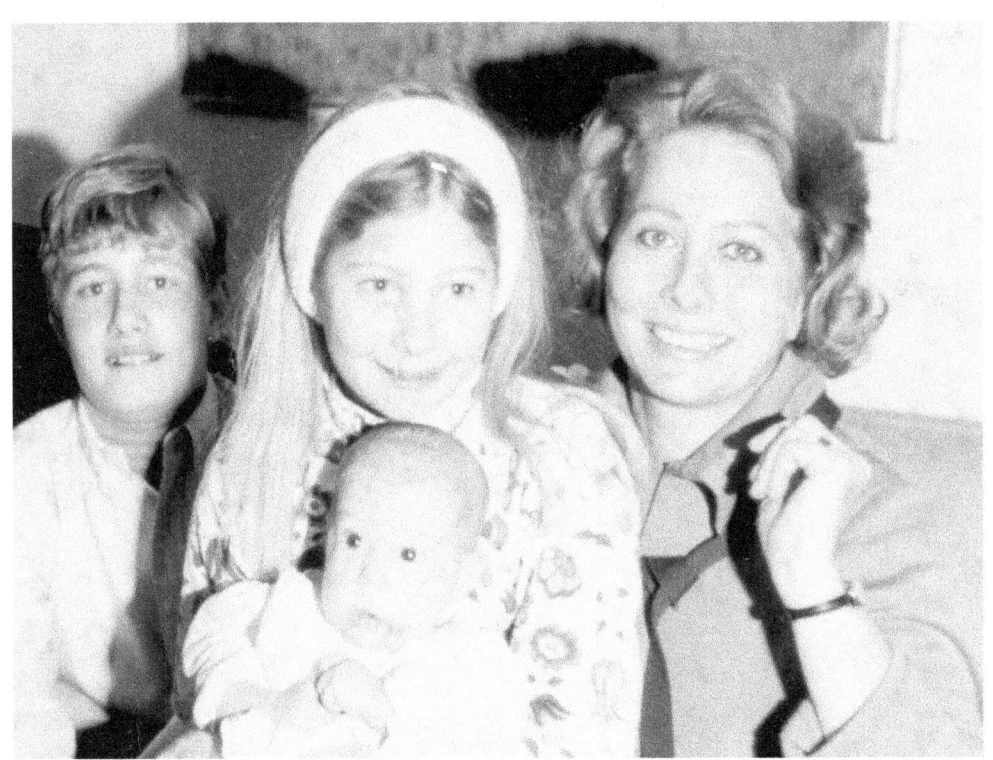

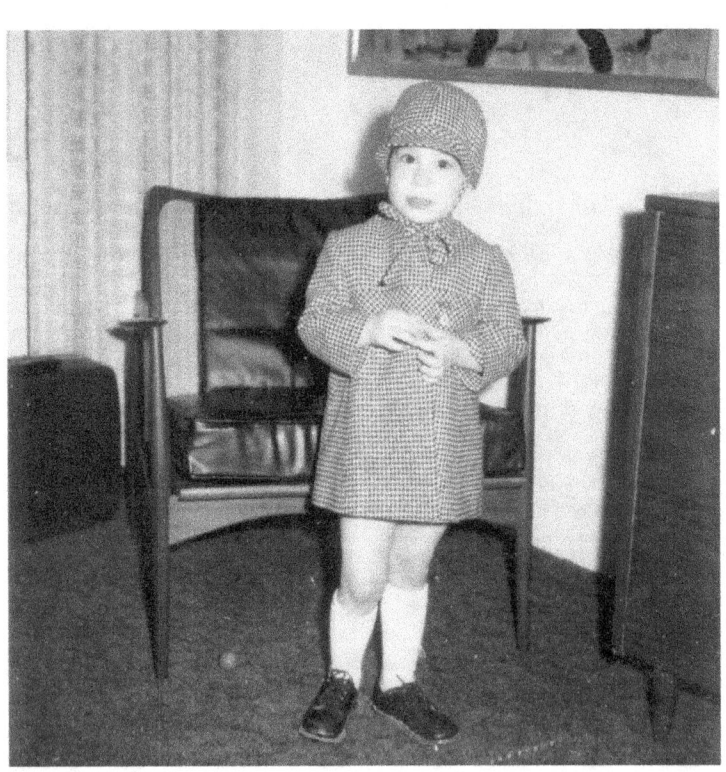

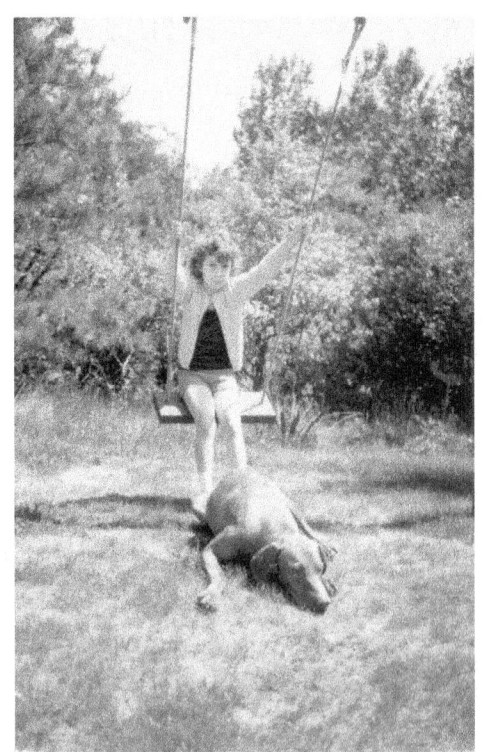

LEFT TOP:

*Frances at the Oyster
Pond, Chatham.*

RIGHT TOP:

*Frances and grandfather
Walter.*

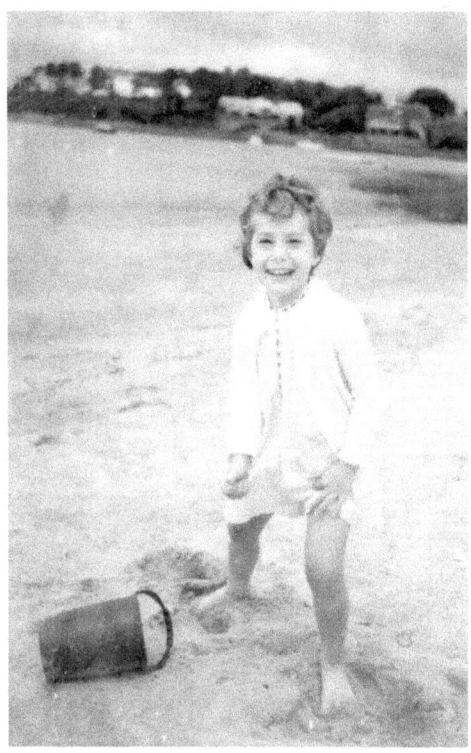

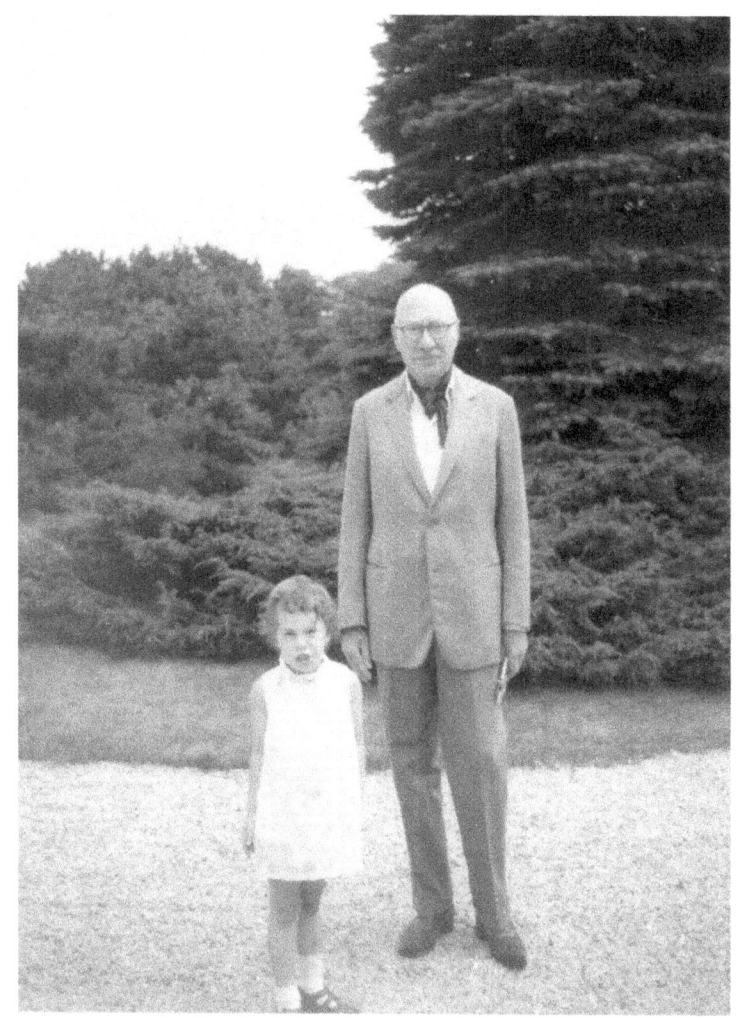

Weeks after Frances' birth, my mother asked me to fly to Washington (on the President's jet) to lunch at the White House and describe "natural childbirth" to President Johnson's wife. Their daughter, Lynda Bird, was expecting a baby and Lady Bird wanted to be informed. There were plenty of D.C. residents who could have enlightened her. I think my mother, always seeking to connect with important people, offered to have me fly down and explain the process to her. And so I sat at the dining room table in the White House showing Lady Bird Johnson how to do the breathing exercises and when to push, etc. She took notes.

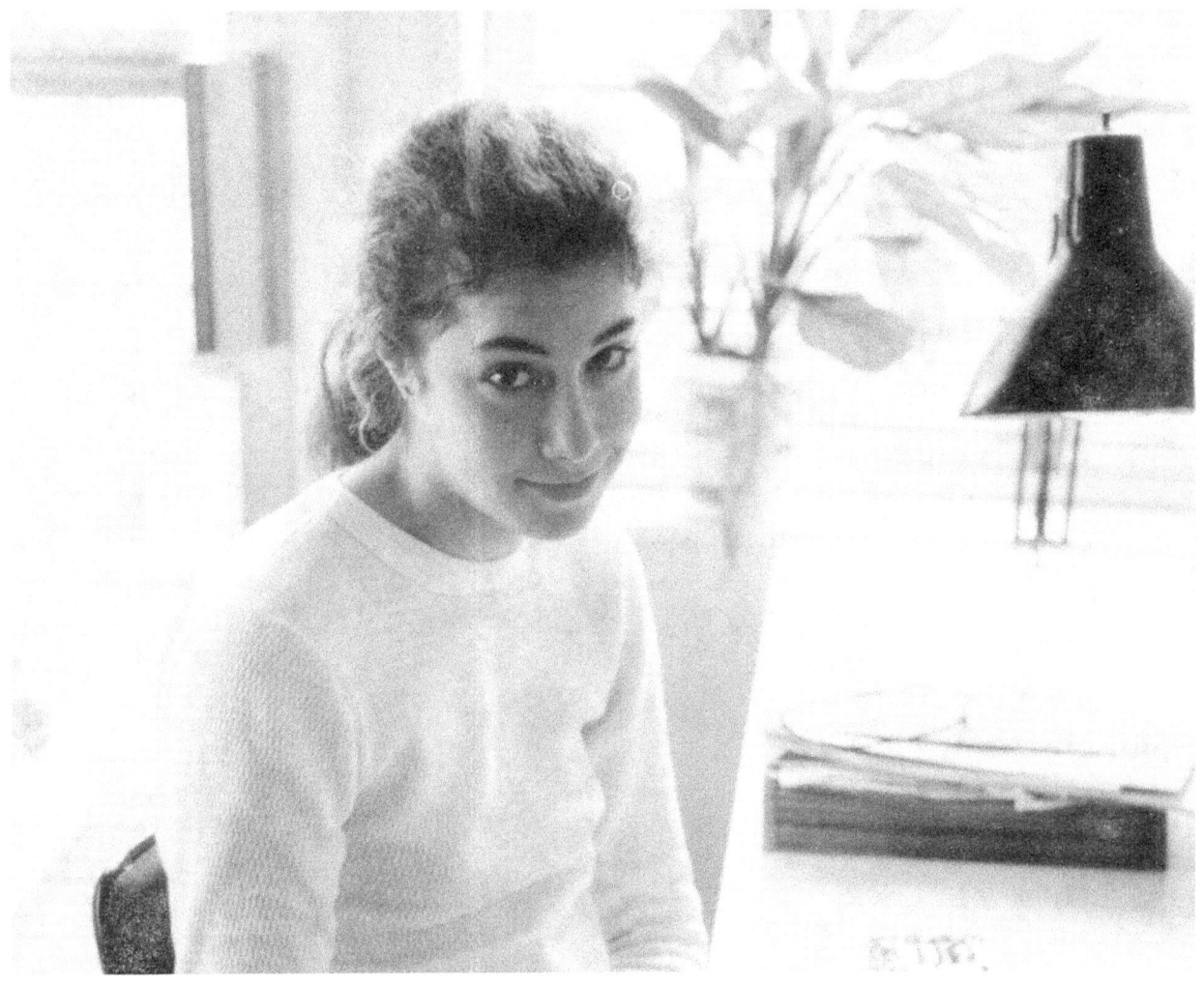

GIRDLE DAYS

Losing the fifty or so pounds I had acquired during my pregnancy was hard, and I joined Weight Watchers, a quasi militaristic organization, bought an elastic girdle—a struggle to tug over my expanded size—and swam twice a week with my new friend, Celia Eisenberg.

126

Frances Anne quickly beguiled us all with her charm. Bud proved to be a doting father, jumping up even a bit too quickly to help her as she blossomed. Inheriting her father's proclivity for clever quips and puns, she developed a sharp sense of humor.

Bud and I struggled on my insurance earnings for a little over a decade. I went to work for Herbert Ernest, selling life insurance for Canada Life, the emotional atmosphere gradually deteriorating as Bud's shopping center expenses accumulated. He continued to borrow from his relatives and from me. After a while, I became thoroughly disenchanted with fielding phone calls. Bud had coached me to say, "Bud will call you back." He meant to, but he never had the cash to repay his debts. Bankruptcy and divorce from Bud created havoc, but by then divorce had become a part of my life. In 1979, Frances and I began a new life in a rental on 89th Street. I belonged to the generation that believed children could survive divorce—as if it were only a matter of moving from one apartment to another. Frances enrolled at the Lenox School. The emotional upheaval of bankruptcy and divorce had taken its toll on both of us. I wasn't any help to her as I drifted along in a soup of poverty and melancholy. My parents were determined to "teach me an overdue lesson" in life and economics. I was told to stop trusting and believing in people so readily. Maybe I should become a *Menschenkenner*? These memories are still painful and remind me that I will never become a real *Menschenkenner*—it just won't happen. I am too easily touched and saddened by the plight of others, including animals, and have dedicated my remaining years to helping Palestinian artists regain their land and sense of self-worth.

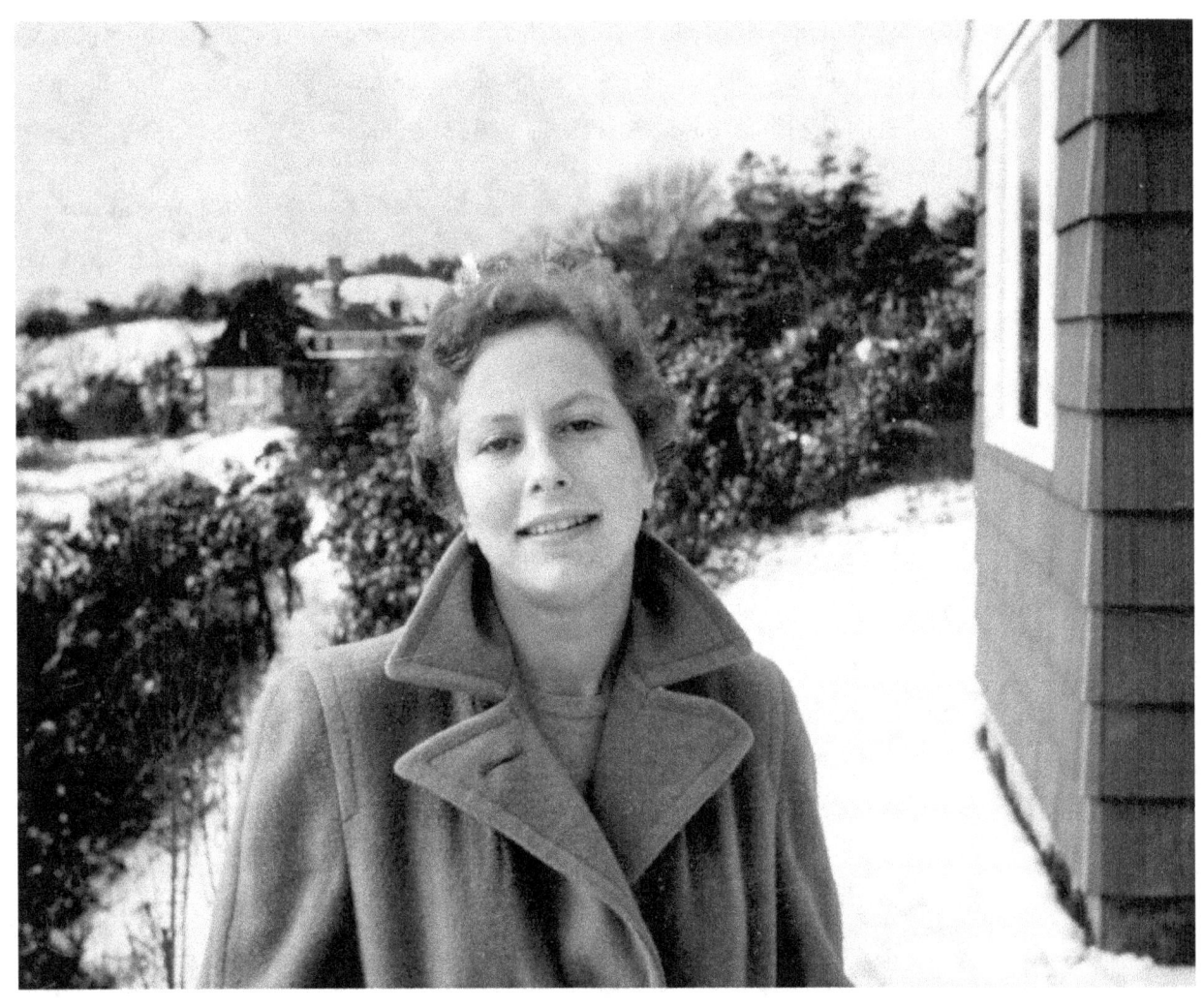

ABOVE:

Mary in front of
Eaglehead house,
Manchester, Mass.

MARY GOES TO WORK
CANADA LIFE AND THE PEUGEOT

I needed a job to help support my family and found work as a life insurance sales person. My insurance sales position was an education in how to sell a product, particularly one I didn't believe in. But a great experience.

After a few tries, I became convincing, sold a bundle of policies, and was named Canada Life Woman of the Year.

To celebrate my success, I went car shopping at the New York Coliseum, spotted a pearl gray Peugeot 403 with many appealing bells and whistles. Seizing an opportunity to practice my now rusty French, I made an incredible deal, buying the car on the showroom floor. After it arrived, we all went for a ride around the neighborhood, opened the sunroof, played the hi-fi radio and inhaled the new car smell. Our romance with the Peugeot lasted about four weeks.

On a visit to Aunt Florence, recovering from an overdose of one of her medications in Noroton, Connecticut, our engine began to heat up. Red lights flashed on the dashboard. The little gray Peugeot came to a halt right in the middle of Interstate 95. A kindly gentleman appeared from nowhere and helped push us to the side of the highway with his Lincoln. That was the last time we drove anywhere in the Peugeot 403 without encountering problems with tires, muffler, radiator or what have you.

Once, we needed a tow of about three hundred miles to a garage that promised Peugeot parts. French distributors, however, decided not to market the 403 in the United States that year. No spare parts were forthcoming.

MASTERCHARGE TO MASTERCARD

In 1974, John Reynolds, Mastercard CEO and former president of Interbank Card Association, was launching a daring new program encouraging women to apply for Mastercards in their own name. Heretofore, men were the major credit card holders. To charge a purchase, women were obliged to borrow their husband's or father's card. John Reynolds felt that I could provide a woman's point of view, promoting his new card directed at women.

I traveled with John to television studios around the U.S., prompting and encouraging him as he responded to questions and comments. When we stopped off in Washington, my mother generously offered her Georgetown garden and invited members of Congress to meet him. It was a rare occasion—my mother and I working together.

M&M

A group of "moms," in a class-action suit, accused M&M Candy Co. of causing cavities in their childrens' teeth. Saturday morning TV, the big all-time babysitter for parents wanting to sleep in, provided cartoons interspersed with M&M candy commercials. I was hired by M&M to elicit written evidence from dentists that M&M's were not the only source of children's cavities.

Visiting a host of dental offices to lure dentists into writing letters, I ended up at the Museum of Natural History, where an expert on dinosaurs wrote the hoped-for letter, declaring that dinosaur cavities came from munching grass and tree leaves. M&M chocolate was redeemed and M&M continued advertising on Saturday morning television. I was rewarded with a lifetime supply of M&M's, a trip to Disney World, and very few dollars.

MATCHMAKING; Networking—bringing people and causes together—was something Grandmother Adele did instinctively and constantly, always finding a common thread. My mother, too, could have made it her profession. Historically, the women in our family made things happen without benefit of formal training. Their strength came from reaching out, connecting and establishing. My great-great-grandmother in Jebenhausen, Germany organized women's clubs and social gatherings at the local synagogue. Clearly, a gift for connecting people was in our genes.

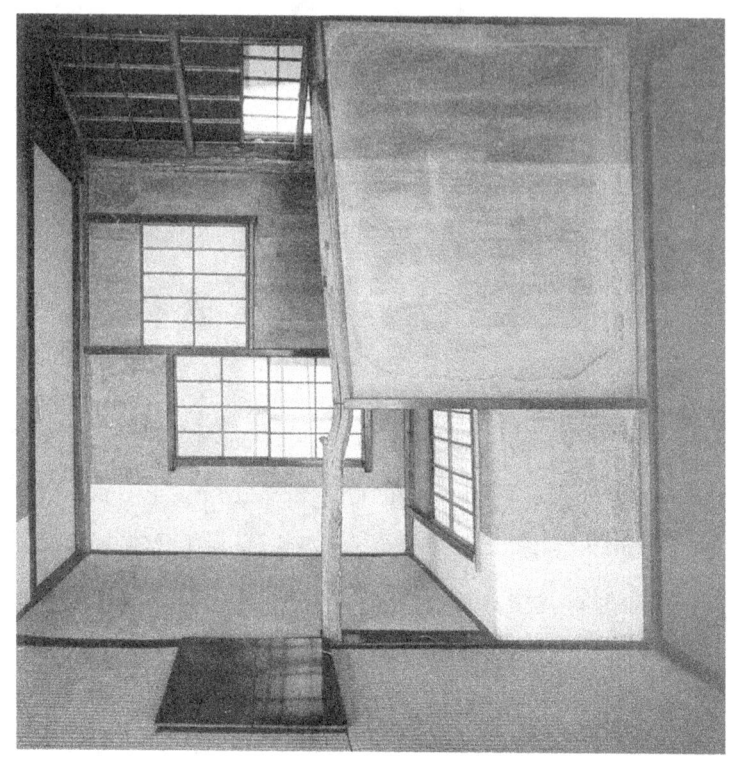

RIGHT:

Katsura Imperial Villa.

KATSURA

With only a slight background in Japanese Edo architecture, I was invited by my parents' friends, Ed and Haru Reischauer, to tag along with a scholarly group from the Aspen Institute touring the Japanese Emperor's Moon-Viewing Pavilion, *Katsura*, in the city of Kyoto. (Ed was a former US ambassador to Japan.) *Katsura*, offering a *shoin*, a tea house and beautiful gardens for strolling, was an irresistible prospect for an American girl who could only say *sayonara* after checking her pocket dictionary. Nevertheless, I felt guilty flying off, while Frances coped with entering a new school, Chapin, without a reassuring hand to hold.

NEW ORLEANS MUSEUM OF ART EXHIBITS ORIGINAL DRAWINGS OF US CAPITOL

The trip to Japan led to a speaking engagement at the Maryland Historical Society describing my favorite Zen temples in Kyoto. After my talk, while chatting with their Director, Romaine Somerville, I learned of some amazingly well-preserved, never-seen competition drawings for the design of the U.S. Capitol building submitted by architects back in 1792, stored in the Historical Society's basement.

BOTTOM:

Sarah and Prescott Dunbar, sponsors of the Bicentennial exhibition for the New Orleans Museum.

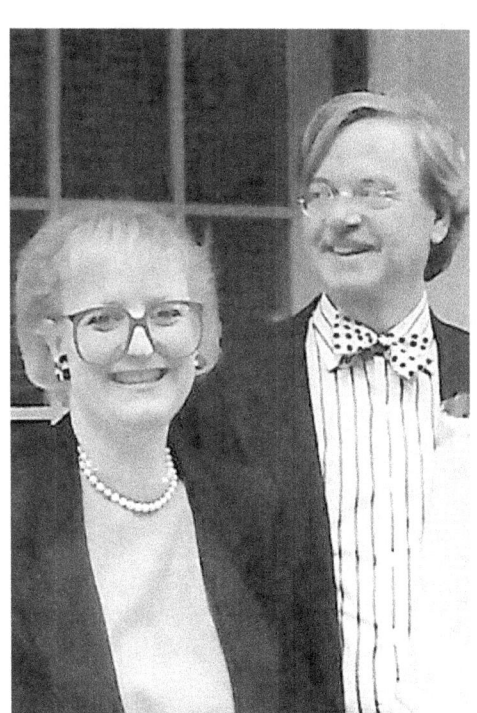

In Chatham, I described the drawings to Sarah and Prescott Dunbar, Trustees of the New Orleans Museum of Art. They hired me to organize a Bicentennial exhibition for the New Orleans Museum, the drawings serving as a magnet to attract other Bicentennial memorabilia. A fee of $10,000, a huge sum, was offered to put the exhibition together—my very first job in the art world.

Borrowing from the Library of Congress, from Kiplinger and a dozen other private collectors, I titled the exhibition *Designing A Nation's Capitol, Competition And Compromise*, and wrote:

"The capitol building is a government workshop to serve the practical requirements of legislative debate."

Citizens of New Orleans turned out in great numbers for the opening and drank mint juleps. My mother sent a plant. Didi came to share the honors with me, the two of us squeezing into the Dunbars' guest bed, a single. It was a beginning.

COMMUNICATE THROUGH ART

Early Matchmaking

Believing that corporations needed help identifying worthy non-profit underwritings, I conceived a company called *Communicate Through Art* offering to enhance corporate images and attract major media coverage by targeting philanthropy in the arts, "a strategic approach to corporate giving." In partnership with Henry Young, we successfully paired The Pennsylvania Ballet Company with Banker's Trust and The Juilliard Music School with American Electric Power.

We rented an overpriced office space on 48th Street and 8th Avenue and persevered for several years, convinced that we were helping arts organizations. As burgeoning philanthropists without remuneration, however, after five years, we were obliged to close our doors.

A CURATOR IS BORN

The Spanish Tourist Office

Once in a while things have a way of falling into place, call it luck, fate, or just timing. Judy Ross, an editor at *Our Town*, a New York City community newspaper, occupied the locker next to mine at the 92nd Street Y. We always ended up in the steam room after a swim, and talked art while the hot steam clouded our vision and choked us. Having recruited me to be an art

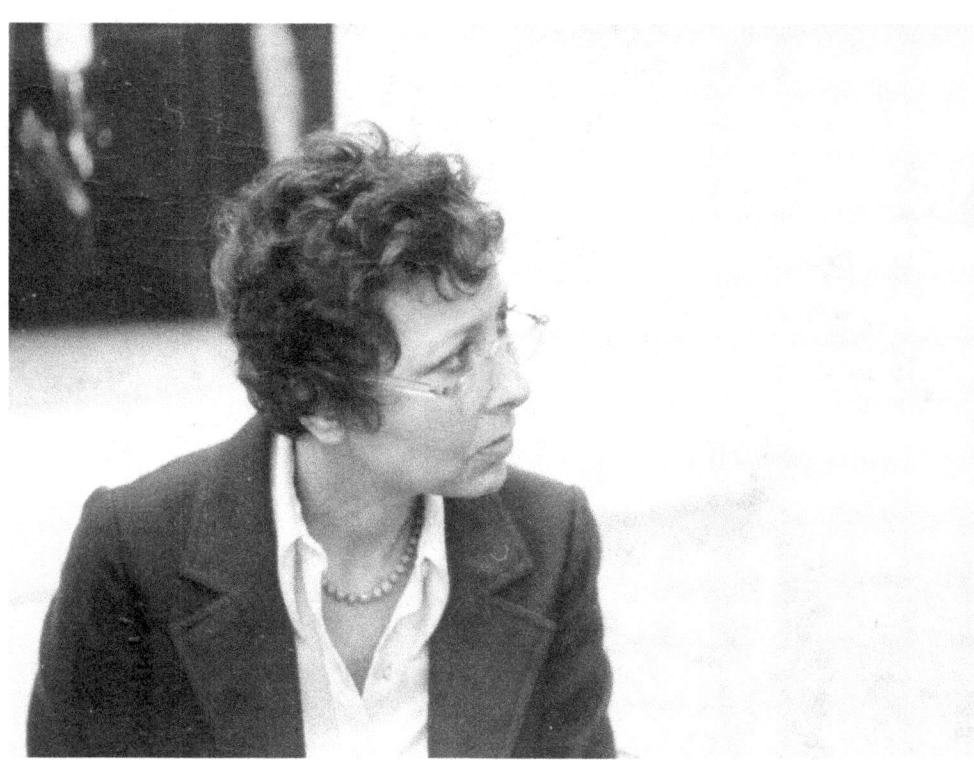

columnist for the newspaper, Judy asked if I wanted to evaluate the art currently on exhibit at the Spanish Tourist Office on lower Fifth Avenue. "Go see it and write something."

I assumed that I would find a Juan Gris, or even a Miró, and was surprised to see forlorn drawings on the Spanish Tourist Office walls. "Haven't you got better art back in Madrid or Barcelona?" I asked. "This can't be representative of Spanish art today."

At first, the director seemed insulted and put off by a brash American woman, and then he brightened. "Why don't you go over there and bring back some better art?"

I was thrilled with such an opportunity. Dictator Francisco Franco had died recently, and the international art world predicted that Spanish contemporary art, now released from a dictator's restrictions, would bloom in all sorts of ways. But I had never been to Spain and couldn't speak Spanish. "Not a problem," I was told. "I'll have a car and an interpreter meet you at the airport."

135

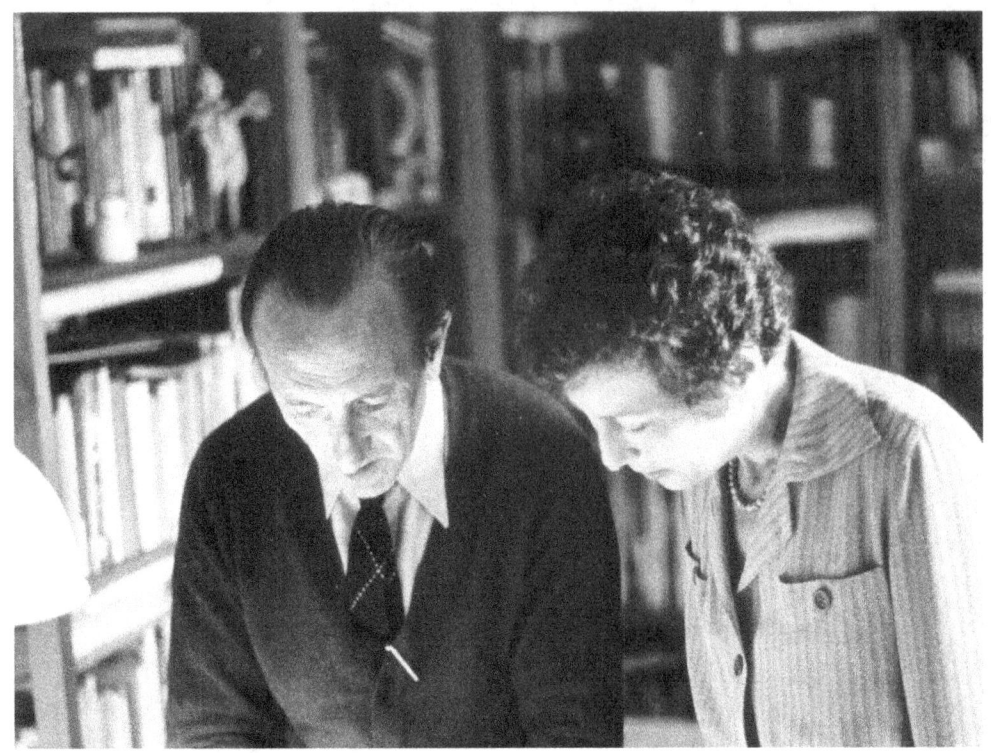

For two weeks I was shepherded around galleries and artists' studios in Madrid and Barcelona, dining with the reigning Prince and Princess—in blue jeans! My red silk suit, recently dry cleaned in New York, had shrunk to unwearable. I couldn't zip or button it. I felt embarrassed dining with Spanish royalty in jeans, I don't think the royal couple ever noticed. They were so intent on firing questions about the New York art scene.

I lodged a complaint against the dry cleaner in Small Claims Court and won my case. It was my first experience at "fighting back"—no longer acting the weakling I had been heretofore.

I penned my impressions of the art scene in a series of articles entitled, "Under the Spanish Easel," for Saturday Review, and organized exhibitions of Spanish artists in eight New York galleries, concluding that Franco's recent demise had had little effect on the work of contemporary Spanish art.

136

GALLERY URBAN

In 1989, Ikan Sawada, a member of the Toyota car family, hired me as director of Gallery Urban, his new venture in the United States. Our staff was made up of young Japanese enthusiasts who could not speak English and knew little about art. When they answered the telephone, they could not write down who called or even make themselves understood. I would soon learn that "director" was a meaningless title. Sawada insisted that I sign in every morning, sign out for lunch, and repeat the whole process when I left for the day. I was not permitted to show or sell artwork by contemporary Japanese artists, only French Impressionists such as Renoir, Degas, Manet and Monet, with ten-figure price tags. Our austere openings were limited to guests who had bid high at Sotheby's and Christie's auctions.

There was great jubilation when we sold a Gauguin landscape. It broke up the monotony of sitting day after day in the scarcely visited gallery. I proposed an exhibition of Fernand Léger's oil paintings, but was told that his work wasn't popular in Japan.

Sawada's attitude toward American women was demeaning. Whenever he and I needed to talk, he would face my assistant, a young man in his twenties, and suggest that he pass the message on to me.

Sawada made several visits to New York from his palatial home in Nagoya and approved our sterile environment. Looking at his accounts after a few years, however, he decided his American venture wasn't working out.

NEW ZEALAND

Living at Seven Gracie Square, a small family building, I never felt that my kids and I were particularly cherished. Penthouse occupant, Nancy Ford made no secret of the fact that we were below her, literally and socially. So, I was really surprised one day to receive a phone call inviting me to "drinks" in her highly decorated apartment overlooking the East River. Bert Aaron jumped up as I came in saying he'd been told that I promoted art from other countries and would I be interested in meeting the Mayoress of Auckland, New Zealand, arriving in the U.S, looking for a compassionate guide.

I accepted eagerly and hours later, Barbara Goodman, not the daunting politician I expected, but a charming face arrived at my door, with her suitcase and a gift of some lamb fleece, shaven from one of her flock. "I need a place in New York where I can hide from the press and the New Zealand Consulate, and Bert Aaron said you would provide it for me." I enjoyed her fresh, almost childlike comments on New York City, likening Auckland to a village. Barbara was well connected to Pan Am airlines and offered me a complimentary roundtrip ticket to come visit her. She offered to drive me around. Cotton was doing some photography work for the Museum of Natural History and suggested that I write something about the Polynesian influence on New Zealand artists, for their magazine. Missing was my confidence in long-distance travel, which I am sure I inherited from my father—a man who thought of travel from D.C. to New York as a trip round the world!

After flying through an honest-to-God typhoon, and eating food cooked in Maori earthen pits, I persuaded a group of tribal leaders to allow me to exhibit contemporary New Zealand

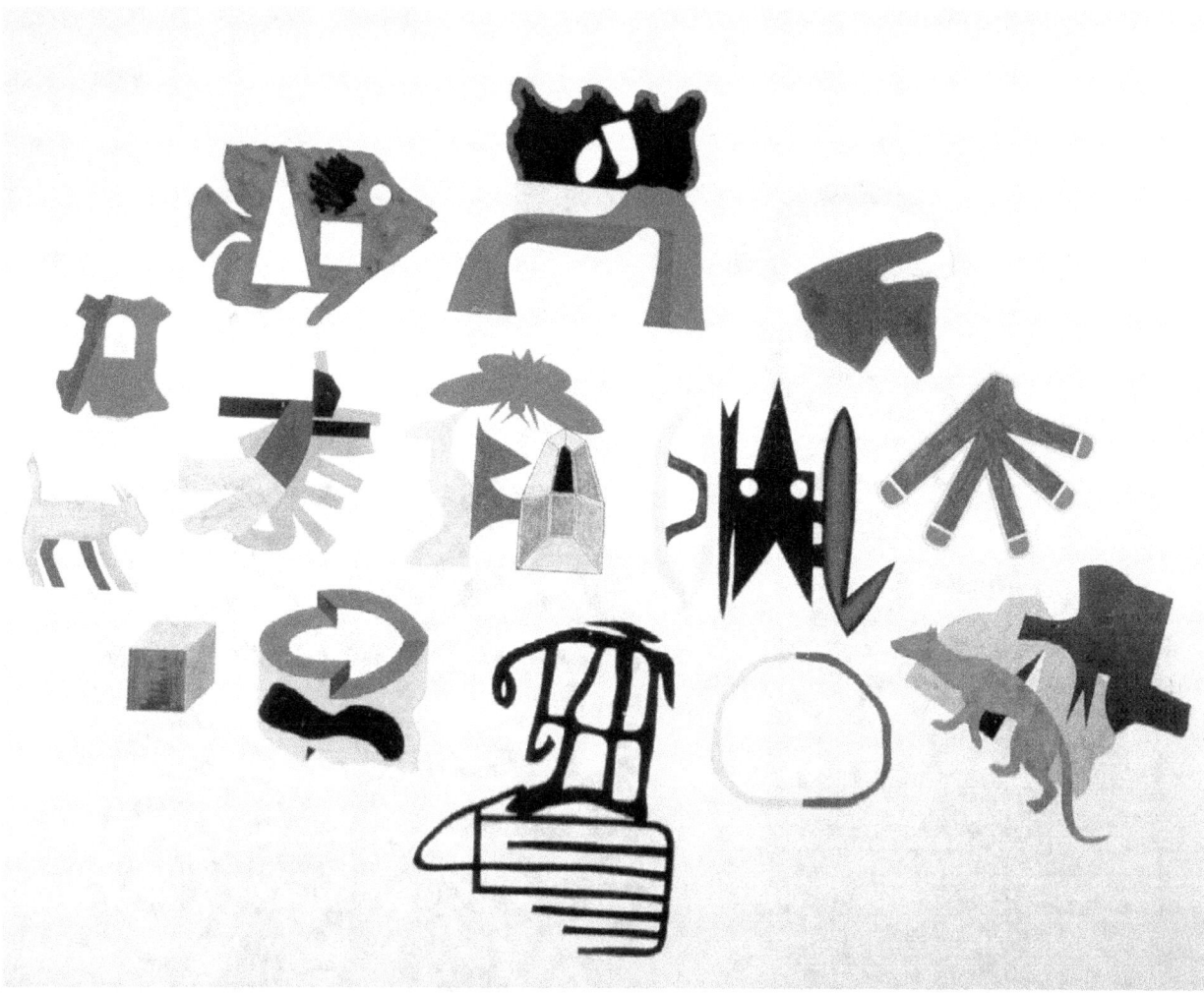

artists while their Maori totem ancestors were being shown in the 1984 exhibition *Te Maori* at the Metropolitan Museum, in New York.

Kara Puketapu, escorting the totems—which are considered an embodiment of living beings with souls—and a member of the te Atiawa tribe, helped me identify Maori elements in the artwork I brought over.

New York Times art critics praised the 17 young New Zealand artists who participated, one of whom, Philippa Blair, became my friend. A new career beckoned. I believed that my New York gallery-owner friends would participate and profit. Had I inherited Aunt Florence's eye?

139

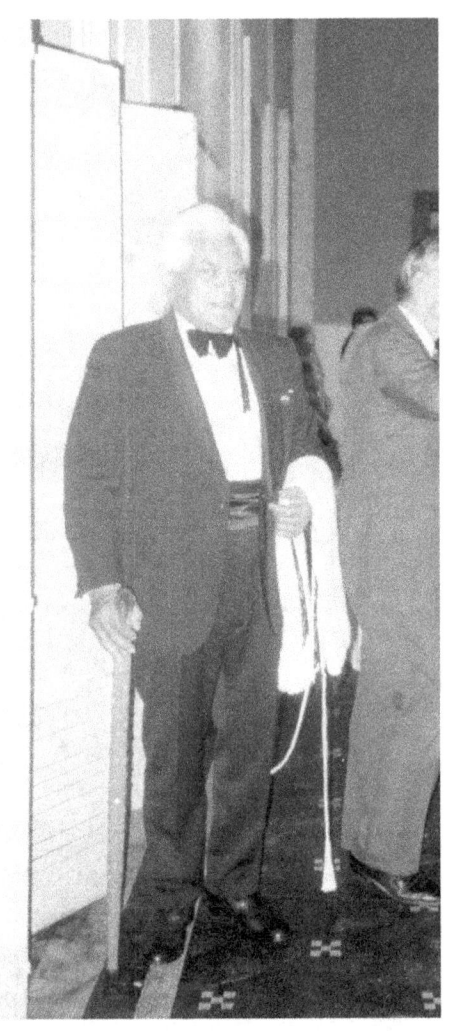

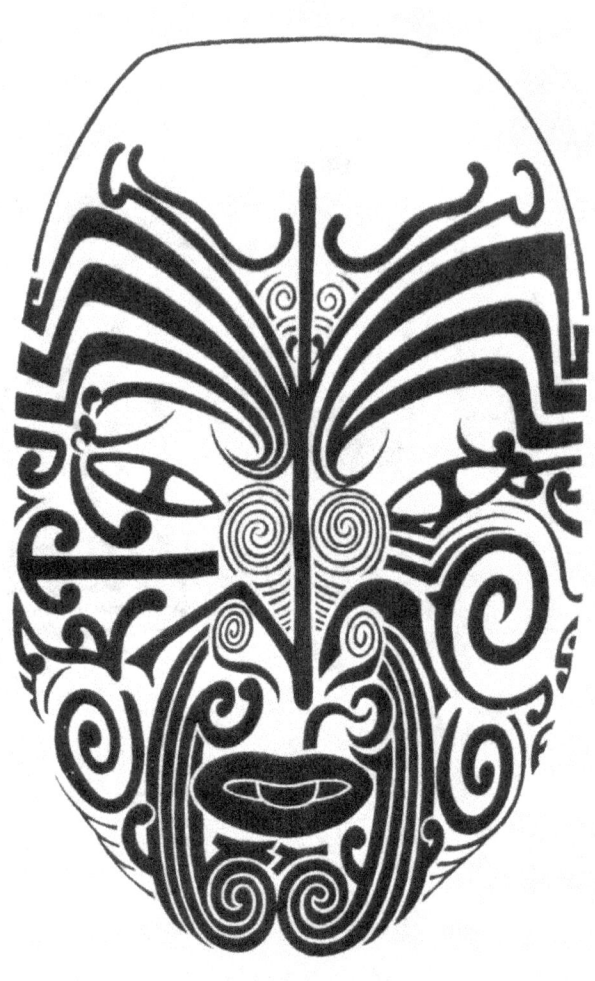

ABOVE LEFT:

*Maori Cheiftain at the
Metropolitian Museum.*

ABOVE RIGHT:

*An image from a Maori
totem.*

140

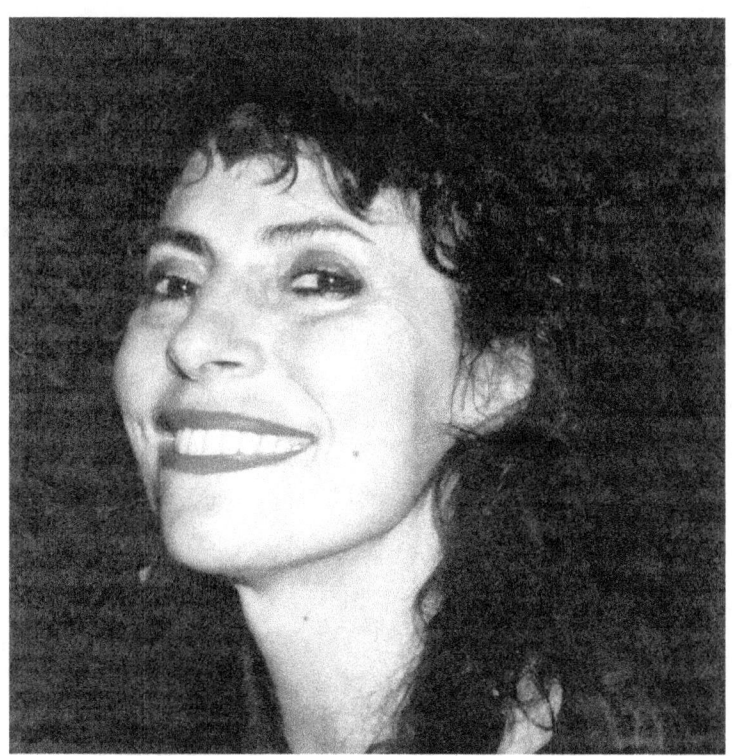

ZITTA AND ISRAEL

I met Israeli pianist, Zitta Finkelstein, and her husband, Adrian Smilovici, at a party given by my German language tutor, Lotte Zernick. "Are you Jewish?" Zitta asked, and "If so, why haven't you visited Israel?" Her bluntness was appealing.

In 1985, *Newsday* asked me to write a colorful view of Jerusalem on Easter Sunday, to sit at the foot of the Via Dolorosa in the Old City, and describe the confluence of religions commemorating the holiday. Still wary of flying, I consulted my daughter Didi, who had spent a summer on an Israeli kibbutz. She encouraged me. My mother thought it a bad idea. "Too many Jews," she declared.

Determined to overcome my travel phobia, and wondering what being in a country of Jews felt like, I signed on and invited Zitta and Adrian to join me. As our El Al flight approached Ben Gurion Airport in Tel Aviv, everyone on the plane broke into song, and a grand harmony of voices accompanied us to our landing. The song was "Havenu Sholem Aleichem"—one I had heard sung frequently at Horty and Max's Passover dinners. I looked down on beautiful white beaches—the Mediterranean sparkling. It was hard not to like Israelis—tough, aggressive, courageous, friendly and warm. I frequently heard the phrase *hamesh dakot*, Hebrew for "five minutes,"—convincing, promising.

Touring Israel—visiting artists' studios—it really mattered that Zitta and Adrian spoke Hebrew. I was amazed at how much had been achieved—efficiency, production, grapes thriving in desert soil. The year was 1984.

I decided to bring some Israeli art to New York. Israel was still a young country in the '80's. Memories of the Holocaust were strong.

In New York, Bertha Urdang, a fireball Israeli dealer, brought Israeli art to the attention of a few major collectors and museum curators with verve and conviction. Bertha preached that the Minimalism with which they were establishing themselves was the new Expressionism of the 'seventies and 'eighties. "The energy in her gallery was always at a crescendo," quipped Josh Neustein, one of her favorite artists. Her passion for art steamrolled over decency, manners and reason. Bertha desperately wanted Israeli art to succeed. She enlisted me in her cause.

My feelings about being Jewish were vague, impersonal, uninvolved.

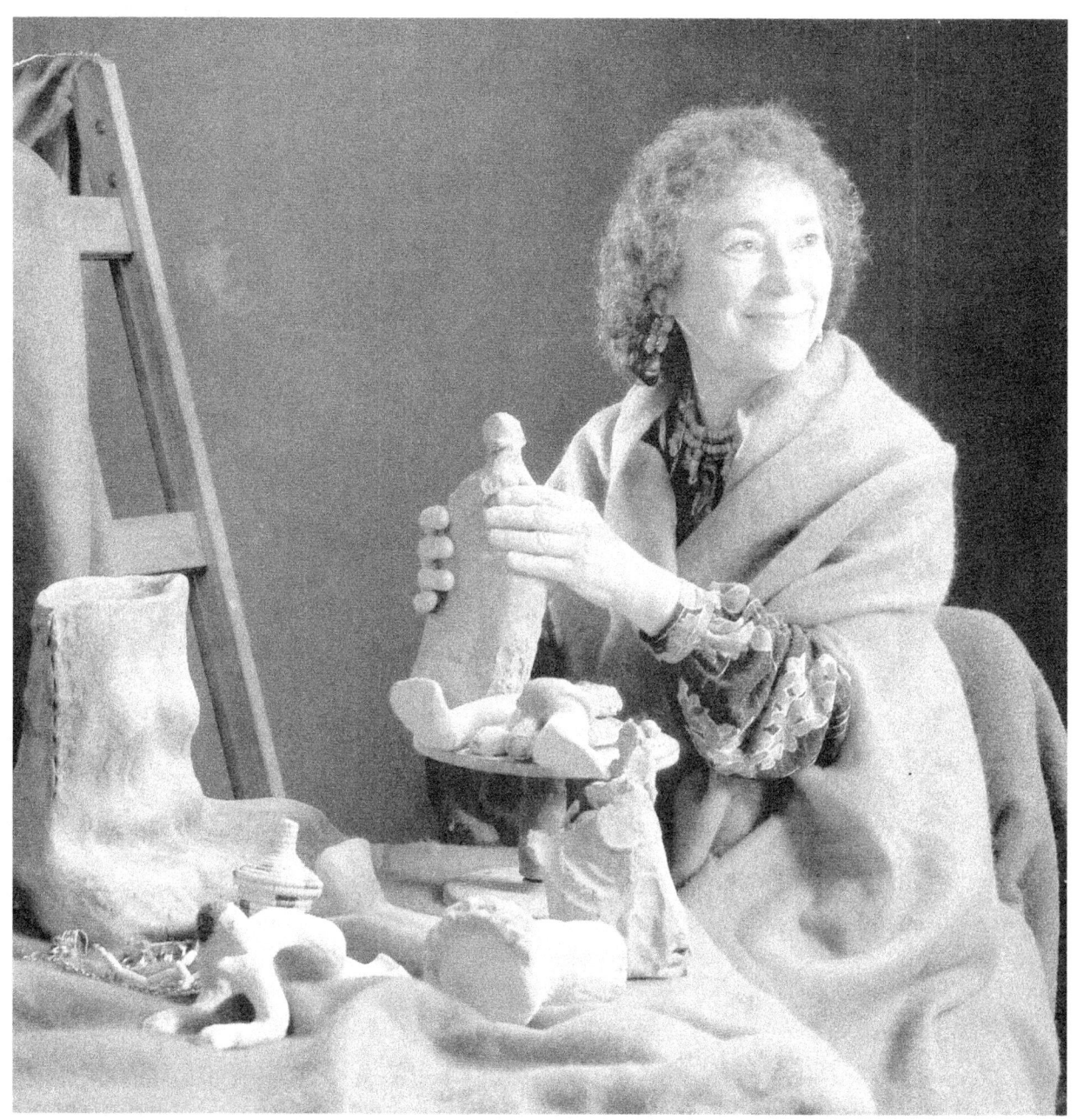

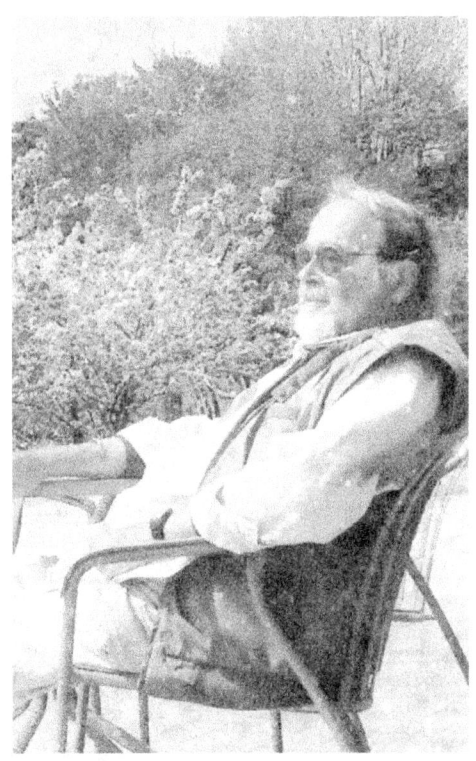

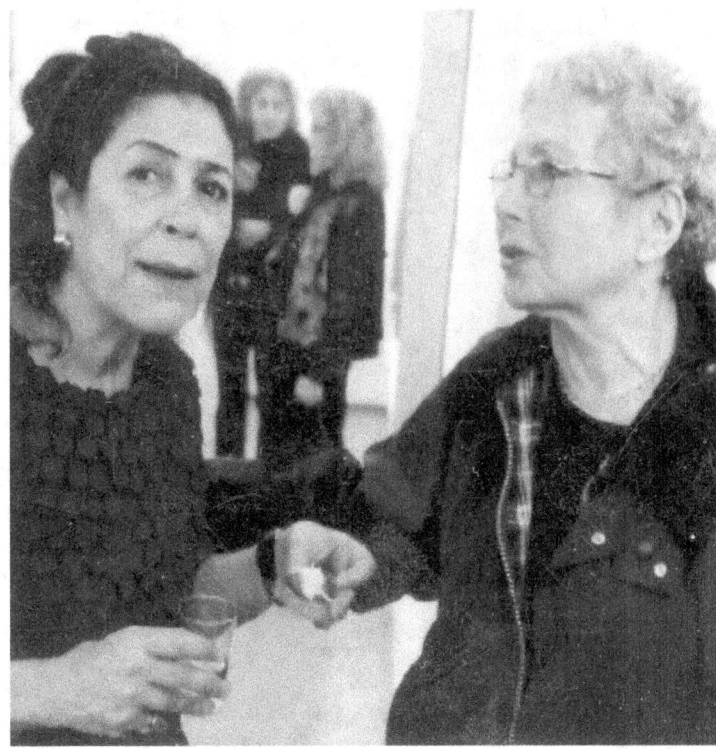

Galleries in Tel Aviv weren't doing well, selling artwork primarily to tourists. Martin Weyl, Director of the Israel Museum, sent an encouraging message:

> What an ideal time to introduce contemporary Israeli artists to New York City—just as your city and the Metropolitan Museum are about to receive our greatest treasures—the Dead Sea Scrolls... If Israelis can be shown in New York, it adds to their measure of success in Israel.

Teddy Kollek, Mayor of Jerusalem, when told about my visits to artists' studios—invited me to stay at Mishkenot Sha'ananim, Jerusalem's official and palatial guest residence. I was given a seven-room suite with a balcony overlooking the desert and a kitchen stocked with Israeli *foie gras*. The writer Saul Bellow had occupied the suite before me and had left wonderfully imaginative scribbles and cartoons scattered about.

TOP LEFT:
Felix Becker, director of Lufthansa.

TOP RIGHT:
Mary with Israeli gallery owner Noemi Givon.

Felix Becker, U.S. Director of Lufthansa German Airlines, offered a barter of $250,000 in air travel, enabling Israeli artists and their art works to travel to New York. Lufthansa was opening a new route between Frankfurt and Tel Aviv; and Felix saw this as a great promotional opportunity.

Zim Shipping, in the port city of Haifa, offered free transport of the heavy sculpture.

ARTisrael, my first big exhibition, opened in New York City in September of 1986. Sixty-eight Israeli artists with their artwork and their families landed at JFK.

Igal Tumarkin's heavy sculpture, a version of the German howitzer Big Bertha, stood in the middle of Spring Street Gallery. On opening night, an eager crowd of 1,400 people including New York City's Mayor Ed Koch, caused part of the sculpture to fall off its track, injuring a young lawyer. Fifteen stitches on her leg and a lawsuit followed.

Memory of such problems faded quickly when, in January 1987, the Israeli Consul General, Moshe Yegar, asked me to mount a second exhibition to honor Israel's forty years of independence.

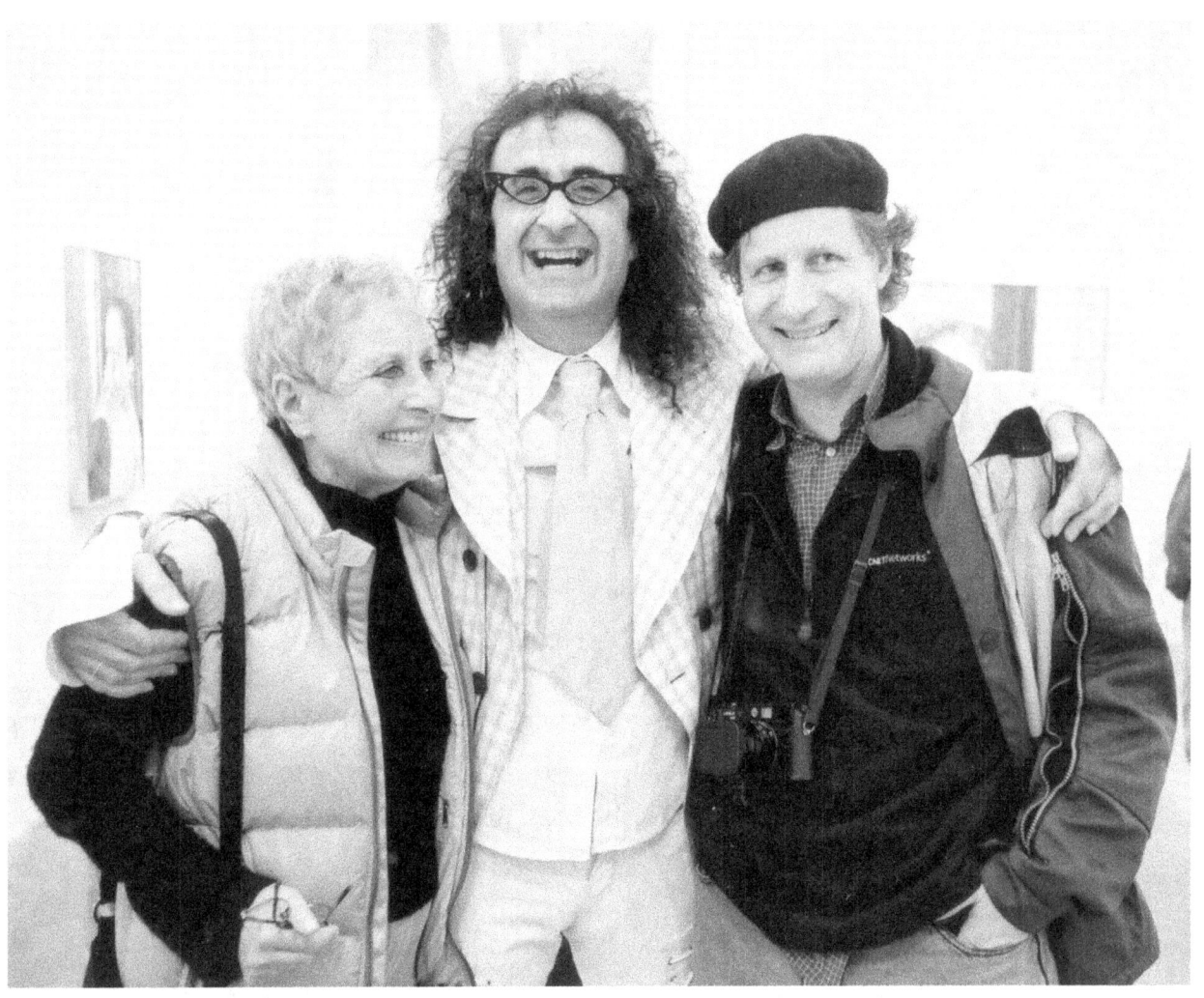

ABOVE:

Mary, Igal Ozeri, Israeli artist, and Cotton.

Ultimately, eleven American museums contracted to show Israeli art between 1988 and 1990. Israeli artists Igal Ozeri and Tsibi Geva linked up with prominent New York galleries. In fact, Igal became an American artist superstar, painting young girls in alluring poses, participating in a current craze for photorealism.

In 2014, I asked Igal to help finance my Palestinian exhibition at White Box gallery, using the money from the sale of one of his exotic girl portraits to cover the costs of shipping Palestinian art from Ramallah. I liked the idea of an Israeli artist contributing to a Palestinian exhibition.

146

TOP RIGHT:

Zena Harman, Chairman of UNICEF 1964 – 66. Zena was warm, intelligent, humble and unassuming, genuinely devoted to social justice. Putting aside her many civic responsibilities she drove me around Israel helping select the art and artists to travel to New York.

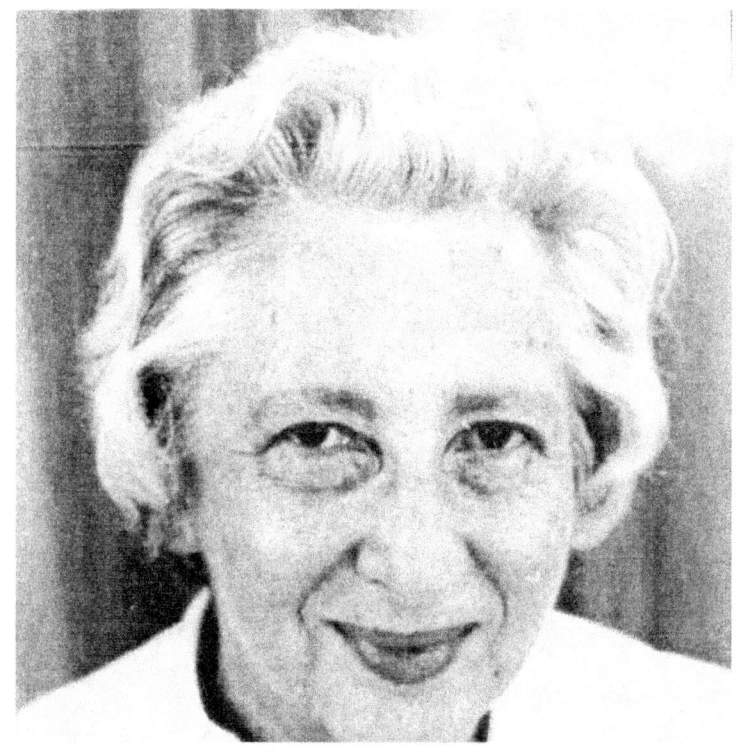

BOTTOM RIGHT:

Mary and former Mayor Ed Koch.

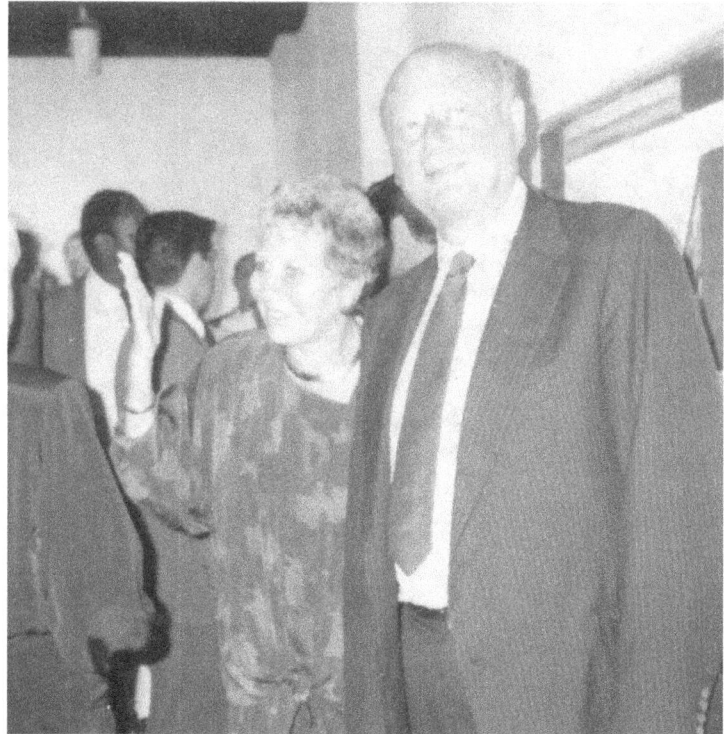

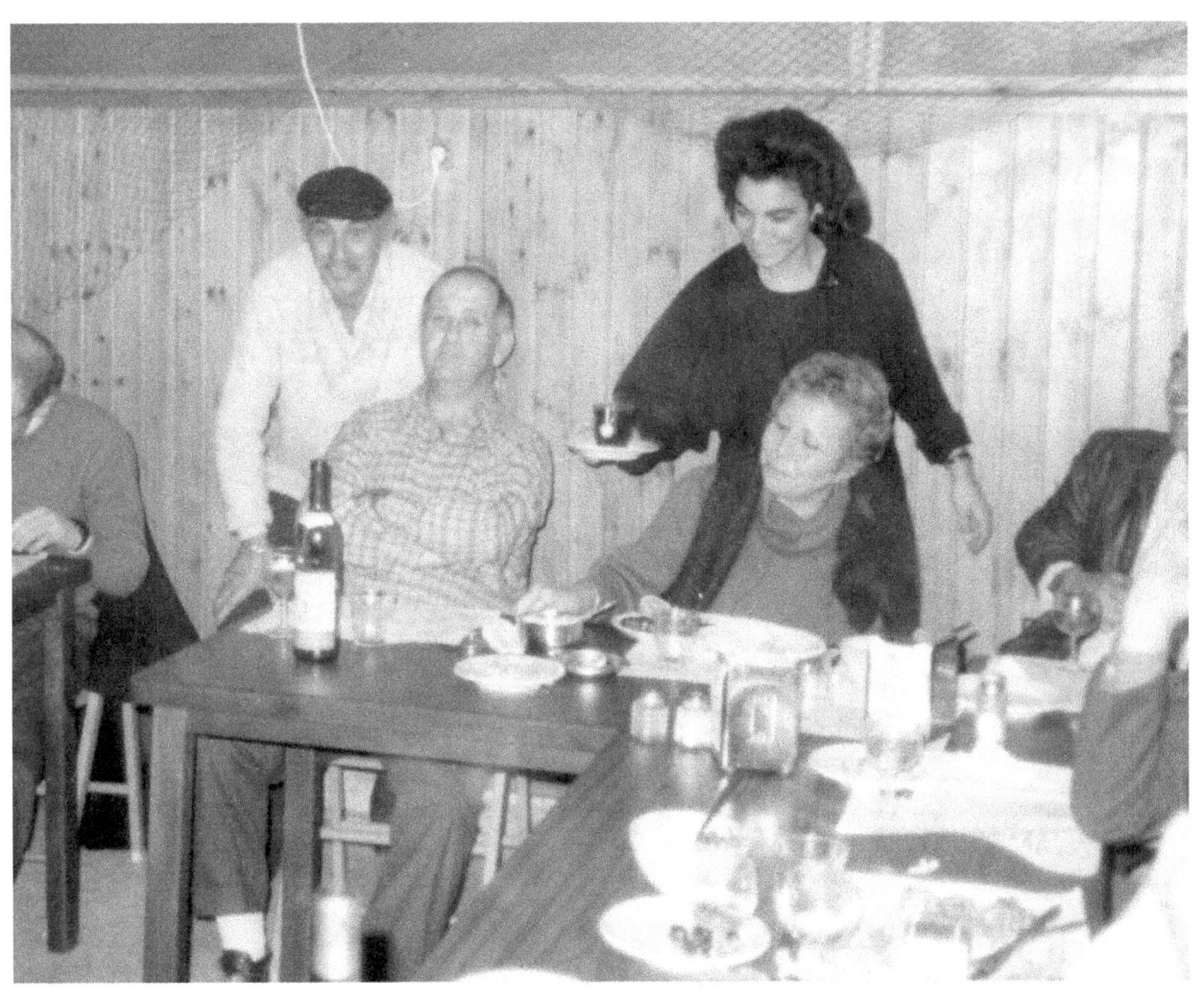

ABOVE:

*Dinner with Israeli
artists in Jaffa.*

148

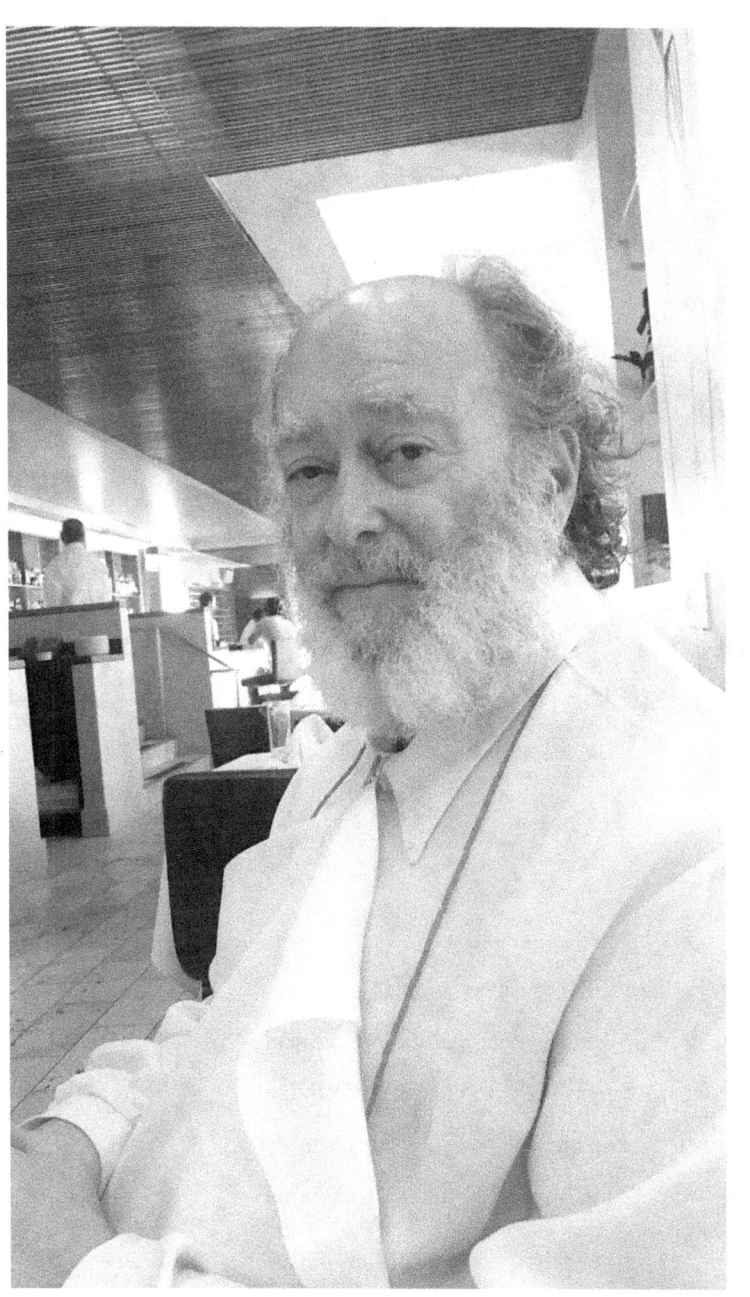

BARRY ROSEN

Inveterate traveler, critic-commentator, and life observer, Barry has been my friend for over 30 years. We met when Barry lost his partner to AIDS and I began working in Israel. We have stayed connected, for which I am glad. I quickly grew to depend on his excellent advice and consummate knowledge of the contemporary international art world.

LEFT:
Barrt Rosen.

149

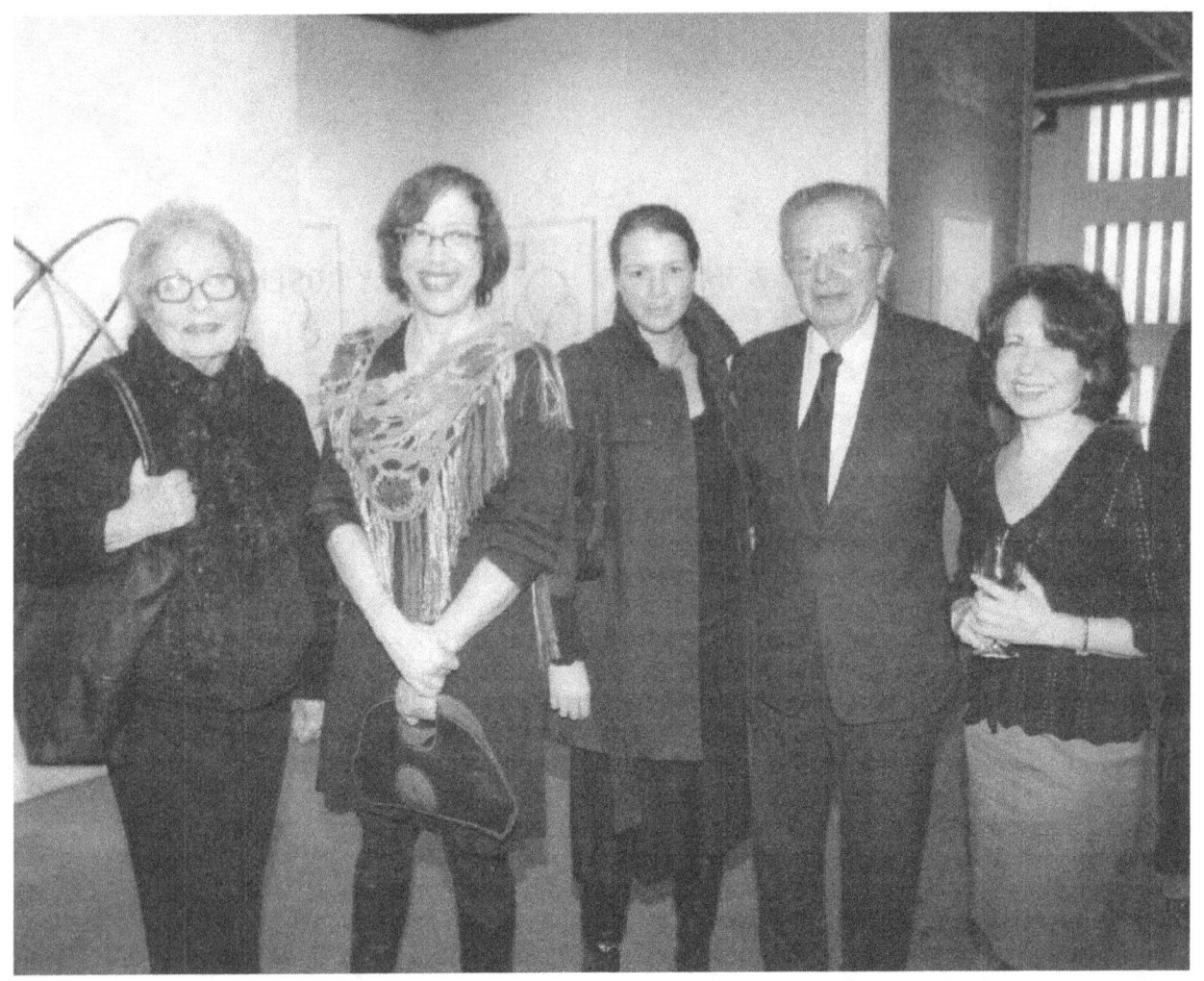

MILTON ESTEROW AND ARTNEWS

ARTnews publisher, Milton Esterow, hired me as Director of International Programs, suggesting that I return to Israel to examine the effects of the Intifada on Israeli and Palestinian art. On this trip, I noticed major changes—the poor treatment of the remaining Palestinian population, the desert sun beating down on them as they stood in line to pass through newly created "checkpoints," suffering for hours while waiting for an Israeli soldier to motion them to pass.

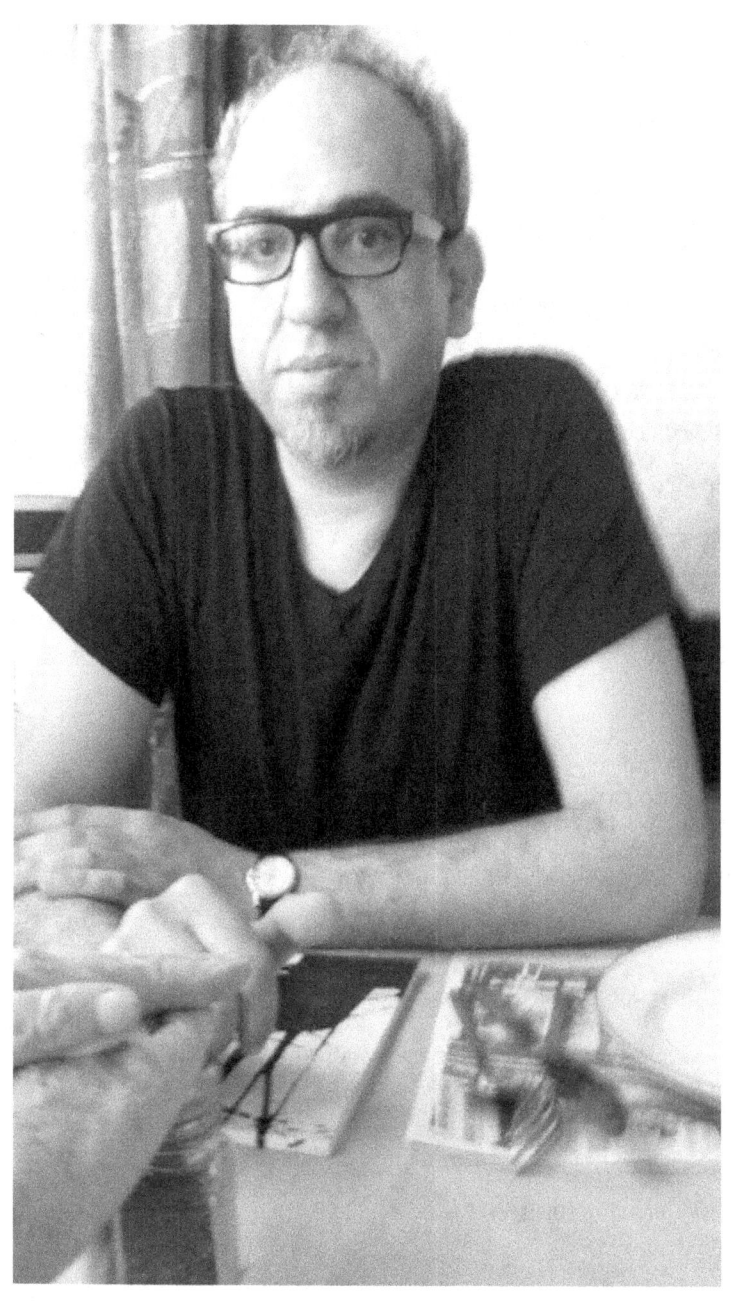

Palestinian cars, restricted to unpaved roads, bore yellow license plates reminiscent of yellow armbands worn by Jews in Germany, during the Nazi regime. Were Jews causing this kind of suffering? Was I contributing?

As I was leaving a Palestinian refugee camp on the outskirts of Jerusalem, an Israeli guard asked, "Do you think this is an amusement park? What were you doing in there?"

Making our way through the checkpoints, Cotton and I discovered Palestinian artists employing photography, video, installation and new media, as well as exploring issues of mobility and migration, depleted natural resources and political marginalization. Palestine had become a fragmented state, a shrinking land broken apart, soon to be

ABOVE:

*Palestinian artist Sharif
Waked.*

permanently devastated by a security wall which would pass through its towns and villages, making it impossible for families to visit and be whole.

In Haifa, an Israeli/Palestinian municipality, we scheduled a visit to Palestinian artist, Sharif Waked. While we waited on the street for an invitation to come up, he looked down on us from his fourth-floor studio and ordered us to come "empty handed." Cotton was told to leave his bulky camera equipment on the sidewalk. This was our first experience with the mistrust that followed us and that soon became part of our everyday experience in the Palestinian Territories.

I visited Israeli Prime Minister, Bibi Netanyahu, in his Tel Aviv office. We met in New York, when he represented Israel at the United Nations in 1986. He had generously contributed to my Israeli exhibitions. I asked him why Israeli Jews had become such tyrannical, insensitive figures? "Don't be too judgmental—don't forget you are one of us," he admonished.

My feelings for Israel, the government and the people, gradually changed. I began to see that their wonderful approach to life—warmth, openness and hospitality—had turned aggressive and hateful. Israel had become a country of people determined to take possession of the land and ruthlessly expel those who lived there. And so disillusionment set in and, like falling in love, I fell out. The article I wrote for ARTnews following this trip was never published. Milton claimed it was too biased.

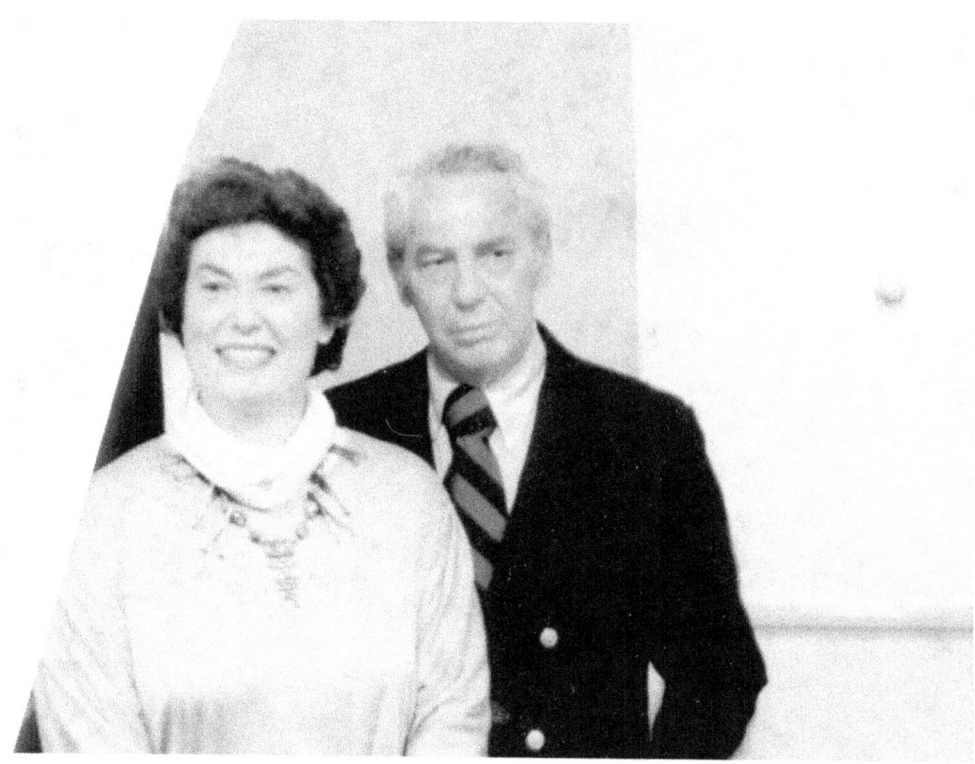

POOR JUDGMENT IN PARTNERS CONTINUED

My friend, Bess Schuyler, had a terrific backhand. We played tennis on the polished wooden floors of New York's Seventh Regiment Armory. Bess always managed to win. Her real estate partner, Dave Lind, a notorious gossip, called one day suggesting that I meet his recently divorced friend, Dan Evangelista, head of the Legal Department at IBM. My parents had always revered IBM.

Dan was unusually tall, six-foot-seven. He described his humble origins—his father, immigrating from Italy, working as a hod carrier, wheeling cement to building sites and in contrast, Dan's remarkable rise to the top of IBM's legal department. Clearly he had developed a personable approach. Awed by him, I was delighted to be invited out to dinner after years

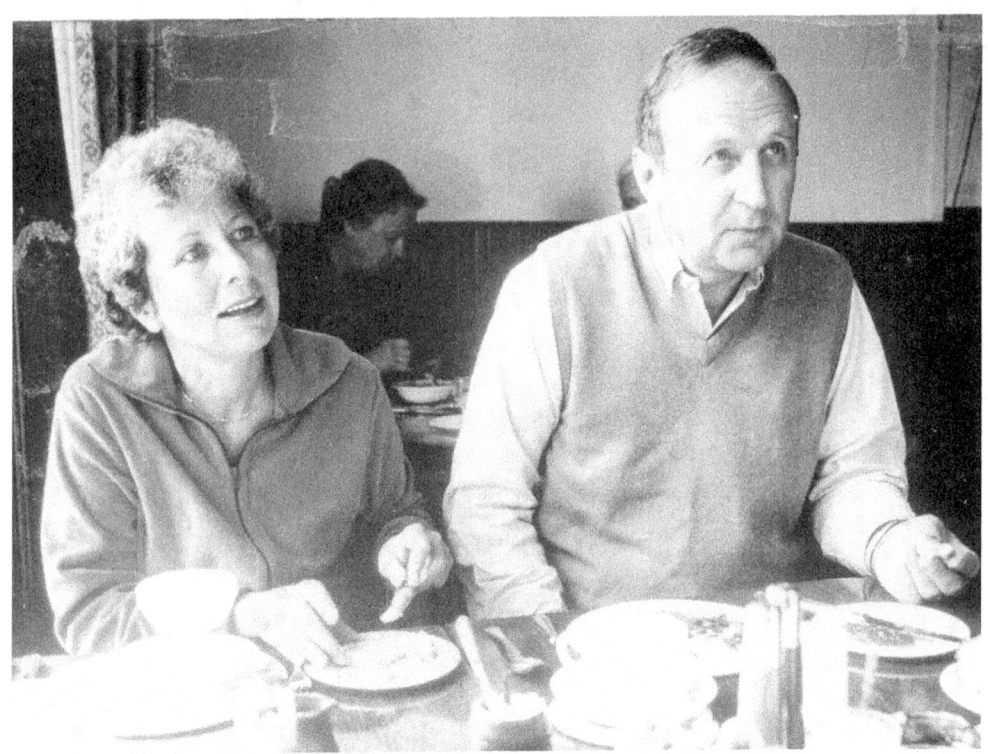

of living in envy of friends who chatted about the many restaurants they had sampled. How wonderful to meet someone who could afford to eat out! And after months of living lavishly, I abandoned what existed of my limited people-assessment powers and accepted Dan's offer to marry.

Dan's three children, Julie, Lynne, and Scott, and my daughter Frances were opposed to our marriage and didn't hide their feelings. Dan's mother, living in a house on Dan's Bedford, New York property, registered her disapproval as well.

Commuting between our Park Avenue apartment and Dan's house in Bedford created scheduling complications in our daily lives. One of us was always in the wrong place. Dan's son, Scott, was in school in Bedford while Frances attended school in New York City. Further complications arose from Dan's trips to many of the outlying branches of IBM. We faced tough choices.

My interest in importing art from other countries had resulted in connections to Israeli artists in Tel Aviv, and I was planning an exhibition of their work in New York City. IBM made it known that they disapproved of my activities. Their policy governing all personnel and their spouses discouraged involvement in geographic regions where IBM was establishing markets. The dictum felt like an over-the-top invasion of my life. Our fragile marriage creaked and groaned.

Dan had seemed intelligent, trustworthy, noble, caring, and—wow—was I surprised to discover door-slamming whenever Frances "disobeyed" him and a Republican/conservative position in political discussions. His executive behavior included getting rid of my cat, which he accomplished one morning, to my horror, by opening the kitchen window as the cat lay sunning on the window sill. His "other self" proved as deceptive as the summer camps I had so believed in. We agreed to separate. As head of the Legal Department at IBM, Dan was a veritable soldier of truth, tall, blue-eyed, convincing. In his capable legalese, he argued that he was the rightful owner of our co-op apartment at 1125 Park Avenue. I testified that I had given the seller, Hugette McClaughlin, my check for $235,000, my inheritance from my grandmother Frankie Louchheim, and that it seemed logical that I be considered the rightful owner. Friends suggested that as an important figure in IBM's legal department, Dan revisit law school and take a refresher course in property. The 1970's narrative that discouraged women from owning marital property, along with my Jewish last name, made me feel I wouldn't be acceptable to the co-op board. I won the battle to keep the apartment.

AN INTERNATIONAL INCIDENT

On one of their many trips to London, my parents had purchased a watercolor entitled *Conglomerate Boulder*, by the celebrated British painter Graham Sutherland. Sutherland gained a reputation in Great Britain when Queen Elizabeth commissioned him to paint Churchill's eightieth birthday portrait. Our Sutherland painting, however, was of a large rock surrounded by some green and yellow bushes. Nothing special.

Judy and I put it up for sale and were contacted by a young dealer named Tim Goldsmith, who listed his home address as 12 Eaton Square, London. For no particular reason, I looked up the address and discovered it to be the home of Sir James Goldsmith, described in the English press as an Anglo-French financial genius with an undeniable Midas touch and a personal life filled with a rich pageant of stolen wives and unconcealed mistresses.

So, his son, Tim Goldsmith, working as an art dealer in New York, took the painting, leaving me a handwritten receipt, and promised to return the painting in twenty-four hours if unsold.

Two weeks later, I panicked. Getting no answer from Tim's phone, I called Scotland Yard. They, of course, knew all about the scandalous Goldsmith family and initiated a search for the missing painting. I have no idea what magic they performed, but the Sutherland painting, in a distressed cardboard box, arrived at my front door twenty-four hours later.

I thanked Scotland Yard profusely, resolving to give them a call the next time I couldn't find my car keys.

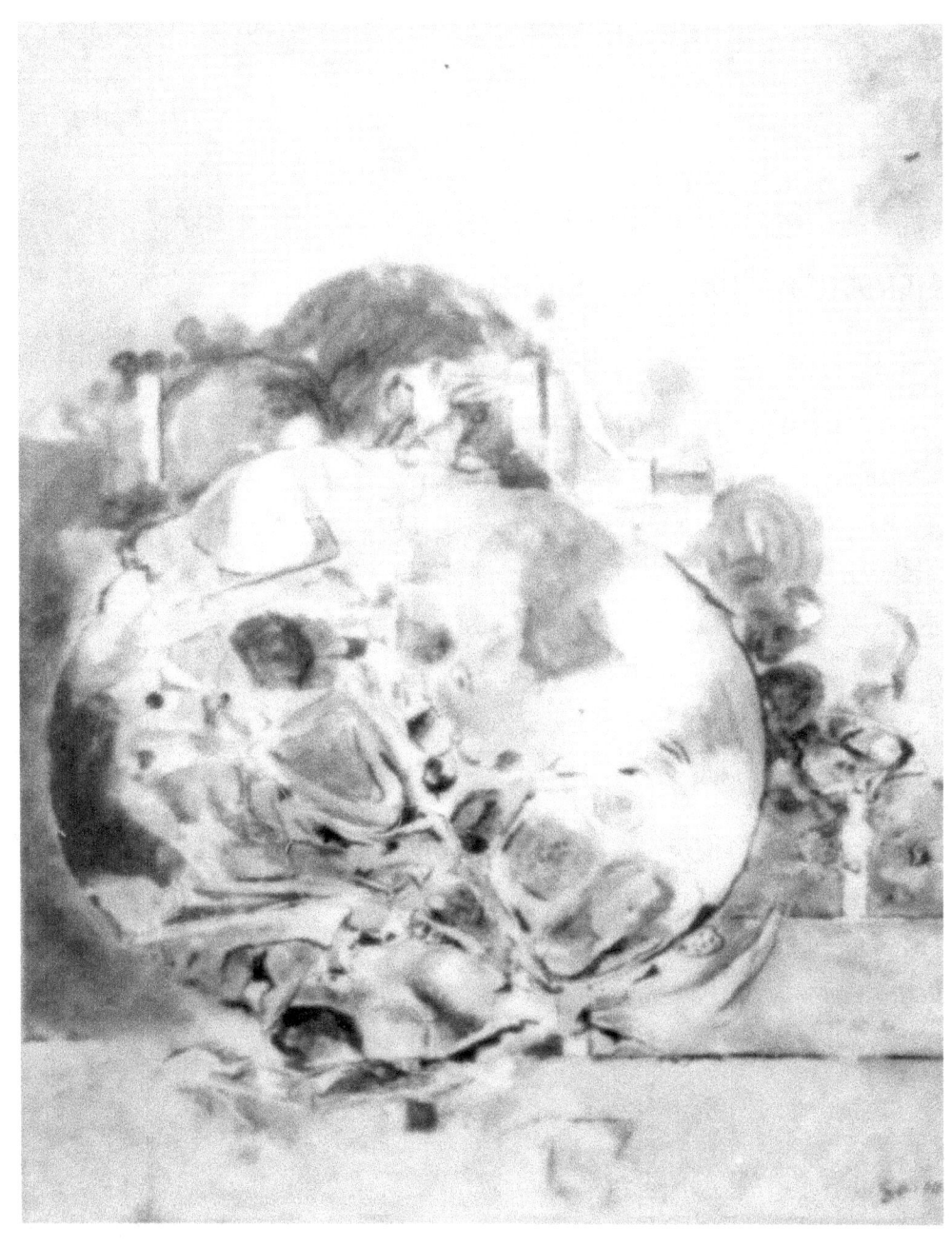

157

MENSCHENKENNER MARY MATURES

Dan demanded that I pay him a finder's fee of $110,000 for spotting the apartment in *The New York Times*. As my indignation and sense of self-worth increased, I became stronger. I even decided to keep the name Evangelista (with the passing thought that Dan might charge me for use of the name.) I liked it better than Louchheim or Lieberthal. Maybe I had inherited my family's anti-Jewish bent.

Solo now at 1125 Park Avenue, I explored ways to justify living in an eight-room space. I rented to E. F. Hutton and Company for photo shoots and placed ads in *The New York Times* offering "bed-and-breakfast,"

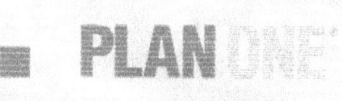

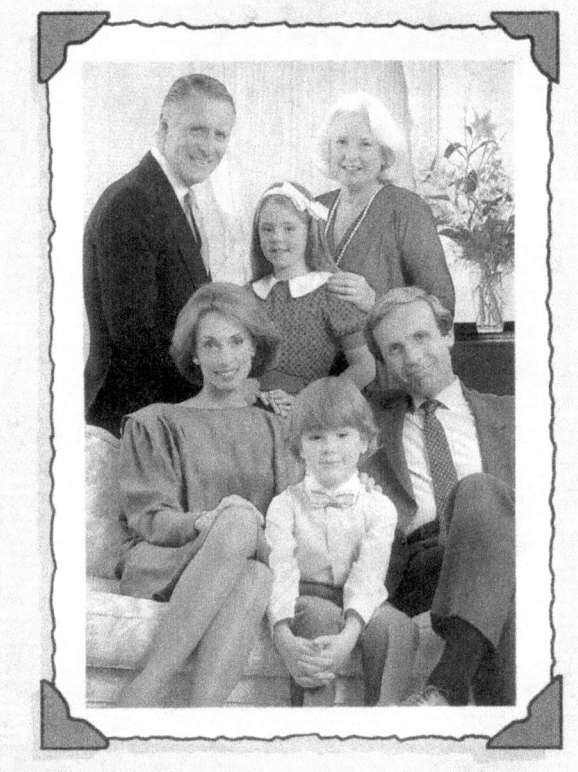

RIGHT:
E. F. Hutton brochure.
Photo shot at 1125
Park Ave.

158

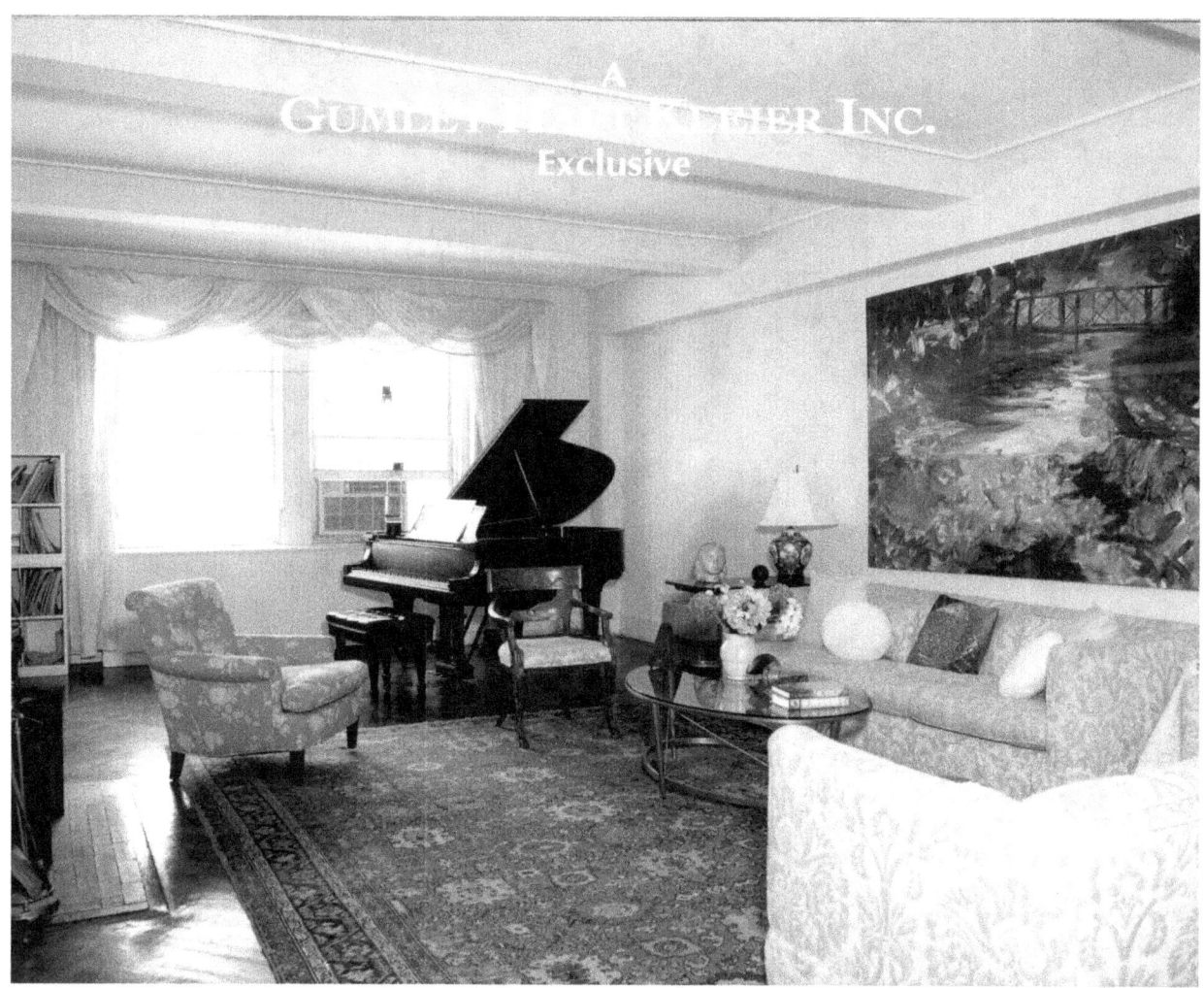

A
GUMLEY HAFT KLEIER INC.
Exclusive

ABOVE:

Living room at 1125 Park Ave.

passed the tests New York City required of amateur innkeepers, and rented rooms to a variety of travelers, some of whom complained bitterly about the torn towels, overcooked poached eggs, and pigeons roosting noisily on window sills.

I held onto that $235,000 apartment for twenty-five years and sold it for $2.9 million— probably the best investment I ever made.

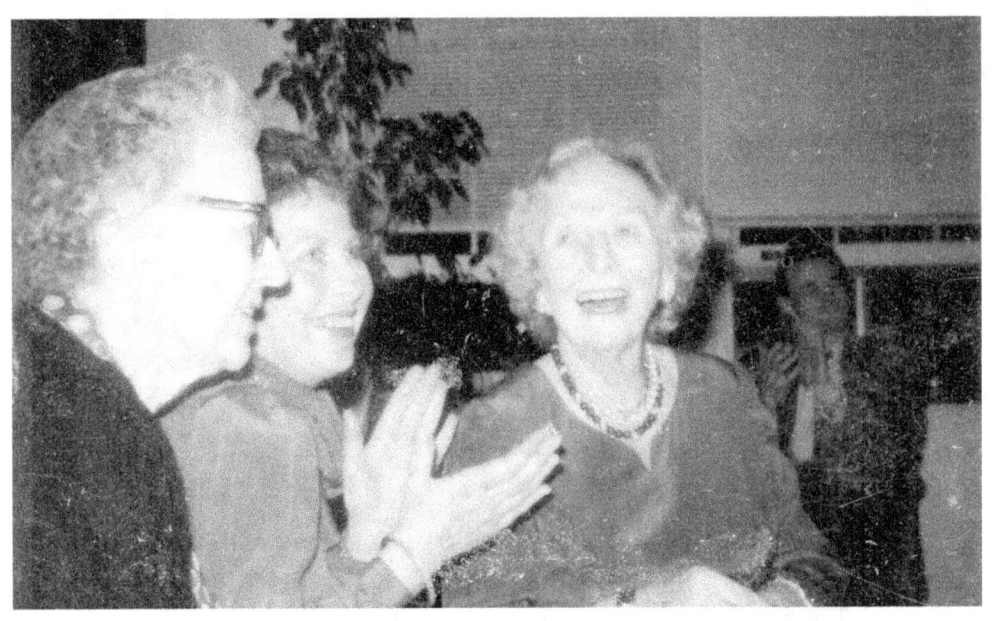

MUSIC RETURNS

KYRIENA SILOTI

1980–1989

Kyriena Siloti's piano lessons were of stern Russian origin. Her father, Alexander Siloti, had studied with composer Franz Liszt. To play the piano correctly one had to hold one's fingers in certain awkward positions and drill with scales and arpeggios until a legato sound was produced. The finger exercises were excruciatingly painful yet helpful in developing finger agility.

Kyriena was hard to please. I would ask if I could play a piece I had heard. She would say, "Ah, but you're not ready for that yet!" Gradually, I grew to resent her rigid methods but enjoyed her company, listening to her tales of Moscow during the Bolshevik Revolution and her escape to Manchuria. She would come for dinner at my apartment carrying handfuls of pills and an old jam bottle filled with skimmed milk. "It's not that I distrust your cooking, but I prefer drinking the milk I buy at the farmer's market and I'm really not hungry for food, at night, just conversation."

FONTAINBLEAU, FRANCE

What professional musician (or even an aspiring amateur such as I) could resist the lure: summer study at Fontainebleau's School of Music, in a setting resonating with the spirit of its co-founder, the late Nadia Boulanger, whose musical legacy lies in the compositions of many of today's best American composers.

It was as a non-professional with fluency in French, gained from a year at the Sorbonne and subsequent visits to France, that I applied for Fontainebleau's 1983 summer session. Three weeks after I sent my audition tape, I received a phone call from Fontainebleau's New York office: the jury had accepted me. My piano performance included the stipulated categories of Classic, Romantic, and Twentieth century French work. I had chosen the Adagio movement from Mozart's Third Sonata, Chopin's Fourth Prelude, and some selections from Ma Mere L'Oye of Ravel.

In the town of Fontainebleau, where we were housed, on a typical day, I would open the double windows to see the rosy sunrise over the red tiled roofs of the waking city. Greeting my ear, the voice of a fish peddler shouted, "des poissons!"; the rattle of the metal grill at the news-stand; the waiter sweeping the sidewalk at the corner cafe while customers at the bar have an early morning "boisson". The aroma was wonderful: black coffee beans freshly ground, strong Gauloise cigarettes, and a unique brand of French petrol intermingled.

At the chateau we were each assigned a room with a piano. Mine was luxurious, facing a formal garden where peacocks strutted and groups of swallows swooped by. Solfege (sight singing) and ear training combined with dictation—selections from Stravinsky and Bartok—challenged me. To pass the final exam, we had to sing a Bach Cantata *a cappella*.

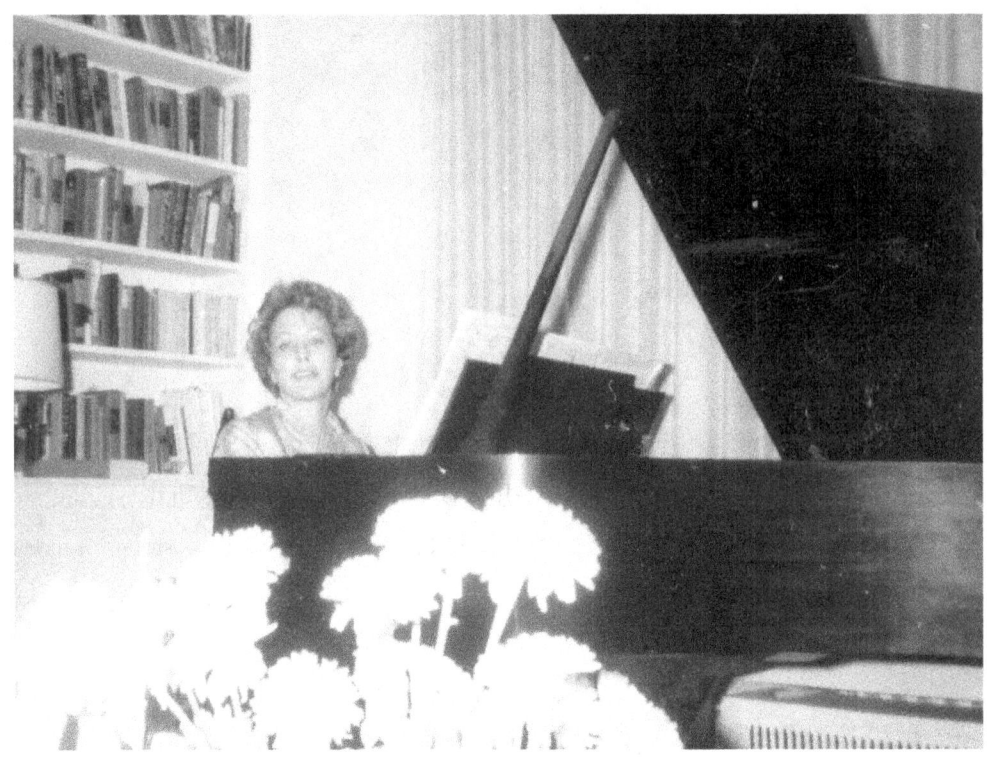

Performances were held in the Jeu de Paumes, an indoor tennis court of kings and now an auditorium for the "concert d'eleves." These performances frequently set in motion pigeons, nesting in the high rafters, who seemed to enjoy distracting the audiences by demonstrating take-off and landing techniques.

Back in New York, I joined the Amateur Chamber Music Society. My first bid to play came from Jerome Bergman, who drove a yellow taxi in Manhattan and carried his violin in the trunk. I had never played with a violinist. My ensemble experience was limited to playing duets with my mother, and she refused to count so we were rarely on the same page. Jerome was a first violinist in the string section of the New Jersey Symphony. It was wonderful to be playing in sync. We played together compatibly for twenty-five years.

When I learned that Jerome was David Kreeger's cousin—David was founder of Geico Insurance, avid amateur violinist, proud owner of a Stradivarius, and my family's friend—I suggested a trip to Washington, D.C. to play some chamber music, hoping that David would

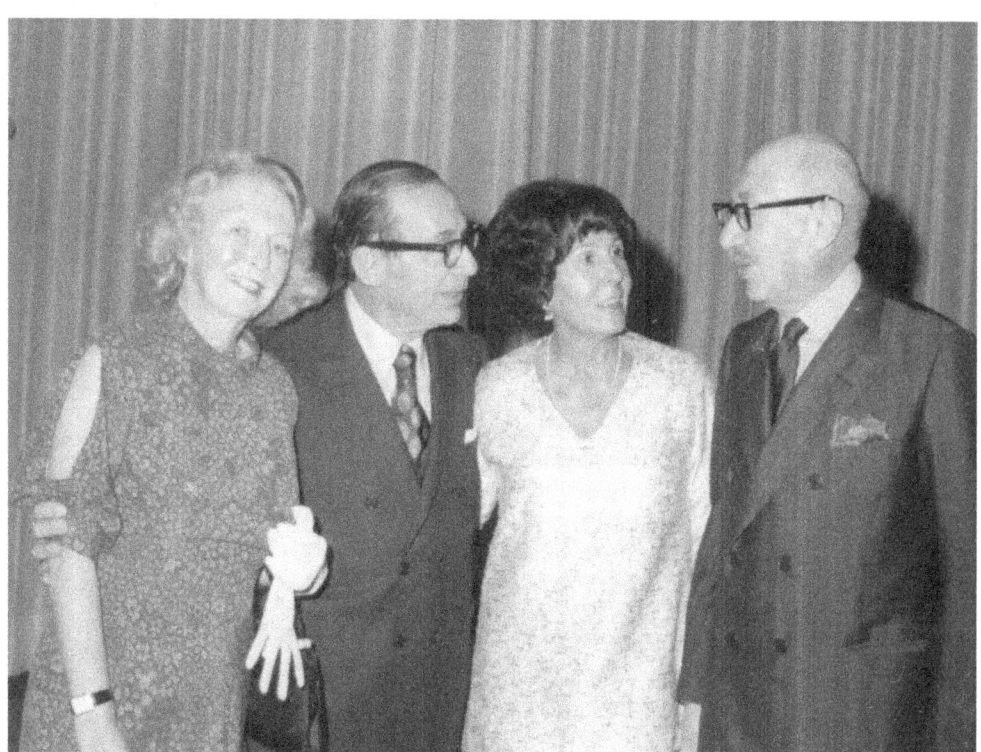

RIGHT:

My Parents with David and Carmen Kreeger.

find a good job for his cousin, perhaps even with Geico. Unfortunately, Jerome's virtuoso playing far exceeded David's musical abilities. I think that was the clincher. No job was offered.

Thanks to Jerome I learned to count, helped by a metronome, and signed up for summer chamber music sessions with accomplished string players at Bennington and Amherst. Winters, I attended New York soirées at Anne Rattner's apartment on 108th street and Joe Machlis's on 57th street, where pianists preparing for Carnegie Hall performances did a run-through. I had picked up good listening habits from attending concerts with my father.

When my mother sold her house in Georgetown, she offered me Grandma Frankie's piano. Because I already had a large Steinway, fitting in a second piano, even one I had revered as a young girl, was challenging. But it fit comfortably back to back with my existing piano, and with it, I eagerly explored the two piano literature with able pianist friends hoping that my neighbors could tolerate the orchestral level of sound we made.

163

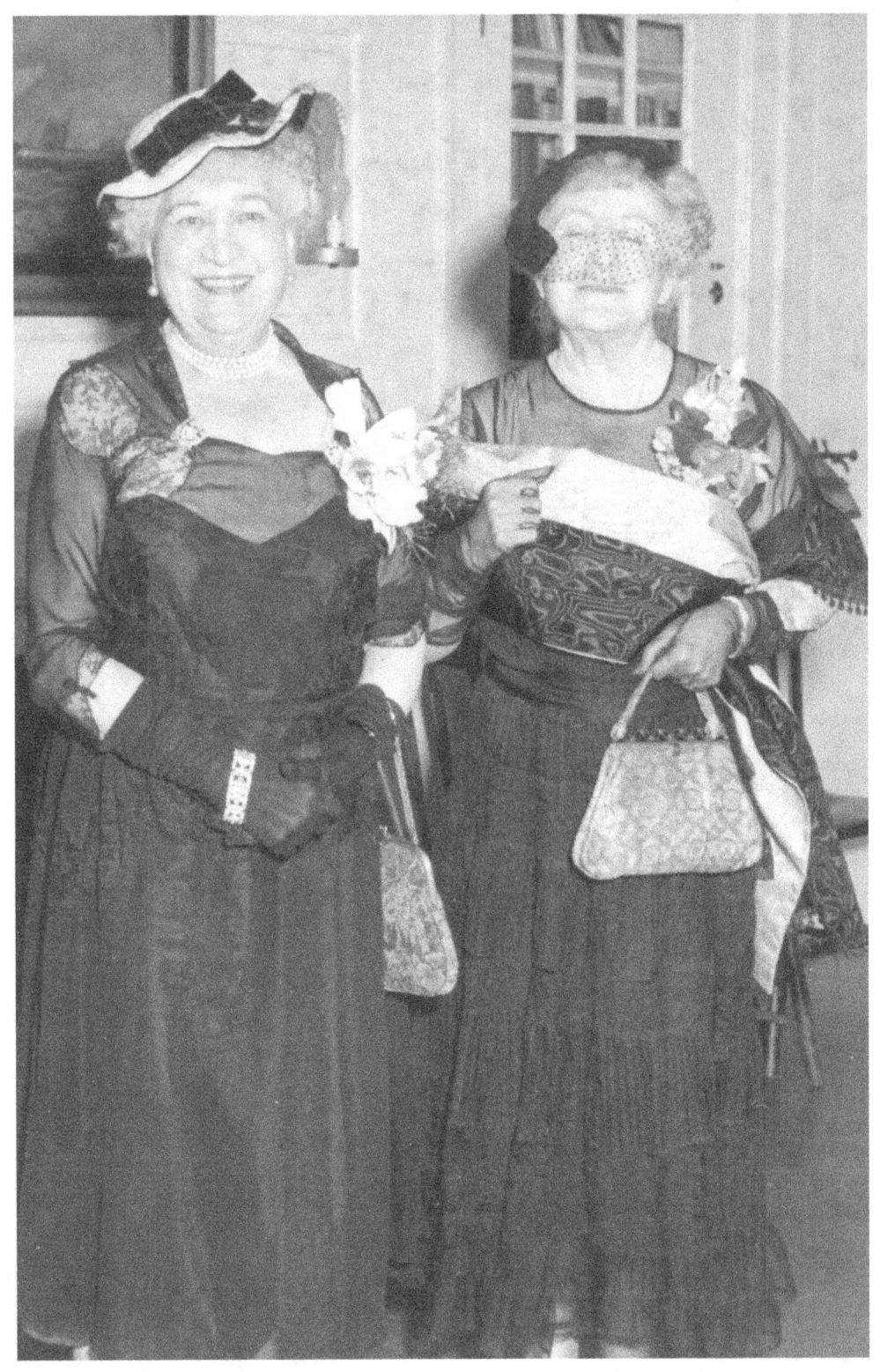

LEFT:

*Grandmother Frankie
Louchheim (left) and
Grandmother Adele
Scofield (right).*

ADELE AND FRANKIE

My two grandmothers lived a few blocks apart in New York City. Envy and rivalry characterized their meetings, most of which took place when some member of our family came to town. Organizing separate visits required careful planning. In many respects they were very much alike. Both were imperious and snide and believed that money conferred status. The difference was that Frankie had money to buy the things that showed the world she was rich—automobiles, fabulous gowns, pearl necklaces and earrings, diamond brooches and rings—while Adele had only memories of great wealth: the great bay windows of the Fifth Avenue house, the bevy of servants at her command at the 86th Street house, polished crystal and china so precious it was kept under lock and key. Little remained to her but a monogramed candy box and the belief that if the household silver was highly polished, nothing could go very wrong. Frankie had an adoring husband, while Adele was not only separated from her husband, but divorced—in those days a social outcast role for a woman of breeding.

Both were parsimonious, Adele out of necessity, Frankie because it pleased her to be. Owning everything, she held back as much as she could. She made one portion serve two when she was dining out of the public eye. Her likes were limited to men, music and small children, in whose presence she brightened.

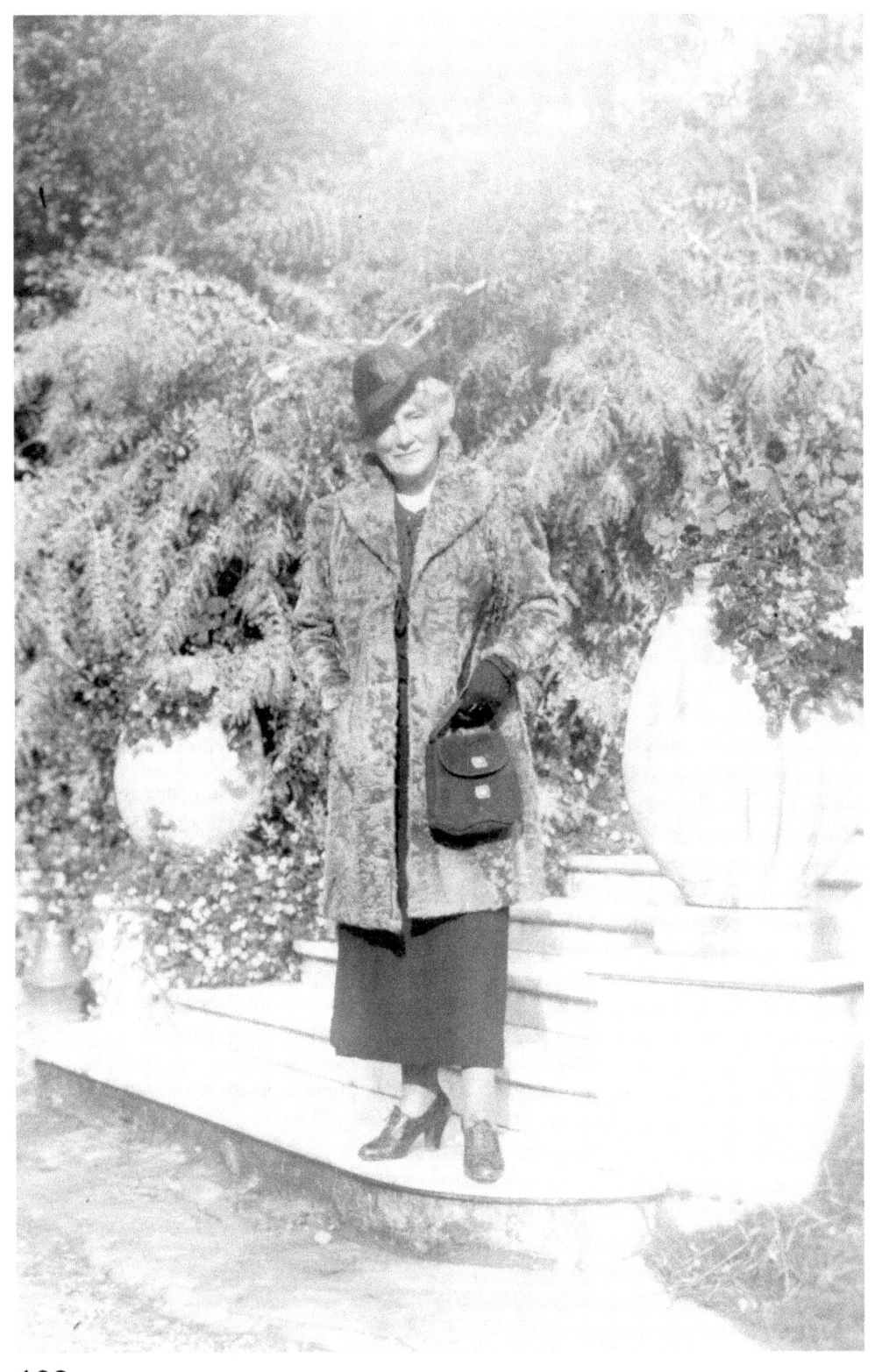

ADELE

Adele was an easy target. Frankie found ample opportunity to criticize her for bragging and telling tales about her titled friends. All my mother could think of saying in defense was: "She does manage on so little."

And Adele did manage to maintain the airs of a wealthy matron as she downsized. I admired the way she reimagined her life. As prices rose at her hairdresser on 86th Street, where she maintained a regular Friday appointment, costs remained the same for her: $2.50 a week, and she always left a 25-cent tip. Detractors referred to her as an "ingratiator." Using her warehouse of received gifts, she would arrive bearing a fanciful box of chocolates or whatever, which she had cleverly rewrapped. She would win over the recipient with little aphorisms of praise, always delivered in French. She entered into a hundred hearts. Every other Monday, she gathered as many family members as she could round up for tea in her studio apartment. Bringing her family together, having them interact and reconfirm their family ties, made her excessively happy.

When Adele shifted her beliefs and adopted Christian Science as her religion, Frankie chided her: *"What's the matter? Isn't being Jewish good enough for you?"*

Adele was demanding and needy, as was my father. Both were possessive of Katie. Christian Science helped calm everyone down a bit.

FRANKIE

Frances Appel Louchheim lived lavishly at the Plaza Hotel on Fifth Avenue, indulged, pampered, elegantly coiffed, diving into her jar of peanut butter every night—a habit I seemed to have acquired. She liked to remind us that her wedding ring came from Cartier.

She looked down on Adele as a "show-off." Frankie could sing and play the piano and had very little interest in the outside world. When her legs became unsteady she succumbed to a wheel chair, refused to leave her apartment and be seen. Her pride overrode the pleasure she might have gotten in Central Park, a few steps away.

Adele conversed in three languages and was a founding member of the politically engaged Women's City Club of New York. I became frightened by the sound of their voices when they argued. What did it mean to hear two respected women verbally attacking each other, and what was the intended outcome? Were we supposed to take sides? A rematch would occur. Adele would return to the arena quoting Marcel Proust or reciting one of Baudelaire's poems, deliberately flaunting a language Frankie had tried to learn but never could. After my daughter Frances Anne was born, in 1965, a truce blossomed. And when Frankie became housebound, and unsteady on her feet, Adele visited her. I like to think that Frances's birth brought them together in harmony.

In 1968, Adele became ill (we never knew with what). Katie took her to Washington where she died on O Street, in my bed. Frankie was not told of Adele's death and frequently asked for her, noting that she hadn't been around recently. I had to deliver the truth—Adele was gone. It was sad to see how Frankie missed her, spoke of her often and told stories about their shared times together.

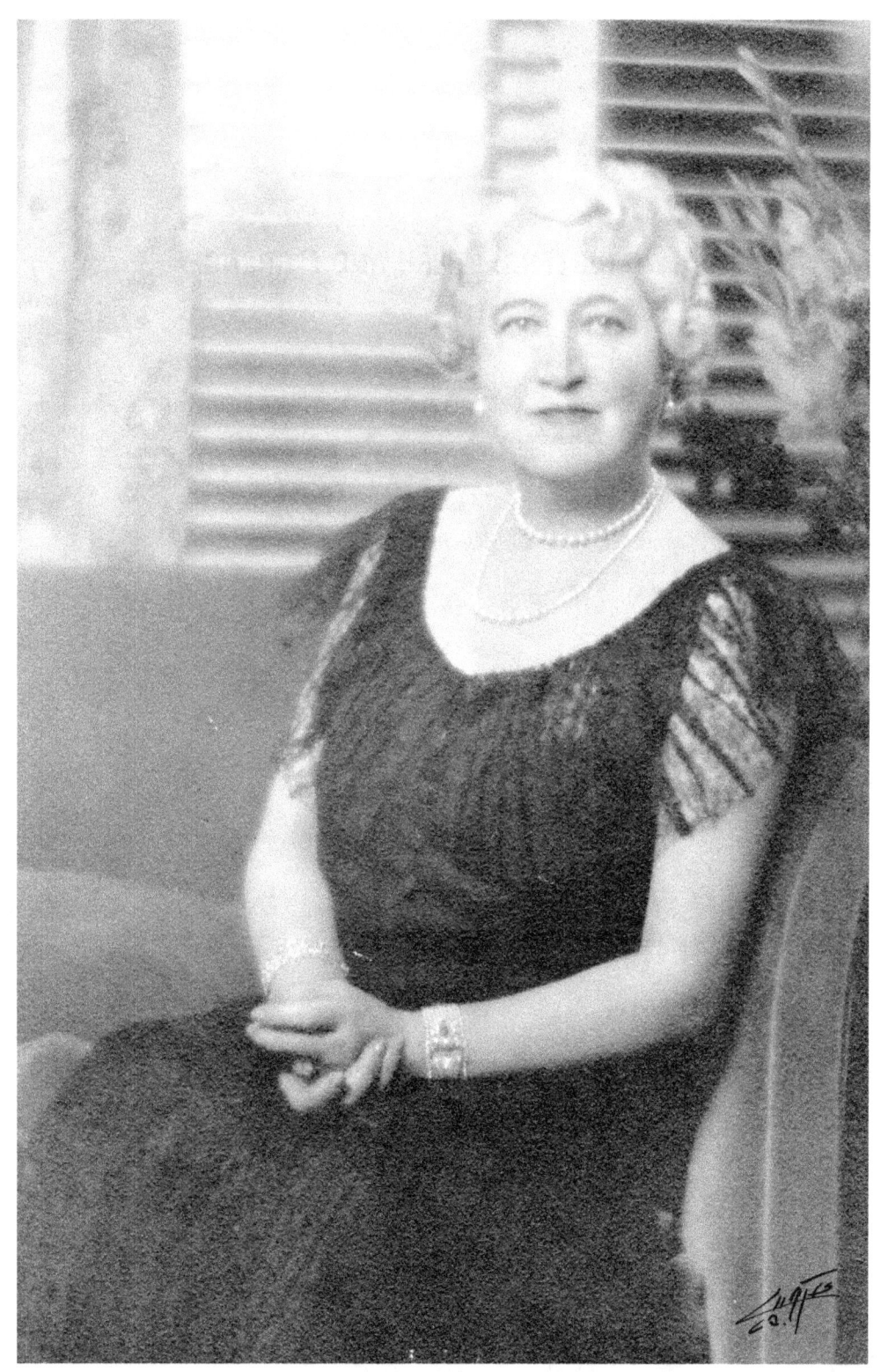

MY FATHER'S TWO SISTERS: HELEN AND FLORENCE

Helen and Florence, my father's two younger sisters, felt like second-class citizens, still living in the era of "boys are better." Shedding husbands and aborting their pregnancies sentenced them both to solitary lives. I became a sort of messenger—the one who would carry the word to my father that they needed money, or were resentful of his privileged life.

HELEN

Aunt Helen, or "Tante Helene" as she preferred, bore no resemblance to Walter or Florence. Helen's New York City apartment at 325 East 57th street resembled a precious jewelry box. An implied Do-Not-Touch! marked every piece of furniture. Her chairs were so small that to sit on one required a whole new concept of comfort.

Judy adopted many of Aunt Helen's idiosyncrasies: she grew fussy and skinny, but beautifully clothed. She suffered from bulimia: eating was a strange process of putting food in her mouth, chewing and then spitting it out—enjoying the taste of food without swallowing. Judy never left home without a baked potato tucked in her purse.

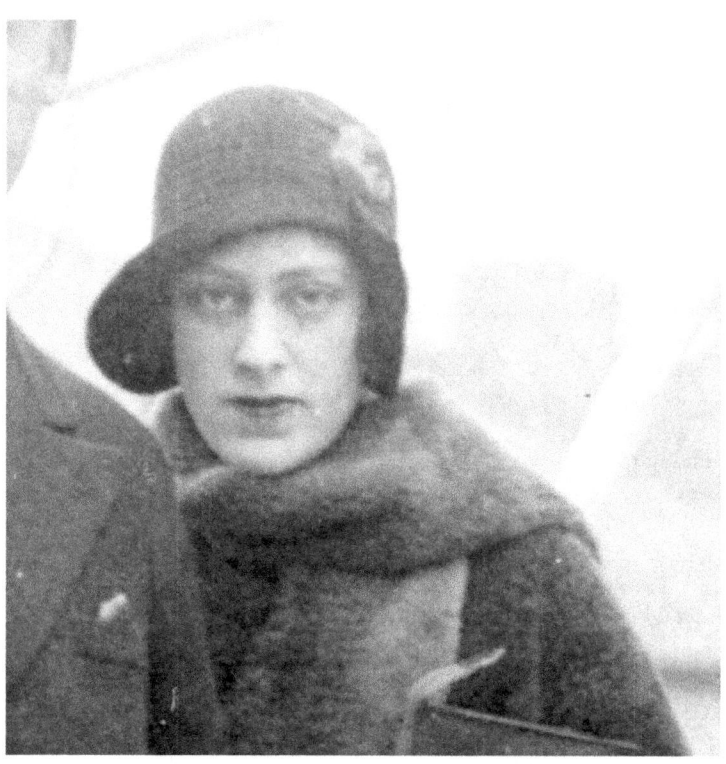

Helen's ambitions took her in the direction of fashion and snobbery. She paraded around Bonwit Teller's *deuxieme etage* (2nd floor), well-coiffed, cigarette in hand, several strands of her mother's pearls hung around her neck, and a very black dress covering her nonexistent breasts—preaching *haute couture* to an admiring group of fashionistas. She excelled at looking down on everyone in a sneering manner—particular scorn directed toward her mother, whom she called "the old trout." There were always some who found her comments droll, amusing. "Puis je fume?" was her plaintiff line at our dinner table.

Over the years, I lost touch with Aunt Helen. She married an Irish titled cartoonist—Sir Patrick Bellew, left her apartment in New York City, and living on dry martinis at noon, moved to Litchfield, Conn. There, in a vintage New England farm house, she became ill and died.

UNCLE PATRICK BELLEW

After Aunt Helen died, Paddy took up with a young nurses' aid who, after a few months, invited her entire family to move in. Arriving one warm afternoon, I came across a professional barber cutting hair in Helen's garage, another woman in the kitchen preparing to sell catered meals, and the young nurse's aid in bed with Uncle Paddy. It was hard to convince Paddy that he was the victim of his nurse's unscrupulous family. I tried unsuccessfully to evict them. And with the young nurse in bed with Paddy it felt like a losing battle.

On one of my visits, a *deus ex machina* occurred. Paddy began to cough uncontrollably. I called 911, and an ambulance arrived. As soon as Paddy was out of the house, I had no trouble getting the nurse and her relatives to pack up and leave.

I became a strong believer in *dei ex machina*, used by the Greeks to suggest an interference from elsewhere or more literally, a god descending from on high, arriving on a stage machine, to correct an unfortunate situation.

When Paddy died in 1982, I learned that all his worldly goods had been willed to Dan, from whom Paddy took orders. Dan had a history of "looking after" older men. When I discovered that Paddy had a son as well as two grandchildren from a previous marriage, I stepped up to the plate and secured the return of my Aunt Helen's property.

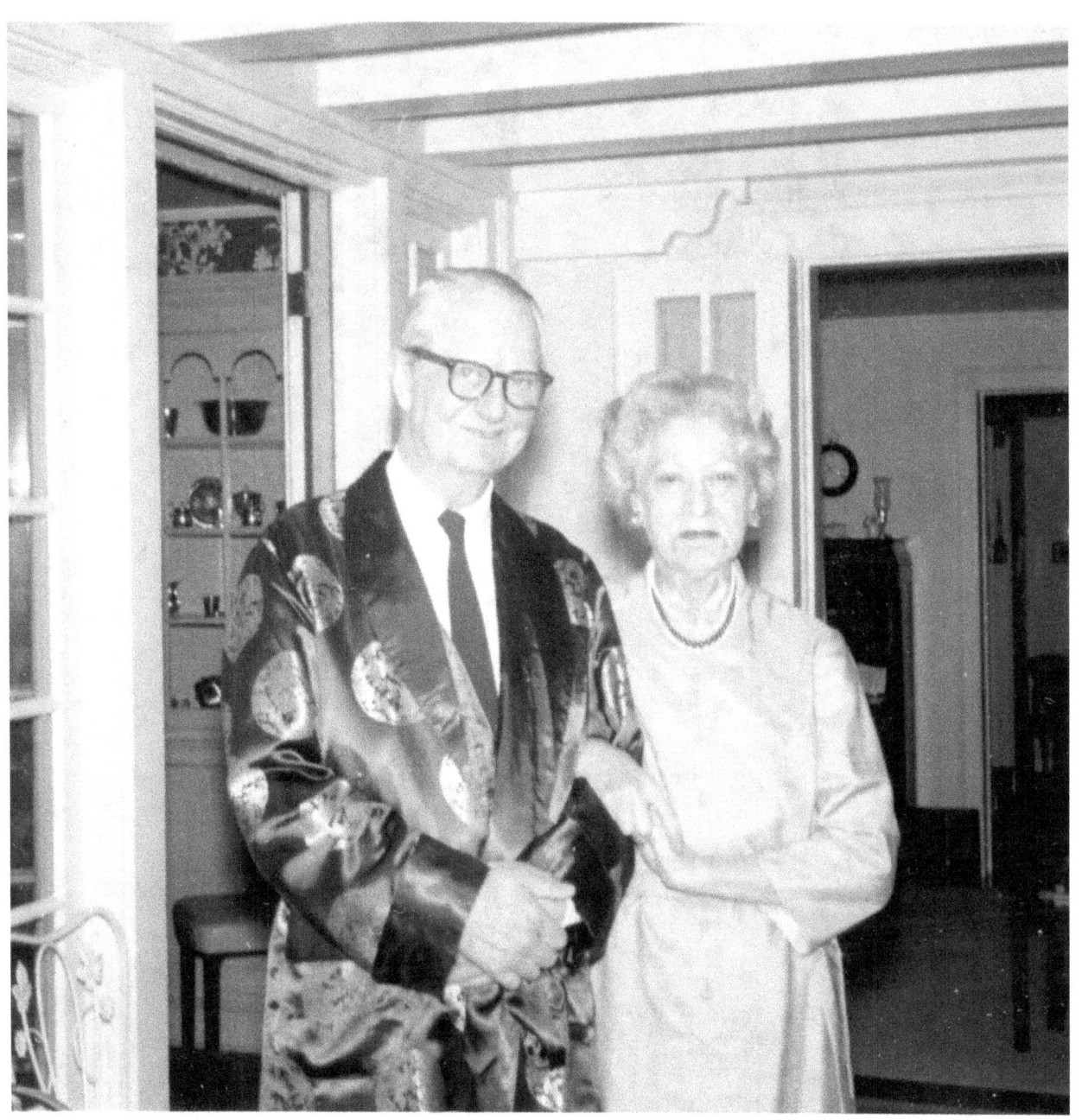

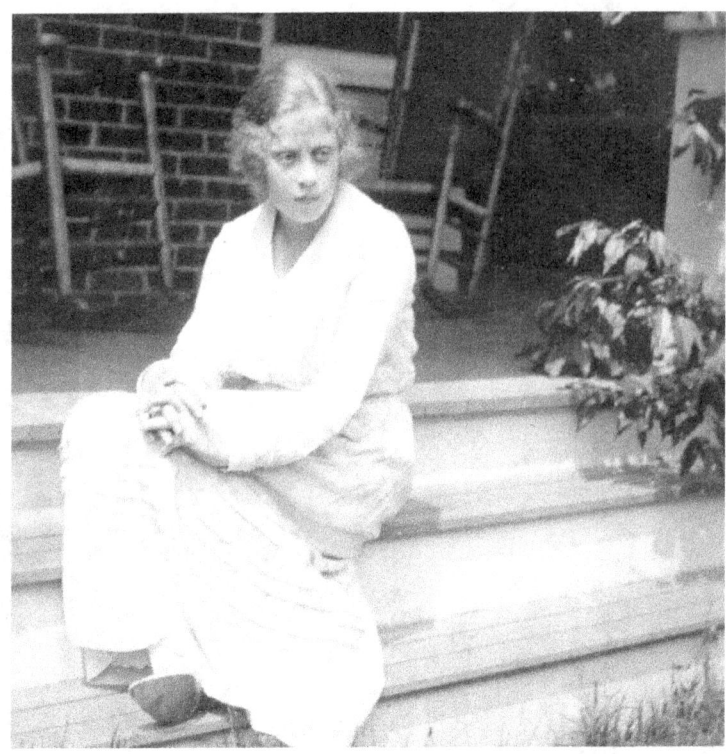

FLORENCE

Like Adele and Frankie, Florence and Katie had trouble accepting each other. Both were trailblazers in an era when women were simply wives and mothers and did not count for much outside the home.

Florence's iconoclasm emerged early. As a girl, she fought the obedience expected of every German-American family. She tried hard to be different from her staid older brother, Walter. She flaunted her non-conformity and any reference to middle class mores caused her to revolt. She refused to live by other people's timetables. Her super conventional parents took her behavior as an affront. They refused to hang her paintings and drawings of artists escaping

174

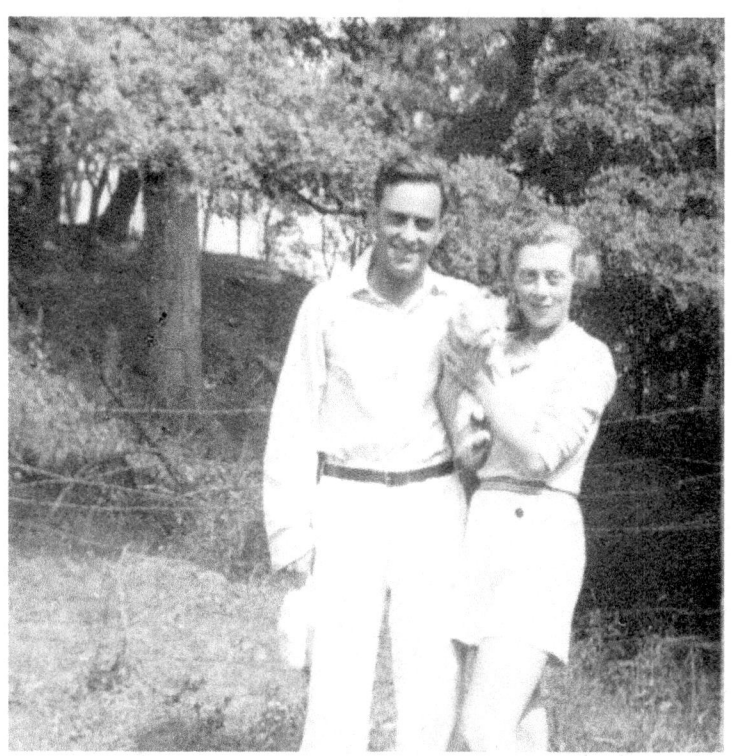

from Europe during World War II.** They mocked and ridiculed her and gave money more freely to my father, who conformed to their view of a responsible person.

Florence had a sharp eye and an appreciation for the unconventional. At Radcliffe College, she and her Harvard classmate, Alfred Barr (who later became a founder of the Museum of Modern Art) benefited from having Paul Sachs as their professor. Paul took his students to visit homes of private collectors, which no doubt gave Florence the impetus to build an art collection of her own. And when Barr suggested that they tour studios of European artists, Florence was delighted to accompany him. That began her youthful years in Europe, meeting artists and collecting their works. With little money she became an outstanding collector, supporting many of the most famous new artists of the time.

**Florence had acquired many of their works and became their den mother teaching them how to comport themselves in New York.

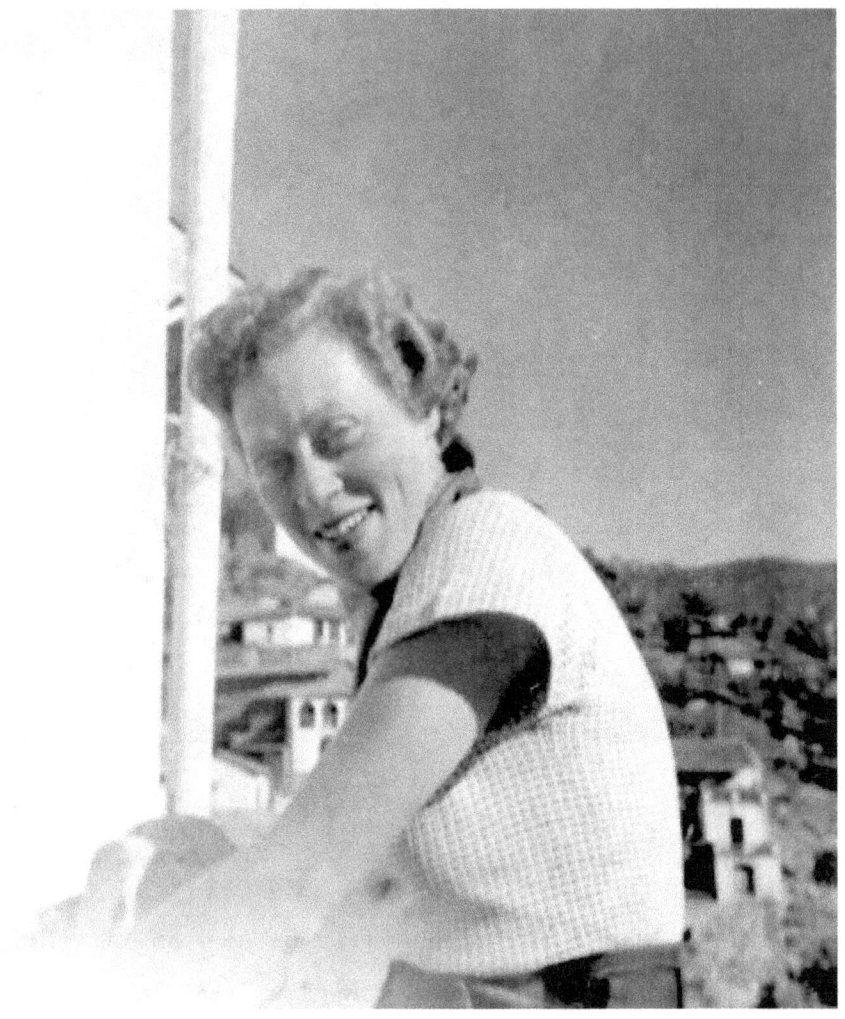

Florence's art collection gained fame and was written up and praised by critics for its brilliant examples of 20th century art. "They have that indefinable unity and charm which characterize all carefully made and much loved private collections. Their owner's taste speaks quietly through them and gives them a certain added significance."

Seven decades later, in Central Park, with our dogs on leashes, I met Paul's nephew, Sam Sachs, Director of New York's Frick Museum who by a strange coincidence, traveled to Japan with me with the Aspen Institute. Sam generously supported my Palestinian art exhibitions and encouraged artists to participate.

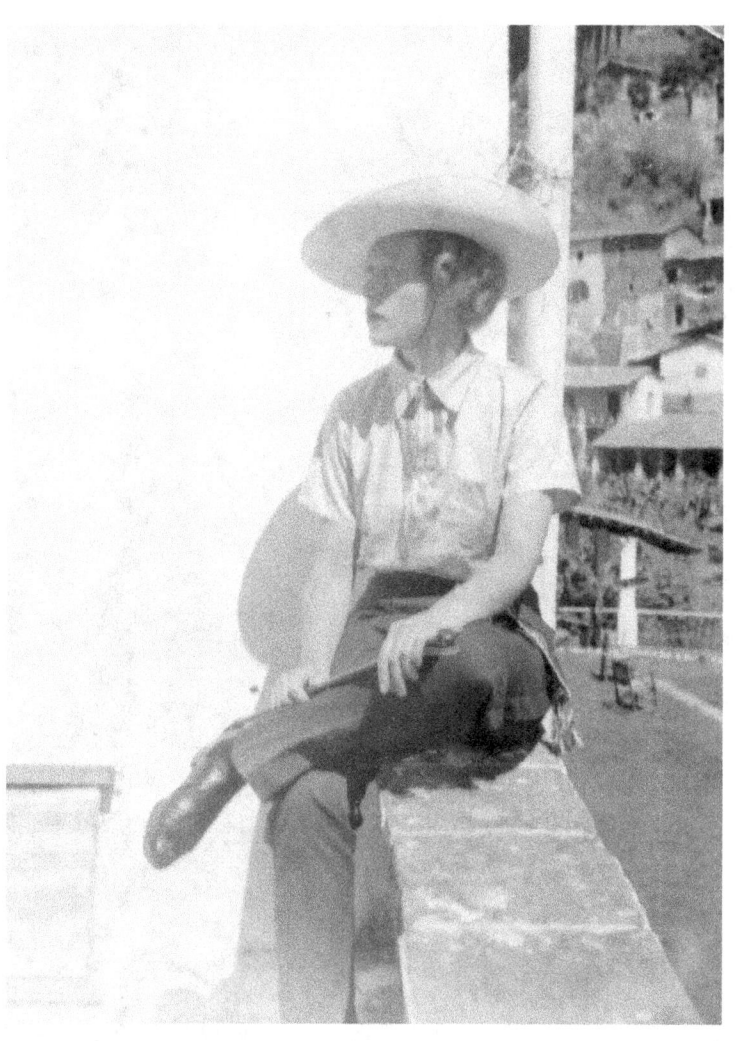

In 1948, Florence bought Governor John Hunt's mansion in Vernon, Vermont. The house, surrounded by majestic pine trees and wooded pastures, was built in 1769 and needed care. I was conscripted to spend my weekends, a short train ride from Providence, scraping off old wallpaper and polishing floor boards. Restoring the house gave Florence great satisfaction. It was her work of art. Because there were several uncultivated acres around the house, Florence rented pastures to a neighboring farmer to graze his cows. The beauty of the Vermont countryside was visible on all sides.

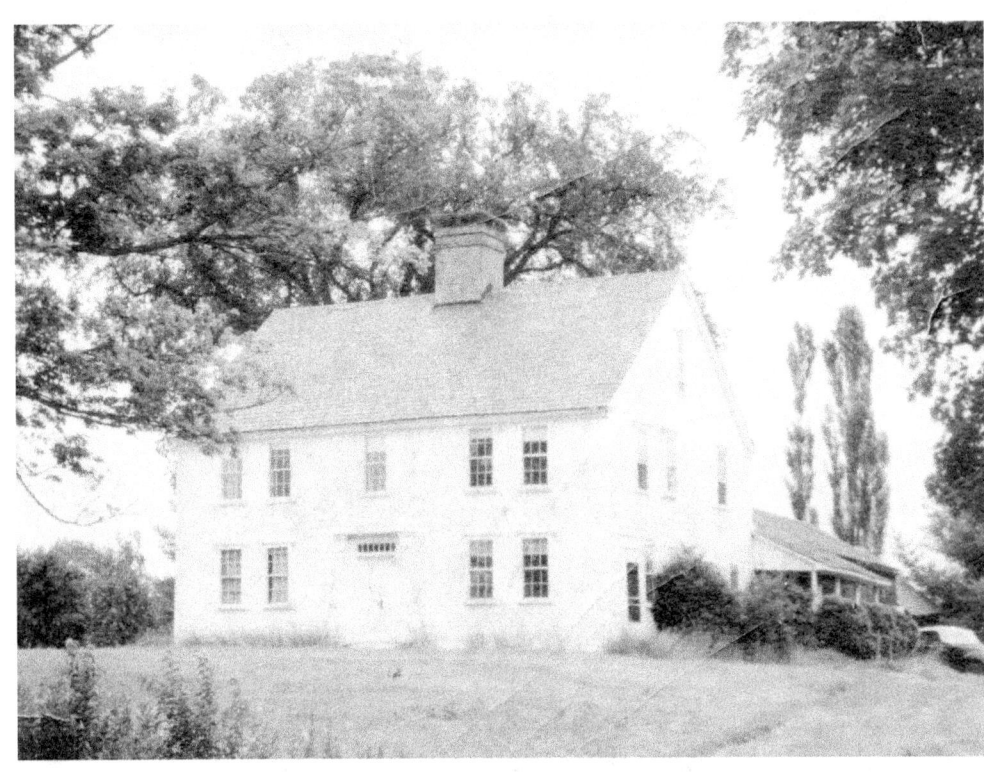

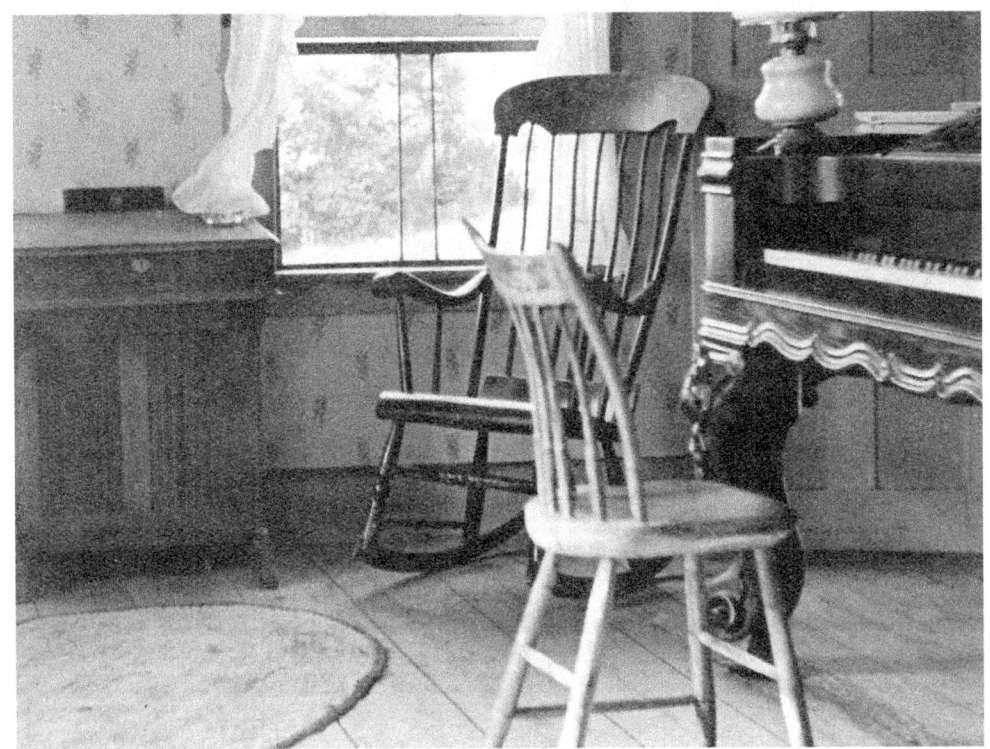

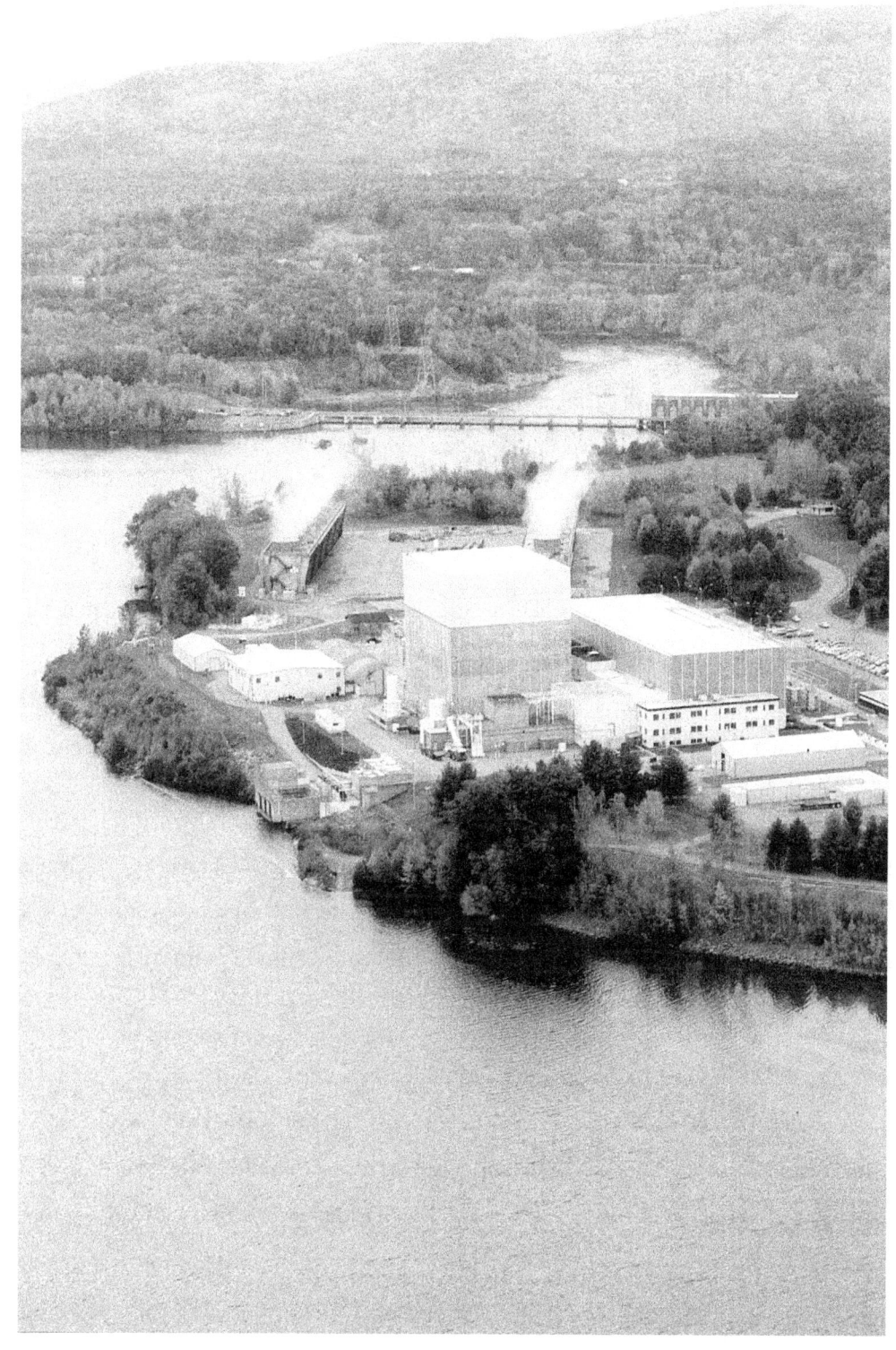

When Florence's 57th street walk-up apartment was robbed, only her costume jewelry was taken, her valuable art overlooked. Increasingly fearful of city life, she left New York and retreated to her home in Vermont. To insure her collection's future—she was adamant about keeping it intact—she asked her lawyer, Bill Price, to write a will leaving everything to the Museum of the University of Michigan on condition that it not be sold. After her death, most of it was indeed sold. She created the Florence Louchheim Stol Foundation, dedicated to supporting young artists, and named me director.

Not long after Florence settled comfortably into her farm house, the Vermont Yankee Power Company without advance warning built a large nuclear power plant on the lot adjoining her property. Florence was enraged yet felt helpless to combat the situation. Having run away from Manhattan because of a robbery in her apartment, she now felt cornered by a different kind of violence seemingly in her own backyard. Her errant behavior in Vernon was not conducive to enlisting sympathy or help from her neighbors.

After she died, Yankee Power bought her house for $48,000, and made it their Visitor Center. It came to resemble a Howard Johnson roadside cafeteria. Recently, I learned that the nuclear reactor was never used, that it leaked radiation, and now stands idle, its obtrusive machinery a curse on the land.

Florence was demanding, yet generous and appealing. She wanted no burial, grave, or ceremony to mourn her death. She asked that her ashes be left at the crematorium in Brattleboro, Vermont. A few years ago, the crematorium closed and called me to come and collect her ashes. I buried her in our family plot in Chatham, next to my father. She may never forgive me for doing that.

In 2012, forty five years after Aunt Florence's death, a professor of Spanish Literature at Boston University wrote me to request photographs and an opportunity to speak about Florence and her family. Professor Christopher Maurer explained that Florence had been the inspiration for an excellent book of poems by the Spanish writer, José Moreno Villa.

According to Maurer, Florence and José met in 1926 in Madrid, where Florence was studying. José, still a bachelor in his forties, was a prominent but modest painter and poet and Florence was a ravishingly beautiful twenty eight year old American girl with money and a Harvard educated taste in Spanish poetry and painting. In November of that year, they decided to marry and in February traveled to New York together with my father and his new bride, Katie. It was not surprising to read that reaching New York, Florence's parents forbade their marriage, and threatened to disown her if she married the penurious poet. José returned to Spain where he wrote the book of poems and several essays about their love affair. It seems that Moreno found American culture and Florence disturbingly unpredictable.

But Florence stayed with him, in a metaphorical sense. Memories of their affair inspired José Moreno to compose a cycle of 40 poems, published in 1929, entitled Jacinta la Pelirroja, (The Red Haired Hyacinth).

José wrote: *That girl [Jacinta, the American girl] is adorable. Besides her physical charms she has certain other inner charms that cast a spell. Tall and elastic, hard and soft, following certain laws of perfection, clean, caressed–rather than swaddled–by clothes thin as veils, with not even a distant memory of nightgowns, corsets, girdles or traditional women's clothing, she comes and goes, rises and falls with sure pulse, with no trembling, flaccid flesh, no trace of intellectual doubt. With a sort of gymnastic impetus she bursts in upon every aspect of life.*

MIRO PAINTINGS

My father was an early admirer of Joan Miro's work. After Florence hung Miro's paintings on my living room walls, he began to visit me more often, offering to buy them. In fact, I think he admired most of the art in Florence's collection. If there hadn't been such great enmity between them, Florence would, I'm sure, have put together a fine group of paintings for him, but his disapproval of her life made them adversaries. Harold Diamond, my friend and an astute art dealer, was also bidding on the Miro paintings.

Bud's debts had risen to a frightening level. And after some heavy borrowing from sympathetic friends, I felt forced to accept my father's offer of 200 shares of GEICO stock in exchange for the two Miro paintings. To this day, I have no idea why he offered stock instead of cash. GEICO, was a very new company, recently founded by his friend, David Kreeger. Months later, Geico stock fell, and I was left with 200 shares no one wanted. Ironically, today GEICO is a winner.

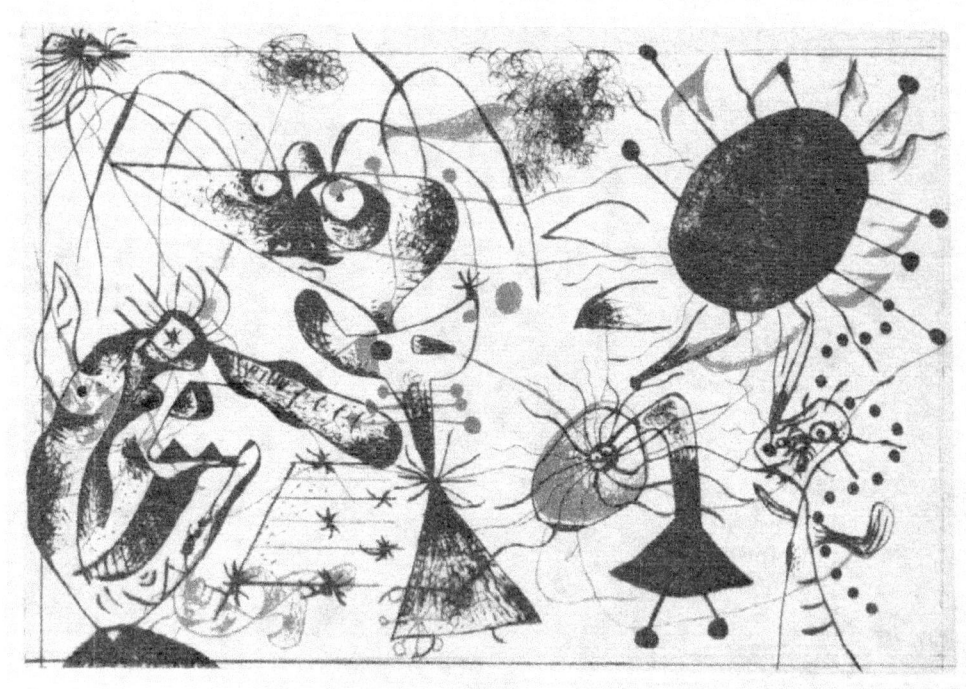

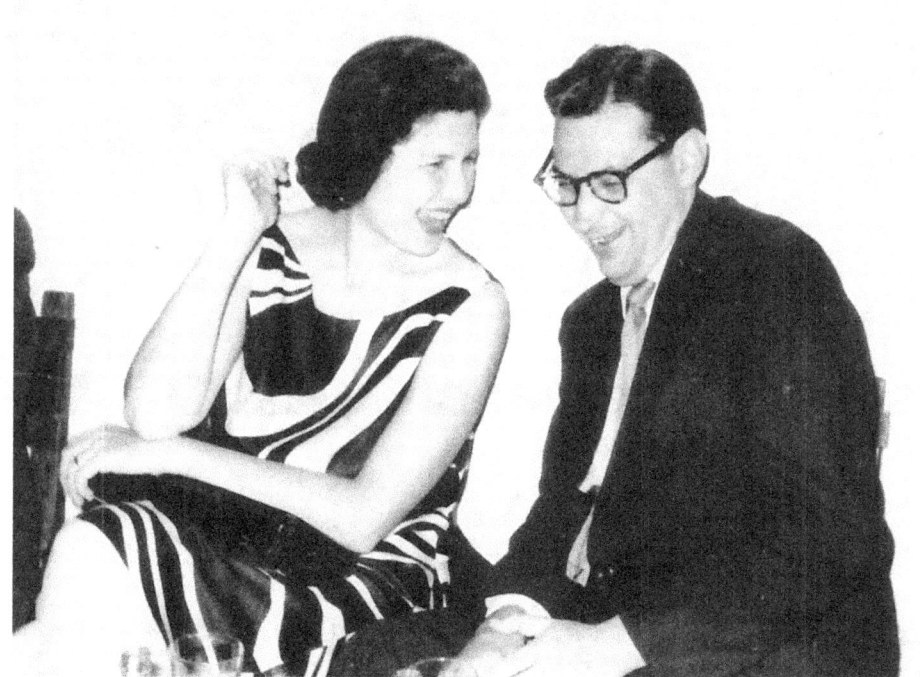

183

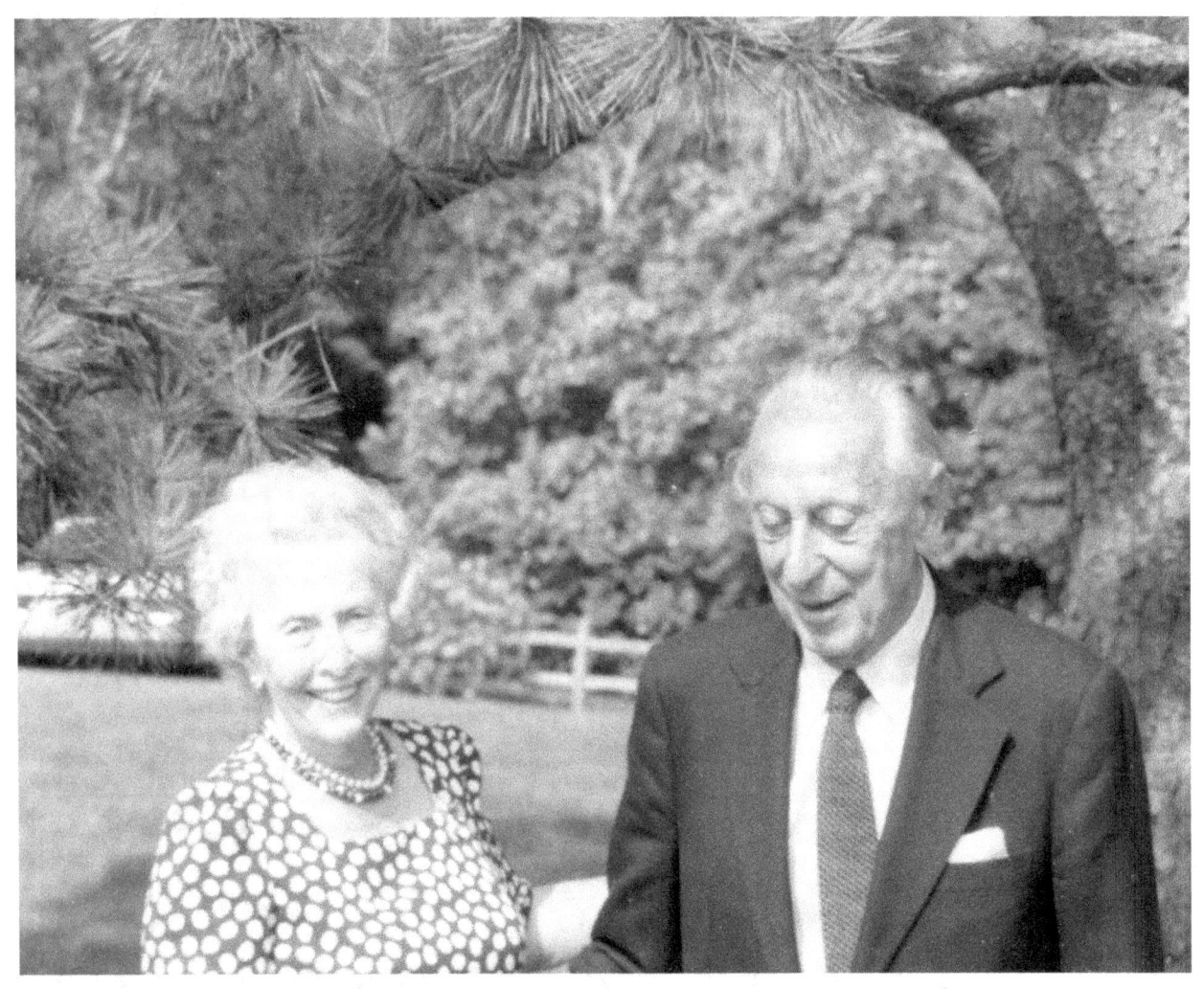

ABOVE:

Katie and Donald.

184

MORE SAD STORIES
KATIE AND DONALD

After my father died, my mother felt lonely in her big brick house and feared the crime wave that had recently hit Georgetown. Money trickled in more slowly, and a sense of poverty overcame her. She did not know how to balance a checkbook and learned from her accountant that Walter had done nothing to reduce the taxes on his estate, believing that the government was a most worthy recipient of his accumulated wealth. Overnight she became extremely frugal, repairing the living room wallpaper with Scotch tape and dismissing her staff, deciding to live in a state of shabby gentility. When Didi asked her why she only dated rich men, she replied, "for security."

THE INDISPENSABLE MAN

from "Observe the Lark"—Collected Poems, Random House, 1985

by Katie Louchheim

Small talk had a bank account, a car,
His dinner coat lapels were just as wide
As the careful smile he took such pride in.
At lunch, he wore old-school ties.

He had no party. Dems or Reps,
They came, they went, he stood on steps
Of hostess power the hour always eight.
Fluent in accents, he could celebrate

The rise and fall of nations small and great.
Protocol and wines, he knew by heart,
Fate alas, had shaped him for a minor part.
Being a man and single, raised him to an art.

On a trip to New York to visit her family, Katie met an old friend, Donald Klopfer, co-founder of Random House. Their families had summered on the Jersey shore, and as young married folk, they lived in the same building, 1112 Park Avenue. Donald had always been a ladies' man, elegant, worldly, aggressive and well connected in New York society. He ranked high with both married and widowed women.

Pat, Donald's wife, was bedridden with an obscure illness attributed to Donald having had an affair with her best friend. Soon after she died, Katie began coming to visit him in New York, each weekend leaving a few more of her things. Within a few months, encouraged by Judy's insistence that she could not "go on living with a man unless they were married"— a recurring mantra in our family—Katie and Donald held a wedding ceremony on the lawn in front of our house in Chatham. Shortly thereafter, heartbreak set in.

Katie assumed that her status as a political grande dame and Georgetown socialite would transport her, like a queen, into Donald's New York publishing world. In fact, no one in New York gave a damn about politics and Katie's financial assets seemed paltry compared to those of other women in Donald's life.

Donald saw Katie as an entrance into a whole new exciting, politically thriving Washington world, but this didn't happen. Katie arrived in Donald's life with her paintings and a phone book of names, most of whom had left the government and retired.

A very strong-minded interior decorator hired by Donald's wife had gussied up Donald's apartment. "There is no room to put any of my things," Katie complained, and resigned herself

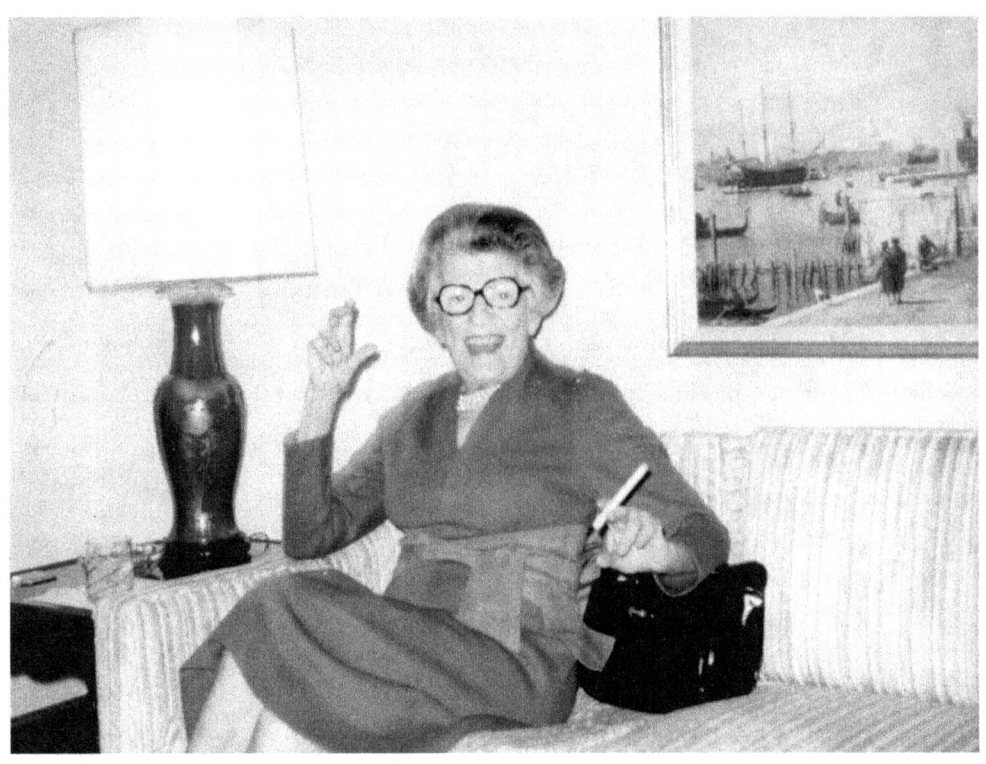

to hanging a few paintings on the celadon-colored walls. Her lifetime *leitmotif*—"gotta have a man"—had suddenly turned sour and imprisoned her in another woman's aesthetic.

Donald regretted his loss of privacy, and once he realized that Katie's VIP connections had evaporated (I always cringed when she did her name-dropping thing), their marriage cooled quickly.

Tempers flared. Katie, often tearful and cast aside, found escape in the commiserative arms of Aunt Louise Joseph**, eight blocks away. She was sorry that she had sold her beautiful Georgetown house for a pittance and that her Washington life was gone.

After Donald's death in 1985, Katie's health deteriorated. She lived on in his penthouse, alone, stricken with dementia, often sitting at her desk leafing through magazines in gestures reminiscent of her work days. Where were the six hundred recipients of her holiday cards?

**Aunt Louise Morgenthau Joseph connected to all of us in warm and wonderful ways. Vivacious, knowledgeable and elegant, the wife of Grandma Adele's older brother Hugo, Louise became a shoulder to lean on, always providing just the right amount of encouragement and advice. A lovely woman with style and reserve, she was also extremely forthright and an attentive listener, qualities we all admired.

KATIE GONE—TIG, AGAIN

Tig, my friend from Chatham summers, came back into my life, sadly only briefly.

My mother suffered in Donald's New York penthouse, alone, politically forgotten, her own sharp memory was a thing of the past. Visitors feared her blank stares. Occasionally, she would cry out, using obscene language. Judy and I argued frequently over her medical care, Judy insisting on a Christian Science approach. After living for several lonely years in this manner, she died alone.

On March 11, 1991, we held a memorial service for her at the Unitarian Church at Lexington Avenue and 80th Street. Ted Sorenson and Eugene McCarthy praised her achievements for women, and cousin Tom Louchheim**, a rabbi, led us in prayers. A mezzo-soprano sang one of Richard Strauss's *Four Last Songs*. Katie had always loved *Rosenkavalier*.

The service was attended by political multitudes. I looked around the church and wondered where all these people were when Katie was sick and alone. Instead, they came to be seen, to gawk at Jacqueline Kennedy and the Moynihans sitting in the back row. Frances read one of Katie's poems with great feeling. I couldn't help contrasting the sadness that filled the church with her Washington merry-go-round life where she played such a vital and lovable role in the lives of so many.

**Tom and his wife, Marcia, named their daughter Katie after my mother. She would have been pleased.

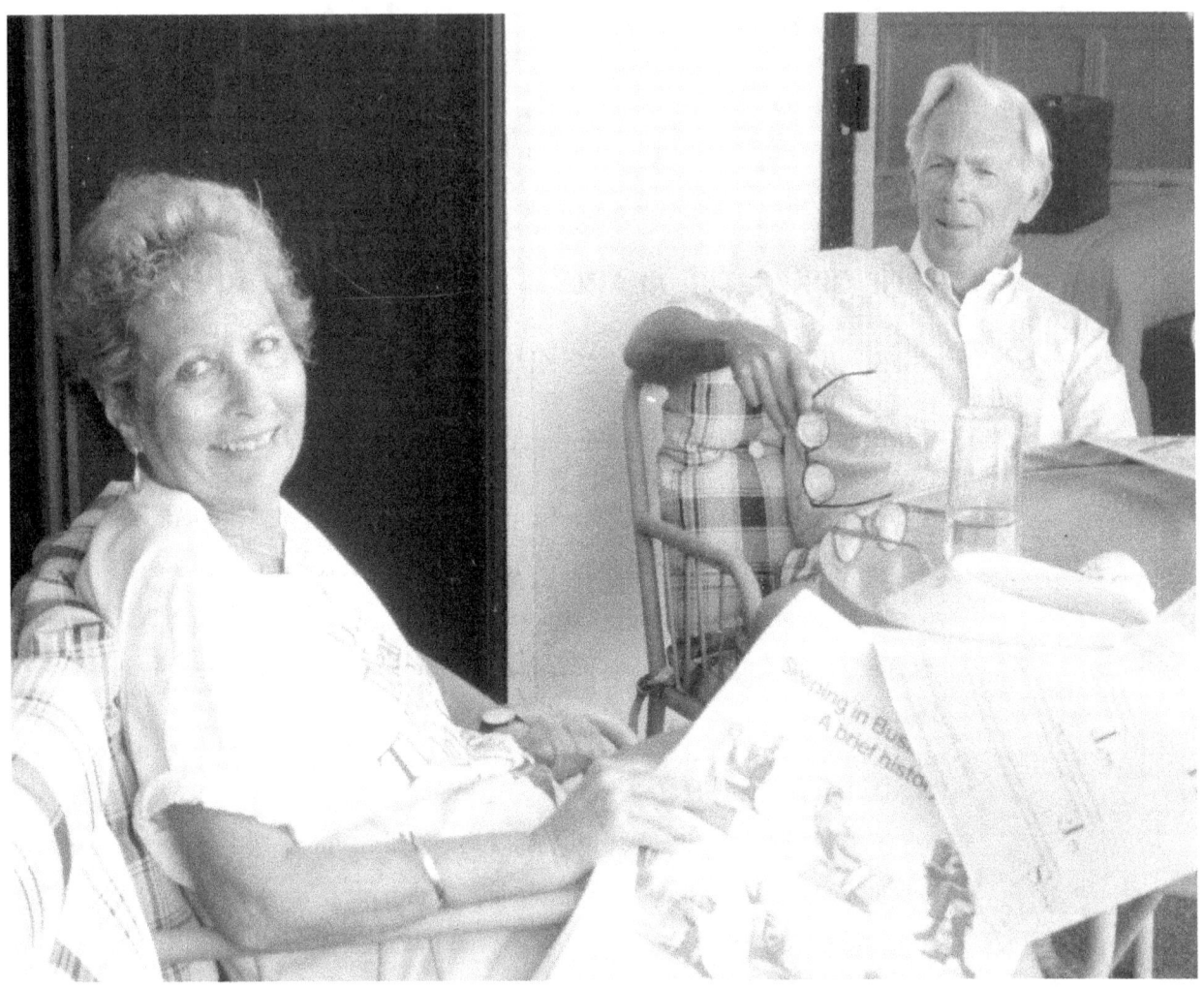

Just before the service began, an usher handed me an envelope. I recognized the handwriting, a backward slanting half-print, half-script. Henry "Tig" Woodland had read of Katie's death in the *New York Times* and sent his condolences, reminding me of her strong opposition to our friendship and asking if we could meet for lunch. My parents had enjoyed lively dialogues on political candidates and issues with Tig, a Republican, but felt that his smoking and barefoot presence were disrespectful.

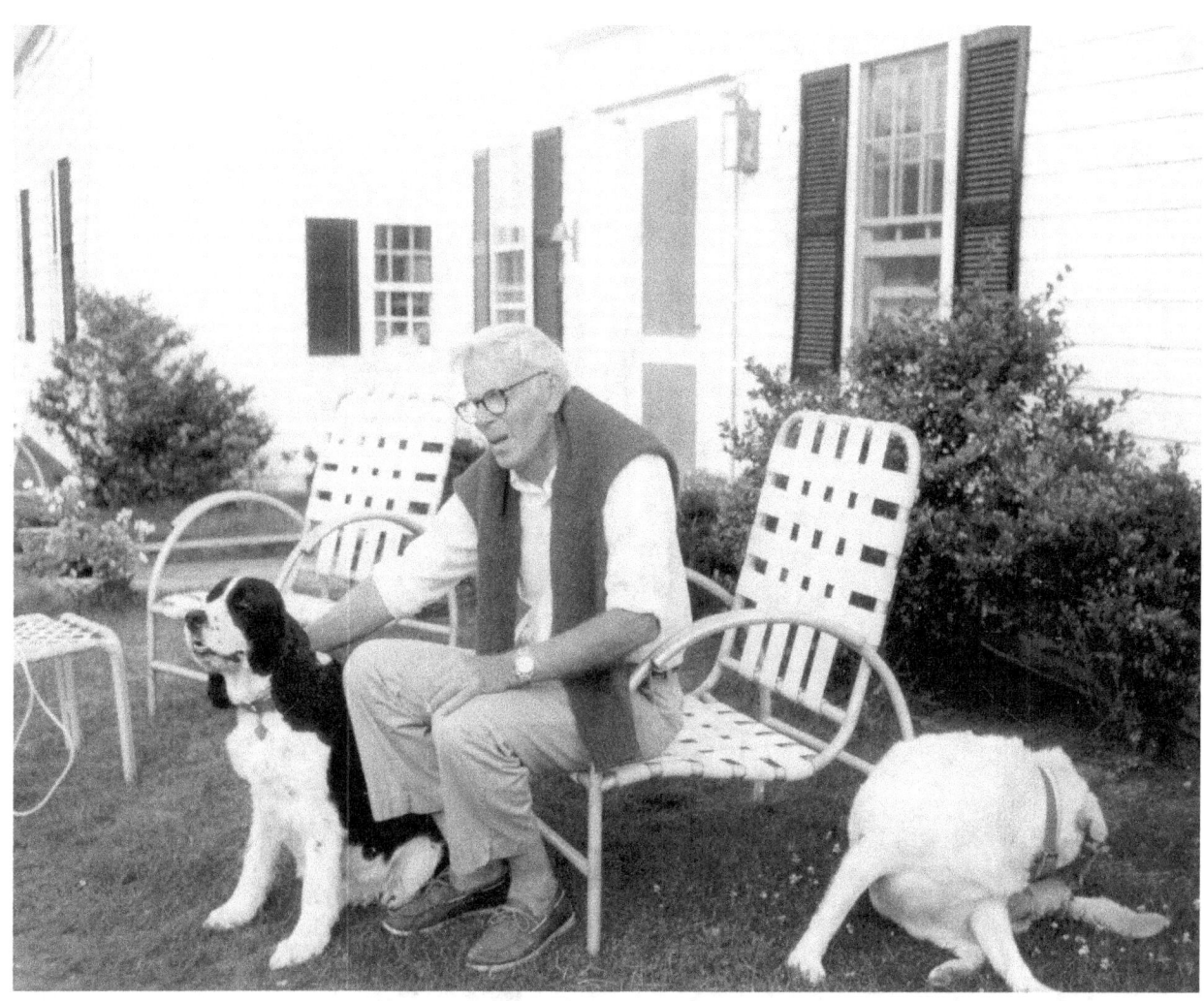

ABOVE:
Tig with his dogs.

Remembering the good times we shared, I boarded the Plymouth & Brockton bus to Fall River, where we milled about the terminal looking for each other. We hadn't connected in more than 30 years. Soon, though, I was in his jeep along with his three dogs, speeding toward his house in Newport.

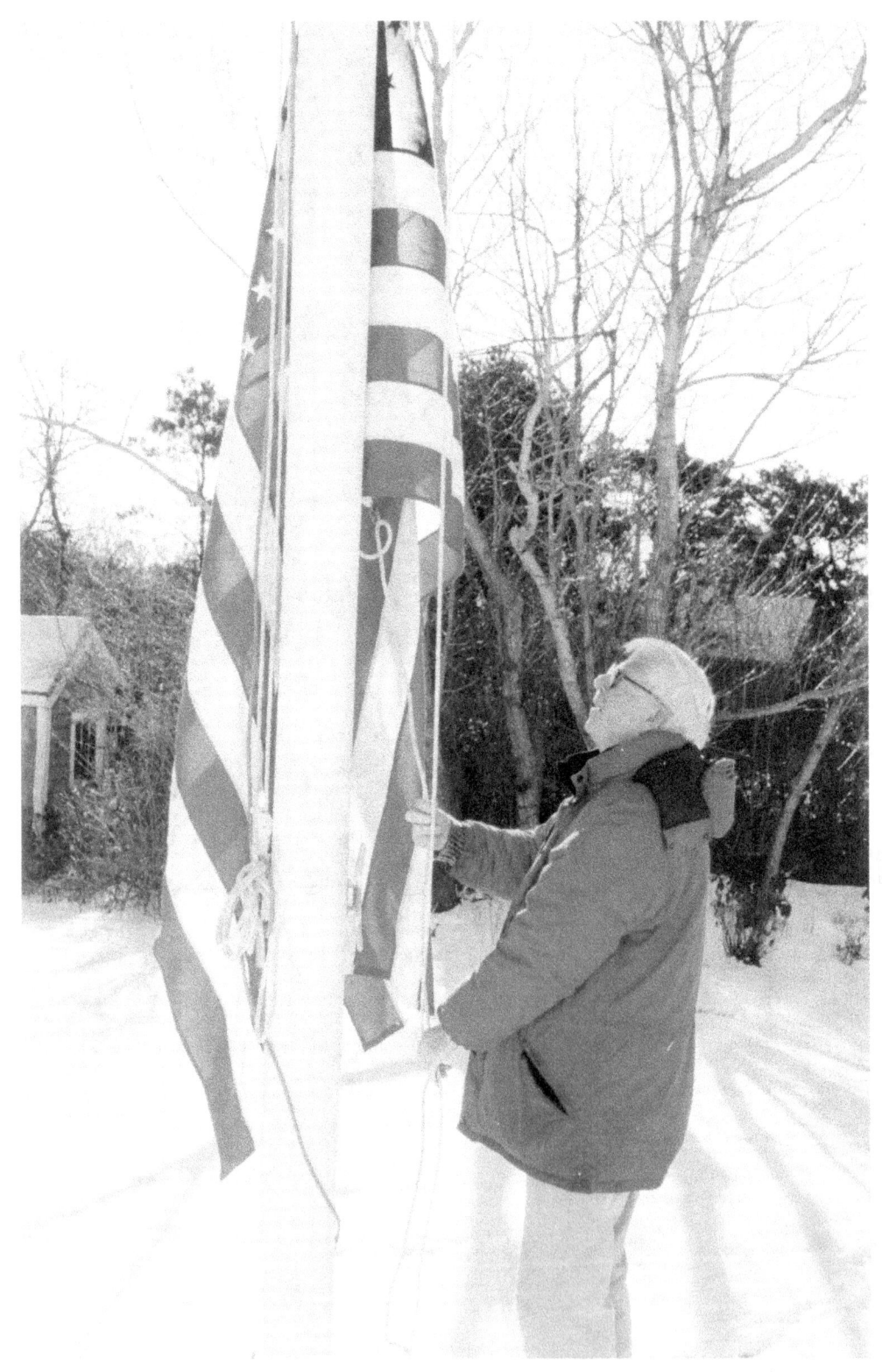

LEFT:

Tig raising the flag.

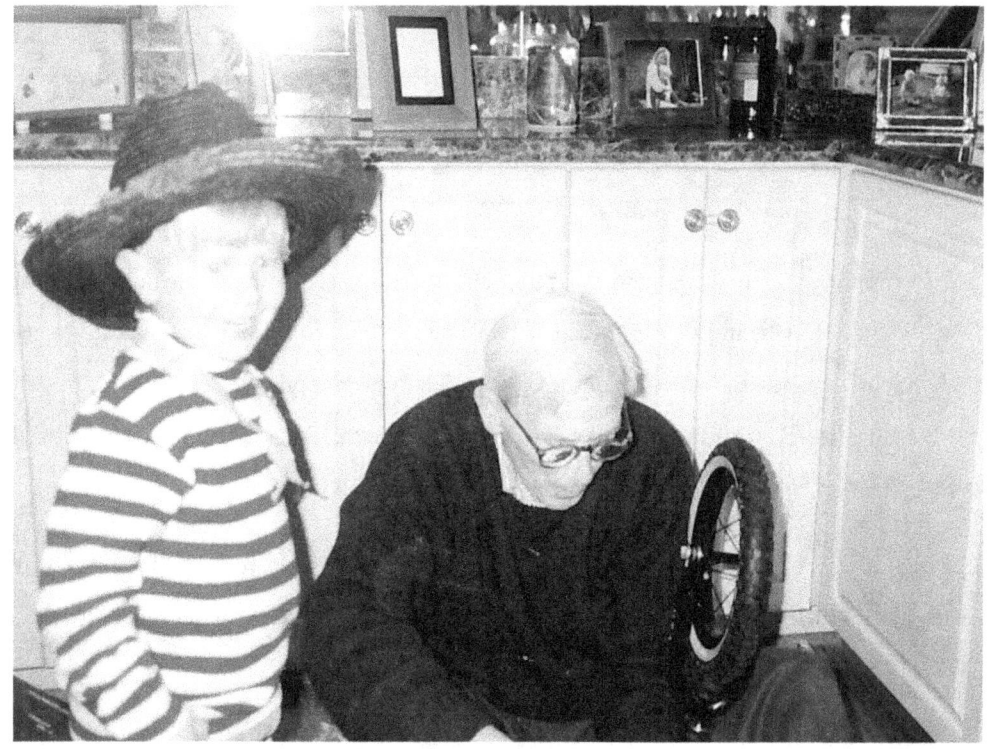

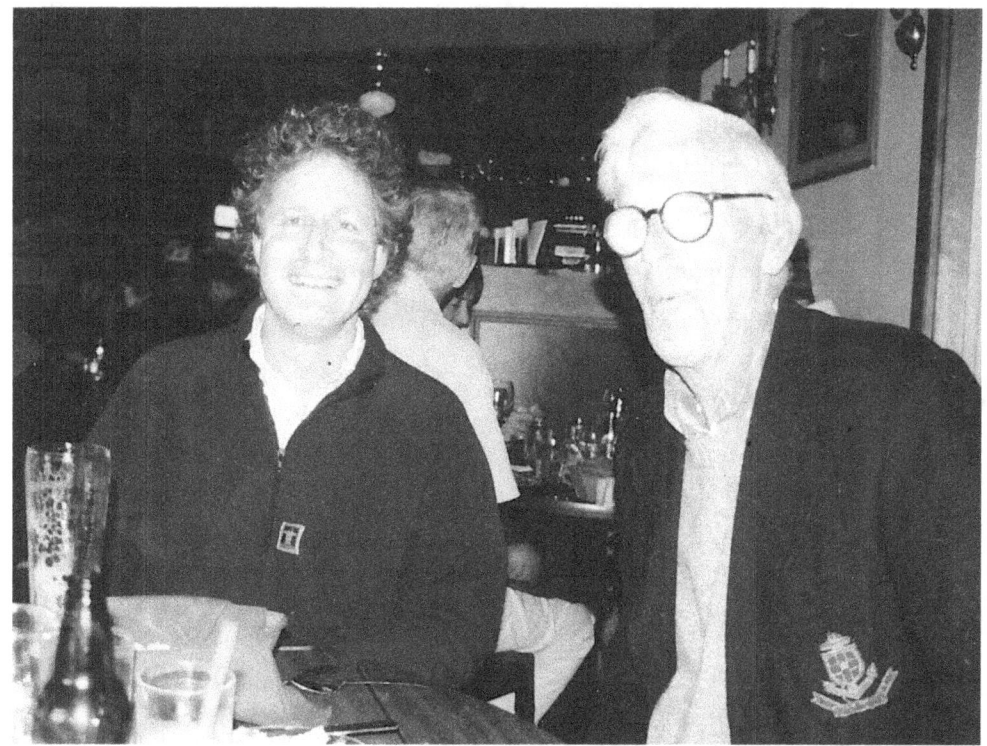

Still loving the sea, Tig kept a powerboat in Newport Harbor for visits to his mother, Edith Woodland Bliss, living in Edgartown. She had taken to serious drinking after the death of her husband and sometimes lost consciousness. Edith had never approved of me, Tig's "Jewish friend." She died shortly after we met again. Within a month, Tig and his three dogs arrived at Stage Harbor Road, where we lived for the remainder of his life.

Leafing through old photographs, we learned that Tig's great-grandparents, Willard and May Sears, had lived in our house on Stage Harbor Road, one hundred years earlier. Although Willard** had built a sea captain's mansion bordering Stage Harbor, his wife, May, had objected to the chilly Northeast winds that frequently blasted through the less than airtight windows, and they had moved inland to 482 Stage Harbor Road. What a coincidence!

Another of Tig's relatives—his great grandfather, Francis Scott Key—wrote the lyrics for *The Star Spangled Banner*. Perhaps as a symbol of their relationship, Tig installed a gigantic flagpole in our garden, making the raising and lowering of the flag a part of his daily routine. A heavy smoker, Tig suddenly fell ill. When he was taken by ambulance to Mt. Sinai Hospital in New York one winter night, I was unable to ride with him, my fear of hospitals and medical procedures overriding my concern for his wellbeing. Cotton came from San Francisco, a great comfort to both of us. Tig died on March 1, 2001—a sad spring for all who loved him.

**Willard Sears was architect of the Isabella Gardiner Museum in Boston.

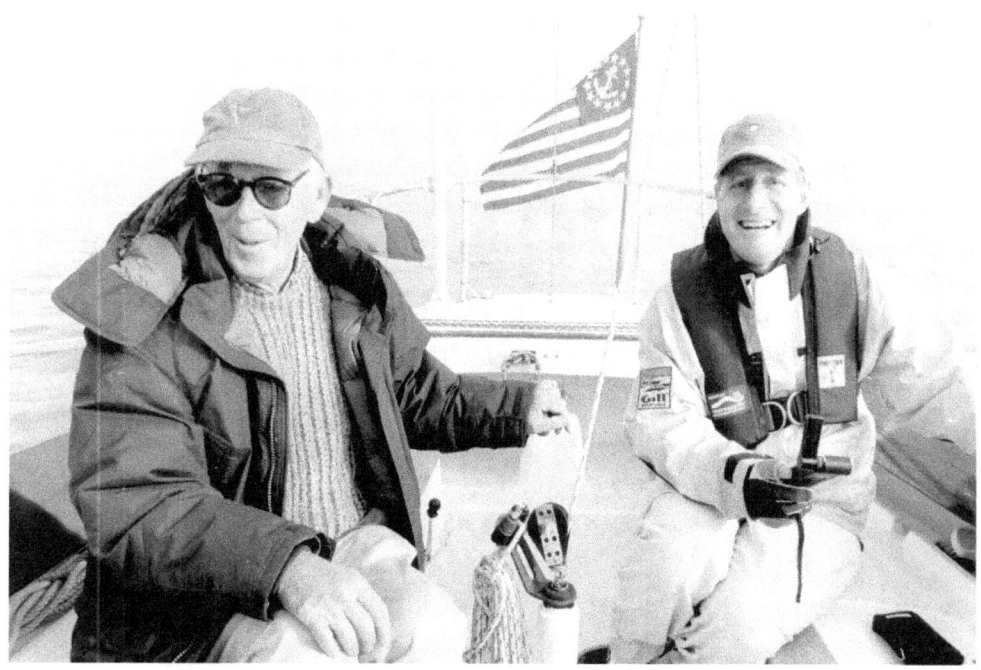

I wrote two poems following his premature death:

A MEMORY

Were our first times better?

We crossed Monomoy—our bare feet squishing through marshes

The sun so strong it burned the insides of our bodies

We fished, we sailed and planned a future.

Or was it forty years later

We encountered each other, partially

Damaged, but still whole

Or is it now ,when what remains are

Memories—the bad parts deleted

Your death, my going on.

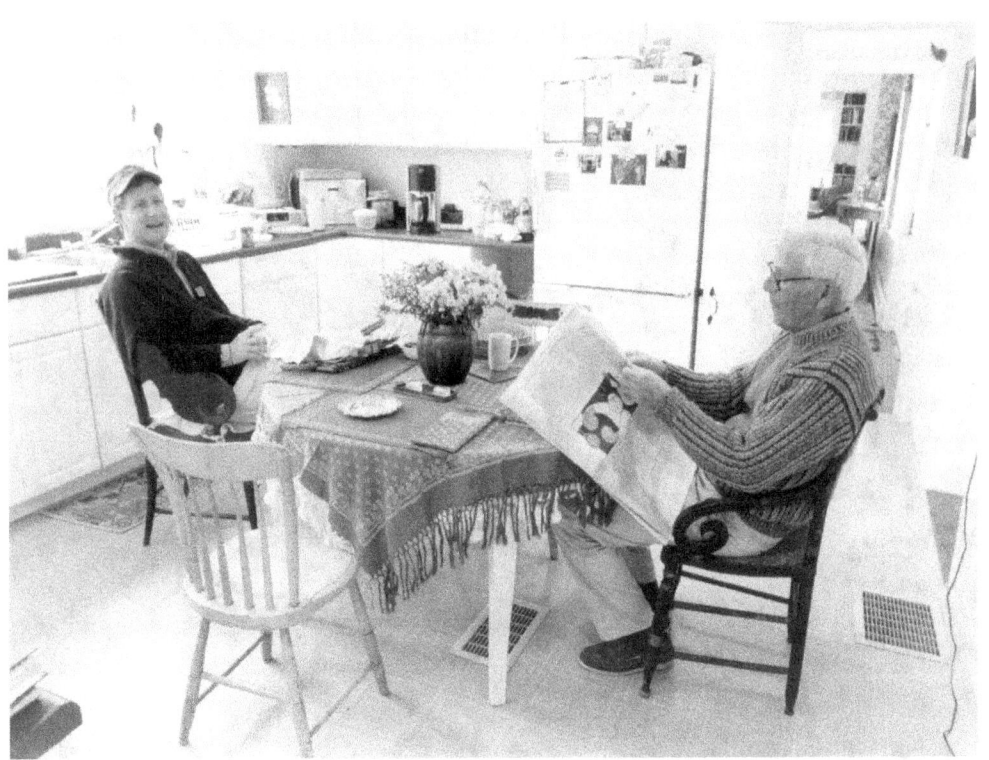

LEFT OVER WOMEN

What's to become of us leftover women?

Like a dish prepared for too many guests we wait to be

Consumed by maybe a late arrival?

In the great master plan, the one we learned at school, there were to be some of each

but were there supposed to be an equal number and were there really to be so many left over?

The women sit in tight rows, legs crossed hair neatly coiffed

Someone will come for them

They look at their watches

Someone is late

Perhaps, they have lost their collective way

"Tig"

I know where Tig is right now.
He's got one hand looped over the steering wheel,
And the other clasping an ice cold Coke,
His eyes are peering through his thick rimmed glasses,
As he makes out the boats in his new harbor.

I know where Tig is right now,
He's building a perfect warm fire as the winter wind howls outside,
Patiently fetching one log after the next,
Then moving toward his chair and sitting,
As he takes one last look to check its flame.

I know where Tig is now,
He's settling into his high backed chair,
Sandy and Eddie lying contented and quiet at his feet,
As he settles into a new good book,
And heaves a quiet sigh.

I know where Tig is now,
He's helping some kids assemble some newfangled
Toys, patiently finding the way through garbled
Directions as he uses his uncommon common sense to
Help.

I know where Tig is now,
He's right here with us,
Looking out over the pier,
Remembering some childhood stunts, running wild with the McClay's,
Of his carefree and barefoot sand torn years of childhood on the Cape.

I know where Tig is now,
He's in our hearts as we remember him with love.

May 12, 2001

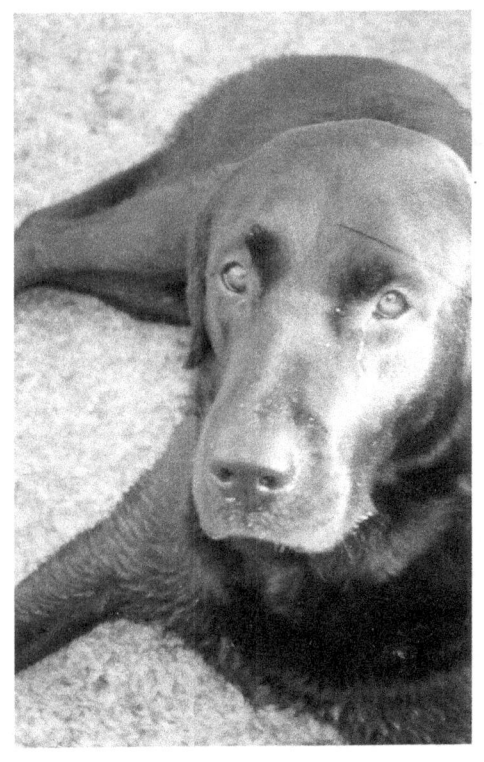
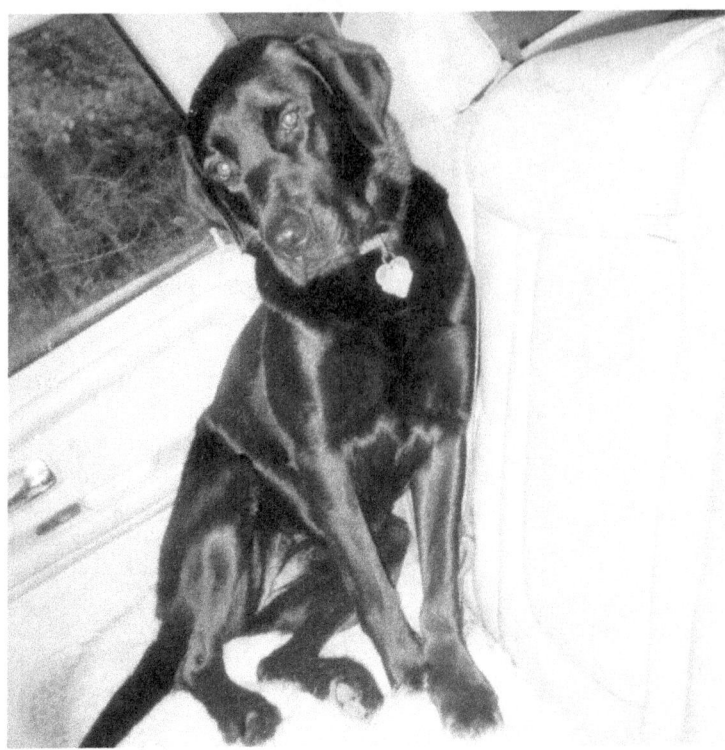

LUCY, A.K.A MICKY-MY-LIFE

We had become a dog family, loving Scout, Frances's Labrador, a famous squirrel hunter. It seemed natural to have a Labrador in our lives. Didi's Tessie, a cherished Border Collie, spread joy and happiness, as did Java, a loving companion to Calder and Saskia. After our hard times, Frances believed that a dog would make everything better and chose Lucy, born behind Ocean State Job Lot in Chatham from a litter of eleven Labrador pups.

Lucy warmed our hearts as she took over the living room couch and dominated our schedule. She uncomplainingly endured our weekly five-hour trips between New York City and the Cape. On city streets and Chatham beaches, she commanded attention. Her sweet nature and handsome appearance attracted many Central Park dog owner friends, who for love of Lucy, contributed generously to my art exhibitions.

JUDY, MY SISTER

Her Slide Into Darkness and Secrecy

Judy had always been the "good child," obedient, submissive, and bright. Her fear of falling into parental disfavor gave me the freedom to be rebellious. I encouraged her to break away, but our parents' hold on her was too strong.

She ran errands, filled in at dinners, attended Christian Science services with her father. As a child, she would rise early Sunday morning, don her Liberty silk print dress, a pink velvet sash loosely tied around her waist, a dainty purse holding the collection dollar and wait, patiently for him by the front door. Even though the stock market wasn't open on Sunday, my father could never leave for church without checking the price of Dupont, which he had fortuitously bought when it was at seven. He also followed IBM, although he hadn't had the courage to buy shares in the rising company. He seldom took risks. His oft-heard advice was "buy and hold."

Judy accepted Christian Science's tenets—God is Love, there is no sickness—like the gold star Sunday school student that she became. She was the reincarnation of Mary Baker Eddy.** She made her father very proud.

Katie's diary confirms the wiles she and Walter exerted to end Judy's engagement to Paul Matisse in 1952. Paul had insulted Katie by calling her breakfast table "bourgeois" when he spotted a Lazy Susan at the center. Katie, retaliating, referred to Paul's long hair as "delinquent."

**Mary Baker Eddy was the founder of Christian Science.

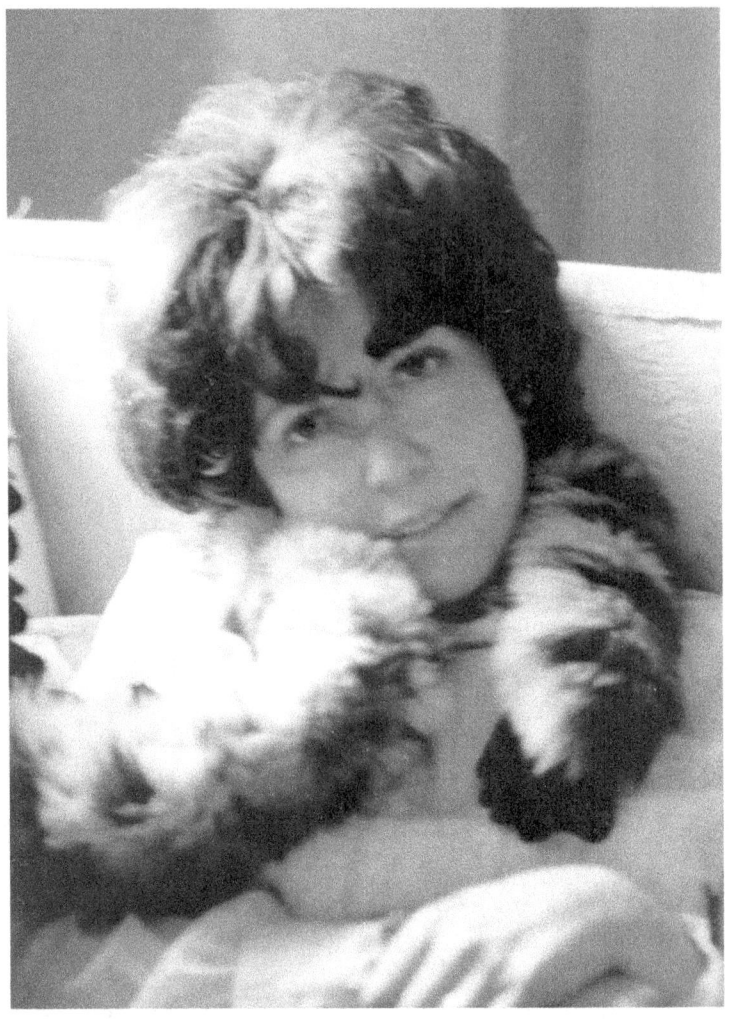

Years later, I received a note from Paul Matisse thanking me for clarifying the mystery of their sudden breakup, saying that he still had "very affectionate" memories of the Judy he once "knew and loved" and could "still easily remember the night they met, and the happiness." My parents had successfully ended the relationship. Katie claimed that Paul had no visible means of support, only the Matisse name he had inherited from his grandfather.

Katie also did not like Judy's attachment to Paul's mother, who was married to the French Dadaist, Marcel Duchamp. It was a situation grand with problems. Judy loved her mother.

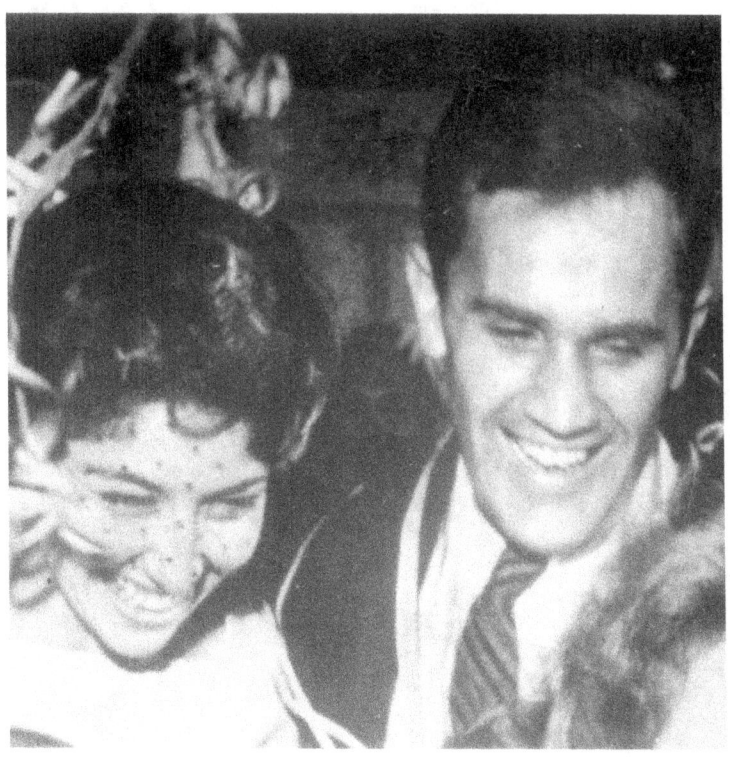

Judy loved Paul. Judy retreated back to Georgetown and married another Paul, Paul Sitton, an obliging and docile government employee from Atlanta, Georgia, Katie's choice.

Paul Sitton had a good job working for Phillip Handler, Director of the National Academy of Science. He and Judy dutifully bought a house in Georgetown, a few blocks away from my parents. Their marriage lasted seven years. They had no children. Paul died of AIDS and Judy became seriously committed to Christian Science, which made her father very happy. She had always identified with her father and, like him, knew exactly how she wanted to live and could not be moved from her course. Nestled in this caring faith, she found contentment.

In 1972, Judy met and secretly married another Southerner and fellow Christian Scientist, Dudley Haupt. In 1988, they moved to Darien, Connecticut, and devoted themselves to gardening.

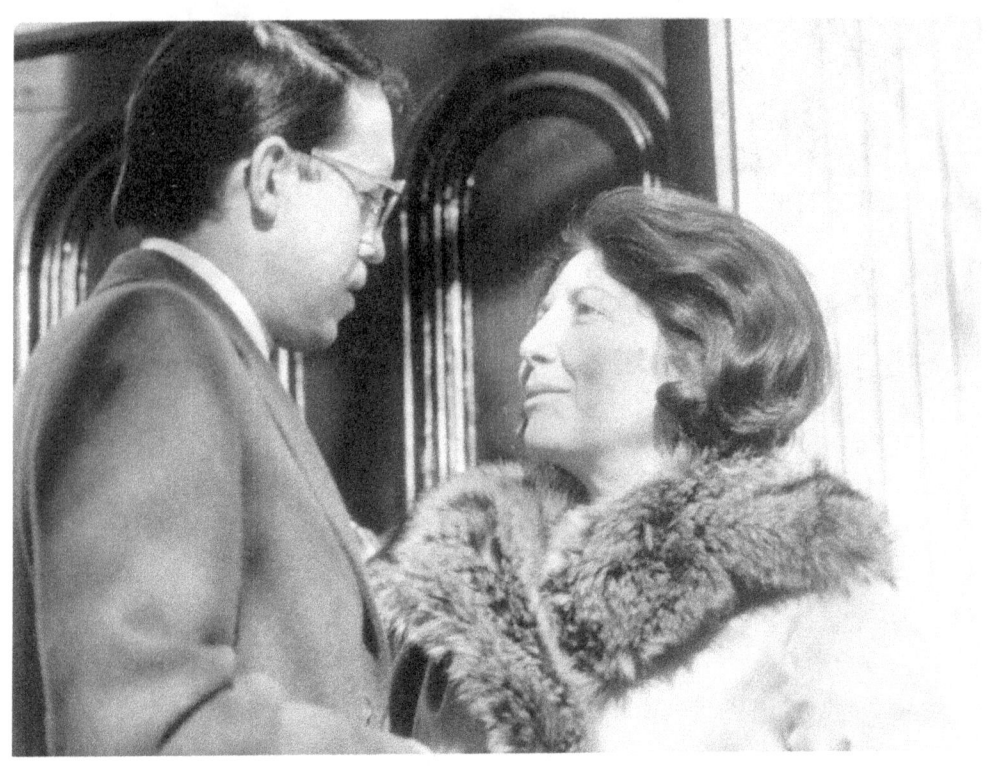

Judy and Dudley Haupt.

One year later, Dudley died very quietly, secretly—had he been sick?

Judy had given no indication that he was suffering. When I visited them in Darien, word came through Judy that Dudley was too busy to see me. I later learned that his mother, Lydia, had flown from Louisville, to read Christian Science teachings to him, and sat by his bedside and prayed. No doctor was called.

As a widow, in Darien, Judy was isolated, lonely and extremely vulnerable, totally separated from her Washington life. Judy and Dudley had never socialized in Darien.

Raymond Beegle, founder of The New York Vocal Arts Ensemble, rescued Judy from her Darien doldrums when he enlisted her help in contacting the press. He reported that she was able to book an appearance for his Ensemble on the Charlie Rose show—quite a coup.

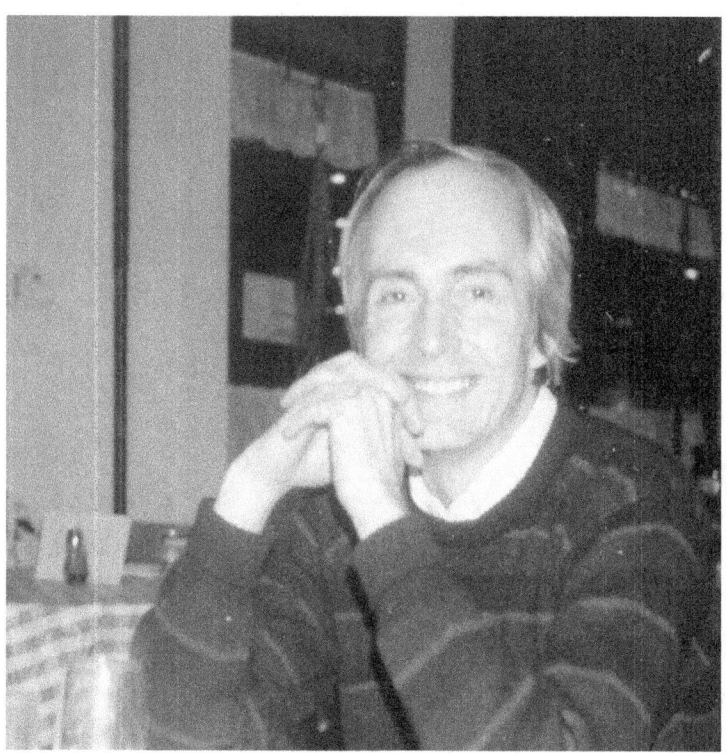

Raymond told me recently that he still missed Judy, remembering her "beautiful dark speaking voice with much laughter in it. There was always excitement and merriment in our conversations, which were often about angels, birds, music, God and her vegetable garden. She loved angels. I believed that she tried to look like Mary Baker Eddy or at least resemble her in all the pictures. She was pencil thin, and seemingly had no kinship to gravity, as if she could float from one place to another. I often felt that she was like a bird caught in a room, fluttering in a confined space—even when she was out of doors."

At a Christian Science church service in Darien, one Sunday, Judy met Claggett Read who generously offered to modernize her kitchen. Their romance developed into a happy marriage. Judy's acceptance of Christian Science prevented her from consulting doctors and shortly after their wedding, a large sore developed under her eye.

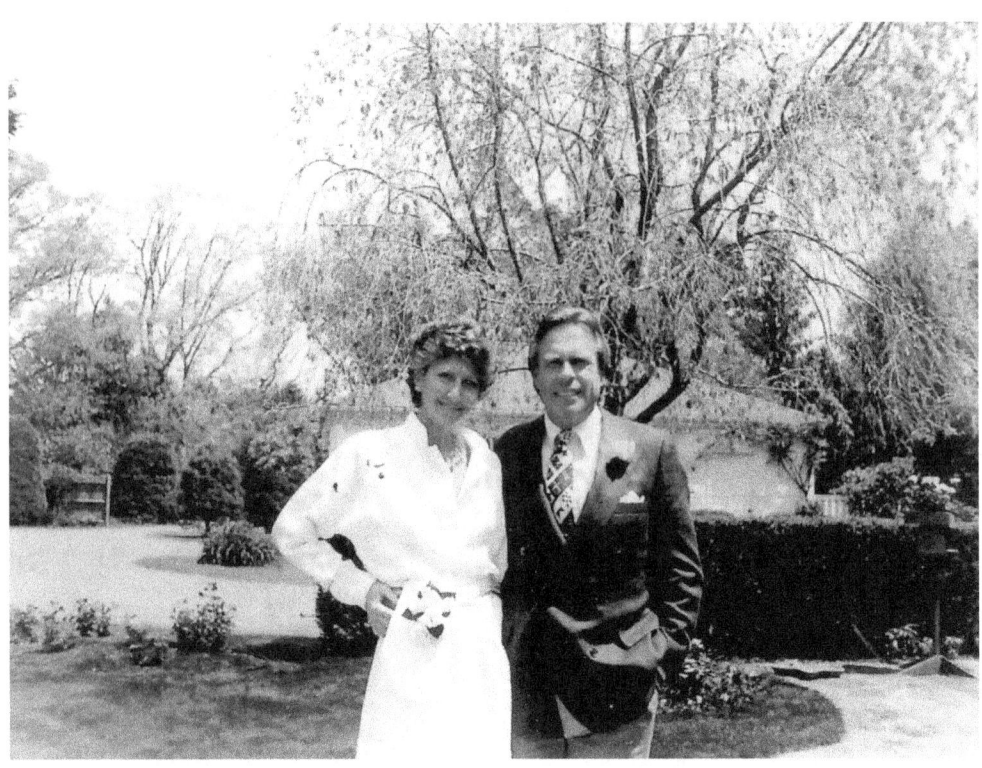

As the melanoma became unwieldy, she covered her cheek with a bandage and Hollywood-size sunglasses. I quizzed her on this masquerade and she withdrew, often refusing to see me. When Tig and I walked her around her bedroom, she was unable to stand on her own.

Judy passed away quietly at her home in Darien. Holding fast to Christian Science precepts and her father's commitment to the religion, she never consulted a medical doctor. She was 62 years old. A phone call from Claggett told me, "Our dear Judy has found her place in heaven." I remembered my grandmother Adele's words to Katie: "Your dear father is now at peace in heaven and looks down on you, lovingly."

Why hadn't I managed to get Judy to a doctor? I searched for a therapist to help. Though Judy's intense suffering was self-imposed, I came to feel responsible for her death.

204

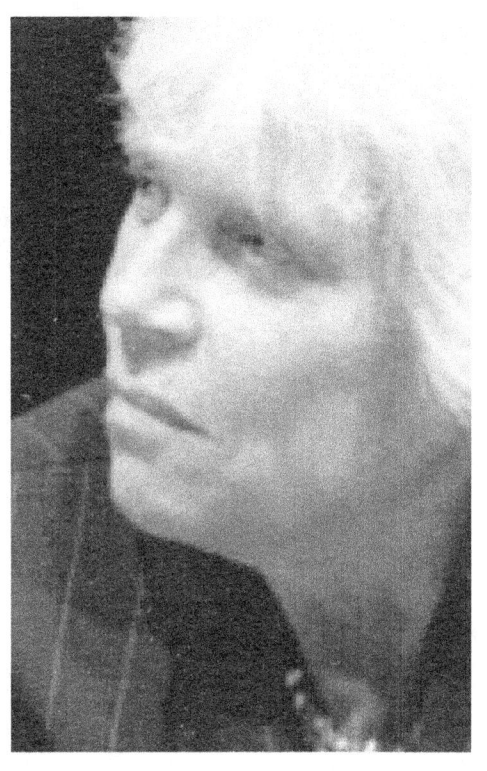

ABOVE:
Elizabeth Young-Bruehl.

BELOW:
*Elizabeth Fry, counselor at
National Cathedral School.*

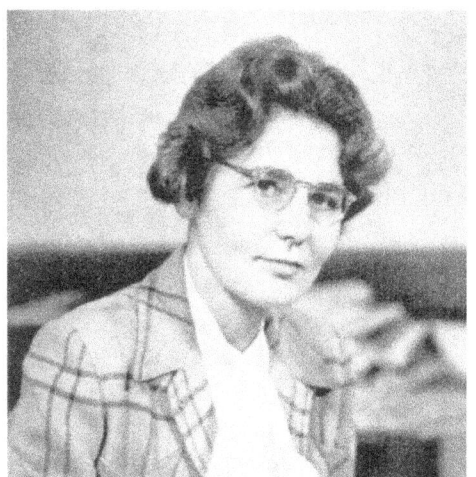

ELIZABETH YOUNG-BRUEHL

In a *New York Times* group photo of some visiting psychiatrists, one woman caught my eye, in many ways resembling a counselor at the National Cathedral School who had shown interest in my studies and in me. Both women had stern but friendly faces. I tracked her down.

Unpretentious, with a warm easy laugh, Elisabeth Young-Bruehl helped me to put things in perspective. Judy's intense suffering was self imposed by holding to her religious beliefs. Elizabeth helped me with another personal loss when Tig died five years later. Elisabeth was both accessible and reserved. She had published outstanding biographies of Hannah Arendt and Anna Freud, two women she held in high regard, and was at work on a study about *childism*—prejudice against children—when she died.

Her death, from an embolism was a great loss to me, as it was for the many others who crowded New York University's School of Law for a memorial celebration of her life.

FROM ISRAEL TO PALESTINE

ArtPalestine

Cousin Wally Marks, in Los Angeles, invited a group of his synagogue friends to help support ArtPalestine, a non-profit organization I put together on my return from Israel. Wally's check for $10,000 gave me the moral and financial boost I needed to move forward. Sadly, he died within a year of our meeting.

In January, 2009, *First Person*, an exhibition of contemporary Palestinian artists, opened at the Jerusalem Fund Gallery in Washington, D.C. Newly-elected U.S. President Barack Obama attended. I had worked on his 2008 presidential campaign, phoning, ringing doorbells, even making soapbox speeches on New York City subway platforms, always accompanied by our Labrador Lucy. Maybe stopping at my exhibition was his way of showing appreciation.

In July of 2009, Michael Connor and I co-curated *The Thousand and One Nights*, an exhibition of Palestinian artists, at Postmaster Gallery on 19th street, in New York. Artists Shadi Habib Allah, Sharif Waked, Jumana Manna, Hannah Farrah, Taysir Batniji, Hani Zurob, and Shuruq Harb participated. Crowds spilled onto the sidewalk. Several artists made good New York connections, two with the Guggenheim Museum.

Then in April of 2014, I brought together nineteen Palestinian art works from Israel's West Bank and the Diaspora in an exhibition at White Box gallery. I called it *How Green was my Valley*, borrowing the title from an MGM film of the same name.

Our website, www.artpalestine.org, registered 4,000 viewers a month.

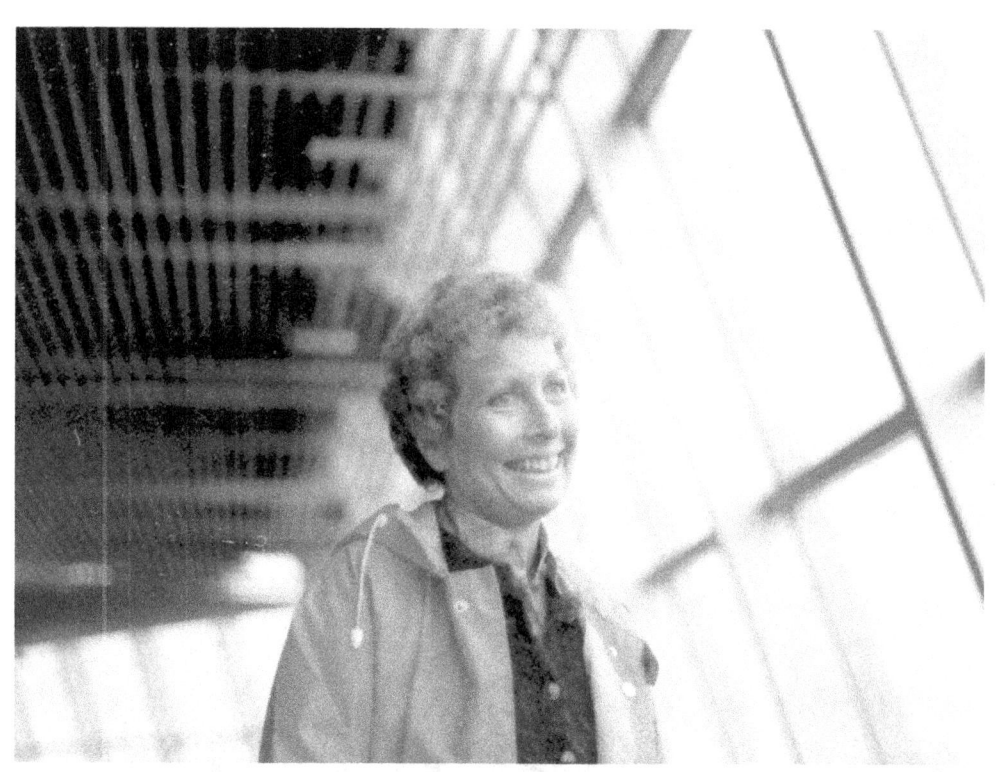

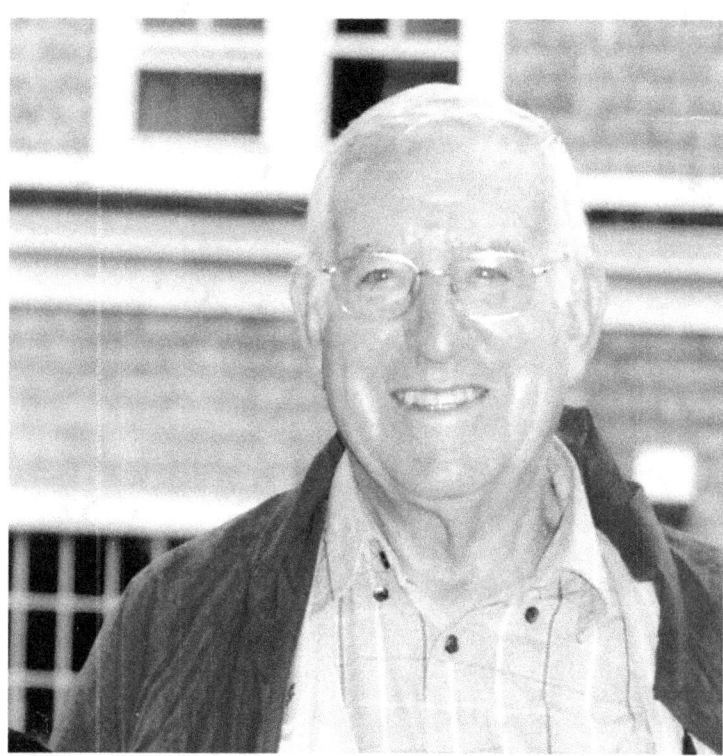

ArtPalestine
International

— an exhibition
highlighting a
new generation of
Palestinian artists

Whitebox
Art Center
329 Broome St.
New York, NY

How Apr 3
Green 2014
Was 5pm
My
Valley

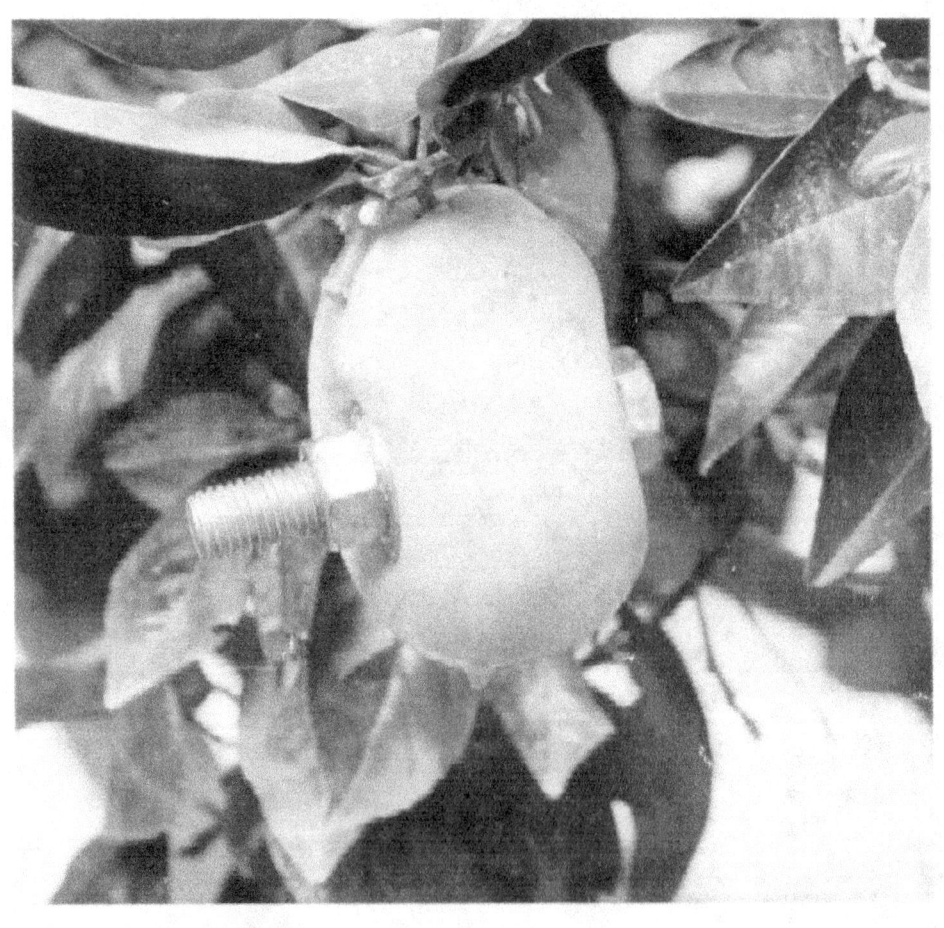

LEFT:

How Green Was My
Valley, featuring a
photograph by artist,
Mohammed Musallam
from Gaza.

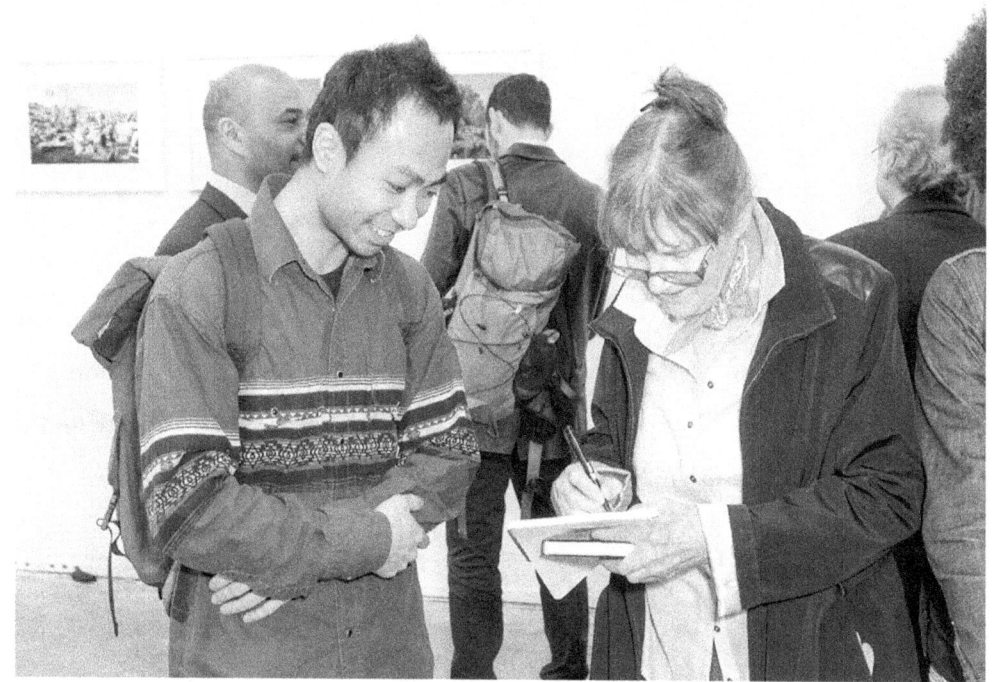

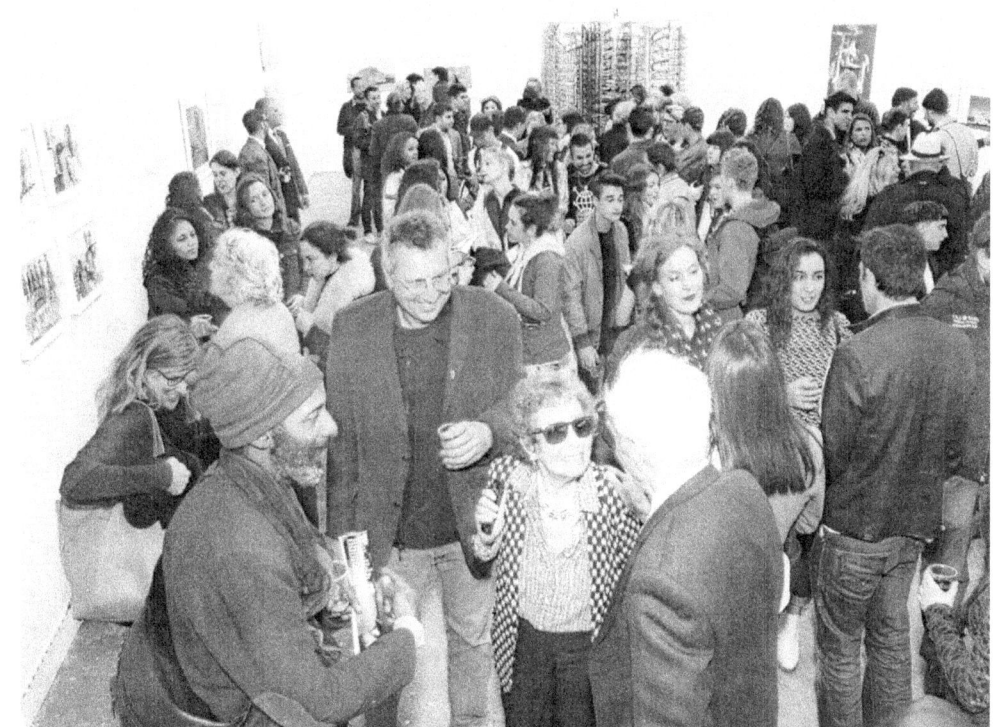

To round off this tale: my identity as a Jew seems to have twisted and turned, so that I'm finishing my life with a distancing from Judaism, not unlike the one my parents imposed on me. Although I am glad to have found my repressed Jewish identity, I find myself strongly opposed to Israel and its treatment of Palestinians. Identifying Israel with Judaism, Israel demands loyalty from American Jews; I do not think they deserve it. Israeli cruelty toward Palestinians has made Jewish identity uncomfortable for me.

MONEY DISASTERS: WIN SOME – LOSE SOME

Clover Hill

Ed Politi, a violinist friend, advised me to buy gold bars from Clover Hill, an alleged hotshot broker with Merrill Lynch, as a hedge against inflation. After a few months, Clover proposed other investment opportunities. Traveling back and forth between Israel and the U.S., I paid little attention to Clover's investments. Returning from Tel Aviv one night, I glanced at my Merrill Lynch account and saw that I had lost a very large chunk of money.

An arbitration suit against Clover, a black man, drew criticisms—I was accused of racial prejudice. The lawsuit dragged on for months and finally came before an arbitration board in Chicago. My lawyers managed to extract a huge fee for themselves before sending me the remainder.

BARRY BLOOM

Barry Bloom provided another example of my financial naivete. I met Barry at a dinner at the home of friends, George and Bernice Yazbek. Bernice was a phenomenal cook and invitations to the Yazbeks were rarely turned down. Their daughter Julianne and Frances were classmates at the Unitarian Church Nursery School and later the Chapin School. Today, by coincidence, they are neighbors in Cambridge, Massachusetts.

When Barry, my dinner partner, explained how his company, Cornell Capital, was renovating neighborhoods in New York City, and paying investors nine percent interest, I was intrigued, and invested. Monthly checks arrived with a certain regularity. I called George and Bernice to thank them for connecting me to this wonderful new source of income.

Something like six months passed when I next phoned Cornell Capital, only to be informed by a recording that the line had been disconnected. I trotted over to the office and found the door bolted and no sign of a human being. The story really ends there, although I was able to connect with a group of other disappointed investors who decided to bring a class action lawsuit against Barry. But what was the point? He had no money personally, and to sue the wind didn't resonate with me.

I swallowed hard and took another sizable loss.

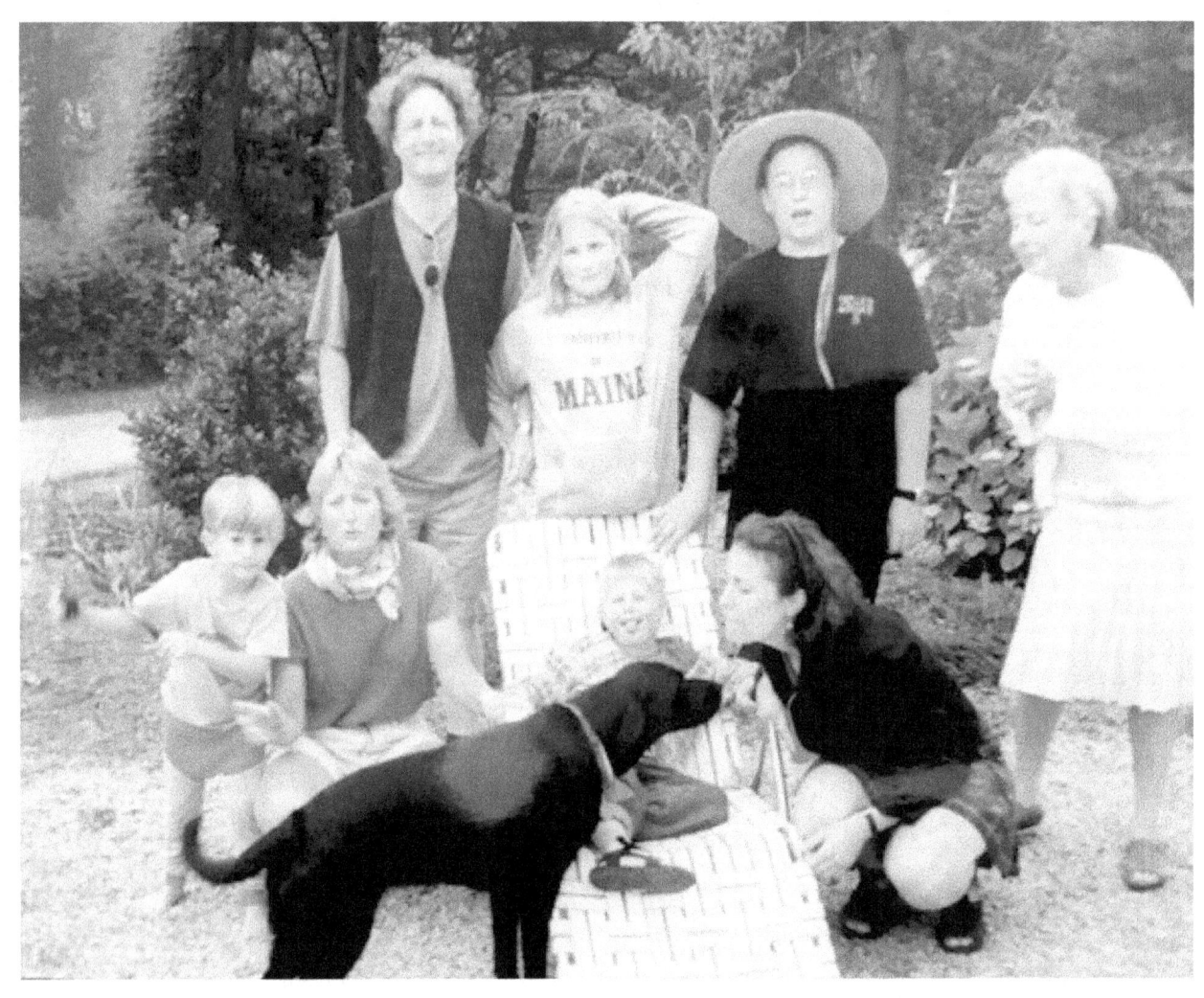

ABOVE:

*Me and my children and
their children.*

TODAY

Today, on New York City's Upper East Side, sidewalks are hosed by attentive doormen, and garbage is seldom left standing. Exotic flowers grow in fanciful tree boxes, and dog feces are rapidly removed by conscientious dog walkers like myself. After spending the first twenty-five years of my life in an apartment that faced brick walls, it's such a treat to look out my window and see cars and people—life happening.

I don't need to remember phone numbers. I can click my laptop or cell phone and order whatever I want. I can warm up dinners in a microwave oven and watch Larry David. I can read what critics have to say about movies and order my choices on Netflix without leaving my living room, Google anything I need to know without trudging to the public library. I can order food without pushing a cart around the A&P. H&M beckons with up-to-the-minute styles at giveaway prices. Imagine: $ 6.00 for a jacket, $ 2.00 for a pocketbook, $ 23.00 for a man's suit!

The #4, #5 and #6 subways take me downtown in minutes. Citibank's cash machines throw dollars at me, and I can swan around the corner to consult my doctors. Sunday on 86th Street is just another day. All shops are open. Churchgoers no longer dominate.

In my later years, I am relatively carefree. Can I compare my life with that of my Lauchheimer antecedants in Jebenhausen who needed a "shutzbrief," a permit, to travel from one village to the next?

IMPATIENCE

I am impatient, it's true. I have trouble waiting for doctors, trains, planes, dogs looking for their spot, children, friends who have lost track of time, elevators, supermarket checkout lines, violinists who lose their place in the music, people who say they will call right back and don't, waiters who see that we are ready to leave and don't bring the bill, people who start to tell an anecdote and never come to the end of it, movies that should have been edited, museum exhibitions that go on forever, traffic lights in Boston that change very slowly, conversations that have no beginning or end—and my own life, which seems to wind and curve.

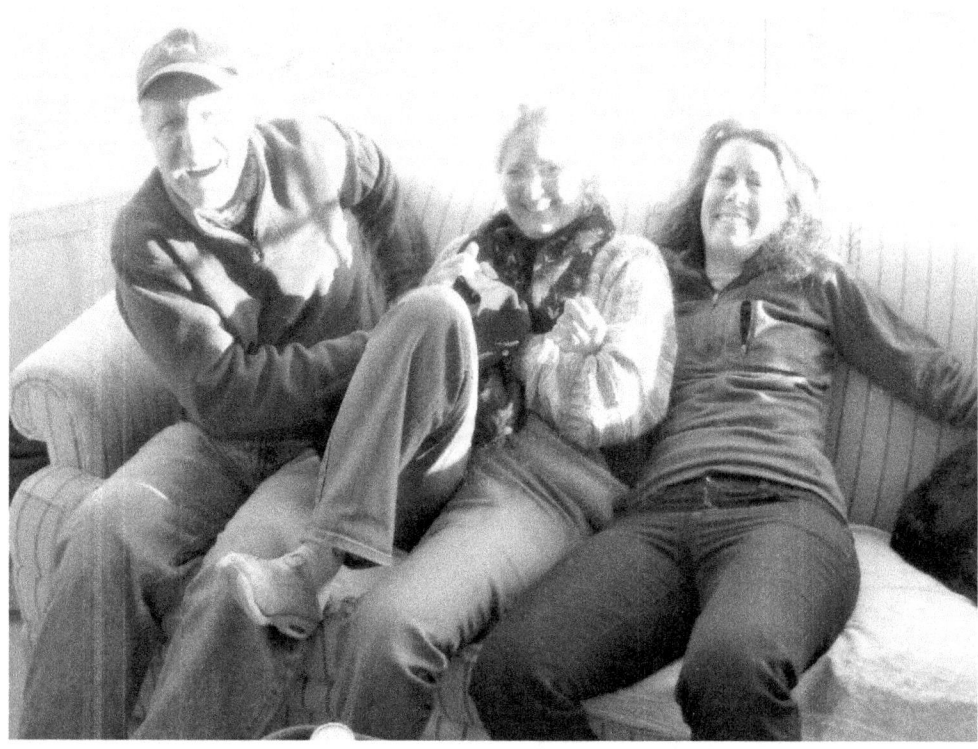

FAMILY TODAY – 2014

Did I succeed as a mother? I managed to carry out the pro forma duties—escorting my children to the park, the dentist, the pediatrician and birthday parties—but I lacked the necessary compassion and concern. I was distracted by trying to build a life for myself. Although I was more physically at home than my mother, I was sometimes emotionally absent, and although I cooked, my children insist to this day that they were raised on TV dinners.

I am a fortunate grandmother. Calder is a chef presiding over a San Francisco bistro, and Dr. Saskia a burgeoning design consultant in Glasgow. Ian and Graham Macnab have chosen careers in finance, following in Craig's footsteps and have already achieved a level of success most unusual for men so young.

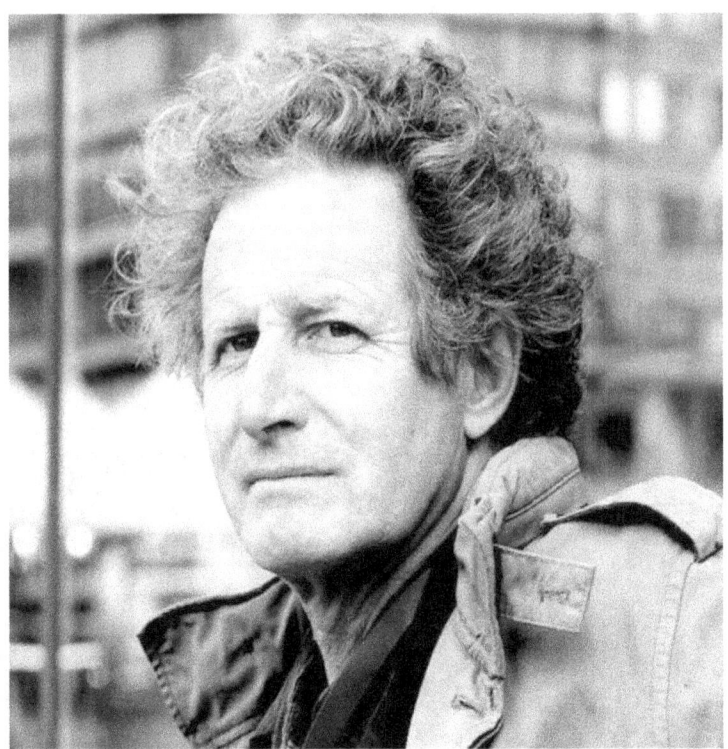

COTTON

From his earliest days as a preemie and victim of many childhood illnesses, Cotton surmounted both his physical challenges and the psychological problems brought on by two immature parents. Despite the negative attitudes I infused in him—"photography is a hobby, not a career" and other such untruths—he became a highly skilled and successful professional photographer.

Cotton led me through the crashing sounds of the Beatles, the drilling regimen of the Knickerbocker Greys, the psychedelic colors on his walls, and the Lycée Français, translating Latin into French. When his photos of the Orkney Islands came to the attention of editors at National Geographic, Cotton's future was secured.

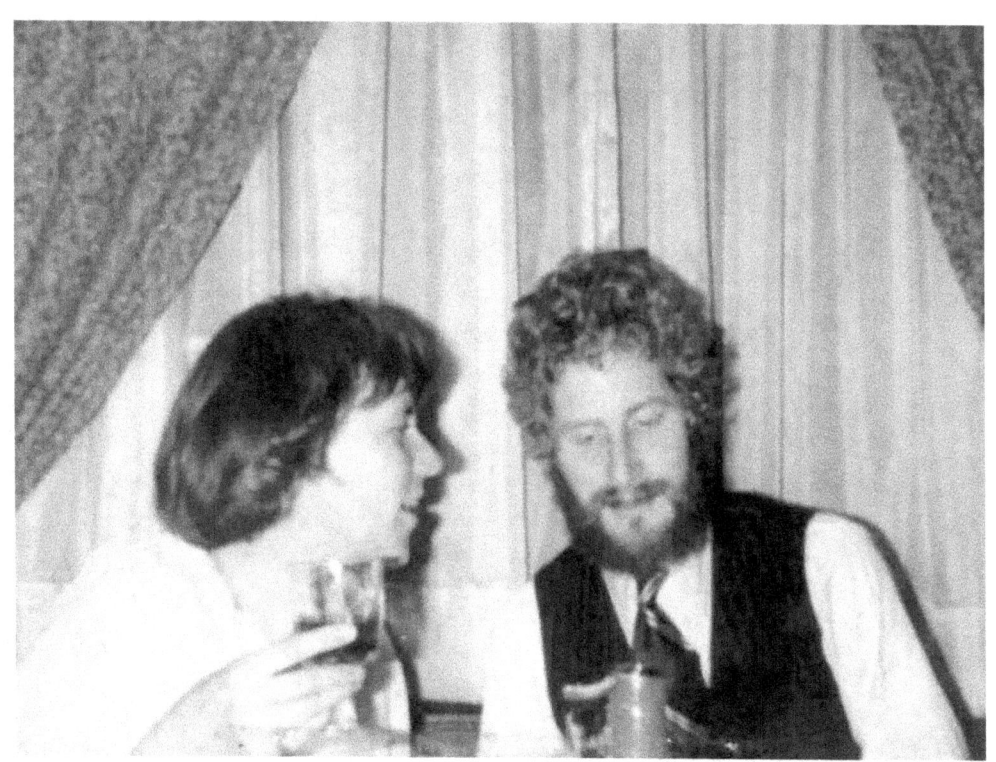

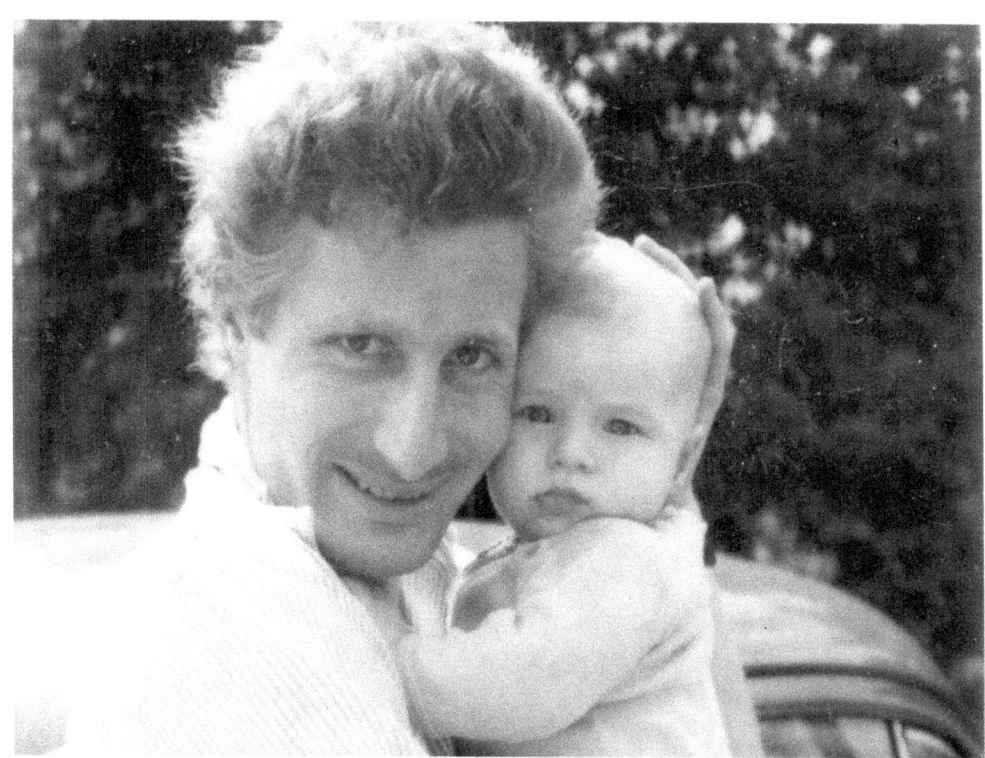

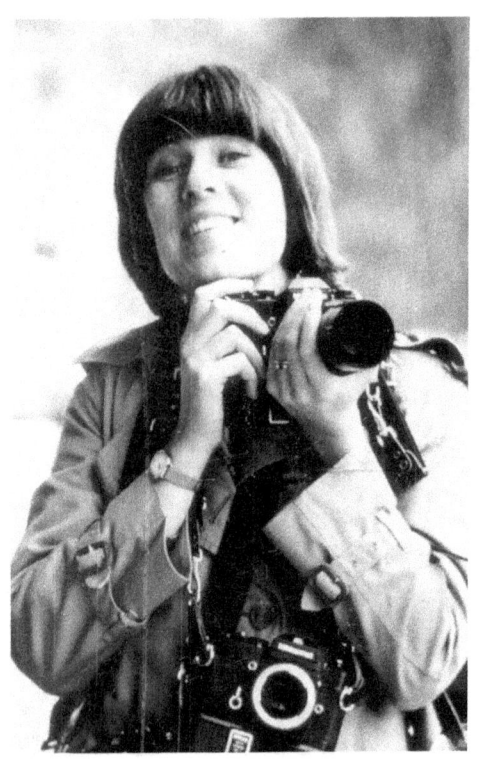

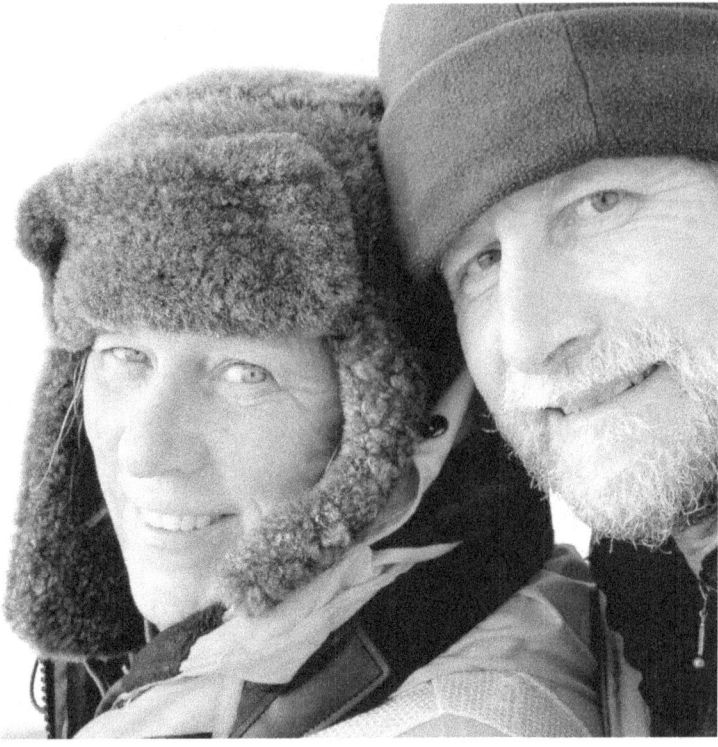

LEFT TOP:
Sisse.

RIGHT TOP:
Sisse and Cotton.

LEFT BOTTOM:
Calder, Saskia, Ian, and Cotton on Tig's boat.

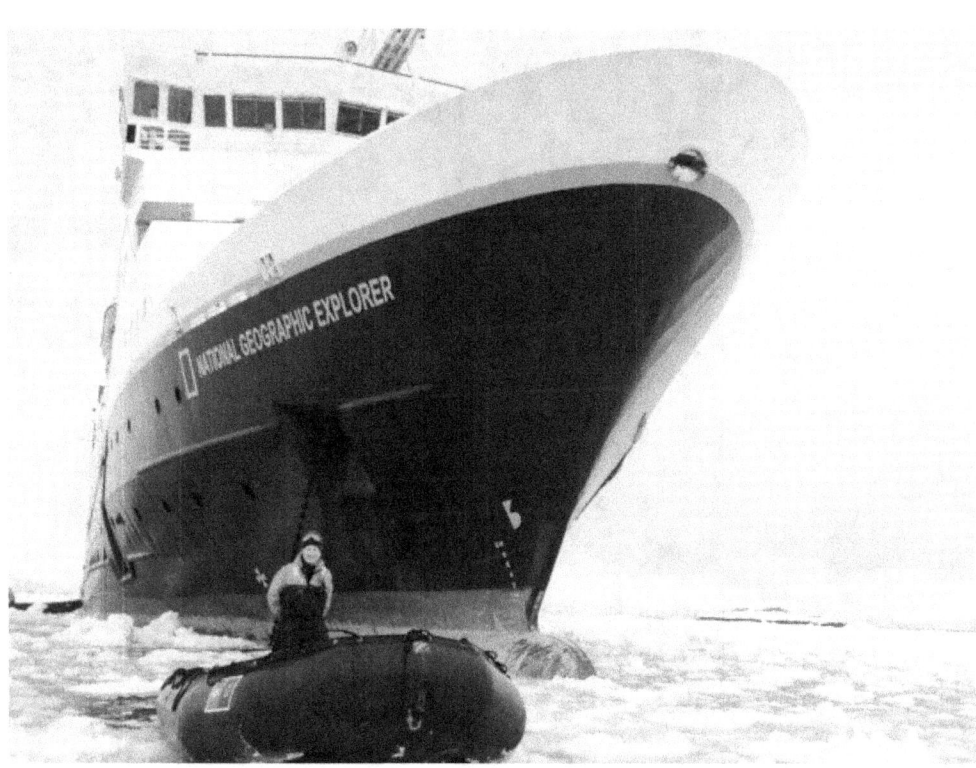

Cotton met Marie-Louise ("Sisse") Brimberg, a legendary National Geographic photographer from Copenhagen. She soon captured his heart.

Calling themselves Keene Press, Cotton and Sisse circled the globe. When Calder and Saskia were born, they juggled assignments with parenting and teaching photography on Lindblad's popular expeditions to the Antarctic. Cotton proudly completed requirements for driving a Zodiac. He then turned to exploring the world below sea level.

Two years ago, on a dive off the Norwegian coast, Cotton suffocated underwater. We lost him on May 28, 2015, my wonderful son, devoted husband and father and friend to so many. Sisse bravely and successfully continues their work with Keene Press and Lindblad Expeditions.

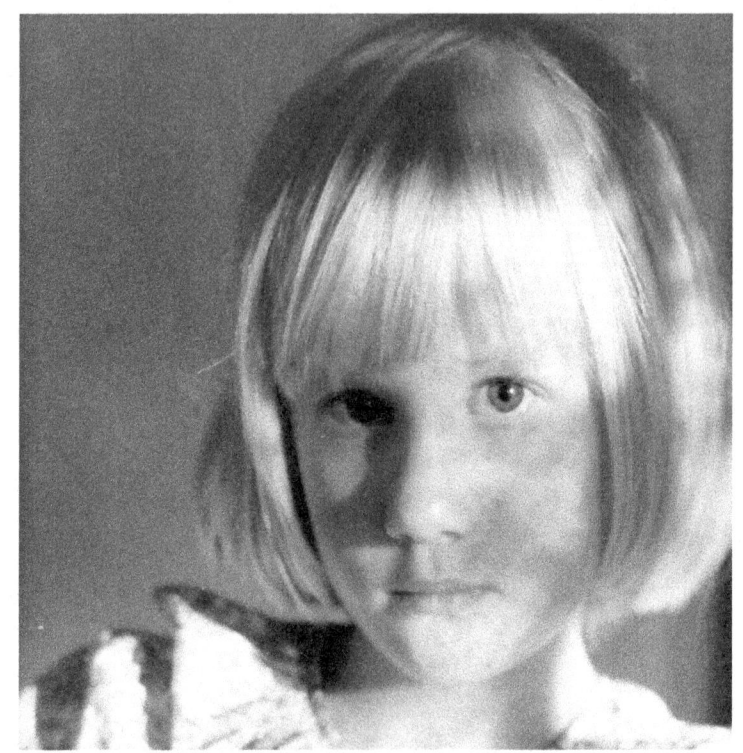

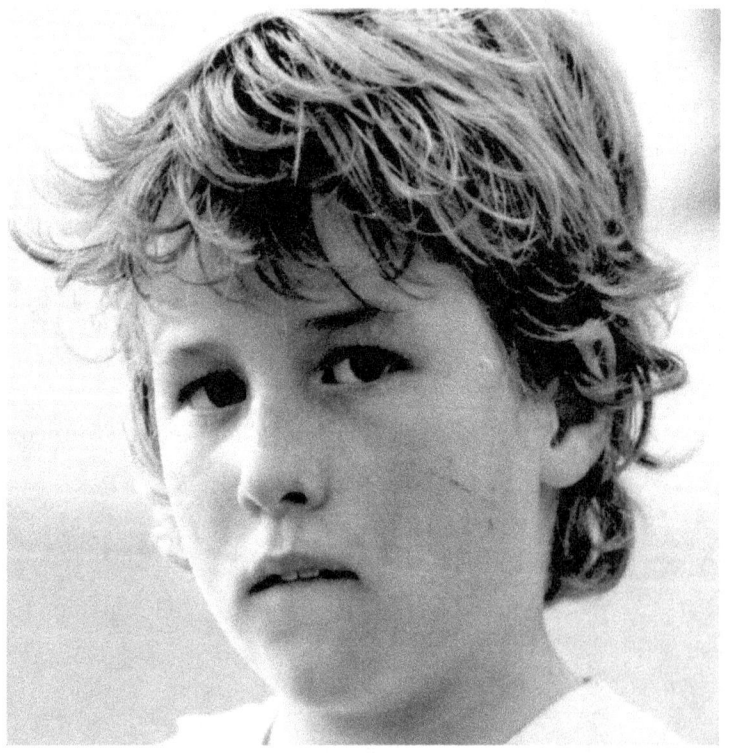

OTHER DEATHS

Many other people, family and friends, died in my lifetime, many too soon, some macabre, all too sad.

Walter died believing in Mary Baker Eddy.

Katie died lonely in Donald Klopfer's New York penthouse, flipping through old magazines as if she were productively occupied.

Aunt Florence died in her frigid Vermont farmhouse, over-medicated, abandoned by her family.

Judy died believing in Christian Science.

Tig died from heavy smoking and drinking and waited 3 weeks for a surgeon, unaware of fast -growing cancer.

Celia Eisenberg was run over by a garbage truck in Truro, on the Cape—an avid walker, wearing earphones and absorbed in listening to music, unaware of an approaching truck.

Nadia Stanley died from a fire caused by her cigarette.

Sally Duplaix was done in by her doctors.

Bess Schuyler intentionally deprived herself of food and water because she had no capable Scrabble partners in her retirement home.

Cousin Laura Kadan drowned in her bathtub in Washington Heights upon learning that she would be bound to a wheel chair and wanted to spare her son the burden and expense of her care.

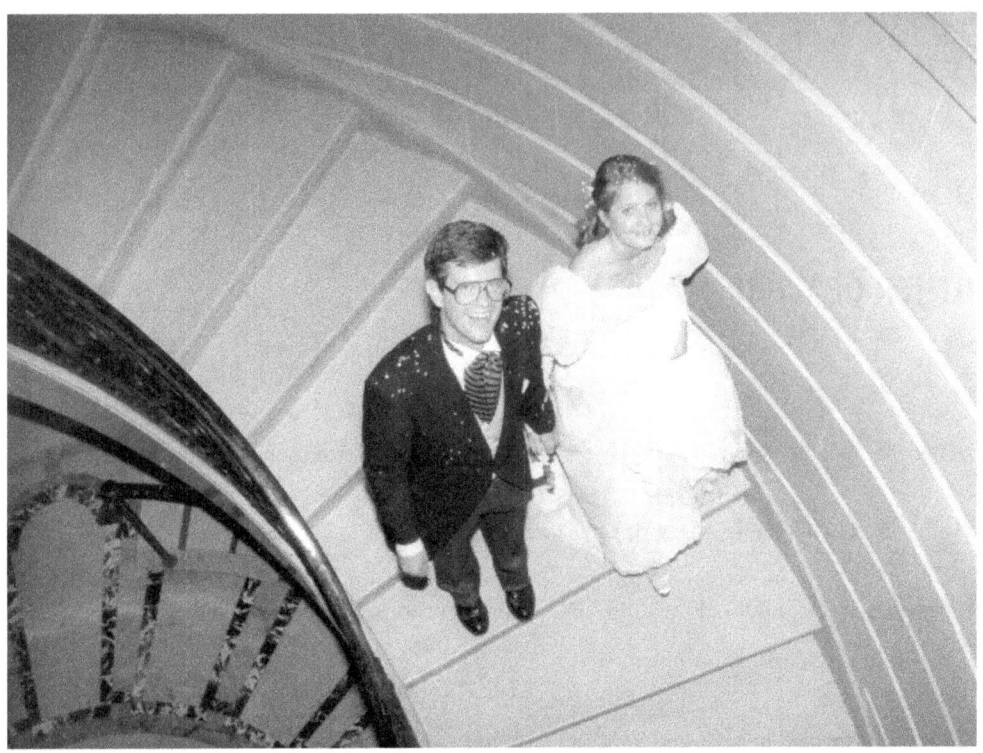

DEIRDRE

After completing four years at New York University, in 1977, Didi moved to Philadelphia to work for Johns Manville, selling industrial building products. She wisely decided to attend Columbia Business School where a friend introduced her to Craig Macnab, from Johannesburg. Theirs was a sweetly romantic courtship.

The wedding reception was held at the National Academy of Design on Fifth Avenue, I worked there and the Museum generously closed to the public for us.

Not lovers of city life, Didi and Craig moved to Nashville, Tennessee, where Ian and Graham, their two handsome sons, were born. Both boys became lacrosse players and scored high marks in their studies. Following in their father's footsteps, they chose careers in real estate and finance.

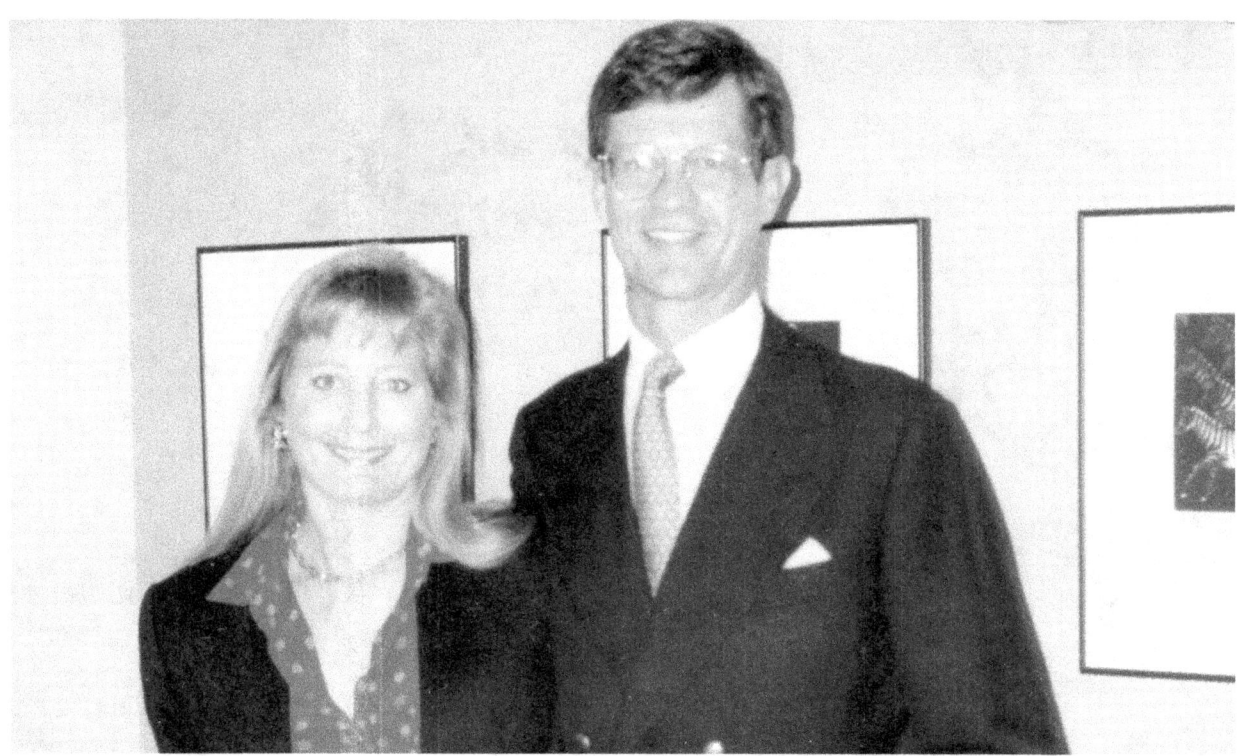

Didi loved horses and learned to ride at Claremont Stables on New York's Upper West Side. During her summer holidays she became even more attached at August Acres in New Hampshire. Now she audaciously drives her four horses across the US, exploring trails around her homes in Winter Park, Florida, and Steamboat Springs, Colorado.

Leadership came naturally with grandmother Katie's genes, as Didi presided over The Florida League of Women Voters and served as their President for five years. She made great strides in promoting Florida voter registration and solar energy usage. I wish my mother could have known how Didi has inherited her love of the political arena.

Ian and Graham are wonderful companions and I cherish my times with them.

Craig loves to ski when he's not playing golf in Scotland or traveling for his highly successful company.

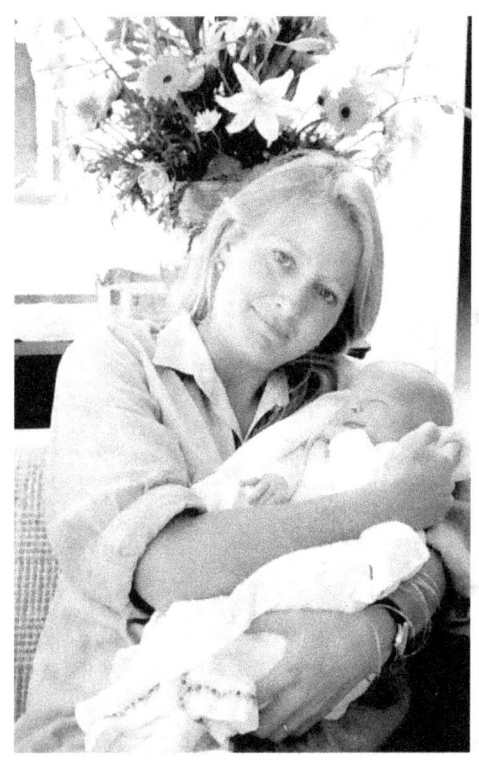

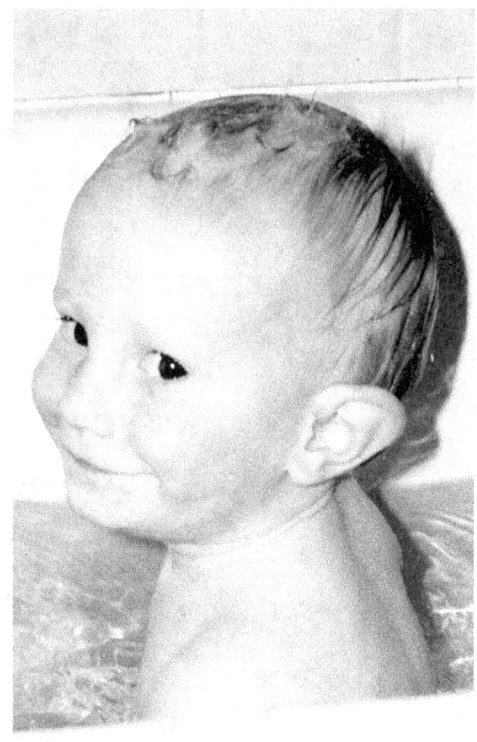

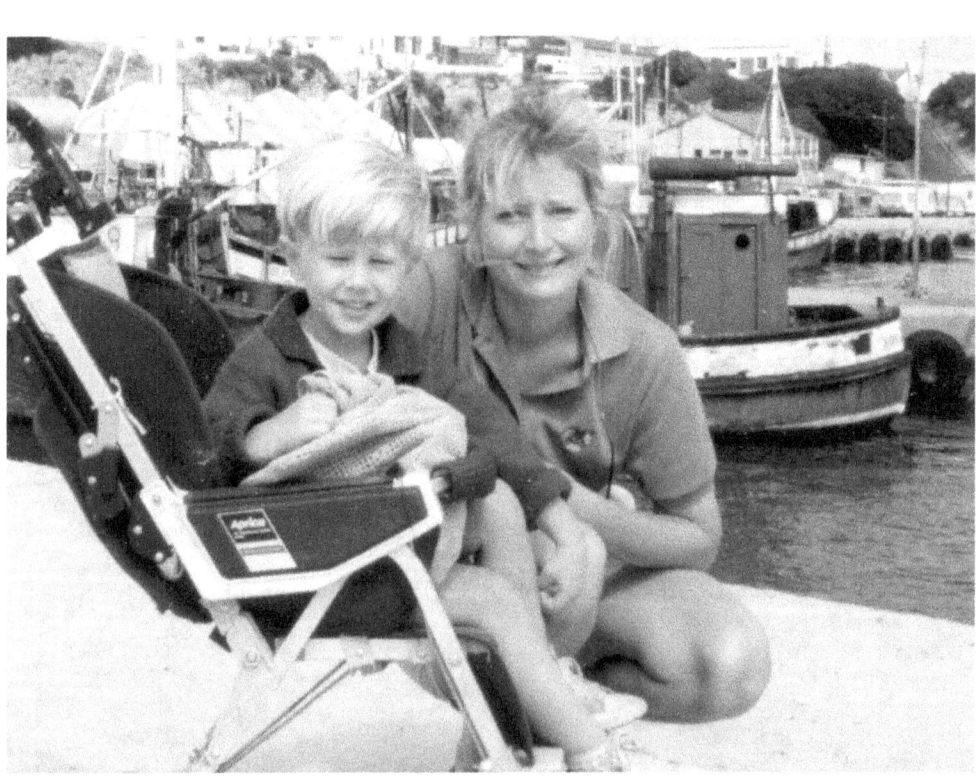

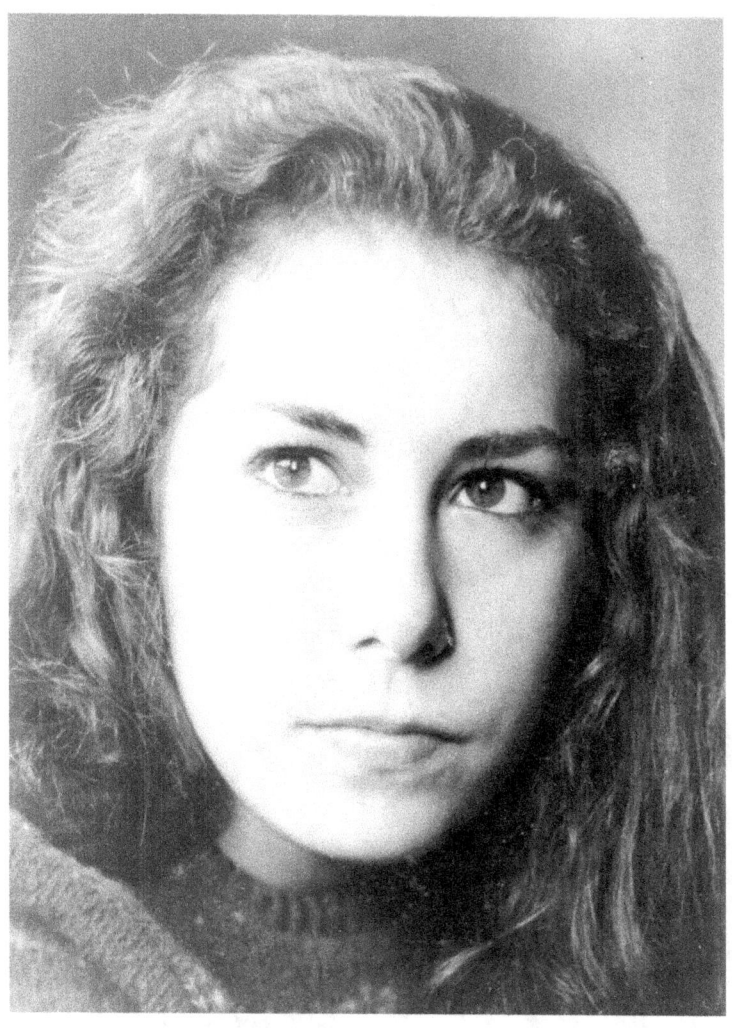

FRANCES ANNE

After graduation from Boston University, Frances did postgraduate work at Pratt Institute in New York City, learning the new age tools and excelling in graphic design. Her creative bent manifested itself with Lycos, in Waltham, Massachusetts, where, as Project Manager, she designed Interface testing for community products.

When Lycos moved elsewhere, Frances shifted to the Harvard School of Public Health and from there to Harvard University Press, where her grandmother's book, *The Making of the New Deal*, was published.

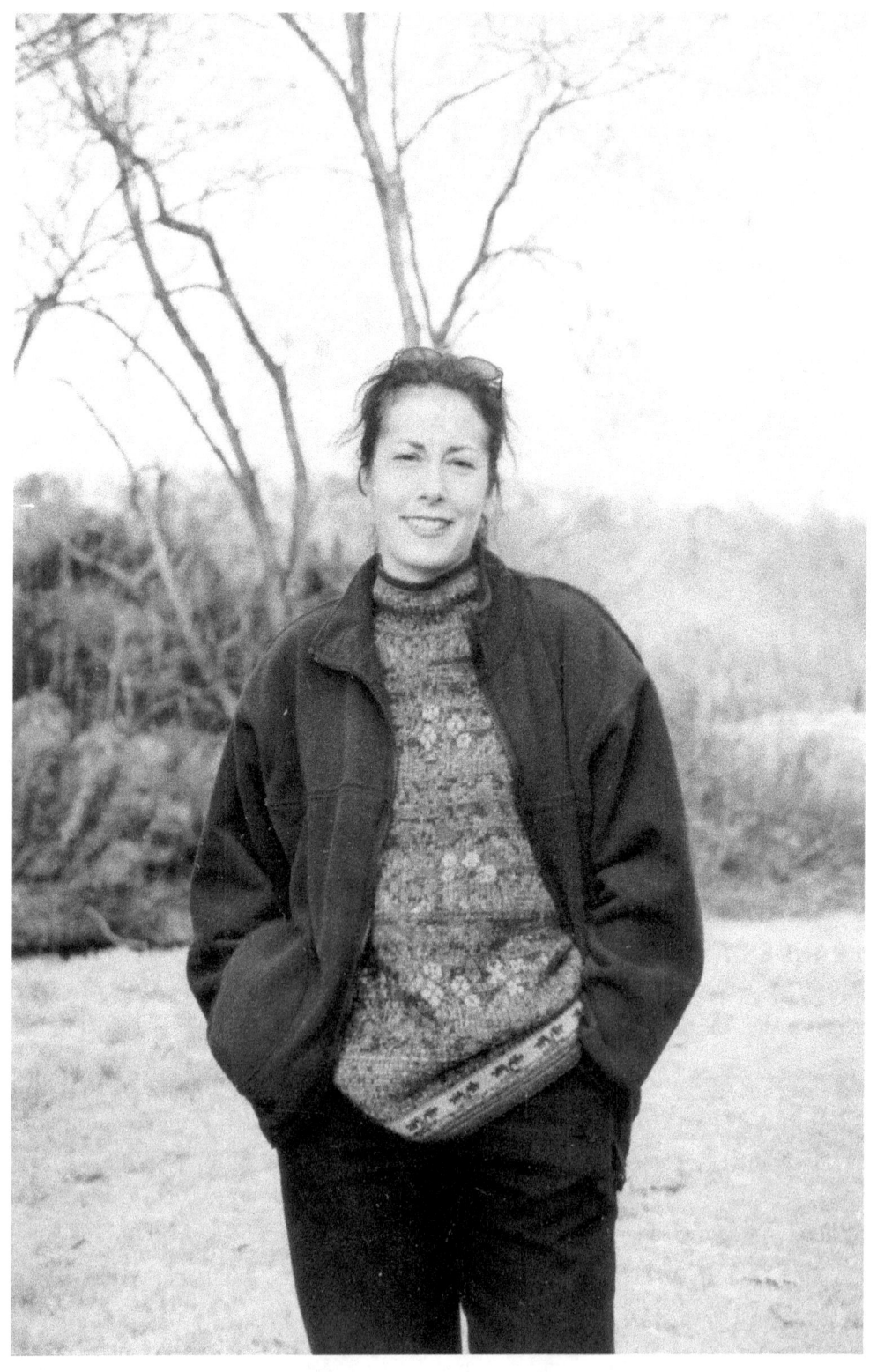

LEFT:

Frances. Photograph
taken by Cotton.

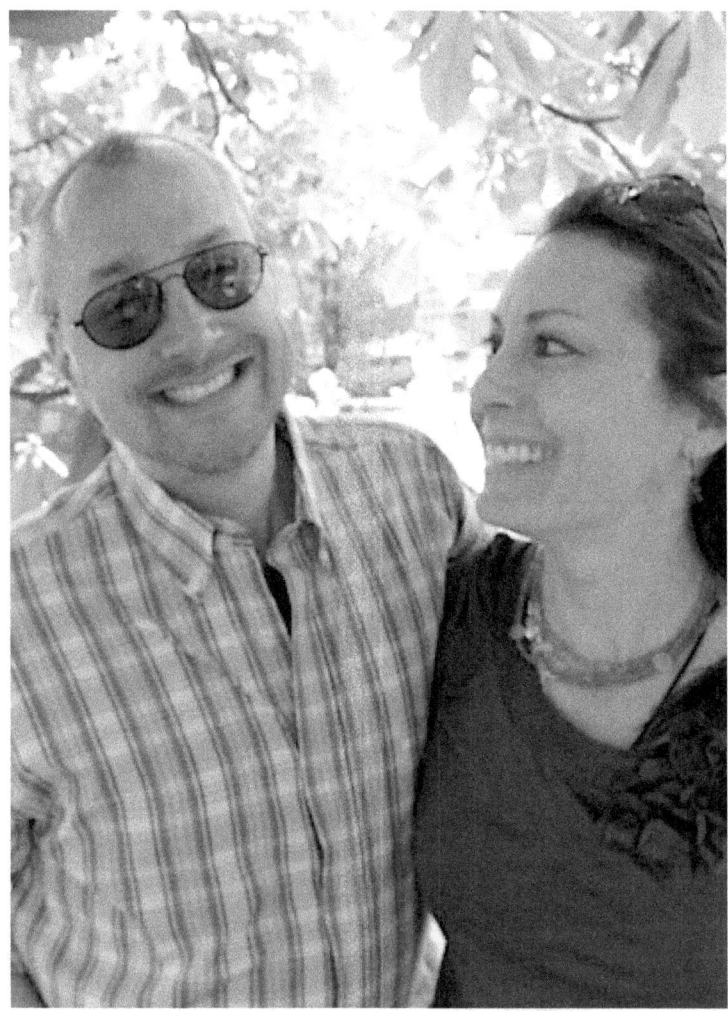

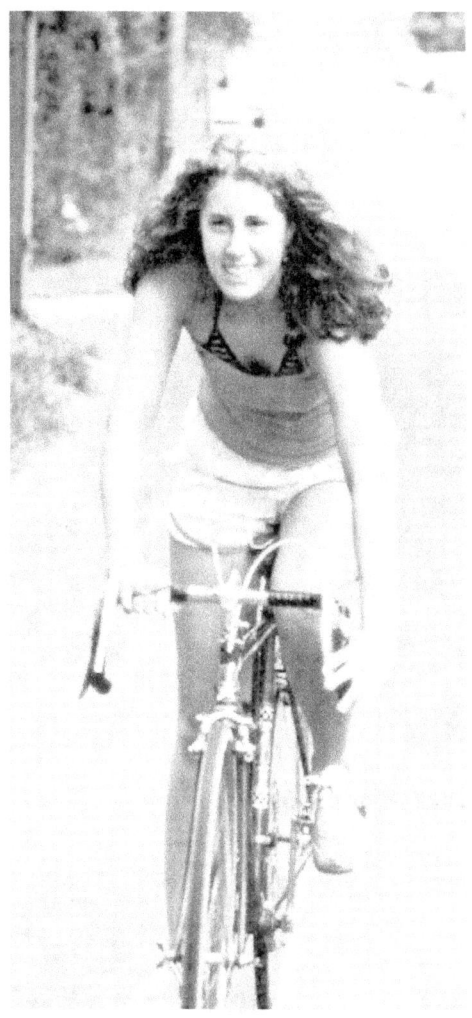

LEFT TOP:
Frances and Matthew.

RIGHT TOP:
Frances on a bike.

Performing a good deed for an officemate, she adopted Blazer, a Labrador pup, which led to a career change in her life. Her compassion for animals would lead to her present work—counseling and caring for dogs in Cambridge, Massachusetts, where she and Matthew Davies—a solver of MIT staff computer-related problems—live cozily in a converted chocolate factory with their youngest "child" Clarabelle, a hound they rescued from an Alabama pet shelter.

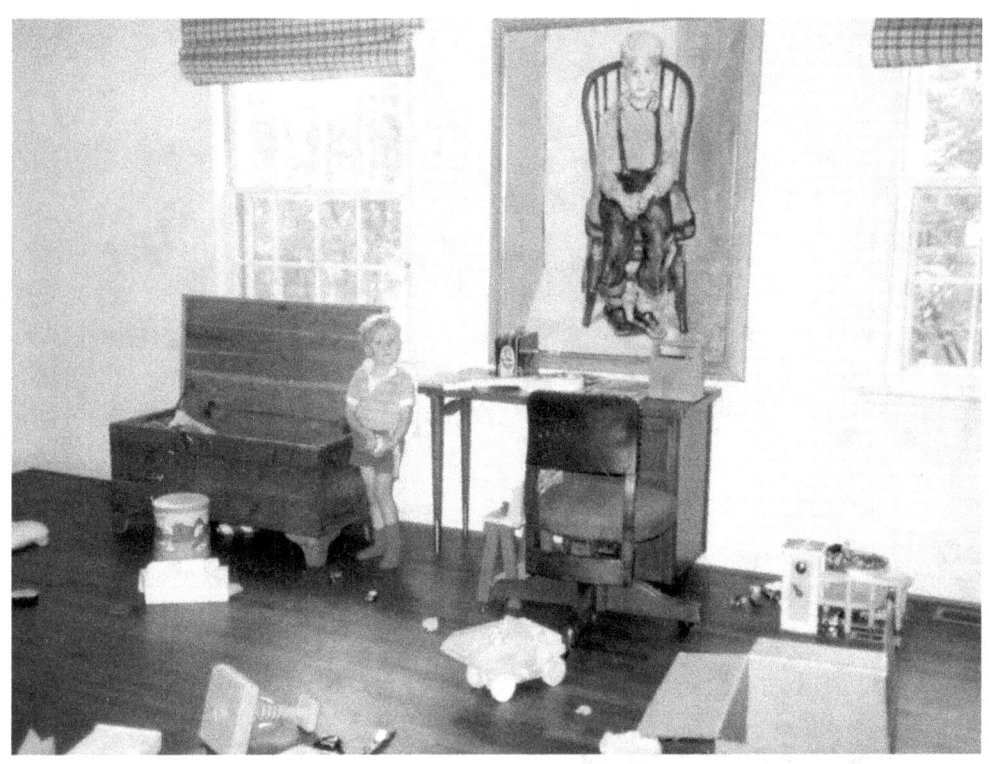

TOP LEFT:

*Cotton's son Calder with
a portrait of his father
– painted by Vincent
Bruno.*

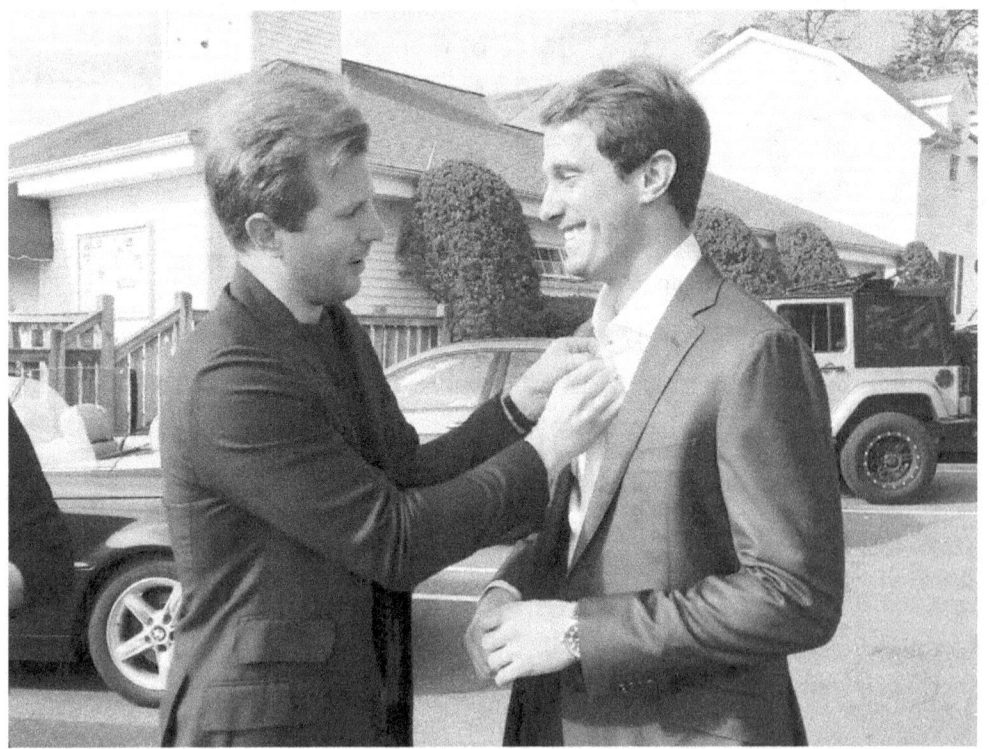

BOTTOM LEFT:

*Ian and Graham
Macnab in Connecticut.*

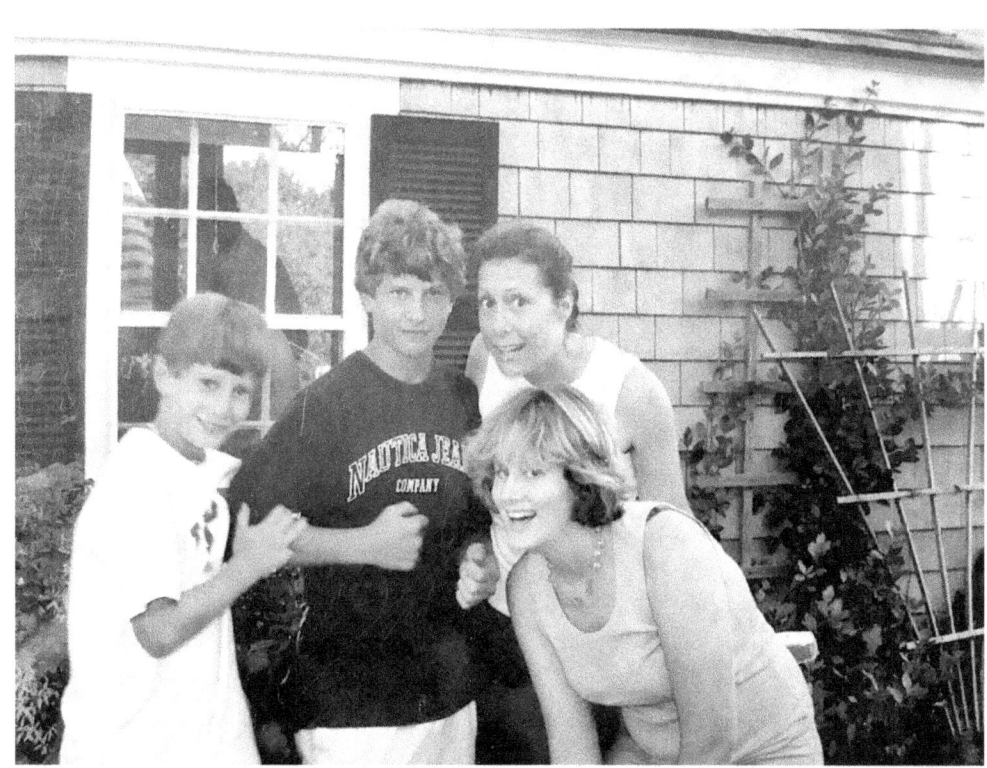

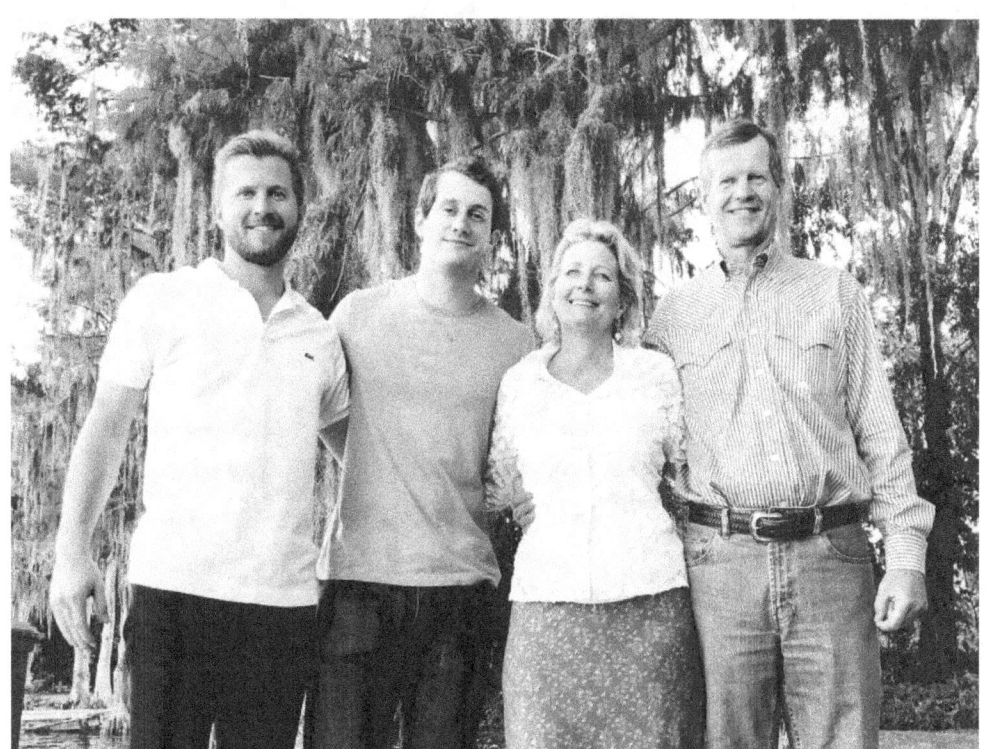

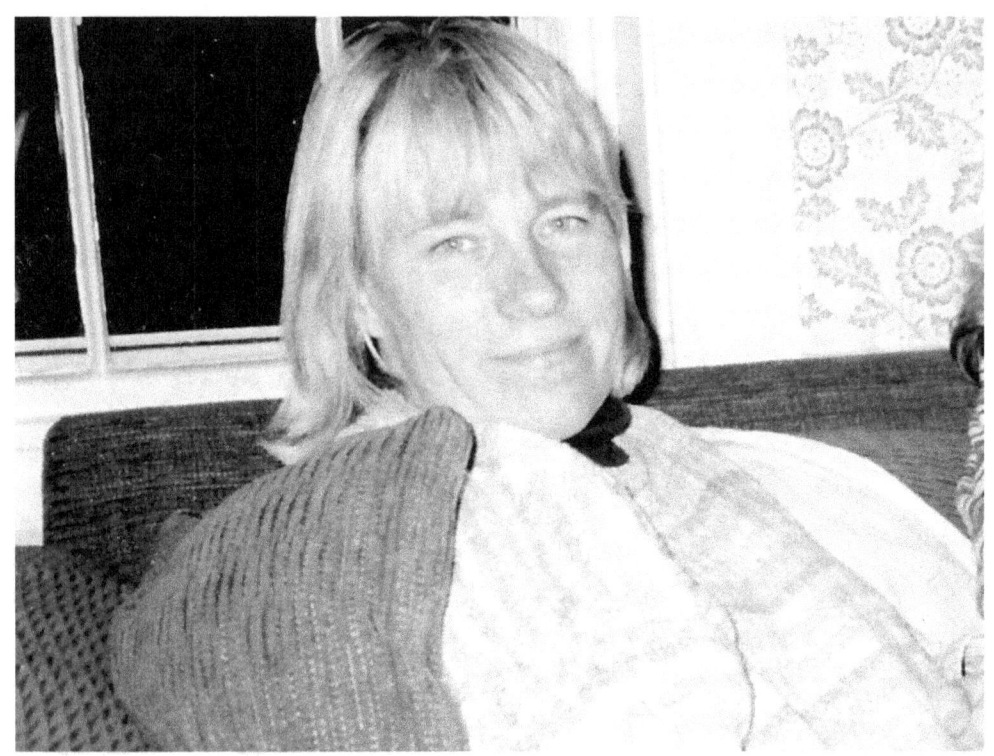

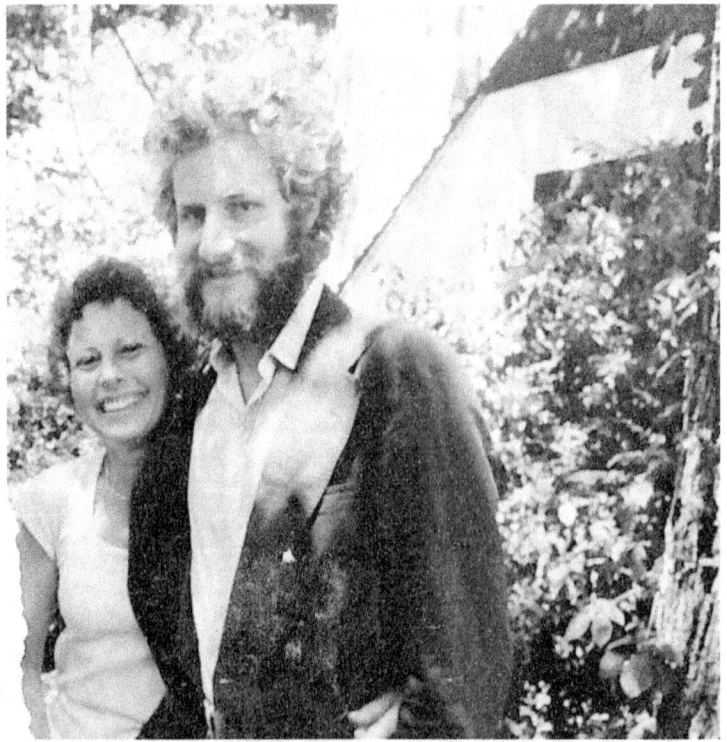

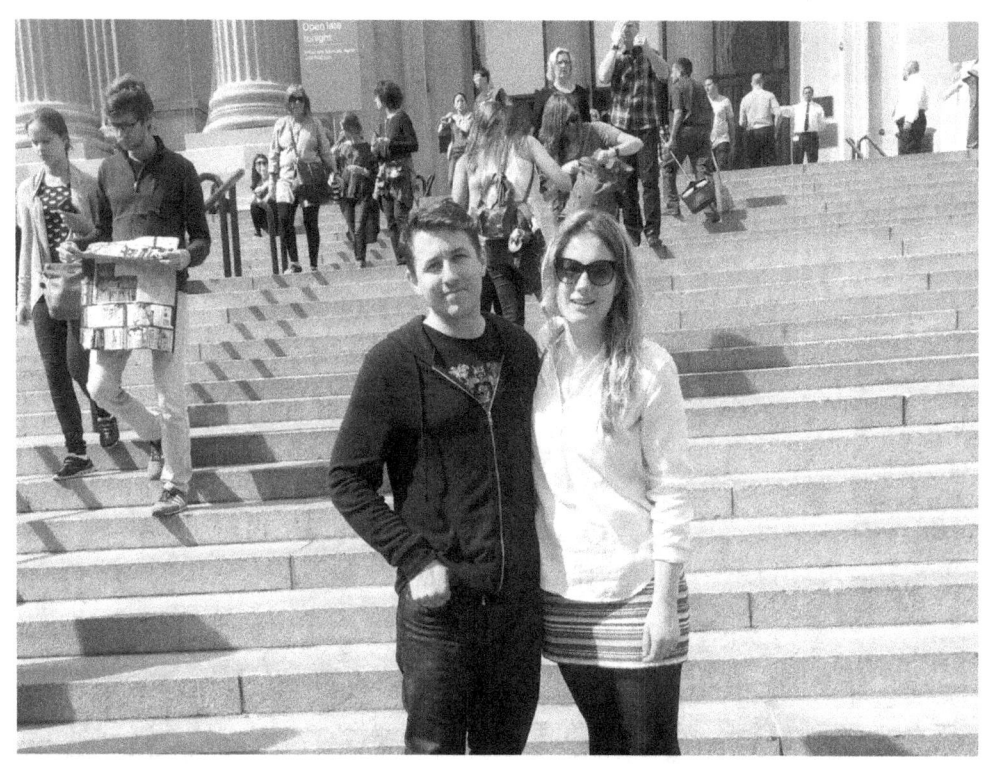

TOP RIGHT:

Calder and Saskia.

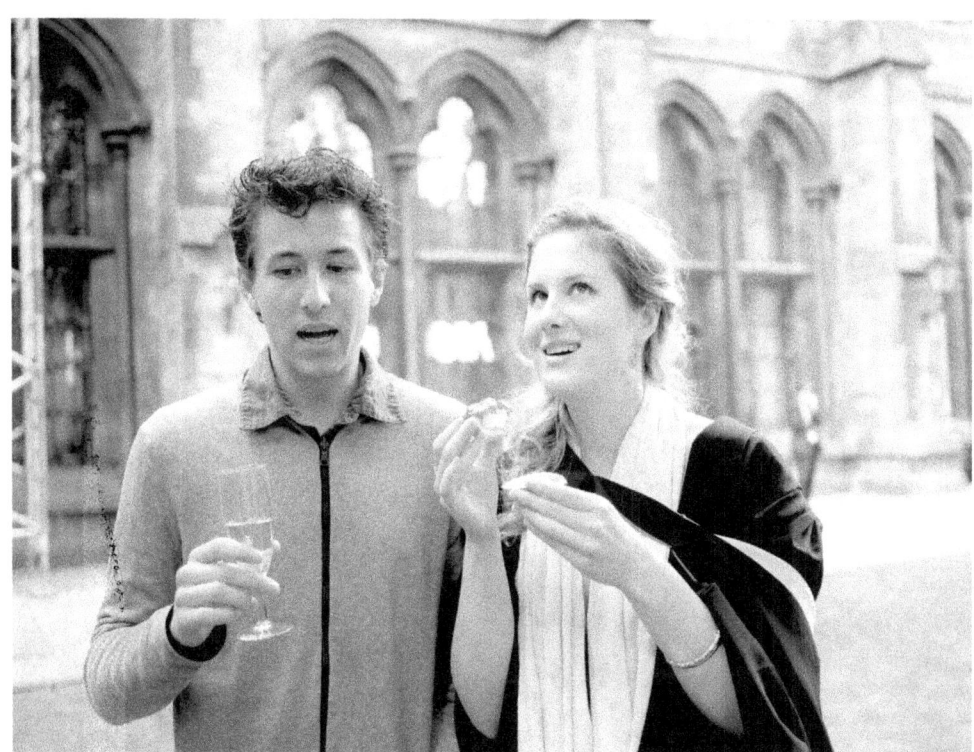

BOTTOM RIGHT:

Calder and Saskia at Saskia's graduation.

231

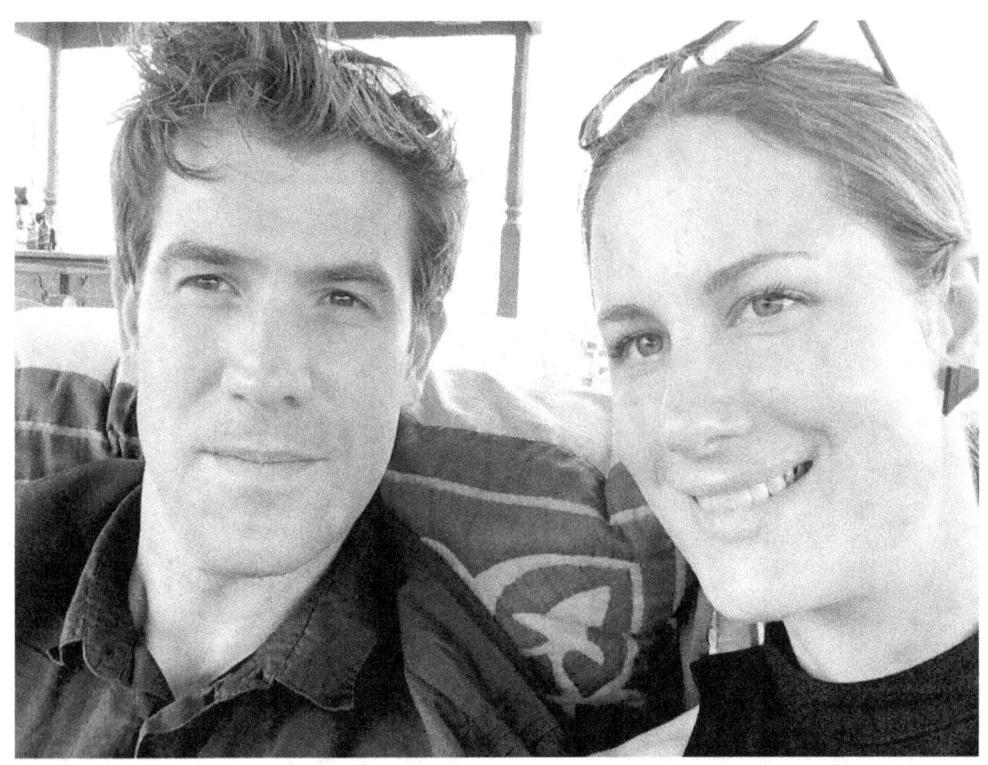

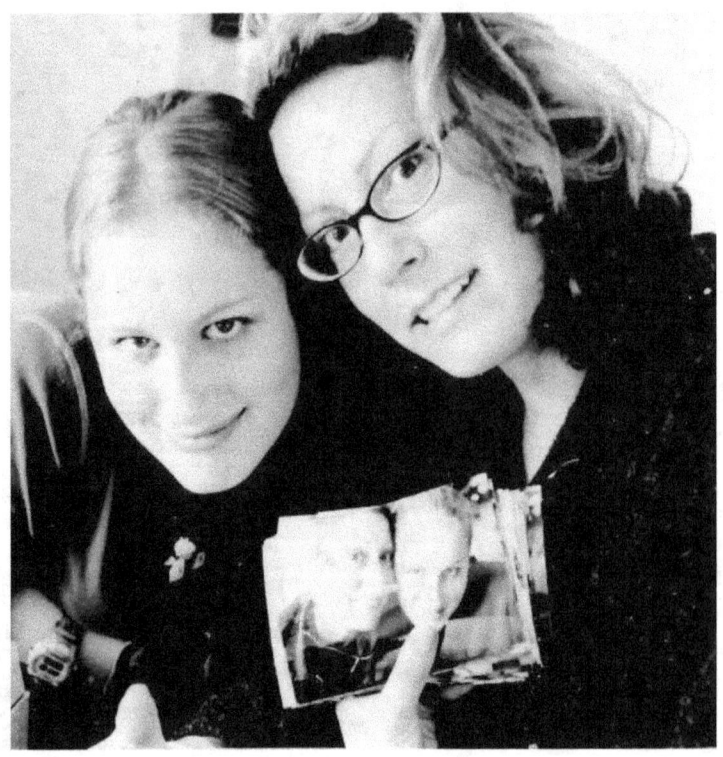

232

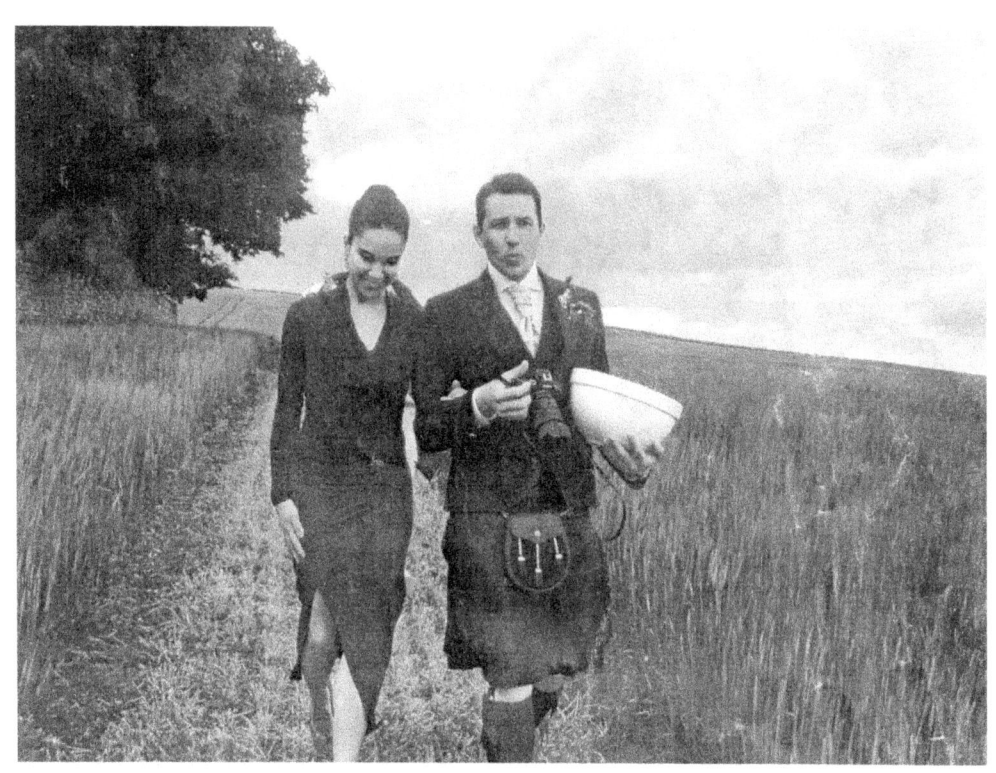

TOP RIGHT:
Kelsey and Calder.

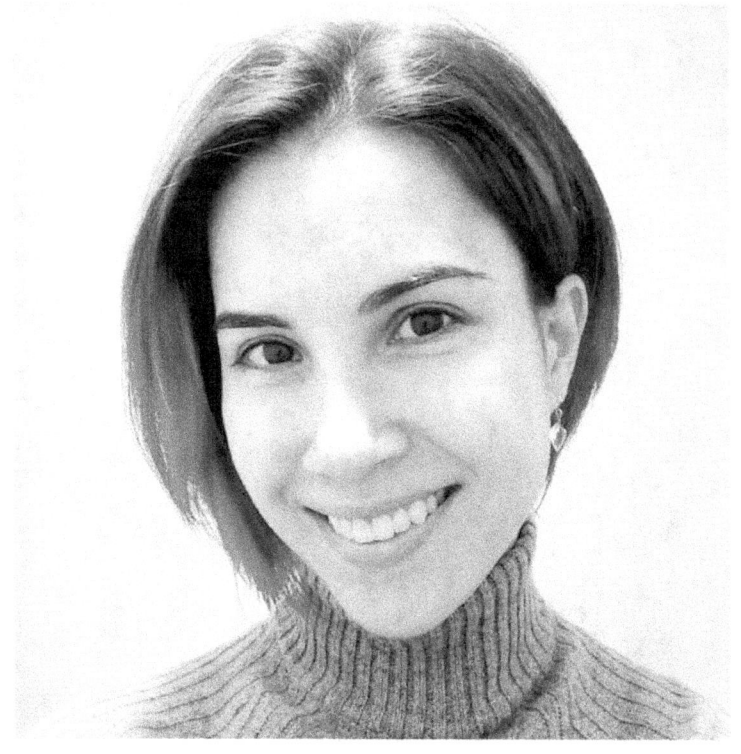

BOTTOM RIGHT:
Kelsey.

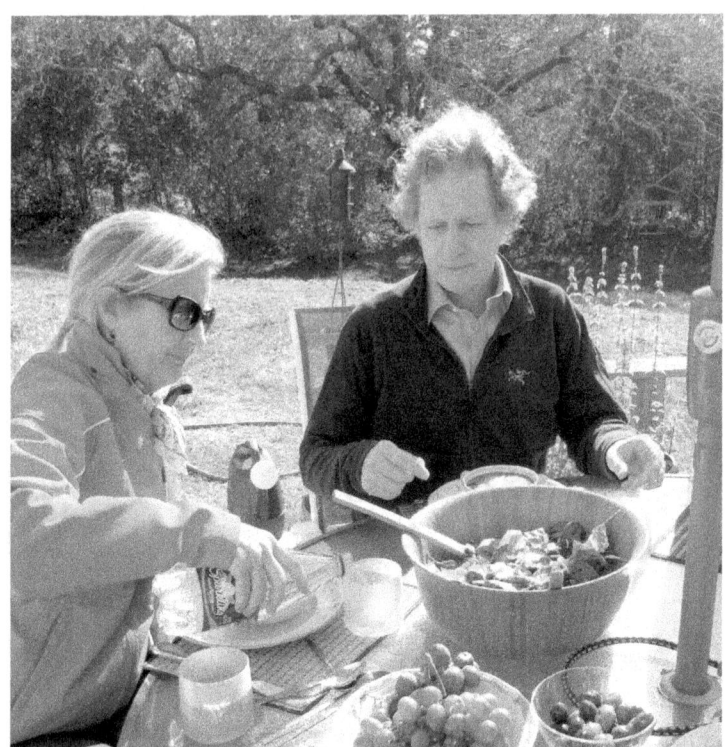

LEFT:

Cotton and Didi.

BOTTOM LEFT:

Saskia.

BOTTOM RIGHT:

Chef Calder.

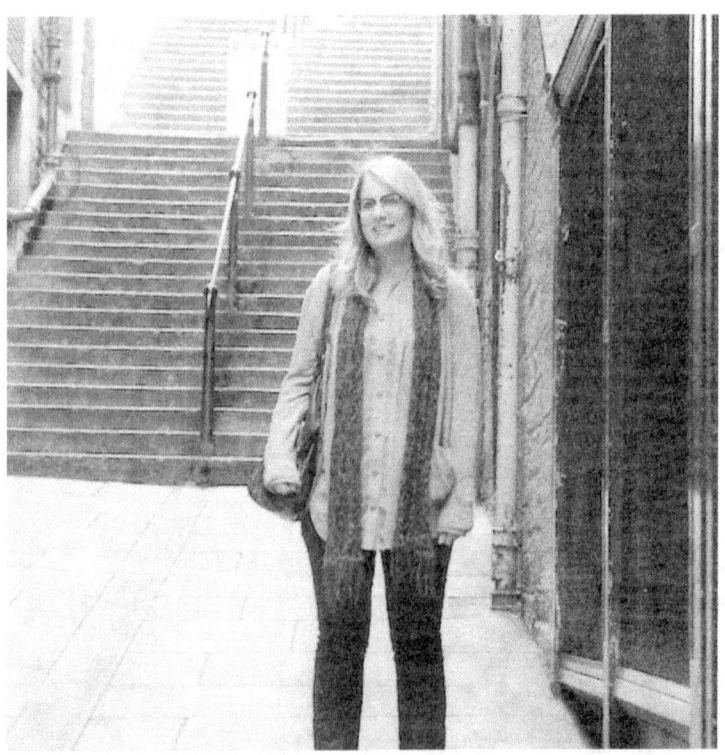

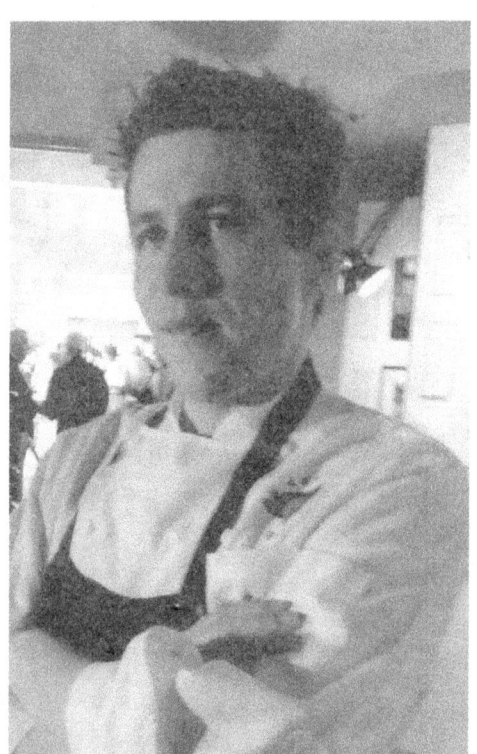

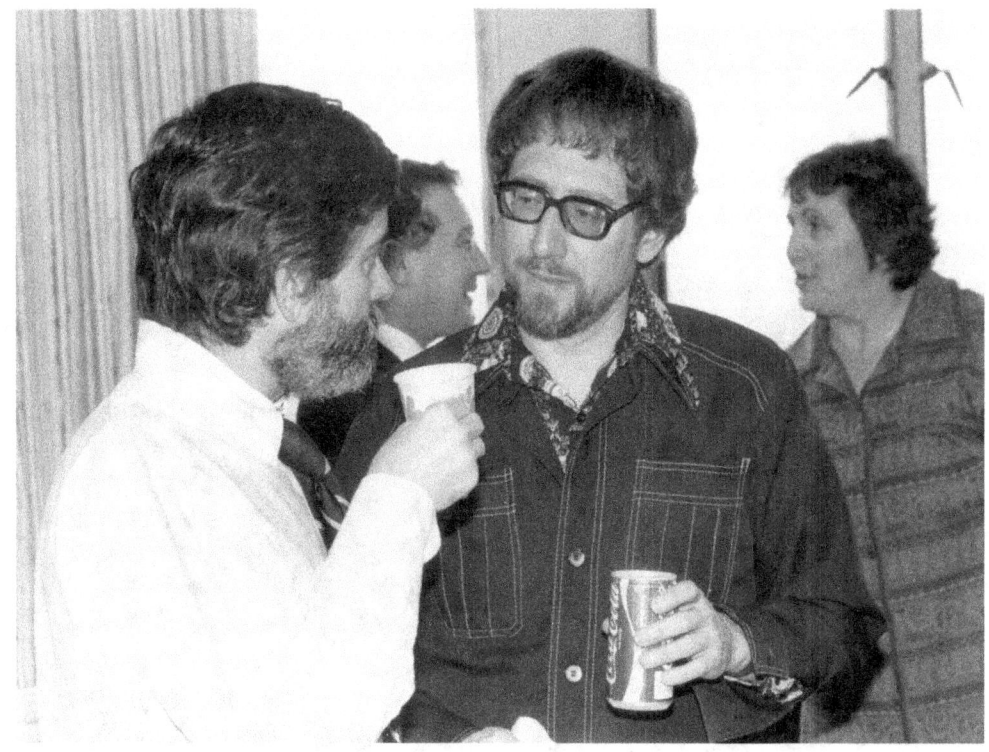

STEPHEN DAVID ROSS

After Tig died, Sally Duplaix persuaded me to sign up with Match.com, an internet site offering to connect men and women with similar backgrounds. Sally claimed living alone was grim, and convinced me to reduce my age by five years. "After all," she said, "everyone thinks you're only 65!"

After many meetings over Starbuck's coffee, dinners, and Central Park walks, I decided that Lucy was my best companion.

One day, I received an email from a Binghamton University professor, who said that I sounded "just like his cup of tea." I reminded him of his music teacher.

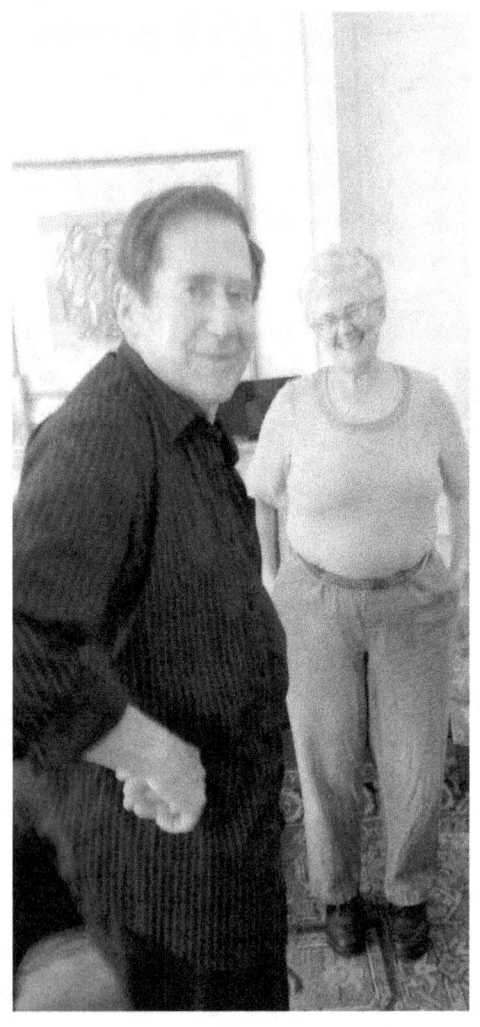

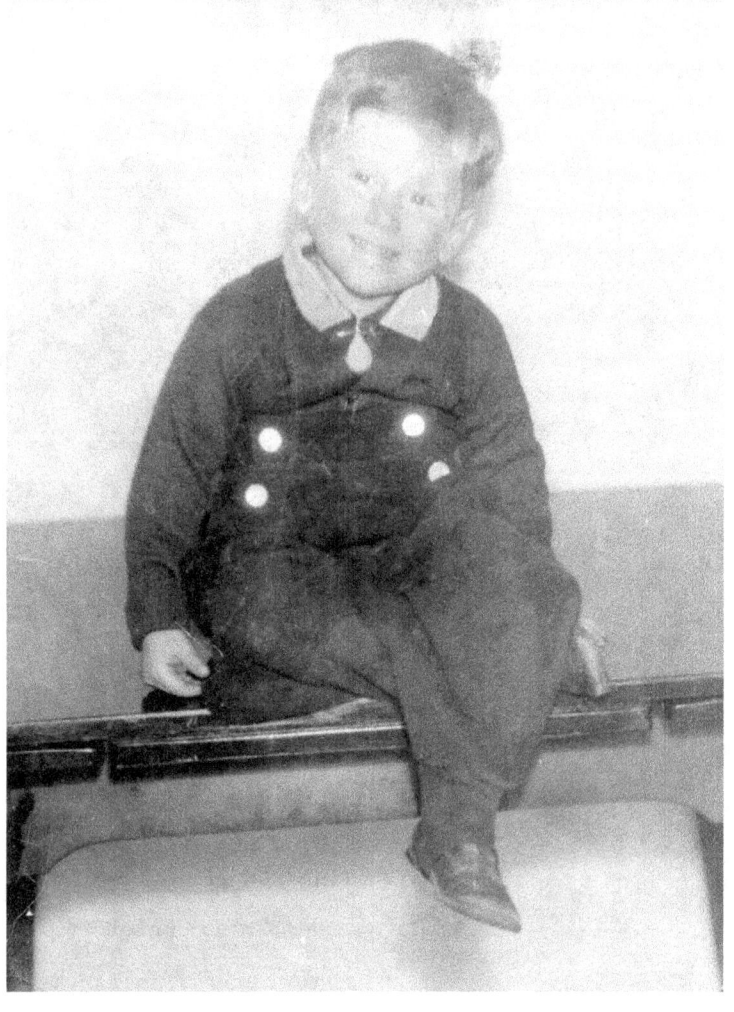

Stephen David Ross drove up to 103 East 86th Street wearing a pair of bright yellow sunglasses. He parked his car and led me to the water turtles floating in Central Park's rowboat pond. He spoke eloquently of his love of animals, adding that he was a vegetarian. "Distinguished Professor of Philosophy, Interpretation, and Culture" was written on his office door. I still don't know what that means.

Several months later, Stephen and his two Russian Blue cats, Dmitri and Vanya, moved into my New York City apartment and Chatham house, along with his collection of philosophy books and a lifetime supply of dried Porcini mushrooms. And here we still are.

LEFT TOP:
Stephen and his sister Deborah.

RIGHT TOP:
Stephen age 4.

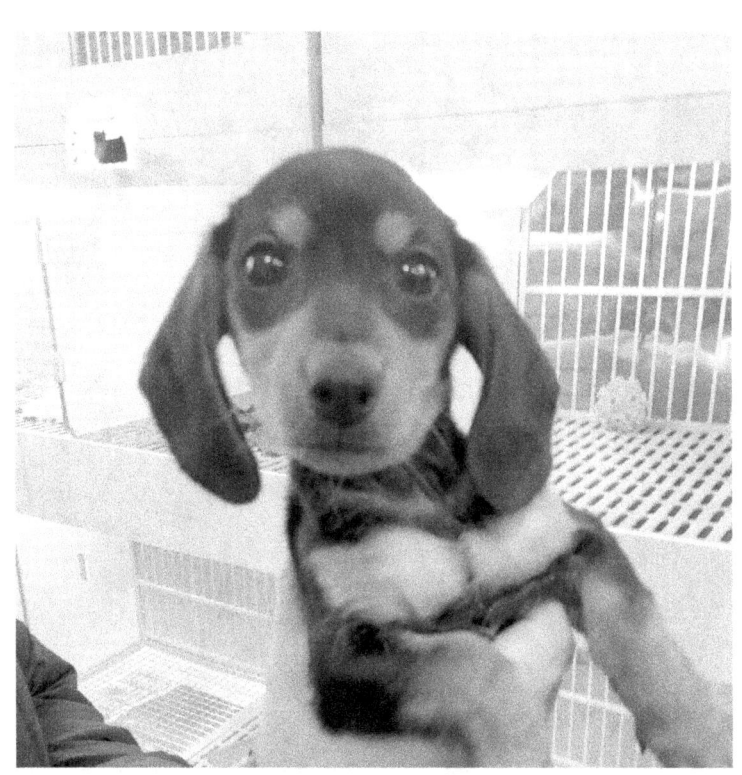

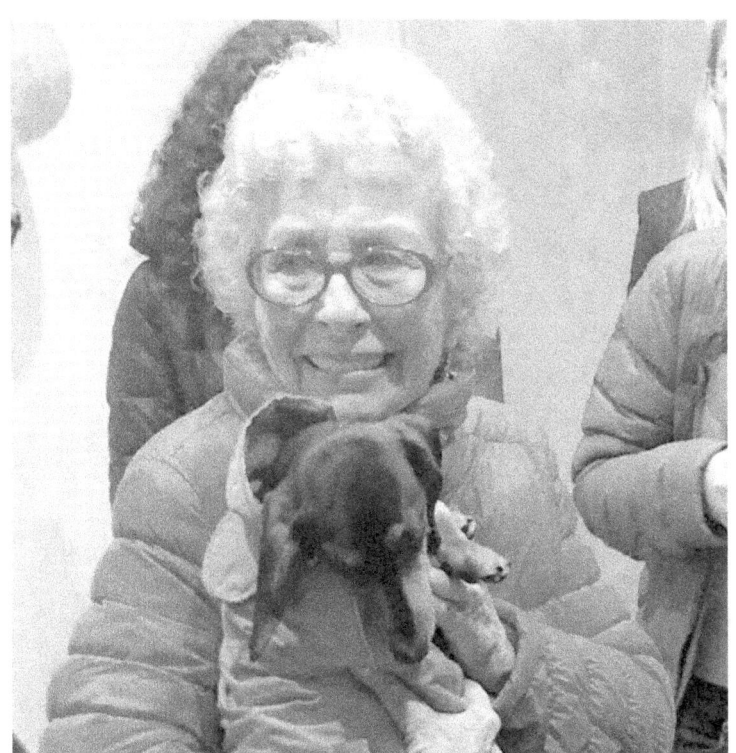

237

www.ingramcontent.com/pod-product-compliance
Lightning Source LLC
Chambersburg PA
CBHW081555220526
45468CB00010B/2669